# Test Bank

*for*

# Weiten and Lloyd's

## Psychology Applied to Modern Life
## Adjustment in the 21st Century

Eighth Edition

**Mary Ann Valentino**
*Fresno City College*

**David Ward**
*Arkansas Tech University*

# Test Bank

*for*

## Weiten and Lloyd's

# Psychology Applied to Modern Life
# Adjustment in the 21st Century

## Eighth Edition

**Mary Ann Valentino**
*Fresno City College*

**David Ward**
*Arkansas Tech University*

Australia • Brazil • Canada • Mexico • Singapore • Spain • United Kingdom • United States

**Thomson Higher Education**
**10 Davis Drive**
**Belmont, CA 94002-3098**
**USA**

For more information about our products,
contact us at:
**Thomson Learning Academic Resource Cent**
**1-800-423-0563**

For permission to use material from this text o
product, submit a request online at
**http://www.thomsonrights.com.**
Any additional questions about permissions can
submitted by email to **thomsonrights@thomson.c**

# TABLE OF CONTENTS

# ABOUT THE AUTHORS

Mary Ann Valentino, Ph.D. is a full-time psychology instructor at Fresno City College and a practicing clinical psychologist.

David Ward obtained his PhD and MS from the University of Georgia and BS from the University of Texas. He has been recognized as an exceptional, experienced and dedicated teacher by the presentation of several teaching awards. In his current position at Arkansas Tech University, he teaches general psychology, social psychology, developmental psychology and research methods. As an extension of his teaching dedication, he stays active reviewing textbooks and contributing to teaching supplements. Currently, Dr. Ward is working to help Arkansas Tech University expand its psychology program to include a graduate curriculum. When not working, he stays active by hiking the Ozarks and coaching basketball and soccer. David and his wife Rebecca are parents to a set of fraternal twins, Casey and Caleb.

# PREFACE

Each chapter of this Test Bank begins with a list of learning objectives. These are the same learning objectives that can be found in the main text, Instructor's Manual, and the Study Guide. Every question includes correct answer, main text page reference, corresponding learning objective, and question-type (note that the short-answer essay questions do not include correct answers and question-type). An asterisk next to a question signifies that the question is new to this edition of the test bank.

Towards the end of every chapter, you will see "multiple choice questions from study guide". Fifteen questions are pulled from each Study Guide chapter and put into this test bank so that you can use some of the Study Questions on your exams. A great way to reward students who utilize their study guide throughout the course is to present them with questions they have already encountered in their Study Guide on the exams.

Following the Study Guide questions, you will see "Multiple Choice Questions on the Web Site". These are 15 multiple-choice questions pulled from the approximately 100 in the main multiple-choice section. Students who utilize their book companion website at http://psychology.wadsworth.com/weiten_lloyd8e, specifically the tutorial quiz for each chapter on the web site.

Finally, you will come to the true/false questions (which are all new to this edition) and the short-answer essay questions.

All items from this test bank are also available in ExamView®, a computerized testing package with online capabilities. The ExamView® testing software is offered at no charge to instructors who adopt the text. ExamView® helps you create, customize and deliver both print and online tests in minutes. Its "what you see is what you get" interface, along with a Quiz Test Wizard and an Online Test Wizard, guide you step-by-step through the test creation process. ExamView® is available on a cross-platform Windows/Macintosh CD-ROM.

# Chapter 1
# ADJUSTING TO MODERN LIFE

## LEARNING OBJECTIVES

1. Describe four examples of the paradox of progress.
2. Explain what is meant by the paradox of progress and how theorists have explained it.
3. Provide some examples of people's search for direction.
4. Describe three problems that are common in popular self-help books.
5. Summarize advice about what to look for in quality self-help books.
6. Summarize the philosophy underlying this textbook.
7. Describe the two key facets of psychology.
8. Explain the concept of adjustment.
9. Explain the nature of empiricism.
10. Explain two advantages of the scientific approach to understanding behavior.
11. Describe the experimental method, distinguishing between independent and dependent variables and between experimental and control groups.
12. Distinguish between positive and negative correlation and explain what the size of a correlation coefficient means.
13. Describe three correlational research methods.
14. Compare the advantages and disadvantages of experimental versus correlational research.
15. Discuss the prevalence of reported happiness in modern society.
16. List the various factors that are surprisingly unrelated to happiness.
17. Explain how health, social activity, and religion are related to happiness.
18. Discuss how love, work, and personality are related to happiness.
19. Summarize the conclusions drawn about the determinants of happiness.
20. List three steps for developing sound study habits.
21. Describe the SQ3R method of effective reading.
22. Summarize advice on how to get more out of lectures.
23. Summarize how memory is influenced by practice, interference, depth of processing, and organization.
24. Describe several verbal and visual mnemonic devices.

**MULTIPLE CHOICE QUESTIONS**

1.    Modern technology has provided us with many time-saving devices, but
a.    most of us don't use them.
b.    they cost too much for most of us.
c.    they never seem to work as advertised.
d.    we still complain about not having enough time.

**ANS: d**          **Pg: 2**
**LO: 1**           **Conceptual**

2.    In spite of countless time-saving devices—automobiles, telephones, photocopiers, fax machines, and so on—most of us complain about a relative lack of
a.    time.
b.    money.
c.    information.
d.    work.

**ANS: a**          **Pg: 2**
**LO: 1**           **Conceptual**

*3.    Modern Western society has made extraordinary technological progress
a.    and therefore, has seen decreases in social problems.
b.    but social and personal problems seem more prevalent and more prominent than ever before.
c.    and therefore, has seen a boom in time spent engaging in leisure activities.
d.    but social and personal problems are just as prevalent as they were in the past.

**ANS: b**          **Pg: 2**
**LO: 1**           **Factual**

4.    Many people share a sense of economic decline today, even though
a.    productivity is on the rise.
b.    cost of living remains stable.
c.    our society is more affluent than ever.
d.    the upper class is probably smaller than previously.

**ANS: c**          **Pgs: 2-3**
**LO: 1**           **Conceptual**

5.    Technology has enabled humankind to exercise unprecedented control over many aspects of the physical world but at the same time has also created serious
a.    environmental problems.
b.    microscopic defects.
c.    medical costs.
d.    under-consumption.

**ANS: a**          **Pg: 4**
**LO: 1**           **Factual**

6.       _____ refers to the idea that technological advances haven't led to perceptible improvement in our collective health and happiness.
a.     Information anxiety
b.     Technology overload
c.     The paradox of progress
d.     The point/counterpoint phenomenon

**ANS: c**          **Pg: 4**
**LO: 2**          **Conceptual**

7.       Many theorists believe that the basic challenge of modern life has become the search for
a.     cultural significance.
b.     a healthy leisure activity.
c.     meaning or a sense of direction.
d.     a significant other to share one's life.

**ANS: c**          **Pg: 5**
**LO: 2**          **Factual**

8.       According to social critics, all of the following are examples of the search for direction gone awry **except**
a.     enrollment in "self-realization" programs.
b.     the desire to spend more time with loved ones.
c.     joining cults and unorthodox religious groups.
d.     the popularity of media figures such as Dr. Laura.

**ANS: b**          **Pgs: 5-6**
**LO: 3**          **Factual**

9.       Most experts characterize "self-realization" programs (e.g., est training, Silva Mind Control) as
a.     intellectually stimulating.
b.     intellectually bankrupt.
c.     spiritually revitalizing.
d.     spiritually self-defeating.

**ANS: b**          **Pgs: 5-6**
**LO: 3**          **Factual**

*10.    The famous radio talk show host Dr. Laura holds a degree in
a.     psychology.
b.     social work.
c.     physiology.
d.     psychiatry.

**ANS: c**          **Pg: 6**
**LO: 3**          **Factual**

*11.    Surveys exploring psychotherapists' opinions of self-help books suggest
a.      there are some excellent books that offer authentic insight and sound advice.
b.      there are some good books that offer adequate insight and advice.
c.      there are some excellent books that offer good general advice but very few that offer good specific advice for particular problems.
d.      psychotherapists do not endorse the use of self-help books because it is bad for business.

**ANS: a**          **Pgs: 7-8**
**LO: 4**           **Factual**

*12.    "Psychobabble" is best defined as
a.      psychological jargon.
b.      textbook definitions.
c.      ill-defined terminology.
d.      technical terminology.

**ANS: c**          **Pg: 8**
**LO: 4**           **Factual**

*13.    Which of the following is the best definition of psychology?
a.      the study of consciousness
b.      the study of behavior and the profession that applies knowledge from these studies to solving practical problems
c.      the study of abnormal behavior and the profession that applies knowledge from these studies to diagnosing and treating people with mental illness
d.      the study of motivation, emotion, and memory

**ANS: b**          **Pg: 11**
**LO: 7**           **Factual**

*14.    Which of the following is the best example of "overt" activity?
a.      eating
b.      thinking
c.      dreaming
d.      reasoning

**ANS: a**          **Pg: 11**
**LO: 7**           **Conceptual**

15.     Which of the following is **not** mentioned in the textbook as a criticism of self-help books?
a.      They tend to sacrifice clarity for jargon.
b.      They are rarely based on solid research.
c.      The topics they cover are often quite narrow.
d.      Most don't provide explicit directions for changing behavior.

**ANS: c**          **Pgs: 8-9**
**LO: 4**           **Conceptual**

16. "Our philosophy is intended to move each person closer to an emotional and spiritual center. Part of the process is helping each individual discover the core of his or her true nature. Once a person is centered, all problems can be managed within the flow, a course of events that is natural and authentic." This statement is
a. an example of psychobabble.
b. just general enough to be helpful.
c. obviously based on empirical research.
d. a good example of sound, specific advice .

**ANS: a**          **Pg: 8**
**LO: 4**          **Conceptual**

17. A high-quality self-help book will
a. give advice on a wide range of problems.
b. be based primarily on the author's speculations about human nature.
c. not promise too much in the way of immediate change.
d. always contain detailed summaries of research supporting the advice given.

**ANS: c**          **Pg: 9**
**LO: 5**          **Conceptual**

18. Which of the following should you look for in self-help books?
a. clarity in communication
b. discussion of what's not known
c. some mention of the theoretical basis for the advice
d. all of these

**ANS: d**          **Pg: 9**
**LO: 5**          **Conceptual**

19. You probably can reasonably expect some assistance from a book that is intended to help you to
a. lose 20 pounds every month.
b. learn to eat more healthily and gradually include more exercise in your weekly routine.
c. build muscle overnight.
d. find the thin person trapped inside of you.

**ANS: b**          **Pg: 9**
**LO: 5**          **Conceptual**

20. Which of the following is **not** one of the underlying assumptions of this textbook?
a. You can change your behavior, if you know the right techniques.
b. The key to effective adjustment is to "take charge" of your own life.
c. The book is a resource that can open other opportunities for change.
d. Knowledge of psychological principles may be of value in everyday life.

**ANS: a**          **Pgs: 9-11**
**LO: 6**          **Conceptual**

21.     Which of the following are essential guidelines for thinking critically?
    1.      Define the problem.
    2.      Avoid emotional reasoning.
    3.      Analyze biases and assumptions.
    4.      Use either-or thinking.

a.      1 only
b.      1 and 3 only
c.      1, 2, and 3 only
d.      1, 2, 3, and 4

**ANS: c**          **Pg: 11**
**LO: 6**           **Conceptual**

22.     "Any overt response or activity by an organism" defines the term
a.      behavior.
b.      empiricism.
c.      psychology.
d.      mental process.

**ANS: a**          **Pg: 11**
**LO: 7**           **Factual**

23.     Some psychologists prefer to study animals rather than humans mainly because
a.      animal subjects tend to be more cooperative than humans.
b.      it's easier to control the factors influencing animals' behavior.
c.      researchers don't have to worry about causing discomfort to animals.
d.      most animals are unable to figure out the hypotheses for a particular study.

**ANS: b**          **Pgs: 11-12**
**LO: 7**           **Conceptual**

24.     Until the 1950s, psychologists were found almost exclusively in
a.      private industry.
b.      academic institutions.
c.      mental health facilities.
d.      the psychiatric wards of hospitals.

**ANS: b**          **Pg: 12**
**LO: 7**           **Factual**

25.     Clinical psychology is primarily concerned with
a.      discovering the mechanisms of learning.
b.      the physiological processes involved in behavior.
c.      research dealing with the structure of consciousness.
d.      the diagnosis and treatment of psychological problems.

**ANS: d**          **Pg: 12**
**LO: 7**           **Factual**

26.    The rapid growth of clinical psychology was stimulated mainly by
a.    the demands of World War II.
b.    growing interest in self-help approaches.
c.    the inability of physicians to cure most psychological disorders.
d.    psychological problems resulting from the Great Depression of the 1930s.

ANS: a            Pg: 12
LO: 7            Factual

27.    The term _____ refers to the psychological processes through which people manage or cope
       with the demands and challenges of everyday life.
a.    adaptation
b.    adjustment
c.    personality
d.    mental health

ANS: b            Pg: 12
LO: 8            Factual

28.    _____ is the premise that knowledge should be acquired through observation.
a.    Self-help
b.    Codependence
c.    Empiricism
d.    Subjectivism

ANS: c            Pg: 13
LO: 9            Factual

29.    Which of the following does **not** represent an empirical technique?
a.    watching people engage in a learning activity
b.    weighing rats after two months of a special diet
c.    gauging the speed with which a patient performs a fine motor activity
d.    speculating about the factors that are related to human happiness

ANS: d            Pg: 13
LO: 9            Factual

30.    Which of the following is the basis of empiricism?
a.    correlation
b.    logic
c.    systematic observation
d.    common sense

ANS: c            Pg: 13
LO: 9            Conceptual

31.	Compared to other methods of drawing conclusions about behavior, the major advantages of the scientific approach are
a.	emphasis on empiricism; subjectivity.
b.	bias; ability to generalize the findings.
c.	clarity and precision; relative intolerance of error.
d.	freedom to make value judgments; use of statistics.

ANS: c		Pg: 13
LO: 10		Conceptual

32.	The two main types of research methods in psychology are _____ research methods and _____ research methods.
a.	biased; unbiased
b.	experimental; control
c.	dependent; independent
d.	experimental; correlational

ANS: d		Pg: 13
LO: 10		Factual

33.	An experiment is a research method in which the investigator manipulates the _____ variable and observes whether any changes occur in a(n) _____ variable as a result.
a.	control; experimental
b.	experimental; control
c.	independent; dependent
d.	dependent; independent

ANS: c		Pgs: 14-15
LO: 11		Factual

*34.	Social psychologist Stanley Schachter hypothesized that increases in anxiety would cause increases in desire to be with others.  In this study, the independent variable was
a.	level of anxiety.
b.	desire to be with others.
c.	anxious subjects.
d.	affiliation.

ANS: a		Pg: 14
LO: 11		Conceptual

35.	A condition or event that an experimenter varies to see its impact on another variable is called a(n) _____ variable.
a.	control
b.	dependent
c.	independent
d.	experimental

ANS: c		Pg: 14
LO: 11		Factual

36.    A measurement of some aspect of the subject's behavior after the experimental manipulation is
       called a(n) _____ variable.
a.     control
b.     dependent
c.     independent
d.     experimental

**ANS: b**          **Pg: 14**
**LO: 11**          **Factual**

37.    A researcher wants to determine whether diet causes children to learn better in school.  In this study,
       the independent variable is
a.     the children.
b.     the type of diet.
c.     the age of the children.
d.     a measure of learning.

**ANS: b**          **Pg: 14**
**LO: 11**          **Conceptual**

38.    A researcher wants to examine the effects of caffeine consumption on memory ability.  In this
       study, the dependent variable is
a.     the children.
b.     memory ability.
c.     caffeine consumption.
d.     the grade level of the children.

**ANS: b**          **Pg: 14**
**LO: 11**          **Conceptual**

39.    An experimental group consists of subjects who
a.     are unaware of the purpose of the study.
b.     merely act as if they are unaware of the purpose.
c.     receive some special treatment in regard to the dependent variable.
d.     receive some special treatment in regard to the independent variable.

**ANS: d**          **Pg: 14**
**LO: 11**          **Factual**

40.    A control group consists of subjects who
a.     are controlled by the experimenter.
b.     are allowed to control the manipulation of the variables.
c.     do not receive the special treatment given to the experimental group.
d.     receive some special treatment in regard to the independent variable.

**ANS: c**          **Pg: 14**
**LO: 11**          **Factual**

41. The experimental and control groups should be the same in every respect except for
a. the number of subjects in each group.
b. the variation created by the manipulation of the independent variable.
c. the assumptions underlying the research question.
d. the method of measuring the dependent variable.

ANS: b          Pg: 14
LO: 11          Conceptual

42. Suppose a researcher wants to know whether a high protein diet causes children to learn better in school. Half of the children in the study eat a high protein diet while the other half eats their norma diet. The control group consists of the
a. male children.
b. older children.
c. children who eat their normal diet.
d. children who eat the high protein diet.

ANS: c          Pg: 14
LO: 11          Conceptual

43. Dr. Brill randomly assigns 100 test-anxious student volunteers to either a group that will receive therapeutic touch treatment or a group that will receive a sham version of the treatment. Based on her results, Dr. Brill will have evidence of
a. how well therapeutic touch works in the treatment of various mood disorders.
b. how test-anxious students behave in a classroom setting.
c. how effective the sham version of the treatment is.
d. whether or not therapeutic touch causes an alleviation of symptoms of test anxiety.

ANS: d          Pg: 14
LO: 11          Conceptual

*44. The logic of the experimental method rests heavily on the assumption that
a. two variables are positively correlated.
b. experimental and control groups are alike in all important matters except for the independent variable.
c. experimental and control groups are alike in all important matters except for the dependent variable.
d. the independent variable is quantifiable and measureable.

ANS: b          Pg: 14
LO: 11          Conceptual

*45. Which of the following is the primary advantage of the experimental method?
a. It lacks the ethical concerns of other methods.
b. It lacks the practical concerns of other methods.
c. It broadens the scope of what psychologists can study scientifically.
d. It allows scientists to draw cause-and-effect conclusions.

ANS: d          Pg: 14
LO: 11          Conceptual

*46.    Which of the following best describes correlational research?
a.      exerting experimental control
b.      manipulating an independent variable
c.      manipulating a dependent variable
d.      making systematic observations

**ANS: d**              **Pg. 15**
**LO: 12**              **Conceptual**

47.     A correlation exists when
a.      two variables are related to each other.
b.      two variables have the same underlying cause.
c.      two variables are affected by a third variable.
d.      a cause-and-effect relationship exists between two variables.

**ANS: a**              **Pg: 15**
**LO: 12**              **Factual**

48.     A(n) _____ is a numerical index of the degree of relationship between two variables.
a.      independent variable
b.      correlation coefficient
c.      survey coefficient
d.      experimental coefficient

**ANS: b**              **Pg: 15**
**LO: 12**              **Factual**

49.     A correlation coefficient indicates the _____ and the _____ of the relationship
        between two variables.
a.      cause; effect
b.      control; manipulation
c.      strength; direction
d.      positive; negative

**ANS: c**              **Pg: 15**
**LO: 12**              **Factual**

50.     The definitive aspect of correlational studies is that
a.      a causal relationship exists between the variables.
b.      researchers can't control the variables under study.
c.      the subjects must constitute a representative sample.
d.      control of one variable interferes with control of another variable.

**ANS: b**              **Pg: 15**
**LO: 12**              **Conceptual**

51. A positive correlation coefficient indicates the two variables covary in the _____ and a negative coefficient indicates that the variables _____ covary.
a. same direction; inversely
b. opposite direction; directly
c. same direction; directly
d. opposite direction; inversely

**ANS: a**        **Pgs: 15-16**
**LO: 12**        **Factual**

52. When two variables covary in the opposite direction, the correlation between those variables will be
a. perfect.
b. positive.
c. negative.
d. nonexistent.

**ANS: c**        **Pg: 15**
**LO: 12**        **Factual**

*53. The textbook author writes, "Those who perform poorly in high school tend to perform poorly in college" as an example of a
a. positive correlation.
b. negative correlation.
c. inverse correlation.
d. indirect correlation.

**ANS: a**        **Pg: 15**
**LO: 12**        **Conceptual**

54. A correlation coefficient of -.80 indicates a
a. mild, inverse correlation.
b. strong, inverse correlation.
c. strong, direct correlation.
d. nonexistent correlation.

**ANS: b**        **Pgs: 16**
**LO: 12**        **Factual**

*55. Which of the following correlation coefficients indicates the weakest relationship between two variables?
a. -4.36
b. -0.97
c. +0.75
d. +0.15

**ANS: d**        **Pg: 16**
**LO: 12**        **Conceptual**

56.  A teacher takes notes while watching students on the playground to see if differences in play behavior are associated with discipline problems in class. The teacher is using which of the following research methods?
a.  survey
b.  case study
c.  experimentation
d.  naturalistic observation

**ANS: d**          **Pgs: 16-17**
**LO: 13**          **Conceptual**

57.  In a case study,
a.  an individual participant is studied in depth.
b.  systematic observation is used to see if a link exists between variables.
c.  behavior is carefully observed without intervening directly with subjects.
d.  a variable is manipulated while another variable is observed for changes.

**ANS: a**          **Pg: 17**
**LO: 13**          **Conceptual**

*58.  Research indicates that
a.  it is unwise for students to change their answers on a multiple choice test.
b.  the more answer changing that students engage in on multiple choice tests, the more they improved their scores.
c.  it doesn't seem to matter whether or not students change their answers on multiple choice tests because they are equally likely to change a wrong answer to a right answer as they are to change a right answer to a wrong answer.
d.  it is unwise for D and F students to change their answers on multiple choice tests but wise for A and B students.

**ANS: b**          **Pg: 17**
**LO: 13**          **Factual**

59.  Suppose a researcher gave you a form to fill out about your attitudes on abortion, school prayer, and drug legalization. This researcher is using which of the following research methods?
a.  experiment
b.  case study
c.  survey
d.  naturalistic observation

**ANS: c**          **Pg: 17**
**LO: 13**          **Conceptual**

60.  Correlational research broadens the scope of phenomena that psychologists can study because it
a.  allows investigators to do research outside a laboratory setting.
b.  provides a way to investigate variables that can't be manipulated.
c.  doesn't require that the variables be causally related to each other.
d.  involves research that doesn't intrude into the subjects' natural settings.

**ANS: b**          **Pg: 18**
**LO: 14**          **Conceptual**

*61. Survey studies show a positive correlation between marital satisfaction and sexual satisfaction. This indicates that
a. a healthy marriage causes good sex.
b. good sex promotes healthy marriages.
c. couples who have a high marital satisfaction are more likely to have high sexual satisfaction than couples who have a low marital satisfaction.
d. marital satisfaction is not related to sexual satisfaction.

**ANS: c**      **Pg: 18**
**LO: 14**      **Conceptual**

62. The major disadvantage of correlational research is that it
a. is costly to carry out.
b. is artificial, and it is hard to apply the results to real-life settings.
c. is time-consuming and impractical to manipulate variables.
d. cannot demonstrate conclusively that two variables are causally related.

**ANS: d**      **Pgs: 18-19**
**LO: 14**      **Conceptual**

*63. The "third variable" problem is associated with
a. the experimental method.
b. the correlational method.
c. the independent method.
d. the control method.

**ANS: b**      **Pg: 19**
**LO: 14**      **Factual**

64. Empirical surveys consistently find that the vast majority of respondents characterize themselves as
a. fairly happy.
b. very unhappy.
c. moderately unhappy.
d. unconcerned about their personal happiness.

**ANS: a**      **Pg: 19**
**LO: 15**      **Factual**

65. Research results suggest that which of the following is **not** very important in determining one's happiness?
a. money
c. gender
b. intelligence
d. None of these is very important.

**ANS: d**      **Pg: 20**
**LO: 16**      **Factual**

56. Which of the following best characterizes the correlation between income and subjective feelings of happiness?
a. negligible
b. negative, but weak
c. positive, but weak
d. positive and strong

ANS: c          Pg: 20
LO: 16          Factual

*67. Research indicates that people who have children
a. are happier than people without children.
b. are less happy than people without children.
c. are neither more or less happy than people without children.
d. are happier than people without children only if they are married.

ANS: c          Pg: 20
LO: 16          Factual

*68. Research indicates that
a. people with high IQ's are happier than people with low IQ's.
b. people with low IQ's are happier than people with high IQ's.
c. there is no association between IQ and happiness.
d. people with really high IQ's and really low IQ's aren't as happy as people with average IQ's.

ANS: c          Pg: 20
LO: 16          Factual

*69. Which of the following is the best description of the relationship between health and happiness?
a. Good health may not, by itself, produce happiness, because people tend to take good health for granted.
b. Good health is one of the best predictors of happiness.
c. Individuals who develop serious health problems have difficulty adjusting and therefore are less happy than those who are healthy.
d. People born with serious health problems are happier than others because they do not take their health for granted.

ANS: a          Pgs: 20-21
LO: 17          Conceptual

70. All of the following appear to have a moderate impact on subjective feelings of well-being **except**
a. health.
b. physical attractiveness.
c. religious belief.
d. social activity.

ANS: b          Pgs: 20-21
LO: 17          Factual

15

71.    Which of the following has been found to be strongly related to overall happiness?
a.    culture
b.    marriage
c.    income
d.    physical attractiveness

**ANS: b**          **Pgs: 21-22**
**LO: 18**          **Factual**

*72.    Research indicates that
a.    married men are happier than married women.
b.    married women are happier than married men.
c.    both married men and women are happier than unmarried men and women.
d.    both unmarried men and women are happier than married men and women.

**ANS: c**          **Pg: 22**
**LO: 18**          **Factual**

73.    The authors suggest that we should be careful about drawing conclusions about causes of happiness because
a.    they would not be based on empirical evidence.
b.    they would be based on experimental data.
c.    they would be based on correlational data.
d.    they have been found to be invalid by some researchers.

**ANS: c**          **Pgs: 22-23**
**LO: 19**          **Conceptual**

74.    An important insight that can be drawn from the research on happiness is that
a.    money can buy happiness.
b.    attractive people are generally happy people.
c.    objective realities are not as important as subjective feelings.
d.    collectivist cultures are happier than individualistic cultures.

**ANS: c**          **Pgs: 22-23**
**LO: 19**          **Conceptual**

75.    _____ occurs when people shift their own mental scale and change the baseline for comparisons of their own circumstances with those of other people.
a.    Codependency
b.    Empiricism
c.    Subjectivism
d.    Hedonic adaptation

**ANS: d**          **Pg: 23**
**LO: 19**          **Conceptual**

*76. Research indicates that hedonic adaptation
a. probably helps protect mental and physical health.
b. hinders mental health but does not affect physical health.
c. is detrimental to physical but not mental health.
d. has a negative effect on both mental and physical health.

**ANS: a**          **Pg: 23**
**LO: 19**          **Factual**

77. In setting up a schedule for studying, you should
a. allow time for study breaks.
b. develop a new set of priorities each day.
c. try to get the simple, routine tasks out of the way first.
d. avoid the temptation to break up major assignments into smaller parts.

**ANS: a**          **Pg: 24**
**LO: 20**          **Factual**

78. A good place to study is one
a. where you can listen to music while studying.
b. that changes occasionally, to provide variety.
c. that is associated with pleasant activities, like eating.
d. that minimizes demands on your willpower to avoid distractions.

**ANS: d**          **Pgs: 24-25**
**LO: 20**          **Conceptual**

79. When you reward yourself for meeting realistic study goals, you're using the principles of
a. SQ3R.
b. classical conditioning.
c. behavior modification.
d. systematic desensitization.

**ANS: c**          **Pg: 25**
**LO: 20**          **Factual**

80. In order for your reading to be effective, it must be done
a. rapidly.
b. actively.
c. repeatedly.
d. in large chunks.

**ANS: b**          **Pgs: 25-26**
**LO: 20**          **Factual**

81.     Which of the following is **not** involved in the survey step of the SQ3R method?
a.      Review the main terms in each chapter.
b.      Consult the chapter outline or summary.
c.      Look over the topic headings in a chapter.
d.      Consider how parts of the chapter are related.

**ANS: a**          **Pgs: 25-26**
**LO: 21**          **Factual**

82.     In the last step of the SQ3R method you should
a.      reread the chapter at a leisurely pace.
b.      reward yourself for all the work you've done.
c.      test your memory by going over key points.
d.      go back to the first step and repeat the process.

**ANS: c**          **Pg: 26**
**LO: 21**          **Conceptual**

*83.    Which of the following is consistent with the information presented in the textbook regarding class attendance?
a.      Among successful students (grade average B or better) class attendance did not seem to matter.
b.      Among unsuccessful students (grade average C- or below) class attendance did not seem to matter.
c.      Even when an instructor delivers hard-to-follow lectures, it is important for all students to go to class.
d.      It is only important for all students to go to class when instructors provide well-organized lectures.

**ANS: c**          **Pgs: 26-27**
**LO: 21**          **Factual**

84.     Which one of the following is **not** included in active listening?
a.      focusing attention on the speaker
b.      asking those around you for clarification
c.      anticipating what's coming next in the lecture
d.      paying attention to the speaker's nonverbal signals

**ANS: b**          **Pg: 27**
**LO: 22**          **Conceptual**

85.     When course material is especially difficult, it's a good idea to prepare for lectures by
a.      reading ahead on the subject of the lecture.
b.      asking fellow classmates to explain the material to you.
c.      writing down questions that you can ask the instructor later.
d.      reviewing previous material that relates to the present topic.

**ANS: a**          **Pg: 27**
**LO: 22**          **Conceptual**

86. A good reason for taking notes in your own words, rather than verbatim, is that
a. most lecturers are quite wordy.
b. "translating" on the spot is a helpful mental exercise.
c. this reduces the likelihood that you'll later engage in plagiarism.
d. this forces you to organize the information in a way that makes sense to you.

ANS: d          Pg: 27
LO: 22          Conceptual

87. When a question occurs to you during a lecture, you should
a. ask it during class.
b. ask a classmate about it after class.
c. write it down and ask the instructor after class.
d. not ask it, since this would interrupt the lecturer.

ANS: a          Pg: 27
LO: 22          Conceptual

88. Which of the following is **not** one of the tips for getting more out of lectures?
a. Ask questions in class.
b. Listen actively to the lecture.
c. Pay attention to the instructor's nonverbal signals.
d. Try to use the instructor's words when taking notes in class.

ANS: d          Pgs: 26-27
LO: 22          Conceptual

89. Overlearning refers to continued practice of material after you
a. have completed your study plan.
b. have already passed the relevant test.
c. have apparently mastered the material.
d. have become exhausted from studying.

ANS: c          Pg: 27
LO: 23          Factual

90. In psychology, the term "interference" refers to
a. being interrupted while trying to learn something.
b. forgetting due to competition from other information.
c. the intrusion of daydreams when you're trying to learn material.
d. being unable to recall material due to the presence of environmental stimuli.

ANS: b          Pgs: 27-28
LO: 23          Factual

91.     On the day before a test in a particular course, it is probably best
a.      to study only material from that course to minimize interference.
b.      not to overlearn the material.
c.      to avoid studying that material.
d.      to take advantage of the massed practice effect.

**ANS: a**          **Pgs: 27-28**
**LO: 23**          **Conceptual**

92.     A useful study technique that helps to organize information is
a.      outlining reading assignments.
b.      studying with a group of students.
c.      underlining important points in textbooks.
d.      memorizing the order of chapter headings.

**ANS: a**          **Pg: 28**
**LO: 23**          **Conceptual**

93.     _____ refers to learning by emphasizing the personal meaningfulness of material that one has learned in a course.
a.      Mnemonics
b.      Deep processing
c.      Distributed practice
d.      Cramming

**ANS: b**          **Pg: 28**
**LO: 23**          **Conceptual**

*94.    Exercising deep processing means
a.      devoting effort to analyzing the meaning of the reading assignments.
b.      engaging in maintenance rehearsal to establish rote memory.
c.      using mnemonic devices.
d.      rereading the assignments over the course of several different sessions.

**ANS: a**          **Pg: 28**
**LO: 23**          **Factual**

95.     A mnemonic device is a strategy used for
a.      reading actively.
b.      enhancing memory.
c.      reducing interference.
d.      promoting overlearning.

**ANS: b**          **Pg: 28**
**LO: 23**          **Factual**

5. Using "Roy G Biv" to remember the order of colors in the light spectrum is an example of how _____ can help us remember information.
   acrostics
   acronyms
   overlearning
   visual imagery

NS: b          Pg: 28
O: 23          Conceptual

7. Using "Every good boy does fine" to remember the order of musical notes is an example of how _____ can help us remember information.
   acrostics
   acronyms
   overlearning
   visual imagery

NS: a          Pg: 28
O: 23          Conceptual

8. The loci method is a mnemonic device that involves
   making up a logical story.
   inventing a useful acronym.
   memorizing a simple poem.
   taking a make-believe walk.

NS: d          Pg: 29
O: 23          Factual


## MULTIPLE CHOICE QUESTIONS FROM STUDY GUIDE

. In spite of our great technological progress, social problems and personal difficulties seem more prevalent than ever before. This issue is known as the
   approach-avoidance conflict.
   paradox of progress.
   self-realization dilemma.
   paradox of paradoxes.

NS: b          Pg: 4
O: 2          Factual

. According to your textbook, one of the major problems with self-help books is that they are dominated by
   psychobabble.
   graphs and tables.
   research results.
   complicated mathematical models.

NS: a          Pg: 8
O: 4          Factual

3.    "Subjecting ideas to systematic, skeptical scrutiny" best describes which of the following processes?
a.    self-realization
b.    critical thinking
c.    self-actualization
d.    psychological adjustment

ANS: b            Pg: 11
LO: 6            Factual

4.    The branch of psychology concerned with the diagnosis and treatment of psychological problems and disorders is called _____ psychology.
a.    social
b.    clinical
c.    cognitive
d.    physiological

ANS: b            Pg: 12
LO: 7            Factual

5.    The emphasis of psychological science on systematic observation best illustrates which of the following concepts?
a.    empiricism
b.    correlation
c.    determinism
d.    self-realization

ANS: a            Pg: 13
LO: 9            Conceptual

6.    Which of the following is not a characteristic of scientists' investigations?
a.    formal
b.    systematic
c.    subjective
d.    empirical

ANS: c            Pg: 13
LO: 10            Factual

7.    Which of the following is **most** likely to be used as an independent variable in a psychological experiment?
a.    reaction time
b.    desire to affiliate
c.    level of noise
d.    aggression

ANS: c            Pg: 14
LO: 11            Factual

8.  A psychological researcher will most likely be able to draw conclusions about cause-and-effect relationships by using which of the following research methods?
a.  survey
b.  case study
c.  experiment
d.  naturalistic observation

**ANS: c**          **Pgs: 13-14**
**LO: 11**          **Factual**

9.  The correlation coefficient measuring the relationship between time spent studying and percent correct on a psychology exam is likely to be
a.  zero.
b.  positive.
c.  negative.
d.  subjective.

**ANS: b**          **Pg: 15**
**LO: 12**          **Conceptual**

10. An in-depth investigation of an individual participant is called a(n)
a.  case study.
b.  experiment.
c.  correlational study.
d.  naturalistic observation.

**ANS: a**          **Pg: 17**
**LO: 13**          **Factual**

11. Which of the following variables is <u>least</u> important in determining an individual's happiness?
a.  health
b.  money
c.  social activity
d.  job satisfaction

**ANS: b**          **Pg: 20**
**LO: 16**          **Factual**

12. The best predictor of individuals' future happiness is their
a.  IQ score.
b.  past happiness.
c.  marital status.
d.  financial status.

**ANS: b**          **Pgs: 21-22**
**LO: 18**          **Factual**

13. An organized study program should include
a. a detailed schedule of when and what to study.
b. a place of your own to study that is free of distractions.
c. rewards that are immediate and satisfying when goals are attained.
d. all of these.

**ANS: d**          **Pgs: 24-25**
**LO: 20**          **Factual**

14. Which of the following is the correct order for the five steps in the SQ3R method?
a. survey, question, recite, read, review
b. question, survey, read, recite, review
c. survey, question, review, read, recite
d. survey, question, read, recite, review

**ANS: d**          **Pgs: 25-26**
**LO: 21**          **Factual**

15. Forgetting learned material because of competition from other learned material
a. is called interference.
b. is called inhibition.
c. seldom happens if the material is really learned.
d. happens only when students use massed practice.

**ANS:**            **Pg: 27**
**LO: 23**          Factual

## MULTIPLE CHOICE QUESTIONS ON WEB SITE

*1.    "Psychobabble" is best defined as
a.    psychological jargon.
b.    textbook definitions.
c.    ill-defined terminology.
d.    technical terminology.

**ANS: c          Pg: 8**
**LO: 4          Factual**

*2.    Which of the following is the best definition of psychology?
a.    the study of consciousness
b.    the study of behavior and the profession that applies knowledge from these studies to solving practical problems
c.    the study of abnormal behavior and the profession that applies knowledge from these studies to diagnosing and treating people with mental illness
d.    the study of motivation, emotion, and memory

**ANS: b          Pg: 11**
**LO: 7          Factual**

3.    "Any overt response or activity by an organism" defines the term
a.    behavior.
b.    empiricism.
c.    psychology.
d.    mental process.

**ANS: a          Pg: 11**
**LO: 7          Factual**

4.    Clinical psychology is primarily concerned with
a.    discovering the mechanisms of learning.
b.    the physiological processes involved in behavior.
c.    research dealing with the structure of consciousness.
d.    the diagnosis and treatment of psychological problems.

**ANS: d          Pg: 12**
**LO: 7          Factual**

5.    Which of the following is the basis of empiricism?
a.    correlation
b.    logic
c.    systematic observation
d.    common sense

**ANS: c          Pg: 13**
**LO: 9          Conceptual**

6.      A condition or event that an experimenter varies to see its impact on another variable is called a(n) _____ variable.
a.      control
b.      dependent
c.      independent
d.      experimental

**ANS: c**            **Pg: 14**
**LO: 11**            **Factual**

7.      An experimental group consists of subjects who
a.      are unaware of the purpose of the study.
b.      merely act as if they are unaware of the purpose.
c.      receive some special treatment in regard to the dependent variable.
d.      receive some special treatment in regard to the independent variable.

**ANS: d**            **Pg: 14**
**LO: 11**            **Factual**

*8.     Which of the following is the primary advantage of the experimental method?
a.      It lacks the ethical concerns of other methods.
b.      It lacks the practical concerns of other methods.
c.      It broadens the scope of what psychologists can study scientifically.
d.      It allows scientists to draw cause-and-effect conclusions.

**ANS: d**            **Pg: 14**
**LO: 11**            **Conceptual**

9.      In a case study,
a.      an individual participant is studied in depth.
b.      systematic observation is used to see if a link exists between variables.
c.      behavior is carefully observed without intervening directly with subjects.
d.      a variable is manipulated while another variable is observed for changes.

**ANS: a**            **Pg: 17**
**LO: 13**            **Conceptual**

10.     The major disadvantage of correlational research is that it
a.      is costly to carry out.
b.      is artificial, and it is hard to apply the results to real-life settings.
c.      is time-consuming and impractical to manipulate variables.
d.      cannot demonstrate conclusively that two variables are causally related.

**ANS: d**            **Pgs: 18-19**
**LO: 14**            **Conceptual**

11.    Which of the following best characterizes the correlation between income and subjective feelings of happiness?
a.    negligible
b.    negative, but weak
c.    positive, but weak
d.    positive and strong

**ANS: c**          **Pg: 20**
**LO: 16**          **Factual**

*12.    Research indicates that
a.    married men are happier than married women.
b.    married women are happier than married men.
c.    both married men and women are happier than unmarried men and women.
d.    both unmarried men and women are happier than married men and women.

**ANS: c**          **Pg: 22**
**LO: 18**          **Factual**

13.    In setting up a schedule for studying, you should
a.    allow time for study breaks.
b.    develop a new set of priorities each day.
c.    try to get the simple, routine tasks out of the way first.
d.    avoid the temptation to break up major assignments into smaller parts.

**ANS: a**          **Pg: 24**
**LO: 20**          **Factual**

14.    In the last step of the SQ3R method you should
a.    reread the chapter at a leisurely pace.
b.    reward yourself for all the work you've done.
c.    test your memory by going over key points.
d.    go back to the first step and repeat the process.

**ANS: c**          **Pg: 26**
**LO: 21**          **Conceptual**

15.    In psychology, the term "interference" refers to
a.    being interrupted while trying to learn something.
b.    forgetting due to competition from other information.
c.    the intrusion of daydreams when you're trying to learn material.
d.    being unable to recall material due to the presence of environmental stimuli.

**ANS: b**          **Pgs: 27-28**
**LO: 23**          **Factual**

## TRUE/FALSE QUESTIONS

1.  Recent decades have provided us with an increased freedom to choose between multiple alternatives. This choice overload appears to be positively correlated with rumination, postdecision regret, and anticipated regret.
**ANS: true**          **Pg: 2**
**LO: 1 & 12**         **Conceptual**

2.  One of the criticisms of self-help books is that they address rare problems that do not apply to very many readers.
**ANS: false**         **Pgs: 7-8**
**LO: 3**              **Factual**

3.  This text attempts to discourage a critical attitude about psychological issues and to decrease the readers' critical thinking.
**ANS: false**         **Pgs: 10-11**
**LO: 6**              **Factual**

4.  Psychology confines itself to the study of human behavior.
**ANS: false**         **Pgs: 11-12**
**LO: 7**              **Factual**

5.  One advantage of the scientific method is its relative intolerance of error.
**ANS: true**          **Pgs: 13**
**LO: 10**             **Factual**

6.  Psychologists have found an association between feelings of hopelessness and suicidal behavior; that is, the more hopeless a person feels the more likely that person is to engage in suicidal behavior. This is a good example of a negative correlation.
**ANS: false**         **Pgs: 15-16**
**LO: 12**             **Conceptual**

7.  According to research, many common sense notions about happiness appear to be accurate.
**ANS: false**         **Pg: 19**
**LO: 15**             **Factual**

8.  People's level of happiness tends to remain remarkably stable over the life span.
**ANS: true**          **Pgs: 22-23**
**LO: 16**             **Factual**

9.  In general women are less happy than men; this is evident in the statistics indicating that women are treated for depression about twice as often as men.
**ANS: false**         **Pg: 20**
**LO: 16**             **Factual**

10. It is important to understand that studying involves hard work.
**ANS: true**          **Pg: 24**
**LO: 20**             **Factual**

## SHORT-ANSWER ESSAY QUESTIONS

1. Explain what is meant by the paradox of progress and give two examples to illustrate your point.

**Pgs: 2-4**
**LO: 2**

2. What are the main qualities to look for in a good self-help book?

**Pg: 9**
**LO: 5**

3. List and briefly describe two advantages of the scientific approach.

**Pg: 13**
**LO: 10**

4. Define and explain the relationship between the dependent and independent variables in a psychological experiment.

**Pgs: 13-14**
**LO: 11**

5. Distinguish between an experimental group and a control group in a psychological experiment.

**Pg: 14**
**LO: 11**

6. Under what specific conditions is correlational research appropriate in psychology?

**Pgs: 15-18**
**LO: 13**

7. What are the main advantages and disadvantages of correlational research methods in psychology?

**Pg: 18**
**LO: 14**

8. List and describe three factors that are surprisingly **not** related to happiness.

**Pg: 20**
**LO: 16**

9. List and briefly describe several factors that have been found to be very important determinants of happiness.

**Pgs: 21-22**
**LO: 18**

10.    Briefly describe several strategies for learning more from your class lectures and studying.

**Pgs: 26-29**
**LO: 22**

# Chapter 2
# THEORIES OF PERSONALITY

## LEARNING OBJECTIVES

1. Explain the concepts of personality and traits.
2. Describe the "Big Five" personality traits.
3. Describe Freud's three components of personality and how they are distributed across levels of awareness.
4. Explain the importance of sexual and aggressive conflicts in Freud's theory.
5. Describe seven defense mechanisms identified by Freud.
6. Outline Freud's stages of psychosexual development and their theorized relations to adult personality.
7. Summarize Jung's views on the unconscious.
8. Summarize Adler's views on key issues relating to personality.
9. Evaluate the strengths and weaknesses of psychodynamic theories of personality.
10. Describe Pavlov's classical conditioning and its contribution to understanding personality.
11. Discuss how Skinner's principles of operant conditioning can be applied to personality development.
12. Describe Bandura's social learning theory and his concept of self-efficacy.
13. Evaluate the strengths and weaknesses of behavioral theories of personality.
14. Discuss humanism as a school of thought in psychology.
15. Explain Rogers's views on self-concept, development, and defensive behavior.
16. Describe Maslow's hierarchy of needs and summarize his findings on self-actualizing persons.
17. Evaluate the strengths and weaknesses of humanistic theories of personality.
18. Describe Eysenck's views on personality structure and development.
19. Summarize recent twin studies that support the idea that personality is largely inherited.
20. Summarize evolutionary analyses of why certain personality traits appear to be important.
21. Evaluate the strengths and weaknesses of biological theories of personality.
22. Explain the chief concepts and hypotheses of terror management theory.
23. Describe how reminders of death influence people's behavior.
24. Discuss why the subject of personality has generated so much theoretical diversity.
25. Compare and contrast the personality theories of Freud, Skinner, Rogers, and Eysenck.
26. Explain the concepts of standardization, test norms, reliability, and validity.
27. Discuss the value and the limitations of self-report inventories.
28. Discuss the value and limitations of projective tests.

## MULTIPLE CHOICE QUESTIONS

1. Which of the following ideas lies at the core of the concept of personality?
a. being true to oneself
b. traits shared with others
c. consistency across situations
d. being able to adjust to different situations

**ANS: c**      **Pg: 34**
**LO: 1**      **Factual**

2. Which of the following ideas is **not** central to the concept of personality?
a. consistency across situations
b. traits that are shared with others
c. distinctiveness of an individual
d. a unique collection of traits possessed by an individual

**ANS: b**      **Pg: 34**
**LO: 1**      **Factual**

3. Psychology uses the concept of personality to explain all of the following **except**
a. stability in a person's behavior over time.
b. stability in a person's behavior across situations.
c. behavioral differences between people in the same situation.
d. differences in people's attitudes across cultures.

**ANS: d**      **Pg: 34**
**LO: 1**      **Conceptual**

4. _____ refers to an individual's unique constellation of consistent behavioral traits.
a. Cognition
b. Personality
c. Consistency
d. Distinctiveness

**ANS: b**      **Pg: 34**
**LO: 1**      **Conceptual**

5. "Impulsive," "mellow," and "shy" are all adjectives that can be used to represent
a. personality theories.
b. personality traits.
c. personality tests.
d. social situations.

**ANS: b**      **Pg: 34**
**LO: 1**      **Conceptual**

6. Sue's friends say that she is sympathetic, trusting, cooperative, and straightforward. Which of the following "Big Five" traits would best describe her?
a. neuroticism
b. extraversion
c. agreeableness
d. conscientiousness

**ANS: c**        **Pg: 35**
**LO: 2**        **Conceptual**

7. Eric studies three hours per day, five days a week. He only misses school when he is sick and is almost never late for class. On which of the following "Big Five" traits would he likely receive a high score?
a. neuroticism
b. extraversion
c. agreeableness
d. conscientiousness

**ANS: d**        **Pg: 35**
**LO: 2**        **Conceptual**

8. Which of the following is/are "Big Five" traits?
1. Neuroticism
2. Openness to experience
3. Fortitude

a. 1 only
b. 2 only
c. 1 and 2 only
d. 1, 2, and 3

**ANS: c**        **Pgs: 34-35**
**LO: 2**        **Factual**

9. All psychodynamic theories stem from the work of
a. Jung.
b. Adler.
c. Freud.
d. Rogers.

**ANS: c**        **Pg: 35**
**LO: 3**        **Factual**

10. Which of the following is **not** considered to be a psychodynamic theory of personality?
a. Adler's individual psychology
b. Jung's analytical psychology
c. Freud's theory of psychoanalysis
d. Rogers' client-centered psychology

ANS: d          Pg: 35
LO: 3           Factual

11. Psychodynamic theories of personality tend to focus on
a. a set of basic personality traits.
b. unconscious mental processes.
c. the unique qualities of human beings.
d. reward and punishment as primary forces in personality.

ANS: b          Pg: 35
LO: 3           Factual

12. Central to the Freudian conceptualization of personality is
a. the effect of reward and punishment.
b. striving for superiority.
c. how people cope with their own sexual and aggressive urges.
d. the need to self-actualize.

ANS: c          Pgs: 35-36
LO: 3           Factual

13. In psychoanalytic theory, the personality component that operates according to the pleasure principle is the
a. id.
b. ego.
c. superego.
d. superid.

ANS: a          Pg: 36
LO: 3           Factual

14. The moral component of personality, according to Freud, is represented by the
a. id.
b. ego.
c. superego.
d. superid.

ANS: c          Pg: 36
LO: 3           Factual

15. Which of the following is **not** one of the three levels of awareness proposed by Freud?
a. conscious
b. unconscious
c. preconscious
d. collective unconscious

**ANS: d**          **Pgs: 36-37**
**LO: 3**           **Factual**

16. According to Freud, the _____ contains thoughts and feelings that are just below the surface of awareness.
a. id
b. libido
c. preconscious
d. collective unconscious

**ANS: c**          **Pg: 37**
**LO: 3**           **Factual**

17. According to Freud, internal conflict among the id, ego, and superego
a. is routine.
b. is relatively rare.
c. occurs only in individuals with extreme anxiety.
d. can be managed only through psychotherapy.

**ANS: a**          **Pgs: 36-37**
**LO: 4**           **Factual**

*18. Which of the following is **not** listed as one of the controversial issues related to Freud's theory?
a. Freud asserted that people are not masters of their own mind.
b. Freud asserted that people are not masters of their own destiny.
c. Freud asserted that personalities are shaped by how people cope with sexual urges.
d. Freud asserted that children require complete, unconditional positive regard from parents to grow up mentally healthy.

**ANS: d**          **Pgs: 35-36**
**LO: 4**           **Factual**

19. According to Freud, conflicts centering on _____ and _____ impulses are especially likely to have far-reaching consequences.
a. sexual; death
b. power; death
c. sexual; aggressive
d. aggressive; achievement

**ANS: c**          **Pg: 37**
**LO: 4**           **Conceptual**

20.     You're feeling guilty after your third bowl of ice cream. You tell yourself it's alright because yesterday you skipped lunch. This is an example of
a.      conceptualization.
b.      rationalization.
c.      displacement.
d.      identification.

**ANS: b**          **Pg: 39**
**LO: 5**           **Conceptual**

21.     A witness to a brutal murder has trouble remembering any details of the crime. According to Freud, which defense mechanism is at work in this example?
a.      projection
b.      reaction formation
c.      regression
d.      repression

**ANS: d**          **Pg: 39**
**LO: 5**           **Conceptual**

22.     Attributing your own thoughts, feelings, or motives to others to ward off anxiety or guilt is called
a.      regression.
b.      displacement.
c.      projection.
d.      reaction formation.

**ANS: c**          **Pg: 39**
**LO: 5**           **Factual**

23.     Two months ago, your best friend did not win a major scholarship that she had been counting on to help pay for graduate school. Now she is always fighting with you, her boyfriend, and her roommates. She is most likely using the defense mechanism called
a.      regression.
b.      displacement.
c.      projection.
d.      identification.

**ANS: b**          **Pg: 39**
**LO: 5**           **Conceptual**

24. In psychoanalytic theory, failure to move forward from one developmental stage to another is called
a. extinction.
b. regression.
c. inertia.
d. fixation.

**ANS: d**       **Pg: 40**
**LO: 6**       **Factual**

25. Which of the following is the correct order of Freud's psychosexual stages?
a. anal, oral, phallic, genital, latency
b. phallic, anal, oral, latency, genital
c. oral, genital, phallic, anal, latency
d. oral, anal, phallic, latency, genital

**ANS: d**       **Pgs: 40-41**
**LO: 6**       **Factual**

26. According to Freud, a newborn baby is in the _____ stage of psychosexual development.
a. anal
b. latency
c. oral
d. phallic

**ANS: c**       **Pg: 40**
**LO: 6**       **Factual**

27. According to Freud, in order to achieve healthy development, a child in the phallic stage must resolve the Oedipal complex and learn to _____ the same sex parent.
a. annoy
b. be fearful of
c. deceive
d. identify with

**ANS: d**       **Pgs: 40-41**
**LO: 6**       **Factual**

*28.    Jan is a very dependent and clingy individual who relies on obsessive eating and smoking to cope with her problems.  According to Freud, Jan is suffering from fixation in the

a.      phallic stage.
b.      oral stage.
c.      anal stage.
d.      genital stage.

**ANS: b**          **Pg: 40**
**LO: 6**           **Conceptual**

29.     Carl Jung proposed that the unconscious consists of two layers, the _____ and the _____.

a.      preconscious; subconscious
b.      personal unconscious; collective unconscious
c.      personal unconscious; archetype
d.      individual archetype; collective archetype

**ANS: b**          **Pgs: 41-42**
**LO: 7**           **Factual**

30.     According to Jung, the collective unconscious is a storehouse of latent memory traces inherited from people's ancestral past, which is
a.      unique to each individual.
b.      shared with the entire human race.
c.      shared with one's blood relatives.
d.      accessible only through free association.

**ANS: b**          **Pgs: 41-42**
**LO: 7**           **Factual**

31.     One idea from Jung's personality theory that has been incorporated into mainstream modern psychology is the notion of
a.      archetypes.
b.      mnemonics.
c.      collective unconscious.
d.      introversion/extraversion.

**ANS: d**          **Pg: 42**
**LO: 7**           **Conceptual**

32.     Alfred Adler emphasized the _____ context of personality development.
a.      cognitive
b.      emotional
c.      sexual
d.      social

**ANS: d**          **Pg: 42**
**LO: 8**           **Factual**

33. According to Adler, _____ involves efforts to overcome imagined or real inferiorities by developing one's abilities.
a. introversion
b. compensation
c. reaction formation
d. individual psychology

**ANS: b**          **Pg: 42**
**LO: 8**           **Factual**

34. John is always putting himself down and expressing doubts in his own abilities. According to Adler, John may have a(n)
a. inferiority complex.
b. Oedipal complex.
c. fixation at the oral stage of development.
d. underdeveloped social interest.

**ANS: a**          **Pg: 42**
**LO: 8**           **Conceptual**

*35. Adler's theory stimulated hundreds of studies on the effect of _____. Although these studies generally failed to find support for their hypotheses, more recent studies focusing on the Big Five traits have found some support.
a. birth order
b. reinforcement histories
c. primary processes
d. self-actualization

**ANS: a**          **Pg: 42**
**LO: 8**           **Factual**

36. Which of the following notions is **not** considered one of the major contributions of psychoanalytic theory?
a. role of childhood experiences in influencing adult personality
b. role of internal conflict in generating psychological distress
c. influence of reinforcement in maintaining specific behaviors
d. importance of unconscious motivation in influencing behavior

**ANS: c**          **Pg: 43**
**LO: 9**           **Conceptual**

37. Critics have described the psychodynamic perspective as:
    1. biased against females
    2. empirically untestable
    3. overemphasizing unconscious desires

a. 1 only
b. 2 only
c. 1 and 2 only
d. 1, 2, and 3

**ANS: c**          **Pgs: 43-44**
**LO: 9**           **Conceptual**

38. Which of the following theoretical orientations asserts that scientific psychology should focus on the study of observable behavior?
a. humanism
b. behaviorism
c. psychoanalysis
d. structuralism

**ANS: b**          **Pg: 44**
**LO: 10**          **Conceptual**

39. Which of the following individuals is generally recognized for initiating the development of behaviorism?
a. John B. Watson
b. Alfred Adler
c. Albert Bandura
d. Hans Eysenck

**ANS: a**          **Pg: 44**
**LO: 10**          **Factual**

40. Which of the following is a behaviorist definition of personality?
a. a collection of response tendencies that arise in various stimulus situations
b. an individual's striving for superiority
c. a person's durable dispositions that arise in a variety of situations
d. the nature of a person's mental processes

**ANS: a**          **Pg: 44**
**LO: 10**          **Factual**

41. Which of the following individuals is credited with discovering classical conditioning?
a. Carl Rogers
b. Ivan Pavlov
c. Sigmund Freud
d. Abraham Maslow

**ANS: b**          **Pgs: 44-45**
**LO: 10**          **Factual**

42. An originally neutral stimulus that acquires the capacity to elicit a conditioned response is called a(n)
a. unconditioned stimulus.
b. conditioned stimulus.
c. response-bound stimulus.
d. association-positive stimulus.

**ANS: b**          **Pg: 45**
**LO: 10**          **Factual**

43. In classical conditioning, responses are said to be
a. emitted.
b. elicited.
c. spontaneous.
d. extinguished.

**ANS: b**          **Pgs: 44-45**
**LO: 10**          **Factual**

44. Which one of the following types of human responses is most likely to be governed by classical conditioning?
a. cognitive
b. emotional
c. psychomotor
d. social

**ANS: b**          **Pg: 46**
**LO: 10**          **Conceptual**

45. Getting hungry upon hearing the advertising jingle for a fast-food chain is an example of _____ conditioning.
a. operant
b. social
c. classical
d. emotional

**ANS: c**          **Pg: 46**
**LO: 10**          **Conceptual**

46.   According to the principles of classical conditioning, the consistent presentation of the CS alone, without the UCS, is likely to lead to which of the following?
a.    extinction
b.    recovery
c.    transference
d.    negative reinforcement

**ANS: a            Pg: 46**
**LO: 10            Factual**

47.   The strengthening of a response tendency by virtue of the fact that the response leads to the removal of an unpleasant stimulus is
a.    positive reinforcement.
b.    negative reinforcement.
c.    primary reinforcement.
d.    secondary reinforcement.

**ANS: b            Pgs: 47-48**
**LO: 11            Factual**

48.   _____ refers to the process of learning as one experiences the consequences of voluntary actions.
a.    Operant conditioning
b.    Classical conditioning
c.    Social learning
d.    Extinction

**ANS: a            Pg: 47**
**LO: 11            Factual**

49.   If you clean your room to put an end to your father's incessant nagging on the subject, your room-cleaning response has been
a.    extinguished.
b.    discriminated.
c.    positively reinforced.
d.    negatively reinforced.

**ANS: d            Pgs: 47-48**
**LO: 11            Conceptual**

50.   Working hard to sell the most widgets for your employer in order to earn a bonus and paid vacation is behavior that is shaped by the prospect of
a.    primary reinforcement.
b.    negative reinforcement.
c.    positive reinforcement.
d.    secondary reinforcement.

**ANS: c            Pg: 47**
**LO: 11            Conceptual**

51.    Attempting to weaken a response by presenting a noxious or aversive stimulus after that
       response is called
a.     punishment.
b.     classical conditioning.
c.     extinction.
d.     negative reinforcement.

**ANS: a**          **Pg: 48**
**LO: 11**          **Factual**

52.    Albert Bandura differed from other behaviorists in that he gave an important role to
       _____ in influencing human behavior.
a.     reflexes
b.     cognition
c.     consequences
d.     punishments

**ANS: b**          **Pg: 49**
**LO: 12**          **Conceptual**

53.    If you are conditioned indirectly by virtue of watching someone else's conditioning, then
       you have learned through the process of
a.     indirect conditioning.
b.     respondent conditioning.
c.     observational learning.
d.     accidental conditioning.

**ANS: c**          **Pg: 49**
**LO: 12**          **Conceptual**

54.    One's belief about one's ability to perform behaviors that should lead to expected
       outcomes is called
a.     self-concept.
b.     self-actualization.
c.     self-confidence.
d.     self-efficacy.

**ANS: d**          **Pgs: 49-50**
**LO: 13**          **Factual**

55.    Behaviorists have provided the most thorough account of why people
a.     are only moderately consistent in their behavior.
b.     become fixated at particular stages of development.
c.     are not influenced by the consequences of their behavior.
d.     tend to react with aggression when they are frustrated .

**ANS: a**          **Pgs: 50-51**
**LO: 13**          **Factual**

56. Humanistic theory emerged in the 1950s as a(n) _____ behavioral and psychodynamic theories.
a. complement to
b. elaboration on
c. backlash against
d. supplement to

**ANS: c**        **Pg: 51**
**LO: 14**       **Conceptual**

57. Humanism is a theoretical orientation that
a. regards human personality as a collection of response tendencies.
b. views self-efficacy as the ultimate goal of personality development.
c. sees personality as resulting mainly from observation of others.
d. emphasizes unique human qualities such as free will and growth potential.

**ANS: d**        **Pg: 51**
**LO: 14**       **Conceptual**

58. Humanistic psychologists' major charge against the behaviorist and psychodynamic theories was that these models were
a. inaccurate.
b. unscientific.
c. dehumanizing.
d. too optimistic.

**ANS: c**        **Pg: 51**
**LO: 14**       **Conceptual**

59. Which of the following is **not** an assumption underlying the humanistic approach to personality?
a. Human nature includes an innate drive toward personal growth.
b. Humans are largely conscious and rational beings.
c. Individuals have the freedom to chart their courses of action.
d. People tend to engage in behaviors that have been rewarded in the past.

**ANS: d**        **Pgs: 51-52**
**LO: 14**       **Conceptual**

60. Which of the following individuals based his theory on the importance of the self-concept?
a. Abraham Maslow
b. Carl Rogers
c. Sigmund Freud
d. Hans Eysenck

**ANS: b**        **Pgs: 51-52**
**LO: 15**       **Factual**

61. According to Rogers, one's self-concept
a. is unchangeable.
b. may be inaccurate.
c. tends to be congruent with reality.
d. is a product of classical conditioning.

**ANS: b**      **Pgs: 51-52**
**LO: 15**      **Conceptual**

62. Daniel feels that he is not living up to his own best image of the person he'd like to be. He experiences upset due to a sense of
a. conditional love.
b. observational distress.
c. incongruence.
d. self-efficacy.

**ANS: c**      **Pg: 52**
**LO: 15**      **Conceptual**

63. Rogers believed that incongruence develops because of the
a. conditional affection we receive from parents.
b. unconditional affection we receive from close friends.
c. uncompromising accuracy of our self-concept.
d. anxiety we feel as a result of our affection for the opposite-sex parent.

**ANS: a**      **Pg: 52**
**LO: 15**      **Conceptual**

64. The humanistic theorist who emphasized the need for self-actualization and the hierarchical organization of needs was
a. J.B. Watson.
b. B. F. Skinner.
c. Alfred Adler.
d. Abraham Maslow.

**ANS: d**      **Pg: 53**
**LO: 16**      **Factual**

65. Which of the following is **least** closely associated with Maslow's theory of personality?
a. notion of self-actualization
b. hierarchy of needs
c. humans' innate need for personal growth
d. distinction between introversion and extraversion

**ANS: d**      **Pgs: 53-54**
**LO: 16**      **Conceptual**

66. In contrast to the Freudian model, Maslow believed that psychology should take a greater interest in the _____ personality.
a. conscious
b. unconscious
c. healthy
d. unhealthy

**ANS: c**        **Pgs: 53-54**
**LO: 16**        **Conceptual**

67. Maslow's hierarchy of needs is based on the idea that
a. many drives are learned through observation.
b. perceived needs are a function of self-concept.
c. some needs are more basic than others.
d. most needs are a reaction to unconscious anxiety.

**ANS: c**        **Pgs: 53-54**
**LO: 16**        **Conceptual**

68. According to Maslow, which of the following categories of needs must be met first?
a. esteem
b. love
c. safety
d. self-actualization

**ANS: c**        **Pgs: 53-54**
**LO: 16**        **Conceptual**

69. According to Maslow, our need to fulfill our potential is called _____.
a. aesthetic need
b. primary need
c. self-actualization
d. self-esteem

**ANS: c**        **Pgs: 53-54**
**LO: 16**        **Factual**

70. Which of the following was **not** described by Maslow as one of the characteristics of a self-actualizing person?
a. autonomous
b. problem-centering
c. self-centered
d. spontaneous

**ANS: c**        **Pg: 54**
**LO: 16**        **Conceptual**

71.  According to Maslow, the self-actualizing person is characterized by
a.   spontaneity.
b.   freshness of appreciation.
c.   peak experiences.
d.   all of these.

**ANS: d**         **Pg: 54**
**LO: 16**         **Conceptual**

72.  According to Maslow, self-actualized people
     1.   always depend on other people
     2.   maintain a balance between polarities
     3.   feel a sense of kinship with the human race

a.   1 only
b.   1 and 2 only
c.   2 and 3 only
d.   1, 2, and 3

**ANS: c**         **Pg: 54**
**LO: 16**         **Conceptual**

73.  Which of the following is one of the significant contributions of humanistic theory?
a.   importance of one's subjective views
b.   more attention to psychological health
c.   more attention to the self-concept
d.   All of these are important contributions.

**ANS: d**         **Pg: 55**
**LO: 17**         **Conceptual**

74.  Humanistic theory has been criticized for
a.   poor testability of hypotheses.
b.   failure to accumulate much empirical evidence.
c.   an unrealistic view of human nature.
d.   all of these.

**ANS: d**         **Pg: 55**
**LO: 17**         **Conceptual**

75.  Which of the following psychologists said that "personality is determined to a large extent by a person's genes"?
a.   Hans Eysenck
b.   Raymond Cattell
c.   Abraham Maslow
d.   Albert Bandura

**ANS: a**         **Pg: 56**
**LO: 18**         **Factual**

76.     Which of the following traits has been of particular interest to Eysenck?
a.      intelligence
b.      autonomic reactivity
c.      conscientiousness
d.      extroversion-introversion

**ANS: d**              **Pg: 56**
**LO: 18**              **Factual**

77.     The area of psychological research that attempts to trace the hereditary influences on personality is called _____.
a.      social learning
b.      psychoanalysis
c.      behaviorism
d.      behavioral genetics

**ANS: d**              **Pg: 57**
**LO: 19**              **Conceptual**

78.     Twin studies allow researchers to assess hereditary influences, in part, because
a.      genetic overlap for fraternal twins is greater than for non-twin siblings.
b.      twins are usually motivated to act similarly.
c.      genetic overlap is 100% for identical twins, 50% for fraternal twins.
d.      environmental influences are eliminated in twin studies.

**ANS: c**              **Pgs: 57-58**
**LO: 19**              **Conceptual**

79.     _____ is an estimate of the proportion of trait variability within a population that is determined by differences in genetic inheritance.
a.      The inheritance ratio
b.      The heritability ratio
c.      The behaviorally genetic percentage
d.      The genetic coefficient

**ANS: b**              **Pg: 57**
**LO: 19**              **Conceptual**

80.     Results of twin studies have supported Eysenck's theory that personality is largely inherited by showing that
a.      environment has less effect on personality than heredity.
b.      identical twins are more similar in personality than fraternal twins.
c.      fraternal twins reared together are as similar as identical twins reared apart.
d.      parent and offspring are more similar than parent and spouse.

**ANS: b**              **Pgs: 57-58**
**LO: 19**              **Conceptual**

81.     Twin studies discussed in your text suggest that genes account for about _____ of peoples' variation in personality.
a.      15%
b.      25%
c.      50%
d.      75%

**ANS: c**          **Pgs: 57-58**
**LO: 19**          **Factual**

82.     Evolutionary psychologists like David Buss have argued that the "Big Five" personality traits exist across a variety of cultures because these traits
a.      tend to be reinforced as societal norms.
b.      have had significant adaptive implications.
c.      are the ones most likely to be classically conditioned.
d.      help each individual evolve to his/her greatest potential.

**ANS: b**          **Pgs: 58-59**
**LO: 20**          **Conceptual**

83.     Which of the following does the textbook cite as a weakness of biological approaches to personality?
a.      lack of adequate theory
b.      overemphasis on mathematical models of personality
c.      the tendency to reduce behavior to genetic mechanisms
d.      lack of attention to the role of conditioning in personality

**ANS: a**          **Pg: 59**
**LO: 21**          **Conceptual**

*84.    One of the chief goals of terror management theory is to explain why people need
a.      death anxiety.
b.      self-esteem.
c.      contact comfort.
d.      defense mechanisms.

**ANS:  b**         **Pgs: 59-60**
**LO: 22**          **Conceptual**

*85.    According to terror management theory, cultural worldviews diminish anxiety by
a.      providing answers to universal, existential questions.
b.      masking the inevitability of death.
c.      providing distractions.
d.      setting traditions.

**ANS: a**          **Pgs: 60-61**
**LO: 22**          **Conceptual**

*86. According to terror management theory, the increase in patriotism following the terrorist attack in New York on September 11 is associated with
a. an increase in depression.
b. a reaction formation.
c. adaptation.
d. increasing mortality salience.

ANS: d                  Pgs: 60-61
LO: 23                  Conceptual

*87. Politically, mortality salience increases subjects' preference for _____ candidates.
a. liberal
b. charismatic
c. radical
d. conservative

ANS: b                  Pg: 60
LO: 23                  Factual

*88. Psychology is marked by theoretical
a. consistency.
b. inconsistencies.
c. diversity.
d. uniformity.

ANS: c                  Pgs: 62-63
LO: 24                  Factual

89. Which of the following is not a major theoretical perspective in psychology?
a. pragmatic
b. behavioral
c. humanistic
d. psychodynamic

ANS: a                  Pg: 63
LO: 25                  Factual

90. A challenge in interpretation of personality test results is posed by
a. the tendency of respondents to unintentionally distort or misrepresent themselves.
b. the lack of systematic observation provided by the test.
c. the lack of standardization of scoring.
d. all of these.

ANS: a                  Pgs: 64-66
LO:    26               Conceptual

91. Most psychological tests can be placed in one of two broad categories:
a. IQ tests and attitude tests.
b. aptitude tests and achievement tests.
c. mental ability tests and personality tests.
d. projective tests and standardized tests.

**ANS: c**      **Pg: 64**
**LO:**   **26**      **Factual**

92. In psychological testing, "standardization" means that
a. a test can be administered in many different ways.
b. the test has a normative base.
c. subjects are expected to reach a certain standard of achievement on a test.
d. uniform procedures are used in administration and scoring of tests.

**ANS: d**      **Pg: 64**
**LO:**   **26**      **Conceptual**

93. Test norms provide information about
a. what is normal for a particular trait.
b. how many people have taken the test previously.
c. where a score ranks in relation to other scores.
d. the "best" or most desirable scores on a test.

**ANS: c**      **Pg: 64**
**LO: 26**      **Conceptual**

94. If the results of a psychological test are consistent across repeated measurements, then the test is said to be
a. valid.
b. reliable.
c. standardized.
d. statistically significant.

**ANS: b**      **Pg: 65**
**LO: 26**      **Conceptual**

*95. Susie scored a 105 on an online test claiming to measure intelligence. One week later she took the same online test and earned a score of 107. Three weeks later she took it again and earned 103. These scores indicate that the online test is
a. valid.
b. standardized.
c. reliable.
d. projective.

**ANS: c**      **Pg: 65**
**LO: 26**      **Conceptual**

96. Compared to mental ability tests, personality tests tend to have _____ reliability.
a. higher
b. lower
c. equal
d. more variable

**ANS: b**          **Pg: 65**
**LO: 26**          **Factual**

97. If a psychological test is found to measure the quality or construct that it was designed to measure, then it is a _____ assessment tool.
a. valid
b. reliable
c. standardized
d. statistically significant

**ANS: a**          **Pg: 65**
**LO: 26**          **Conceptual**

98. When test results correlate strongly with other measures of the same trait, the test is said to be
a. valid.
b. reliable.
c. significant.
d. standardized.

**ANS: a**          **Pg: 65**
**LO: 26**          **Conceptual**

99. The vast majority of personality tests take the form of
a. self-report inventories.
b. projective techniques.
c. attitude inventories.
d. achievement tests.

**ANS: a**          **Pg: 65**
**LO: 27**          **Factual**

100. One of the strengths of self-report inventories is that they
a. allow for comparing one's behavior with others' behavior.
b. take into account the influence of social desirability.
c. minimize unconscious distortion by respondents.
d. are good at detecting deliberate deception.

**ANS: a**          **Pg: 66**
**LO: 27**          **Conceptual**

101. _____ test requires people to respond to ambiguous stimuli. Inferences about needs, emotions, and personality traits are drawn from the responses.
a. An achievement
b. A projective
c. A self-report inventory
d. A psychological aptitude

**ANS: b**          **Pgs: 66-67**
**LO: 28**          **Factual**


## MULTIPLE CHOICE QUESTIONS FROM STUDY GUIDE

1. Which of the following is **not** one of the "big five" in the five-factor model of personality?
a. consistency
b. neuroticism
c. agreeableness
d. conscientiousness

**ANS: a**          **Pgs: 34-35**
**LO: 2**          **Factual**

2. Most of Sigmund Freud's contemporaries were uncomfortable with his theory of personality, because he said that
a. unconscious forces govern our behavior.
b. childhood experiences strongly determine adult personality.
c. our personalities are shaped by how we cope with our sexual urges.
d. all of these.

**ANS: d**          **Pg: 36**
**LO: 3**          **Factual**

3. According to Freud, the decision-making component of personality that operates according to the reality principle is called the
a. id.
b ego.
c. superego.
d. preconscious.

**ANS: b**          **Pg: 36**
**LO: 3**          **Factual**

4. According to Alfred Adler, the foremost human drive is a striving for
a. congruence.
b. aggression.
c. superiority.
d. self-actualization.

**ANS: c**        **Pg: 42**
**LO: 8**         **Factual**

5. Which of the following behaviors is most likely to be acquired through classical conditioning?
a. phobia
b. study habits
c. driving a car
d. playing tennis

**ANS: a**        **Pg: 46**
**LO: 10**        **Conceptual**

6. Which of the following concepts is least likely to be emphasized in a strict behavioral view of personality?
a. response
b. stimulus
c. cognition
d. consequences

**ANS: c**        **Pgs: 48-49**
**LO: 11**        **Conceptual**

7. According to Carl Rogers, which of the following is likely to be the main cause of troublesome anxiety?
a. childhood trauma
b. unconscious sexual urges
c. experiences that threaten one's self-concept
d. the inability to achieve self-actualization

**ANS: c**        **Pg: 52**
**LO: 15**        **Conceptual**

8. Abraham Maslow argued that humans have an innate drive toward
a. superiority.
b. personal growth.
c. Oedipal resolution.
d. reproductive fitness.

**ANS: b**        **Pg: 53**
**LO: 16**        **Factual**

9.	Which of the following theoretical orientations is most likely to rely on evidence from twin studies for support?
a.	psychodynamic
b.	behavioral
c.	humanistic
d.	biological

**ANS: d**			**Pg: 57**
**LO: 25**			**Conceptual**

10.	According to terror management theory, which of the following helps humans reconcile their self-preservation instinct with the notion that death is inevitable?
a.	a cultural worldview
b.	striving for self-actualization
c.	the use of defense mechanisms
d.	the acquisition of material goods

**ANS: a**			**Pg: 59**
**LO: 22**			**Conceptual**

11.	Which of the following theoretical orientations is most likely to rely on evidence from research on animal subjects for support?
a.	psychodynamic
b.	behavioral
c.	humanistic
d.	biological

**ANS: d**			**Pg: 63**
**LO: 25**			**Conceptual**

12.	Hans Eysenck is most closely associated with which of the following theoretical orientations?
a.	psychodynamic
b.	behavioral
c.	humanistic
d.	biological

**ANS: d**			**Pg: 63**
**LO: 18**			**Conceptual**

13.	Which of the following theoretical orientations takes the most optimistic view of human nature?
a.	psychodynamic
b.	behavioral
c.	humanistic
d.	biological

**ANS: c**			**Pg: 55**
**LO: 14**			**Conceptual**

14. Suppose an individual takes an intelligence test on two separate occasions, three years apart. The finding that the two scores are nearly identical exemplifies which of the following concepts?
a. validity
b. reliability
c. standardization
d. self-actualization

ANS: b          Pg: 65
LO: 26          Conceptual


15. A projective test is generally used to measure
a. attitudes.
b. intelligence.
c. academic achievement.
d. personality traits.

ANS: d          Pg: 66
LO: 28          Factual


## MULTIPLE CHOICE QUESTIONS ON WEB SITE

1. Which of the following ideas is **not** central to the concept of personality?
a. consistency across situations
b. traits that are shared with others
c. distinctiveness of an individual
d. a unique collection of traits possessed by an individual

ANS: b          Pg: 34
LO: 1           Factual


2. Eric studies three hours per day, five days a week. He only misses school when he is sick and is almost never late for class. On which of the following "Big Five" traits would he likely receive a high score?
a. neuroticism
b. extraversion
c. agreeableness
d. conscientiousness

ANS: d          Pg: 35
LO: 2           Conceptual

3.	Psychodynamic theories of personality tend to focus on
a.	a set of basic personality traits.
b.	unconscious mental processes.
c.	the unique qualities of human beings.
d.	reward and punishment as primary forces in personality.

**ANS: b**          **Pg: 35**
**LO: 3**          **Factual**

4.	According to Freud, internal conflict among the id, ego, and superego
a.	is routine.
b.	is relatively rare.
c.	occurs only in individuals with extreme anxiety.
d.	can be managed only through psychotherapy.

**ANS: a**          **Pgs: 36-37**
**LO: 4**          **Factual**

5.	According to Freud, in order to achieve healthy development, a child in the phallic stage must resolve the Oedipal complex and learn to _____ the same sex parent.
a.	annoy
b.	be fearful of
c.	deceive
d.	identify with

**ANS: d**          **Pgs: 40-41**
**LO: 6**          **Factual**

6.	One idea from Jung's personality theory that has been incorporated into mainstream modern psychology is the notion of
a.	archetypes.
b.	mnemonics.
c.	collective unconscious.
d.	introversion/extraversion.

**ANS: d**          **Pg: 42**
**LO: 7**          **Conceptual**

7.	Which of the following individuals is generally recognized for initiating the development of behaviorism?
a.	John B. Watson
b.	Alfred Adler
c.	Albert Bandura
d.	Hans Eysenck

**ANS: a**          **Pg: 44**
**LO: 10**          **Factual**

8. In classical conditioning, responses are said to be
a. emitted.
b. elicited.
c. spontaneous.
d. extinguished.

**ANS: b**          **Pgs: 44-45**
**LO: 10**          **Factual**

9. If you clean your room to put an end to your father's incessant nagging on the subject, your room-cleaning response has been
a. extinguished.
b. discriminated.
c. positively reinforced.
d. negatively reinforced.

**ANS: d**          **Pgs: 47-48**
**LO: 11**          **Conceptual**

10. Humanistic psychologists' major charge against the behaviorist and psychodynamic theories was that these models were
a. inaccurate.
b. unscientific.
c. dehumanizing.
d. too optimistic.

**ANS: c**          **Pg: 51**
**LO: 14**          **Conceptual**

11. According to Maslow, our need to fulfill our potential is called _____.
a. aesthetic need
b. primary need
c. self-actualization
d. self-esteem

**ANS: c**          **Pgs: 53-54**
**LO: 16**          **Factual**

12. Humanistic theory has been criticized for
a. poor testability of hypotheses.
b. failure to accumulate much empirical evidence.
c. an unrealistic view of human nature.
d. all of these.

**ANS: d**          **Pg: 55**
**LO: 17**          **Conceptual**

13.    Twin studies discussed in your text suggest that genes account for about _____ of peoples' variation in personality.
a.    15%
b.    25%
c.    50%
d.    75%

**ANS: c**          **Pgs: 57-58**
**LO: 19**          **Factual**

14.    Which of the following is not a major theoretical perspective in psychology?
a.    pragmatic
b.    behavioral
c.    humanistic
d.    psychodynamic

**ANS: a**          **Pg: 63**
**LO: 25**          **Factual**

*15.    Susie scored a 105 on an online test claiming to measure intelligence. One week later she took the same online test and earned a score of 107. Three weeks later she took it again and earned 103. These scores indicate that the online test is
a.    valid.
b.    standardized.
c.    reliable.
d.    projective.

**ANS: c**          **Pg: 65**
**LO: 26**          **Conceptual**


**TRUE/FALSE QUESTIONS**

1.    Neuroticism is referred to as "negative emotionality" in some trait models.

**ANS: true**          **Pgs: 34-35**
**LO: 2**          **Factual**

2.    McCrae and Costa maintain that personality can be described adequately by measuring the nine basic traits that they have identified.

**ANS: false**          **Pg: 34**
**LO: 2**          **Factual**

3.    The id engages in primary process thinking, while the ego engages in secondary process thinking.

**ANS: true**          **Pg: 36**
**LO: 3**          **Factual**

4.     Defense mechanisms are largely unconscious reactions that protect a person from painful emotions.

**ANS: true**          **Pg: 37**
**LO: 5**               **Factual**

5.     Freud asserted that the foundation for an individual's personality is laid down by 12 years of age.

**ANS: false**         **Pgs: 40-41**
**LO: 6**               **Factual**

6.     Dominant themes in folk art represented by images of nurturing mothers and protective fathers are examples of Jung's conceptualization of archetypes.

**ANS: true**          **Pgs: 41-42**
**LO: 7**               **Conceptual**

7.     Many critics have argued that humanistic theories of personality harbor a bias against women.

**ANS: false**         **Pg: 43**
**LO: 9**               **Factual**

8.     A parent who laughs when her child uses profanity is negatively reinforcing bad language.

**ANS: false**         **Pg: 47**
**LO: 11**              **Conceptual**

9.     Many critics have argued that behavioral theories have relied too heavily on animal research.

**ANS: true**          **Pgs: 50-51**
**LO: 13**              **Factual**

10.    Modern psychologists increasingly view theoretical diversity as a weakness that needs to be overcome, so that psychology can be accepted as a science.

**ANS: false**         **Pgs: 62-63**
**LO: 25**              **Conceptual**


**SHORT-ANSWER ESSAY QUESTIONS**

1.     Identify and briefly describe the "Big Five" personality traits.

**Pgs: 34-35**
**LO: 2**

2.      Identify and briefly describe three different defense mechanisms, and give an example of each.

**Pg: 39**
**LO: 5**

3.      Compare and contrast the psychodynamic theories of personality proposed by Freud, Jung, and Adler. What are the main differences and similarities?

**Pgs: 39-43**
**LO: 9**

4.      Describe one instance of the influence of classical conditioning that occurs in everyday life.

**Pg: 46**
**LO: 10**

5.      Distinguish between positive and negative reinforcement, and give an example of each.

**Pgs: 47-48**
**LO: 11**

6.      Distinguish between how people generally describe punishment and B.F. Skinner's description of the concept of punishment.

**Pg: 48**
**LO: 11**

7.      Explain how social learning theory incorporates cognitive concepts.

**Pg: 49**
**LO: 12**

8.      Explain how the notion of self-concept figures in the development of personality according to Carl Rogers.

**Pgs: 51-52**
**LO: 15**

9.      What are the main contributions and criticisms of humanistic theories of personality?

**Pg: 55**
**LO: 17**

10.     Discuss the relative strengths and weaknesses of self-report inventories and projective techniques for assessing personality.

**Pgs: 64-67**
**LO: 27 & 28**

# Chapter 3
# STRESS AND ITS EFFECTS

## LEARNING OBJECTIVES

1. Describe the nature of stress and discuss how common it is.
2. Distinguish between primary and secondary appraisal of stress.
3. Summarize the evidence on ambient stress.
4. Explain how culture and ethnicity are related to stress.
5. Distinguish between acute and chronic stressors.
6. Describe frustration as a form of stress.
7. Outline the three types of conflict and discuss typical reactions to conflicts.
8. Summarize evidence on life change as a form of stress.
9. Discuss evidence on pressure as a form of stress.
10. List three categories of negative emotions commonly elicited by stress.
11. Discuss the role of positive emotions in the stress process.
12. Explain the effects of emotional arousal on coping efforts and describe the inverted-U hypothesis.
13. Describe the fight-or-flight response and the three stages of the general adaptation syndrome.
14. Distinguish between the two major pathways along which the brain sends signals to the endocrine system in response to stress.
15. Explain the concept of coping.
16. Explain the phenomenon of choking under pressure.
17. Summarize evidence on how stress can affect cognitive functioning.
18. Describe the symptoms and causes of burnout.
19. Discuss the prevalence, symptoms, and causes of posttraumatic stress disorder.
20. Discuss the potential impact of stress on mental and physical health.
21. Describe positive psychology and three ways in which stress might lead to beneficial effects.
22. Explain how social support moderates the impact of stress.
23. Describe the hardiness syndrome and how it influences stress tolerance.
24. Discuss how optimism is related to stress tolerance.
25. List five problems with the SRRS.
26. Summarize how the LES corrects some of the problems that are characteristic of the SRRS.
27. Explain why one should be cautious in interpreting scores on stress scales.

## MULTIPLE CHOICE QUESTIONS

1.  The emerging consensus among contemporary researchers is that stress is
a.  a stimulus event that presents difficult demands.
b.  the response of physiological arousal elicited by a troublesome event.
c.  a special stimulus-response transaction in which one feels threatened.
d.  a series of events that tend to elicit overwhelming feelings of anxiety.

**ANS: c**          **Pg: 72**
**LO: 1**           **Factual**

2.  One accepted definition of stress is
a.  any potentially upsetting event that occurs in one's environment.
b.  any circumstance that threatens well-being and taxes coping abilities.
c.  any negative change that occurs in the course of life.
d.  anything that causes chronic illness in organisms.

**ANS: b**          **Pg: 72**
**LO: 1**           **Conceptual**

3.  Which of the following statements regarding the nature of stress is correct?
a.  Routine hassles may have significant negative effects on mental and physical health.
b.  Major stressful events are more strongly related to mental health than are minor hassles.
c.  Most people effectively deal with everyday stress through the use of defense mechanisms.
d.  Experts generally agree that major and minor stressors are independent of each other.

**ANS: a**          **Pg: 72**
**LO: 1**           **Conceptual**

4.  Lazarus's findings on hassles suggest that the effects of stress are
a.  cumulative.
b.  mutually exclusive.
c.  specific to different domains.
d.  inversely related to the number of demands.

**ANS: a**          **Pg: 72**
**LO: 1**           **Conceptual**

5.  Whether or not an event is stressful is most likely to depend on
a.  how much physiological arousal it causes.
b.  how much change there is.
c.  how one appraises and adapts to the event.
d.  whether one is prepared for the event.

**ANS: c**          **Pgs: 72-73**
**LO: 2**           **Conceptual**

6.     Primary appraisal is an initial evaluation of whether an event is
a.     imminent.
b.     detrimental to one's health.
c.     relevant and stressful.
d.     expected.

**ANS: c**          **Pgs: 72-73**
**LO: 2**          **Factual**

7.     Secondary appraisal involves
a.     making plans to avoid the situation.
b.     tapping into your defense mechanisms.
c.     soliciting a second opinion about a stressful event.
d.     considering your coping resources and options.

**ANS: d**          **Pgs: 72-73**
**LO: 2**          **Factual**

8.     The notion that "stress lies in the eye of the beholder" suggests that
a.     coping strategies tend to vary from individual to individual.
b.     people's appraisals of stressful events are highly subjective.
c.     there are certain events that just about everyone finds stressful.
d.     the appraisal of stress generally involves the use of visual imagery.

**ANS: b**          **Pgs: 72-73**
**LO: 2**          **Conceptual**

9.     The term "ambient stress" refers to
a.     stress that seems to have no identifiable source.
b.     specific situations in which stress is most likely to occur.
c.     chronic environmental conditions that place adaptive demands on people.
d.     stressful situations that result from demands placed on us by others.

**ANS: c**          **Pg: 73**
**LO: 3**          **Factual**

*10.    Urban poverty and violence have been identified as sources of _____ that have been found to be modestly correlated with depression and hostility.
a.     acute stress
b.     traumatic stress
c.     ambient stress
d.     rational stress

**ANS:   c**          **Pg: 74**
**LO: 3**          **Factual**

11. _____ has been a major source of stress in many societies around the world.
a. Religious conflict
b. Cultural change
c. Intergenerational disagreement
d. Coping deficiency

**ANS: b**          **Pg: 74**
**LO: 4**           **Conceptual**

12. Which of the following may be a significant cause of stress for ethnic minorities in Western societies?
a. cultural change
b. overt interracial conflict
c. effects of subtle discrimination
d. effects of modernization

**ANS: c**          **Pg: 75**
**LO: 4**           **Conceptual**

13. One challenge faced by members of ethnic minorities in dealing with everyday discrimination is that manifestations of such discrimination are often
a. imaginary.
b. ambiguous.
c. minor.
d. consistent.

**ANS: b**          **Pg: 75**
**LO: 4**           **Conceptual**

14. Which of the following is **not** a major source of stress described in your textbook?
a. change
b. conflict
c. frustration
d. socialization

**ANS: d**          **Pg: 76**
**LO: 5**           **Conceptual**

15. Acute stressors are
a. threatening events that have a relatively short duration and clear endpoint.
b. unpleasant environmental conditions to which one must adjust.
c. conditions that have a relatively long duration and no apparent time limit.
d. shown by researchers to lead directly to physical illness.

**ANS: a**          **Pg: 75**
**LO: 5**           **Conceptual**

16. Threatening events that have a relatively long duration and no apparent time limit are referred to as
a. ambient stressors.
b. cultural stressors.
c. acute stressors.
d. chronic stressors.

**ANS: d**         **Pgs: 75-76**
**LO: 5**         **Conceptual**

17. Dealing with a rude store clerk and waiting for the results of an examination are two examples of
a. acute stressors.
b. ambient stressors.
c. environmental stressors.
d. chronic stressors.

**ANS: a**         **Pg: 75**
**LO: 5**         **Conceptual**

18. The four major types of stress described in your textbook are
a. pressure, anxiety, environment, social demands.
b. frustration, anger, pressure, and change.
c. frustration, conflict, pressure, and change.
d. conflict, pressure, anxiety, and social demands.

**ANS: c**         **Pg: 76**
**LO: 5**         **Factual**

19. According to psychologists, frustration occurs when
a. feelings of anger are aroused.
b. the pursuit of some goal is thwarted.
c. incompatible motivations are activated.
d. individuals perceive subjective threat.

**ANS: b**         **Pg: 76**
**LO: 6**         **Factual**

20. Which of the following is a common kind of frustration leading to stress?
a. anger
b. anxiety
c. losses
d. subjective threat

**ANS: c**         **Pg: 76**
**LO: 6**         **Conceptual**

21. _____ may be a common effect of environmental or ambient stress.
a. Conflict
b. Frustration
c. Change
d. Trauma

**ANS: b**        **Pg: 76**
**LO: 6**        **Conceptual**

22. Conflict occurs when
a. pursuit of an important goal is thwarted.
b. an event is perceived as threatening.
c. two incompatible behavioral impulses compete for expression.
d. ambiguous stimuli are encountered in the environment.

**ANS: c**        **Pg: 76**
**LO: 7**        **Factual**

23. Generally, which kind of conflict tends to be the least stressful?
a. approach-approach
b. avoidance-avoidance
c. approach-avoidance
d. All types are equally stressful.

**ANS: a**        **Pgs: 76-77**
**LO: 7**        **Conceptual**

24. You want to ask someone for a date, but you're afraid of being rejected. Which of the following types of conflict applies to your situation?
a. approach-approach
b. avoidance-avoidance
c. approach-avoidance
d. frustration-aggression

**ANS: c**        **Pgs: 77-78**
**LO: 7**        **Conceptual**

25. You are a talented artist and you are good at mathematics. You enjoy both and don't know which to major in at college. Which of the following types of conflict applies to your situation?
a. approach-approach
b. avoidance-avoidance
c. approach-avoidance
d. frustration-aggression

**ANS: a**        **Pgs: 76-77**
**LO: 7**        **Conceptual**

26.    Approach-avoidance conflicts often produce
a.    vacillation.
b.    frustration.
c.    aggression.
d.    self-directed anger.

**ANS: a**            **Pgs: 77-78**
**LO: 7**              **Factual**

27.    An approach-avoidance conflict may best be resolved by _____ the avoidance
       motivation rather than _____ the approach motivation.
a.    decreasing; decreasing
b.    decreasing; increasing
c.    increasing; decreasing
d.    increasing; increasing

**ANS: b**            **Pgs: 77-78**
**LO: 7**              **Factual**

*28.   Your friend Judy is trying to decide whether or not to take a college class with you.
       Research indicates that the best way to help Judy resolve this conflict is to
a.    downplay the negative aspects of taking the class.
b.    focus on the positive educational aspects of taking the class.
c.    make a list of pros and cons and spend an equal amount of time pondering each.
d.    focus on the positive social aspects of taking the class.

**ANS: a**            **Pg: 78**
**LO: 7**                        **Conceptual**

29.    _____ is any noticeable alteration in one's life circumstances.
a.    Stress
b.    Life conflict
c.    Life change
d.    Dissonance

**ANS: c**            **Pg: 78**
**LO: 8**              **Factual**

30.    Holmes and Rahe concluded that change is stressful
a.    only when it is undesirable.
b.    only when it is overwhelming.
c.    whether it is undesirable or desirable.
d.    only when accompanied by pressure.

**ANS: c**            **Pg: 78**
**LO: 8**              **Factual**

31. The Social Readjustment Rating Scale was designed to measure
a. frustration.
b. all kinds of stress.
c. change-related stress.
d. the anxiety produced by certain events.

**ANS: c**          **Pgs: 78-79**
**LO: 8**           **Factual**

32. Research with the Social Readjustment Rating Scale has shown that people with higher scores
a. are less susceptible to stress.
b. know from experience how to handle stress.
c. tend to have pessimistic outlooks on life.
d. are vulnerable to physical and psychological problems.

**ANS: d**          **Pgs: 78-79**
**LO: 8**           **Factual**

*33. Current research indicates that
a. positive change is typically more stressful than negative change.
b. only negative change is stressful.
c. we have little reason to believe that change is inherently stressful.
d. all change is inevitably stressful.

**ANS: c**          **Pg: 79**
**LO: 9**           **Factual**

34. Whenever others expect you to conform to their expectations or perform in certain ways, you tend to experience
a. anger.
b. conflict.
c. frustration.
d. pressure.

**ANS: d**          **Pg: 80**
**LO: 9**           **Factual**

35. Which of the following researchers designed a scale to measure pressure as a form of life stress?
a. Albert Bandura
b. Thomas Holmes
c. Neil Miller
d. Wayne Weiten

**ANS: d**          **Pg: 81**
**LO: 9**           **Factual**

36. Weiten's research on the stressful effects of pressure indicates that there is a strong relationship between pressure and
a. the appraisal of stress.
b. measures of procrastination.
c. a variety of psychological problems.
d. stress-induced physiological arousal.

**ANS: c**          **Pg: 81**
**LO: 9**          **Conceptual**

37. Psychologists study responses to stress at which of the following levels?
a. behavioral
b. emotional
c. physiological
d. all of these

**ANS: d**          **Pg: 81**
**LO: 10**          **Factual**

38. _____ are largely uncontrollable and are accompanied by physiological changes.
a. Conflicts
b. Pressures
c. Stressors
d. Emotions

**ANS: d**          **Pgs: 81-82**
**LO: 10**          **Factual**

39. Research findings indicate that cognitive appraisals may influence a person's _____ responses to stressors.
a. emotional
b. social
c. controllable
d. perceptual

**ANS: a**          **Pg: 81**
**LO: 10**          **Factual**

*40. Fredrickson et al. (2003) found that the frequency of pleasant emotions correlated _____ with resilience, and the frequency of negative emotions correlated _____ with resilience.
a. positive; negative
b. negative; positive
c. positive; positive
d. negative; negative

**ANS: a**          **Pg: 83**
**LO: 11**          **Factual**

41. Research suggests that positive emotional reactions to stress may have the adaptive quality of enhancing
a. recovery from psychological trauma.
b. creativity and flexibility in problem solving.
c. avoidance strategies.
d. use of defense mechanisms.

**ANS: b**          **Pg: 83**
**LO: 11**          **Factual**

42. The correlation between test-related anxiety and exam performance is thought to be
a. positive.
b. negative.
c. U-shaped.
d. non-existent.

**ANS: b**          **Pg: 84**
**LO: 12**          **Factual**

43. The negative effects of test anxiety on test performance are mostly due to
a. blocking of memory retrieval.
b. disruption of attention to the test.
c. negative thoughts about oneself.
d. inability to engage in effective studying.

**ANS: b**          **Pg: 84**
**LO: 12**          **Conceptual**

44. Optimal level of arousal is related to
a. level of self-esteem.
b. the complexity of the task.
c. personality type.
d. optimism of the individual.

**ANS: b**          **Pg: 84**
**LO: 12**          **Conceptual**

*45. In theory, the optimal level of arousal for writing a standard daily report at work would be _____ the optimal level for giving the annual oral report presentation for the company.
a. less than
b. greater than
c. equal to
d. less than (for men only)

**ANS: b**          **Pg: 84**
**LO: 12**          **Conceptual**

46.     The inverted-U hypothesis was proposed to explain the relationship between _____ and
        _____.
a.      test anxiety; coping strategy
b.      level of arousal; task performance
c.      level of arousal; physiological changes
d.      familiarity of event; effectiveness of coping strategies

**ANS: b**          **Pg: 84**
**LO: 12**          **Factual**

47.     The "fight-or-flight" response was first described by
a.      Martin Seligman
b.      Ray Rosenman
c.      Walter Cannon
d.      Hans Selye

**ANS: c**          **Pg: 85**
**LO: 13**          **Factual**

*48.    New research on gender and the fight-or-flight response indicates that
a.      fighting may be more adaptive for females than males because females need to fight off
        predators from their offspring.
b.      fighting and fleeing may be less adaptive for females because both responses my
        endanger offspring.
c.      men are more likely to fight and women are more likely to flee.
d.      men and women are equally likely to expend a lot of effort on the care of offspring in
        times of stress.

**ANS: b**          **Pg: 85**
**LO: 13**          **Conceptual**

*49.    An alternative to the fight-or-flight response that may be present for females is the
a.      tend and befriend response.
b.      lock and load response.
c.      freeze and free-up response.
d.      cat and mouse response.

**ANS: a**          **Pgs: 85-86**
**LO: 13**          **Factual**

50.     The fight-or-flight response occurs in the
a.      cerebral cortex.
b.      limbic system.
c.      autonomic nervous system.
d.      synaptic vesicles in the brain.

**ANS: c**          **Pgs: 85-86**
**LO: 13**          **Factual**

51. The parasympathetic division of the autonomic nervous system
a. conserves bodily resources.
b. stimulates the fight-or-flight response.
c. arouses the endocrine system in times of stress.
d. shuts down immediately following a stressful event.

**ANS: a** **Pg: 85**
**LO: 13** **Factual**

52. The sympathetic division of the autonomic nervous system
a. conserves bodily resources.
b. arouses sympathy for those in stressful circumstances.
c. mobilizes bodily resources for emergencies.
d. calms the body after the fight-or-flight response.

**ANS: c** **Pg: 85**
**LO: 13** **Factual**

53. In humans the fight-or-flight response is less adaptive than it is in animals because
a. our stresses are usually of short duration.
b. social evolution has surpassed biological evolution.
c. most modern human stresses can't be managed with these strategies.
d. humans don't have adequate equipment to fight or flee from threats.

**ANS: c** **Pgs: 85-86**
**LO: 13** **Conceptual**

*54. Hans Seyle's work was important because it showed
a. how prolonged physiological arousal that is meant to be adaptive could lead to diseases.
b. how ambient stress could lead to a traumatic stress response.
c. that positive change is just as stressful as negative change.
d. that children do not react to stress the same way that adults do.

**ANS: a** **Pgs: 86-87**
**LO: 13** **Conceptual**

55. Being followed when walking home late at night or narrowly escaping a car accident are experiences that would activate your
a. parasympathetic nervous system.
b. sympathetic nervous system.
c. nonsympathetic nervous system.
d. auxiliary nervous system.

**ANS: b** **Pg: 86**
**LO: 13** **Conceptual**

56.    _____ is credited with formulating the theory of stress reactions called the general adaptation syndrome.
a.    Hans Selye
b.    Neal Miller
c.    Walter Cannon
d.    Michael Scheier

**ANS: a**          **Pg: 86**
**LO: 13**          **Factual**

57.    Selye exposed lab animals to various stressors and found that
a.    each individual animal responded to stress differently.
b.    each type of stress caused a particular physiological response.
c.    patterns of physiological arousal were similar, regardless of the type of stress.
d.    patterns of physiological arousal seemed to depend on the intensity of the stress.

**ANS: c**          **Pg: 86**
**LO: 13**          **Conceptual**

58.    The general adaptation syndrome is a
a.    general coping strategy for dealing with stress.
b.    severe stress-related psychological disorder.
c.    set of nonspecific bodily responses to stress.
d.    physiological-based solution for stressful problems.

**ANS: c**          **Pg: 86**
**LO: 13**          **Factual**

59.    The correct order of stages in the general adaptation syndrome is
a.    resistance, alarm, exhaustion.
b.    alarm, exhaustion, resistance.
c.    resistance, exhaustion, alarm.
d.    alarm, resistance, exhaustion.

**ANS: d**          **Pgs: 86-87**
**LO: 13**          **Factual**

60.    In the _____ stage of the general adaptation syndrome, the body attempts to adapt to continued stress.
a.    alarm
b.    exhaustion
c.    resistance
d.    extinction

**ANS: c**          **Pg: 87**
**LO: 13**          **Conceptual**

61.    You hate mathematics and you feel a knot forming in your stomach when you read in the college catalog that Calculus I is required for your chosen major. You are in the _____ stage of the general adaptation syndrome.
a.    alarm
b.    exhaustion
c.    resistance
d.    extinction

**ANS: a**          **Pg: 86**
**LO: 13**          **Conceptual**

62.    You realize that no matter how much you hate mathematics you will not be able to drop out of calculus class this semester if you want to go to the graduate school of your choice. You hunker down for a miserable semester of hard and studious labor. You are in the _____ stage of the general adaptation syndrome.
a.    alarm
b.    exhaustion
c.    resistance
d.    extinction

**ANS: c**          **Pg: 87**
**LO: 13**          **Conceptual**

63.    After barely squeezing through Calculus I with a B, you sleep 16 hours a day for the first 10 days of summer break and refuse to see any of your friends. You are in the _____ stage of the general adaptation syndrome.
a.    alarm
b.    exhaustion
c.    resistance
d.    extinction

**ANS: b**          **Pg: 87**
**LO: 13**          **Conceptual**

64.    Seyle's general adaptation model has been criticized because
a.    it ignores cultural influences on stress.
b.    the order in which the stages occur may vary between individuals.
c.    it ignores individual differences in the appraisal of stress.
d.    there is no link between stress and physical illness.

**ANS: c**          **Pg: 87**
**LO: 13**          **Conceptual**

65.	_____ are hormones that help mobilize the body for action.
a.	Amphetamines
b.	Endocrines
c.	Catecholamines
d.	Neurotransmitters

**ANS: c**	**Pg: 88**
**LO: 14**	**Factual**

*66.	Which of the following is LEAST likely to have a negative impact on the immune system?
a.	caring for an elderly parent
b.	receiving long-term disability following an automobile accident
c.	remaining in a hostile work environment while waiting for a better job opportunity to come along
d.	spending the weekend with hostile family members

**ANS: d**	**Pgs: 87-88**
**LO: 14**	**Conceptual**

67.	The "master gland" of the endocrine system is the
a.	pituitary.
b.	adrenal cortex.
c.	adrenal medulla.
d.	hypothalamus.

**ANS: a**	**Pg: 88**
**LO: 14**	**Factual**

68.	Mounting evidence from research indicates that stress may _____ the functioning of the immune system.
a.	stimulate
b.	destroy
c.	suppress
d.	enhance

**ANS: c**	**Pg: 88**
**LO: 14**	**Factual**

69.	_____ involves active efforts to master, reduce, or tolerate the demands of stress.
a.	Coping
b.	Adjustment
c.	Stress tolerance
d.	General adaptation

**ANS: a**	**Pgs: 88-89**
**LO: 15**	**Factual**

*70. By definition coping efforts are
a. not necessarily adaptive or maladaptive.
b. necessarily healthy.
c. permanent.
d. effective.

**ANS: a**           **Pgs: 88-89**
**LO: 15**           **Factual**

71. Pressure may disrupt attention to task performance by
a. making one feel self-conscious.
b. making one forget the guidelines for the task.
c. encouraging one to focus on the source of the pressure.
d. overemphasizing the importance of the task.

**ANS: a**           **Pg: 89**
**LO: 16**           **Conceptual**

72. Recent research on the effect of pressure on task performance in "normal" subjects suggests that
a. choking under pressure is fairly common.
b. people actually tend to perform better under extreme pressure.
c. choking under pressure is a phenomenon unique to the athletic domain.
d. normal people are less likely to choke under pressure than are professional athletes.

**ANS: a**           **Pg: 89**
**LO: 16**           **Conceptual**

*73. Your friend Terry, who has been practicing free throw shots in the backyard, just won the chance to shoot a half court basket for a $10,000 prize at a professional basketball game. Research indicates that Terry is
a. more likely to make the shot in front of a large crowd than in the backyard, because the added pressure increases the ability to filter out distractions.
b. less likely to choke under the pressure than a professional athlete, because professionals have their job on the line.
c. very likely to choke under pressure.
d. likely to catch a cold just before the game because of a reduced immune system from the acute stress.

**ANS: c**           **Pg: 89**
**LO: 16**           **Conceptual**

74. Research findings indicate that on a cognitive task, stress may increase one's tendency to
a. become overly sensitive to criticism.
b. jump to conclusions too quickly.
c. consider a variety of options.
d. organize information into categories.

**ANS: b**        **Pgs: 89-90**
**LO: 17**        **Conceptual**

75. Which of the following was **not** cited in your text as a disruptive effect of severe stress on cognitive functioning?
a. a dazed, confused state
b. an emotional numbness
c. inability to deal with interpersonal issues
d. difficulty maintaining a coherent train of thought

**ANS: c**        **Pgs: 89-90**
**LO: 17**        **Conceptual**

76. Physical, mental, and emotional exhaustion due to work-related stress is called
a. burnout.
b. reaction formation disorder.
c. the general adaptation syndrome.
d. posttraumatic stress disorder.

**ANS: a**        **Pg: 90**
**LO: 18**        **Factual**

77. Which of the following is **not** a symptom of burnout?
a. chronic fatigue
b. re-experiencing traumatic events
c. negative attitudes toward oneself
d. feelings of hopelessness

**ANS: b**        **Pg: 90**
**LO: 18**        **Conceptual**

78. According to Ayala Pines, what causes burnout?
a. traumatic experiences in the workplace
b. accumulation of heavy, chronic, job-related stress
c. physical, mental, emotional exhaustion
d. lack of sufficient variety in one's work

**ANS: b**        **Pg: 90**
**LO: 18**        **Factual**

*79.    Which of the following has NOT been identified as a major factor that promotes burnout?
a.      work overload
b.      interpersonal conflicts at work
c.      flaws or weaknesses within the individual
d.      inadequate recognition for one's work

ANS: c                  Pg: 90
LO: 18                  Conceptual

80.     Posttraumatic stress disorder involves
a.      the delayed effects of stressful war experiences.
b.      stress reactions in anticipation of a traumatic event.
c.      psychological disturbance due to the experience of a major traumatic event.
d.      psychotic reactions to chronic stress, which emerge after one leaves the stressful
        environment.

ANS: c                  Pgs: 90-91
LO: 19                  Factual

*81.    Which of the following appears to be a key factor in predicting who is most likely to
        develop PTSD following a traumatic event?
a.      the age of the victim
b.      the place of the traumatic event
c.      the intensity of the traumatic event
d.      biological aspects of the individual

ANS: c                  Pg: 91
LO: 19                  Factual

82.     Research reveals that stress often contributes to the onset of all but which of the
        following?
a.      depression
b.      schizophrenia
c.      eating disorders
d.      autistic disorder

ANS: d                  Pg: 92
LO: 20                  Factual

83.     Psychosomatic diseases are
a.      common reactions to single traumatic events.
b.      psychological disturbances associated with burnout.
c.      imaginary physical ailments caused partly by psychological factors.
d.      genuine physical ailments caused partly by psychological factors.

ANS: d                  Pg: 92
LO: 20                  Factual

84. Which of the following is **not** a beneficial effect that may result from stress?
a. satisfies the need for stimulation and challenge
b. increases optimism
c. promotes personal growth
d. inoculates against later stresses

**ANS: b**          **Pg: 93**
**LO: 21**          **Conceptual**

85. The school of modern psychology that was developed to offset the perceived emphasis in psychology on pathology and suffering is called _____.
a. psychodynamic psychology
b. behaviorism
c. positive psychology
d. coping psychology

**ANS: c**          **Pg: 93**
**LO: 21**          **Conceptual**

86. _____ variables are factors that can soften the impact of stress on physical and mental health.
a. Intervening
b. Dependent
c. Moderator
d. Extraneous

**ANS: c**          **Pg: 94**
**LO: 22**          **Factual**

87. Social support involves
a. charity work to take one's mind off stressful problems.
b. support from various social agencies.
c. various types of aid from one's social networks.
d. one's ability to aid others in need of support.

**ANS: c**          **Pgs: 94-95**
**LO: 22**          **Conceptual**

*88. People who lack social support are
a. more prone to developing infectious diseases, such as colds, under stress.
b. less prone to developing infectious diseases, such as colds under stress, because they are less likely to be exposed to infectious germs.
c. have less intense physiological reactions to stress, because they keep it to themselves.
d. are equally likely to develop infectious diseases as those with high social support.

**ANS: a**          **Pgs: 94-95**
**LO: 22**          **Factual**

*89. Who of the following people is most likely to develop stress-related illness?
a. Susan who lives alone but volunteers at the local skilled nursing home two times per month
b. John who lives with two good friends from high school
c. Jaime who lives with a quiet roommate, belongs to a big family, works for a growing company, and is described as a very "sociable" guy by all who know him
d. Dora who lives alone, works from her home, and prefers to keep to herself

**ANS: d**      **Pgs: 94-95**
**LO: 22**      **Conceptual**

90. Kobasa found strong stress tolerance to be related to
a. belief that situational variables control one's destiny.
b. a passive approach to life.
c. a sense of commitment.
d. all of these.

**ANS: c**      **Pg: 95**
**LO: 23**      **Factual**

*91. Which of the following executives is NOT exhibiting a quality related to hardiness?
a. Al is very committed to his work and sees his job as a part of his identity.
b. Bob finds a way to reframe problems at work as challenges rather than burdens.
c. Clara maintains an illusion of control at work even when deadlines are outside of her control.
d. Drew sees everything as a competition and works hard to outdo all of the other employees.

**ANS: d**      **Pg: 95**
**LO: 23**      **Conceptual**

92. A behavior pattern marked by commitment, challenge, and control that appears to be related to stress resistance is called
a. hardiness.
b. optimism.
c. autonomic passivity.
d. autonomic reactivity.

**ANS: a**      **Pg: 95**
**LO: 23**      **Factual**

93. The general tendency to expect good outcomes is called
a. hardiness.
b. optimism.
c. social support.
d. sensation seeking.

**ANS: b**      **Pg: 96**
**LO: 24**      **Factual**

\*94. People who exhibit an optimistic explanatory style tend to attribute setbacks to
a. other's shortcomings.
b. temporary situational factors.
c. bad luck.
d. personal traits.

**ANS: b**        **Pg: 96-97**
**LO: 24**        **Factual**

95. The Life Orientation Test (LOT) was designed to measure
a. optimism.
b. hardiness.
c. conscientiousness.
d. sensation seeking.

**ANS: a**        **Pg: 96**
**LO: 24**        **Factual**

96. In stressful circumstances, optimists are more likely than pessimists to
a. be realistic about the situation.
b. decline any offers of social support.
c. use their most effective defense mechanisms.
d. engage in action-oriented, problem-focused coping.

**ANS: d**        **Pgs: 96-97**
**LO: 24**        **Conceptual**

97. The pessimistic explanatory style may be related to relatively poor health because
a. pessimists expect to have poor health.
b. pessimism may lead to passive coping efforts.
c. pessimists explain their ailments to doctors inaccurately.
d. pessimists don't elicit much social support.

**ANS: b**        **Pg: 96**
**LO: 24**        **Conceptual**

98. Modern researchers tend to view the Social Readjustment Rating Scale as a measure of
a. diverse forms of stress.
b. change-related stress only.
c. conflict-generated stress.
d. the effectiveness of coping strategies.

**ANS: a**        **Pgs: 97-98**
**LO: 25**        **Conceptual**

99. The correlations between scores on the Social Readjustment Rating Scale and health outcomes may be inflated because subjects' _____ affects both their responses to stress scales and their self-reports of health problems.
a. optimism
b. neuroticism
c. agreeableness
d. conscientiousness

**ANS: b**      **Pg: 98**
**LO: 25**      **Factual**

100. All of the following are criticisms of the SRRS **except**
a. the SRRS fails to take into account differences in subjective perceptions of stress.
b. some of the items of the SRRS are highly ambiguous.
c. the SRRS does not measure physiological reactions such as fight-or-flight.
d. the SRRS does not sample thoroughly from the domain of all stressful events.

**ANS: c**      **Pgs: 97-98**
**LO: 25**      **Factual**

101. The Life Experiences Survey corrects one of the problems of the Social Readjustment Rating Scale by presenting items that are
a. less ambiguous.
b. less individualized.
c. more change-oriented.
d. focused on conflict-related stress.

**ANS: a**      **Pgs: 98-99**
**LO: 26**      **Conceptual**

102. Which of the following statements about the Life Experiences Survey is **not** true?
a. It recognizes that stress involves more than mere change.
b. It allows respondents to indicate whether events are negative or positive.
c. It recognizes that people tend to respond to most events in similar ways.
d. It allows for differences in how people appraise stress.

**ANS: c**      **Pgs: 98-100**
**LO: 26**      **Conceptual**

103. As a reminder that the results of stress scales should be interpreted with caution, you should note that many people who experience high levels of stress
a. fail to develop significant problems.
b. never complain though they become quite ill.
c. demonstrate novel coping techniques.
d. don't answer questions on stress scales honestly or accurately.

**ANS: a**      **Pg: 101**
**LO: 27**      **Factual**

**MULTIPLE CHOICE QUESTIONS FROM STUDY GUIDE**

1. Researchers have found that stress
   a. is healthy because it presents a challenge to the person.
   b. almost always comes from crises that are overwhelming and traumatic.
   c. leads to poor mental health and an eventual breakdown if it is not resolved.
   d. can come from everyday problems and minor nuisances as well as major crises.

   **ANS: d**          **Pg: 72**
   **LO: 1**           **Factual**

2. Which of the following would <u>not</u> be considered a form of ambient stress?
   a. crowding
   b. air pollution
   c. excessive heat
   d. unrealistic expectations

   **ANS: d**          **Pgs: 73-74**
   **LO: 3**           **Factual**

3. Which of the following would be considered an example of an acute stressor?
   a. having your home threatened by severe flooding
   b. ongoing pressures from a hostile boss at work
   c. persistent financial strains produced by huge credit card debts
   d. the demands of caring for a sick family member for an extensive period of time

   **ANS: a**          **Pg: 75**
   **LO: 5**           **Factual**

4. Research on life change and stress began when Thomas Holmes, Richard Rahe, and their colleagues set out to explore the relation between stressful life events and
   a. frustration.
   b. aggressive behavior.
   c. physical illness.
   d. Schizophrenia.

   **ANS: c**          **Pgs: 78-79**
   **LO: 8**           **Factual**

5. According to the inverted-U hypothesis, performance on a task
   a. usually decreases with emotional arousal.
   b. usually increases with emotional arousal.
   c. peaks at the optimal level of arousal for the particular task.
   d. peaks at about the same level no matter what the task is.

   **ANS: c**          **Pg: 84**
   **LO: 12**          **Factual**

6.  A physiological reaction that mobilizes an organism for attacking or fleeing is
    a.  called the fight-or-flight response.
    b.  called the autonomic nervous system response.
    c.  a function of the parasympathetic nervous system.
    d.  seen only in animals, not in humans.

**ANS: a**           **Pg: 85**
**LO: 13**           **Factual**

7.  In contrast to the traditional fight-or-flight model of responding to stress, Shelley Taylor and her colleagues have suggested that females may be more likely to engage in a _____ response.
    a.  run-and-hide
    b.  tend-and-befriend
    c.  lock-and-load
    d.  wait-and-see

**ANS: b**           **Pgs: 85-86**
**LO: 13**           **Factual**

8.  Which of the following is the <u>correct</u> order for the three stages of the general adaptation syndrome?
    a.  alarm, resistance, exhaustion
    b.  resistance, alarm, exhaustion
    c.  exhaustion, resistance, alarm
    d.  alarm, exhaustion, resistance

**ANS: a**           **Pgs: 86-87**
**LO: 13**           **Factual**

9.  When a person experiences stress, the brain sends signals to the endocrine system along two pathways. The structure that appears to initiate action along both pathways is the
    a.  adrenal gland.
    b.  catecholamine.
    c.  hypothalamus.
    d.  pituitary gland.

**ANS: c**           **Pg: 87**
**LO: 14**           **Factual**

10. Laboratory research on "normal" subjects suggests that choking under pressure
    a.  is fairly common
    b.  occurs only in athletic events
    c.  is common only for "high-anxious" individuals
    d.  rarely occurs outside of professional sports

**ANS: a**           **Pg: 89**
**LO: 16**           **Factual**

11. Burnout is associated with all but which of the following?
   a. increased absenteeism
   b. increased sense of self-efficacy
   c. reduced productivity at work
   d. increased vulnerability to health problems

ANS: b                **Pg: 90**
LO: 18              **Factual**

12. Posttraumatic stress disorder (PTSD) is associated with an elevated risk for which of the following?
   a. depression
   b. anxiety disorders
   c. substance abuse
   d. all of these

ANS: d                **Pgs: 90-91**
LO: 19              **Factual**

13. Which of the following statements regarding the effects of social support on stress is not accurate?
   a. Social support is favorably related to physical health.
   b. Social support seems to be unrelated to mental health.
   c. Providing social support to others can be beneficial.
   d. Social support may serve as a protective buffer from stress.

ANS: b                **Pgs: 94-95**
LO: 22              **Factual**

14. Hardiness tends to reduce the effects of stress by altering one's
   a. stress appraisals.
   b. frustration level.
   c. need for sensory stimulation.
   d. autonomic reactivity.

ANS: a                **Pg: 95**
LO: 23              **Factual**

15. Which of the following is not one of the main criticisms of the Social Readjustment Rating Scale (SRRS)?
   a. The list of stressful events on the SRRS is too lengthy.
   b. Many of the events listed on the SRRS are highly ambiguous.
   c. The impact of neuroticism is overemphasized on the SRRS.
   d. The SRRS measures change-related stress exclusively.

ANS: a                **Pgs: 97-98**
LO: 25              **Factual**

# MULTIPLE CHOICE QUESTIONS ON WEB SITE

1.  Whether or not an event is stressful is most likely to depend on
a.  how much physiological arousal it causes.
b.  how much change there is.
c.  how one appraises and adapts to the event.
d.  whether one is prepared for the event.

**ANS: c**          **Pgs: 72-73**
**LO: 2**           **Conceptual**

2.  One challenge faced by members of ethnic minorities in dealing with everyday discrimination is that manifestations of such discrimination are often
a.  imaginary.
b.  ambiguous.
c.  minor.
d.  consistent.

**ANS: b**          **Pg: 75**
**LO: 4**           **Conceptual**

3.  The four major types of stress described in your textbook are
a.  pressure, anxiety, environment, social demands.
b.  frustration, anger, pressure, and change.
c.  frustration, conflict, pressure, and change.
d.  conflict, pressure, anxiety, and social demands.

**ANS: c**          **Pg: 76**
**LO: 5**           **Factual**

4.  Approach-avoidance conflicts often produce
a.  vacillation.
b.  frustration.
c.  aggression.
d.  self-directed anger.

**ANS: a**          **Pgs: 77-78**
**LO: 7**           **Factual**

5.  Whenever others expect you to conform to their expectations or perform in certain ways, you tend to experience
a.  anger.
b.  conflict.
c.  frustration.
d.  pressure.

**ANS: d**          **Pg: 80**
**LO: 9**           **Factual**

6. Research suggests that positive emotional reactions to stress may have the adaptive quality of enhancing
a. recovery from psychological trauma.
b. creativity and flexibility in problem solving.
c. avoidance strategies.
d. use of defense mechanisms.

**ANS: b**        **Pg: 83**
**LO: 11**      **Factual**

7. The "fight-or-flight" response was first described by
a. Martin Seligman
b. Ray Rosenman
c. Walter Cannon
d. Hans Selye

**ANS: c**        **Pg: 85**
**LO: 13**      **Factual**

8. The sympathetic division of the autonomic nervous system
a. conserves bodily resources.
b. arouses sympathy for those in stressful circumstances.
c. mobilizes bodily resources for emergencies.
d. calms the body after the fight-or-flight response.

**ANS: c**        **Pg: 85**
**LO: 13**      **Factual**

9. The correct order of stages in the general adaptation syndrome is
a. resistance, alarm, exhaustion.
b. alarm, exhaustion, resistance.
c. resistance, exhaustion, alarm.
d. alarm, resistance, exhaustion.

**ANS: d**        **Pgs: 86-87**
**LO: 13**      **Factual**

10. You realize that no matter how much you hate mathematics you will not be able to drop out of calculus class this semester if you want to go to the graduate school of your choice. You hunker down for a miserable semester of hard and studious labor. You are in the _____ stage of the general adaptation syndrome.
a. alarm
b. exhaustion
c. resistance
d. extinction

**ANS: c**        **Pg: 87**
**LO: 13**      **Conceptual**

11.    _____ involves active efforts to master, reduce, or tolerate the demands of stress.
a.    Coping
b.    Adjustment
c.    Stress tolerance
d.    General adaptation

**ANS: a**          **Pgs: 88-89**
**LO: 15**          **Factual**

12.    Physical, mental, and emotional exhaustion due to work-related stress is called
a.    burnout.
b.    reaction formation disorder.
c.    the general adaptation syndrome.
d.    posttraumatic stress disorder.

**ANS: a**          **Pg: 90**
**LO: 18**          **Factual**

*13.    Which of the following appears to be a key factor in predicting who is most likely to
        develop PTSD following a traumatic event?
a.    the age of the victim
b.    the place of the traumatic event
c.    the intensity of the traumatic event
d.    biological aspects of the individual

**ANS: c**          **Pg: 91**
**LO: 19**          **Factual**

14.    _____ variables are factors that can soften the impact of stress on physical and mental
        health.
a.    Intervening
b.    Dependent
c.    Moderator
d.    Extraneous

**ANS: c**          **Pg: 94**
**LO: 22**          **Factual**

15.    The pessimistic explanatory style may be related to relatively poor health because
a.    pessimists expect to have poor health.
b.    pessimism may lead to passive coping efforts.
c.    pessimists explain their ailments to doctors inaccurately.
d.    pessimists don't elicit much social support.

**ANS: b**          **Pg: 96**
**LO: 24**          **Conceptual**

## TRUE/FALSE QUESTIONS

1.      Everyday hassles have NOT been found to be predictive of mental or physical health.

**ANS: false**          **Pg: 72**
**LO: 1**               **Factual**

2.      When trying to resolve an approach-avoidance conflict, it is best to focus on lowering the avoidance gradient.

**ANS: true**           **Pg: 78**
**LO: 7**               **Conceptual**

3.      Individuals who score low on the Social Readjustment Rating Scale are more likely to develop illnesses than those who score low.

**ANS: false**          **Pgs: 78-79**
**LO: 8**               **Factual**

4.      Current research indicates that change is inherently and inevitably stressful.

**ANS: false**          **Pg: 80**
**LO: 8**               **Conceptual**

5.      Corticosteriods help inhibit tissue inflammation in case of injury during times of stress.

**ANS: true**           **Pg: 88**
**LO: 14**              **Factual**

6.      On well-learned tasks that should be executed almost automatically, the self-conscious person may focus *too little* attention on the task.

**ANS: false**          **Pg: 89**
**LO: 16**              **Conceptual**

7.      The types of traumas that can cause PTSD are more common than most people realize.

**ANS: true**           **Pg: 90**
**LO: 19**              **Factual**

8.      Psychosomatic diseases are unique to heart and lung problems.

**ANS: false**          **Pg: 92**
**LO: 20**              **Factual**

9.      Strong social support has been found to be a key factor in reducing the likelihood of PTSD among Vietnam veterans.

**ANS: true**           **Pg: 92**
**LO: 22**              **Factual**

10.    Positive change is a crucial factor for predicting adaptational outcomes.

**ANS: false          Pg: 100**
**LO: 26              Conceptual**


## SHORT-ANSWER ESSAY QUESTIONS

1.    Explain what is meant by the statement, "Stress is in the eye of the beholder."

**Pgs: 72-73**
**LO: 2**

2.    Briefly describe the three types of conflict and give an example of each.  Which type of conflict is most likely to produce vacillation.  Why?

**Pgs: 76-78**
**LO: 7**

*3.    How do positive emotions promote resilience in the face of stress?

**Pgs:  83-84**
**LO: 11**

4.    Describe two criticisms of Hans Selye's model of the general adaptation syndrome.

**Pgs: 86-88**
**LO: 13**

5.    Explain how coping responses may be either healthy or unhealthy.

**Pgs: 88-89**
**LO: 15**

6.    Describe burnout and its possible causes.  Do you think it's possible for college students to suffer from "academic burnout"?

**Pg: 90**
**LO: 18**

7.    Define the term "positive psychology" and explain the rationale for this movement.

**Pg: 93**
**LO: 21**

8.     Briefly explain how social networks can be beneficial or detrimental to efforts to cope with stress.

**Pgs: 94-95**
**LO: 22**

9.     Define the term "explanatory style." What are some of the things that optimists do that are helpful in coping with stress?

**Pgs: 96-97**
**LO: 24**

10.    Why is it important to use caution when interpreting scores on instruments designed to measure stress?

**Pg: 101**
**LO: 27**

# Chapter 4
# COPING PROCESSES

## LEARNING OBJECTIVES

1. Describe the variety of coping strategies that people use.
2. Discuss whether individuals display distinctive styles of coping.
3. Analyze the adaptive value of giving up as a response to stress.
4. Describe the adaptive value of aggression as a response to stress.
5. Evaluate the adaptive value of indulging yourself as a response to stress.
6. Discuss the adaptive value of negative self-talk as a response to stress.
7. Explain how defense mechanisms work.
8. Evaluate the adaptive value of defense mechanisms, including recent work on healthy illusions.
9. Discuss whether constructive coping is related to intelligence.
10. Describe the nature of constructive coping.
11. Explain Ellis's analysis of the causes of maladaptive emotions.
12. Describe some assumptions that contribute to catastrophic thinking.
13. Discuss the merits of positive reinterpretation and humor as coping strategies.
14. List and describe four steps in systematic problem solving.
15. Discuss the adaptive value of seeking help as a coping strategy.
16. Explain five common causes of wasted time.
17. Describe evidence on the causes and consequences of procrastination.
18. Summarize advice on managing time effectively.
19. Describe the nature and value of emotional intelligence.
20. Analyze the adaptive value of releasing pent-up emotions and distracting yourself.
21. Discuss the importance of managing hostility and forgiving others' transgressions.
22. Summarize the evidence on the effects of meditation.
23. Describe the requirements and procedure for Benson's relaxation response.
24. Explain why traits cannot be target behaviors in self-modification programs.
25. Describe the three kinds of information you should pursue in gathering your baseline data.
26. Discuss how to use reinforcement to increase the strength of a response.
27. Explain how to use reinforcement, control of antecedents, and punishment to decrease the strength of a response.
28. Analyze issues related to fine-tuning and ending a self-modification program.

## MULTIPLE CHOICE QUESTIONS

1.      Efforts to master, reduce, or tolerate the demands caused by stress in one's life are collectively known as
a.      catharsis.
b.      defense mechanisms.
c.      procrastination.
d.      coping.

**ANS: d**          **Pg: 106**
**LO: 1**           **Factual**

2.      Which of the following statements about the use of coping strategies is **not** true?
a.      Most people come to rely on some strategies more than others.
b.      An individual's coping strategies are influenced by situational demands.
c.      People's coping strategies show moderate stability across a wide variety of situations.
d.      People are most likely to use problem-focused coping in situations involving uncontrollable stress.

**ANS: d**          **Pgs: 106-107**
**LO: 2**           **Conceptual**

3.      The adaptive value of a coping technique depends on the
a.      nature of the situation.
b.      individual's coping strengths.
c.      age of the individual.
d.      degree of social support available.

**ANS: a**          **Pg: 107**
**LO: 2**           **Conceptual**

4.      Researchers have argued that _____ is a desirable quality in applying coping strategies across various situations.
a.      consistency
b.      flexibility
c.      aggression
d.      indulgence

**ANS: b**          **Pg: 107**
**LO: 2**           **Conceptual**

5.      Learned helplessness results when humans are subjected to aversive events that
a.      are unavoidable.
b.      negatively reinforce aggressiveness.
c.      positively reinforce aggressiveness.
d.      are high in control, but low in predictability.

**ANS: a**          **Pg: 107**
**LO: 3**           **Conceptual**

6.	_____ developed the learned helplessness model.
a.	Sigmund Freud
b.	Albert Bandura
c.	Martin Seligman
d.	Abraham Maslow

**ANS: c**		**Pg: 107**
**LO: 3**		**Conceptual**

7.	Whether someone develops learned helplessness under conditions of unavoidable aversive events is most likely to depend on
a.	the intensity of the aversive events.
b.	prior experience in similar circumstances.
c.	conditioning experiences in childhood.
d.	one's beliefs about their control over events.

**ANS: d**		**Pg: 107**
**LO: 3**		**Conceptual**

8.	The belief that events are beyond one's control is particularly likely to emerge in people who
a.	are considered true optimists.
b.	show symptoms of bipolar disorder.
c.	exhibit a pessimistic explanatory style.
d.	score extremely high in sensation seeking.

**ANS: c**		**Pg: 107**
**LO: 3**		**Conceptual**

9.	Withdrawal could be an adaptive response to stress under which of the following circumstances?
	1.	when one is not equipped to handle a situation
	2.	when the stressful event can be ignored
	3.	when the pressure associated with the event will be short-term

a.	I only
b.	I and II only
c.	II and III only
d.	I, II, and III

**ANS: a**		**Pg: 108**
**LO: 3**		**Conceptual**

10.     If you enter a 10K race without training adequately, _____ might be the most adaptive coping strategy.
a.      catharsis
b.      denial
c.      quitting
d.      displacement

**ANS: c          Pg: 108**
**LO: 3           Conceptual**

*11.    Which of the following is an example of the coping strategy known as behavioral disengagement?
a.      arguing with one's best friend because of anger toward one's boss
b.      dropping a class because it is evident that one needs to take one of the recommended prerequisites
c.      using drugs following a significant loss
d.      blaming one's parents for one's character flaws

**ANS: b          Pg: 108**
**LO: 3           Conceptual**

12.     Which of the following was NOT included by Berkowitz among the qualifications to the frustration-aggression hypothesis?
a.      Frustration does not necessarily lead to aggression.
b.      Many factors besides frustration affect the likelihood of aggression.
c.      Aggression leads to frustration as often as frustration leads to aggression.
d.      Frustration may produce responses other than aggression.

**ANS: c          Pgs: 108-109**
**LO: 4           Conceptual**

13.     Diversion of anger toward a substitute target was noted by Sigmund Freud, who called it
a.      displacement.
b.      projection.
c.      rationalization.
d.      reaction formation.

**ANS: a          Pg: 109**
**LO: 4           Factual**

14.     If you yell at your little sister after having a fight with your girlfriend, you may be diverting your anger through the use of
a.      sublimation.
b.      catharsis.
c.      displacement.
d.      denial.

**ANS: c          Pg: 109**
**LO: 4           Factual**

15.     Freud coined the term _____ to refer to the release of pent-up emotion.
a.      aggression
b.      implosion
c.      frustration
d.      catharsis

**ANS: d**          **Pg: 109**
**LO: 4**           **Factual**

16.     Experimental research indicates that aggressive behavior
a.      is basically uncontrollable.
b.      does not reliably lead to catharsis.
c.      is often adaptive in interpersonal relationships.
d.      is an instinctual approach for dealing with frustration.

**ANS: b**          **Pg: 109**
**LO: 4**           **Conceptual**

*17.    Which of the following is the most accurate reflection of the research findings regarding catharsis?
a.      Behaving in an aggressive manner is a good way to "blow off steam."
b.      Behaving in a passive-aggressive manner is an effective way to discharge pent-up emotions.
c.      Behaving in an aggressive manner tends to fuel more anger and aggression.
d.      Aggressive behavior is likely to alleviate frustration only if directed toward an irrelevant someone.

**ANS: c**          **Pg: 109**
**LO: 4**           **Conceptual**

18.     There is evidence that stress is related to
            1.      overeating
            2.      increased smoking
            3.      consumption of alcohol
a.      1 only
b.      2 and 3 only
c.      3 only
d.      1, 2, and 3

**ANS: d**          **Pg: 109**
**LO: 5**           **Factual**

19. When things are going poorly in one area of life, one may compensate by pursuing substitute forms of satisfaction. This coping strategy is referred to as
a. a defense mechanism.
b. developing alternative rewards.
c. addiction.
d. catharsis.

**ANS: b**            **Pg: 109**
**LO: 5**             **Factual**

20. Albert Ellis believes that problematic emotional reactions to stress are caused by
a. unpleasant events.
b. catastrophic thinking.
c. excessively logical thinking.
d. the over-reliance on defense mechanisms.

**ANS: b**            **Pg: 111**
**LO: 6**             **Factual**

21. Which of the following is NOT a category of negative self-talk described by Beck?
a. focusing on negative feedback
b. making unduly pessimistic projections about the future
c. unfairly blaming one's parents for personal trouble
d. unrealistic attribution of failure to one's own shortcomings

**ANS: c**            **Pg: 111**
**LO: 6**             **Conceptual**

22. Who originally developed the concept of defense mechanisms?
a. Albert Bandura
b. Sigmund Freud
c. Albert Ellis
d. Martin Seligman

**ANS: b**            **Pg: 111**
**LO: 7**             **Factual**

23. Defense mechanisms are unconscious reactions that protect a person from
a. interpersonal deception.
b. unpleasant emotions.
c. catastrophic thinking.
d. potential failure in social relationships.

**ANS: b**            **Pg: 111**
**LO: 7**             **Factual**

*24.    Joan compulsively washes and meticulously irons her husbands cloths following an explosive argument with him. Joan's behavior is consistent with the defense mechanism:
a.    displacement.
b.    projection.
c.    denial.
d.    undoing.

**ANS: d**          **Pg: 111**
**LO: 7**            **Conceptual**

25.    The defense mechanism that involves suppressing unpleasant emotions or circumstances and refusing to acknowledge that they exist is referred to as
a.    displacement.
b.    reaction formation.
c.    intellectualization.
d.    denial.

**ANS: d**          **Pg: 111**
**LO: 7**            **Factual**

26.    Gratifying frustrated desires by thinking about imaginary achievements and satisfactions refers to the defense mechanism called
a.    overcompensation.
b.    fantasy.
c.    regression.
d.    identification.

**ANS: b**          **Pg: 111**
**LO: 7**            **Factual**

27.    Defense mechanisms work primarily through
a.    distorting reality so it does not seem so unpleasant and threatening.
b.    reducing a person's impulse control.
c.    allowing a person to release pent-up emotions.
d.    promoting adaptive coping whenever they are employed.

**ANS: a**          **Pg: 112**
**LO: 7**            **Conceptual**

28. Joe has been arrested three times in the past five years for driving under the influence of alcohol. When you ask him about how he is managing his drinking problem, he says "I don't have a drinking problem; I have a **getting caught** problem!" He is most likely using _____ to manage his difficulties.
a. overcompensation
b. undoing
c. projection
d. denial

**ANS: d**          **Pg: 111**
**LO: 7**            **Conceptual**

29. Defense mechanisms can operate at
a. the unconscious level only.
b. the conscious level only.
c. the preconscious level only.
d. both the conscious and unconscious levels.

**ANS: d**          **Pg: 112**
**LO: 7**            **Conceptual**

30. Freud believed that defense mechanisms operate at
a. the unconscious level only.
b. the conscious level only.
c. the preconscious level only.
d. both the conscious and unconscious levels.

**ANS: a**          **Pg: 112**
**LO: 7**            **Factual**

31. Defense mechanisms are largely _____ and entirely _____.
a. unconscious; normal
b. unconscious; abnormal
c. conscious; normal
d. conscious; abnormal

**ANS: a**          **Pg: 112**
**LO: 7**            **Conceptual**

32. Which of the following statements about defense mechanisms is **not** true?
a. Defensive coping is an avoidance strategy.
b. They typically operate at the unconscious level.
c. They are generally considered poor ways of coping.
d. Their use is considered an indication of psychological maladjustment.

**ANS: d**          **Pg: 112**
**LO: 8**            **Conceptual**

33. According to Taylor and Brown, depressed subjects exhibit _____ favorable and _____ realistic self-concepts than do "normal" people.
a. more; more
b. less; less
c. less; more
d. more; less

**ANS: c**      **Pg: 113**
**LO: 8**      **Factual**

34. Defense mechanisms are
a. usually always healthy to use.
b. probably almost never healthy to use.
c. probably not healthy to use, with a few exceptions.
d. none of these.

**ANS: c**      **Pgs: 112-113**
**LO: 8**      **Conceptual**

35. Compared to depressed people, "normal" people tend to _____ the degree to which they control chance events.
a. underestimate
b. overestimate
c. less accurately estimate
d. more accurately estimate

**ANS: b**      **Pg: 113**
**LO: 8**      **Factual**

36. In making projections about the future, "normal" people are more likely than depressed people to
a. be realistic.
b. make accurate projections.
c. rely on empirical evidence.
d. be unrealistically optimistic.

**ANS: d**      **Pg: 113**
**LO: 8**      **Factual**

37. According to Baumeister, the use of illusions tends to become unhealthy when the illusions
a. involve extreme distortions of reality.
b. include the participation of others.
c. incorporate more than one defense mechanism.
d. operate at the unconscious level.

**ANS: a**      **Pg: 113**
**LO: 8**      **Conceptual**

38.     Epstein and Meier found that constructive thinking is favorably related to
a.      wealth.
b.      mental and physical health.
c.      intelligence.
d.      altruism.

**ANS: b**          **Pg: 113**
**LO: 9**           **Factual**

39.     _____ refers broadly to the use of relatively healthful strategies for managing stressful events.
a.      Defending
b.      Compensating
c.      Catharsis
d.      Constructive coping

**ANS: d**          **Pg: 113**
**LO: 9**           **Factual**

40.     Which of the following is not involved in constructive coping?
a.      confronting problems directly
b.      applying basic principles of classical conditioning
c.      exerting some control over potentially harmful behaviors
d.      recognizing potentially disruptive emotional reactions to stress

**ANS: b**          **Pgs: 113-114**
**LO: 10**          **Conceptual**

41.     Constructive coping involves
a.      confronting problems directly.
b.      realistically appraising stress.
c.      learning to manage some emotional reactions to stress.
d.      all of these.

**ANS: d**          **Pgs: 113-114**
**LO: 10**          **Conceptual**

42.     Constructive coping involves all of the following **except**
a.      confronting problems directly.
b.      realistically appraising stress.
c.      exerting total and complete control over one's bad habits.
d.      learning to manage some emotional reactions to stress.

**ANS: c**          **Pgs: 113-114**
**LO: 10**          **Conceptual**

43. Which of the following is **not** a type of constructive coping described in your text?
a. appraisal-focused
b. emotion-focused
c. problem-focused
d. cognition-focused

ANS: d        Pgs: 113-114
LO: 10        Factual

44. According to Albert Ellis, our emotional reactions to life events result mainly from
a. our activation level at the time.
b. our appraisals of the events.
c. the consequences of the events.
d. congruence between events and expectations.

ANS: b        Pg: 115
LO: 11        Conceptual

45. Albert Ellis developed _____ therapy, a system of psychotherapy based on altering clients' appraisals of events in order to reduce maladaptive emotions and behaviors.
a. client-centered
b. psychodynamic
c. rational-emotive behavior
d. social learning

ANS: c        Pg: 115
LO: 11        Conceptual

46. Which of the following is **not** one of the main components of Ellis's model of catastrophic thinking?
a. consequence
b. unconditioned response
c. belief system
d. activating agent

ANS: b        Pg: 115
LO: 11        Factual

47. Which of the following is **not** one of the assumptions that can cause catastrophic thinking and emotional distress, according to Ellis?
a. I must perform well at everything I do.
b. I should be liked by everyone I come into contact with.
c. I should be able to control my destructive emotions
d. Other people should be competent and considerate.

ANS: c        Pgs: 116-117
LO: 12        Conceptual

48.     According to Ellis, which of the following would be an example of irrational thinking?
a.      "I would like to succeed in my chosen profession."
b.      "I must be admired and liked by everyone who meets me."
c.      "I would prefer to have a certain amount of free time on the weekends."
d.      "I think it is important to have a happy marriage."

ANS: b              Pgs: 116-117
LO: 12              Conceptual


*49.    According to Albert Ellis, the goal of therapy is to replace catastrophic thinking with
        more low-key, _____ analysis.
a.      intuitive
b.      natural
c.      rational
d.      congruent

ANS: c              Pg: 117
LO: 12              Factual

50.     Finding humor in the situation is considered a(n) _____-focused strategy of constructive
        coping.
a.      appraisal
b.      emotion
c.      problem
d.      cognition

ANS: a              Pg: 117
LO: 13              Factual

51.     According to research, which of the following usually effectively moderates the negative
        impact of stress?
a.      dissonance
b.      catharsis
c.      repression
d.      humor

ANS: d              Pg: 117
LO: 13              Factual

52.     Comparing your stressful situation favorably with someone else's exemplifies which of
        the following?
a.      cognitive dissonance
b.      reaction formation
c.      positive reinterpretation
d.      systematic problem solving

ANS: c              Pg: 118
LO: 13              Factual

53. Which of the following is an example of positive reinterpretation?
a. cutting your losses
b. learning the hard way
c. comparing yourself to those who are better off
d. looking for something good in a bad experience

**ANS: d**      **Pg: 118**
**LO: 13**      **Conceptual**

*54. Which of the following has NOT be proposed as an explanation for how humor helps to reduce the effects of stress and promote wellness?
a. Humor increases the experience of positive emotions.
b. Humor facilitates rewarding social interactions.
c. Humor facilitates the release of stress-relieving neurotransmitters.
d. Humor affects appraisals of stressful events.

**ANS: c**      **Pg: 117**
**LO: 13**      **Factual**

*55. Susan was wiped out from her third chemotherapy treatment, yet when asked about how she was doing through all of this she replied, "Now I am able to have a lot more compassion for my grandmother who went through this, too, and it has brought us closer together." Susan illustrates the use of _____ as a coping strategy.
a. positive reinterpretation
b. reaction formation
c. learned helplessness
d. catharsis

**ANS: a**      **Pg: 118**
**LO: 13**      **Conceptual**

56. Efforts to remedy or conquer the stress-producing problem itself are called _____-focused coping.
a. problem
b. thought
c. emotion
d. situation

**ANS: a**      **Pg: 118**
**LO: 14**      **Factual**

57. Which of the following is **not** a step in systematic problem solving?
a. clarify the problem
b. think of alternative courses of action
c. try several different alternatives simultaneously
d. act, while remaining flexible

**ANS: c**      **Pgs: 118-119**
**LO: 14**      **Factual**

58. According to D'Zurilla and Sheedy, the first step in systematic problem solving is
a. taking action.
b. clarifying the problem.
c. selecting a course of action.
d. generating alternative courses of action.

**ANS: b          Pgs: 118-119**
**LO: 14          Factual**

59. Which of the following is most likely to hinder people's efforts to clarify their problems?
a. describing problems in vague generalities
b. focusing too much on positive feelings
c. emphasizing the humorous aspects of the problem
d. generating alternative courses of action

**ANS: a          Pgs: 118-119**
**LO: 14          Conceptual**

*60. Which of the following is the BEST example of a clearly identified problem?
a. "My life isn't going anywhere."
b. "I am so nervous that I can't think straight."
c. "I never have enough time."
d. "I need to get a job."

**ANS: d          Pgs: 118-119**
**LO: 14          Conceptual**

61. _____ is a strategy for generating as many alternative courses of action as possible while withholding criticism and evaluation.
a. Brainstorming
b. Overcompensating
c. Cognitive dissonance
d. Appraising

**ANS: a          Pg: 119**
**LO: 14          Factual**

*62. Systematic problem solving involves
a. generating alternative courses of action.
b. listing only plausible resolutions.
c. focusing on guaranteed solutions.
d. focusing on emotional outcomes.

**ANS: a          Pg: 119**
**LO: 14          Factual**

63. Seeking social support is considered a(n) _____-focused strategy of constructive coping.
a. appraisal
b. emotion
c. problem
d. cognition

**ANS: c**      **Pg: 119**
**LO: 15**      **Factual**

64. Which of the following statements about seeking help from others is **not** true?
a. Social support can help buffer the deleterious effects of stress.
b. Some people have more social support than others.
c. Social support is generally considered a stable, external resource.
d. Many people are reluctant to acknowledge their problems and seek help from others.

**ANS: c**      **Pgs: 119-120**
**LO: 15**      **Conceptual**

65. Which of the following is **not** listed in your text as a cause of wasted time?
a. inability to set priorities
b. inability to delay gratification
c. inability to delegate responsibility
d. inability to throw things away

**ANS: b**      **Pg: 121**
**LO: 16**      **Factual**

66. Which of the following is considered a common cause of wasted time?
a. accepting less than the best from yourself and others
b. inability to find things because you threw them away
c. too quickly assigning to others tasks you could do
d. being reluctant to refuse requests from others

**ANS: d**      **Pg: 121**
**LO: 16**      **Conceptual**

67. Which of the following is **not** one of the personality factors that contribute to procrastination?
a. fear of success
b. low self-efficacy
c. low conscientiousness
d. excessive perfectionism

**ANS: a**      **Pg: 122**
**LO: 17**      **Conceptual**

68. Time management experts agree that the key to better time management is increased
a. enjoyment.
b. effectiveness.
c. self-discipline.
d. efficiency.

**ANS: b**          **Pg: 122**
**LO: 18**          **Factual**

69. The first step in attempting to use your time more effectively is to
a. protect your prime time.
b. plan activities using a schedule.
c. clarify your goals.
d. monitor your use of time.

**ANS: d**          **Pg: 123**
**LO: 18**          **Factual**

70. In order to achieve increased effectiveness, one must learn to _____ important tasks.
a. control the number of
b. enjoy
c. allocate appropriate time to
d. monitor the occurrence of

**ANS: c**          **Pg: 123**
**LO: 18**          **Factual**

71. The first step in clarifying your goals is to
a. identify your lifetime goals.
b. recognize your daily concerns.
c. review your past accomplishments.
d. distinguish between personal and career goals.

**ANS: a**          **Pg: 124**
**LO: 18**          **Factual**

*72. Which of the following is NOT an essential component of emotional intelligence?
a. the ability to perceive emotion
b. dissociating emotion from thought
c. reasoning with emotion
d. regulating emotion

**ANS: b**          **Pg: 125**
**LO: 19**          **Factual**

*73.     Mayer-Salovey-Caruso Emotional Intelligence Test authors are striving to make this test
a.       a measure of personality characteristics.
b.       a measure of emotional temperament.
c.       a performance based measure of the ability to deal effectively with emotions.
d.       a verbal based measure of the ability to articulate effectively about emotions.

**ANS: c**          **Pg: 125**
**LO: 19**          **Factual**

74.      A person who has the quality of _____ can monitor, identify, express and
         regulate emotions, and comprehend the emotions of others
a.       adaptive coping
b.       good self-esteem
c.       appropriate catharsis
d.       emotional intelligence

**ANS: d**          **Pg: 125**
**LO: 19**          **Factual**

75.      Research suggests that efforts to actively suppress emotions result in
a.       increased autonomic arousal.
b.       more efficient time management.
c.       inevitable outbursts of physical aggression.
d.       deficiencies in one's ability to deal with others.

**ANS: a**          **Pg: 126**
**LO: 20**          **Factual**

76.      A recent study of the repercussions of "psychological inhibition" in gay men who conceal
         their sexual identity suggests that this inhibition is detrimental to one's
a.       health.
b.       self-esteem.
c.       interpersonal relationships.
d.       ability to maintain an active sex life.

**ANS: a**          **Pg: 126**
**LO: 20**          **Factual**

*77.     Which of the following is NOT one of the suggested guidelines for using writing about
         emotional experiences as a coping strategy?
a.       Explore how this topic is related to a variety of issues in your life.
b.       Write continuously without regard for spelling or grammar.
c.       Remember that the writing is for you, not someone else.
d.       Write only every other day or so, rather than consecutive days.

**ANS: d**          **Pgs: 126-127**
**LO: 20**          **Factual**

78.     There is substantial evidence that _____ is related to increased risk for heart attacks and other ailments.
a.      denial
b.      addiction
c.      releasing emotions
d.      hostility

**ANS: d**          **Pg: 127**
**LO: 21**          **Factual**

*79.    Research suggests that forgiving is an effective _____-focused coping strategy.
a.      emotion
b.      problem
c.      solution
d.      interpersonal

**ANS: a**          **Pg: 127**
**LO: 21**          **Factual**

80.     Mental exercises in which a conscious attempt is made to focus attention in a non-analytic way are referred to as
a.      meditation.
b.      behavior modification.
c.      the relaxation response.
d.      systematic desensitization.

**ANS: a**          **Pg: 128**
**LO: 22**          **Factual**

81.     The most widely practiced approaches to meditation have their origins in
a.      classical conditioning.
b.      behavior modification techniques.
c.      Eastern religions such as Hinduism.
d.      Freud's theory of psychoanalysis.

**ANS: c**          **Pg: 128**
**LO: 22**          **Factual**

82.     Evidence indicates that meditation can lead to
a.      a beneficial physiological state.
b.      decreases in skin resistance.
c.      activation of arousal.
d.      all of these.

**ANS: a**          **Pgs: 128-129**
**LO: 22**          **Factual**

83. The physiological changes often seen in meditation
a. are unique to religion-based techniques.
b. are best considered a type of catharsis.
c. often result in elevated levels of arousal.
d. can also be seen with other relaxation training procedures.

**ANS: d**  **Pg: 129**
**LO: 22**  **Conceptual**

84. According to Herbert Benson, the relaxation response is **not** aided by a(n)
a. mental device.
b. active attitude.
c. comfortable position.
d. quiet environment.

**ANS: b**  **Pg: 129**
**LO: 23**  **Factual**

85. The first step in a self-modification program is
a. design your program.
b. gather baseline data.
c. specify your target behavior.
d. Any of these can be used as the first step.

**ANS: c**  **Pg: 131**
**LO: 24**  **Factual**

*86. Advocates of behavior modification assume that behavior is a product of all of the
following **except**
a. learning.
b. conditioning.
c. unconscious processes.
d. environmental control.

**ANS: c**  **Pg: 131**
**LO: 24**  **Factual**

87. A common problem in developing self-modification programs is that
a. people think in terms of traits rather than behaviors.
b. people fail to use punishment as often as they should.
c. contracts bother people and undermine their motivation.
d. people tend to want to list too many target behaviors.

**ANS: a**  **Pg: 131**
**LO: 24**  **Conceptual**

88. Personality traits cannot be used as targets because they
a. are simply too hard to change.
b. are not specific behaviors.
c. are too often associated with negative emotions.
d. cannot be changed except through psychotherapy.

**ANS: b**        **Pg: 131**
**LO: 24**        **Factual**

*89. Which of the following would NOT be a good target behavior for a self-modification program?
a. smoking
b. yelling at one's children
c. eating junk food
d. getting embarrassed

**ANS: d**        **Pg: 131**
**LO: 24**        **Conceptual**

90. A period prior to a behavioral intervention during which a target behavior is observed carefully is called the _____ period.
a. preliminary survey
b. baseline
c. preparation
d. contingency

**ANS: b**        **Pgs: 131-132**
**LO: 25**        **Factual**

91. Which of the following is **not** information you need in gathering baseline data for a self-modification program?
a. events that typically precede the target behavior
b. initial frequency of the target behavior
c. kind of emotions that surround the target behavior
d. typical consequences of the target behavior

**ANS: c**        **Pgs: 131-132**
**LO: 25**        **Conceptual**

92. If you recognize that an undesirable behavior is preceded by a particular event, you have
a. identified an antecedent.
b. recognized a reinforcer.
c. established a baseline.
d. eliminated an unconditioned response.

**ANS: a**        **Pg: 132**
**LO: 25**        **Factual**

93. It is useful to know about the common antecedents of a behavior you wish to change because the antecedents may
a. be punishments for your target behavior.
b. be reinforcing your target behavior.
c. produce disruptive emotional responses.
d. trigger the undesirable behavior.

**ANS: d**          **Pg: 132**
**LO: 25**          **Conceptual**

*94. Jim, who was working on quitting smoking, noticed that he smoked a cigarette immediately following every meal, including snacks. Thus Jim identified a(n) _____ to his smoking behavior.
a. antecedent
b. positive reinforcement
c. negative reinforcement
d. punishment

**ANS: a**          **Pg: 132**
**LO: 25**          **Conceptual**

*95. Susan, who was working on quitting smoking, noticed that she smoked whenever she was feeling anxious. Thus Susan identified a(n) _____ to her smoking behavior.
a. antecedent
b. positive reinforcement
c. negative reinforcement
d. punishment

**ANS: c**          **Pg: 132**
**LO: 25**          **Conceptual**

96. In selecting a reinforcer for a self-modification program, you should
a. select the strongest reinforcer possible.
b. try to select an appropriate negative rather than positive reinforcer.
c. not be concerned with the reinforcer's availability.
d. remember that you can use a reinforcer that you're already getting.

**ANS: d**          **Pg: 132**
**LO: 26**          **Conceptual**

97. Reinforcement contingencies are
a. stimuli that operate unconsciously.
b. responses that tend to occur infrequently.
c. guidelines regulating the delivery of reinforcers.
d. negative reinforcers that work irregularly.

**ANS: c**          **Pg: 132**
**LO: 26**          **Conceptual**

98.  In arranging contingencies for a self-modification program, you should set behavioral goals that are both _____ and _____.
a.  challenging; realistic
b.  realistic; easily attainable
c.  clear; unrealistically high
d.  attainable; relatively vague

ANS: a                    Pgs: 132-133
LO: 26                    Conceptual

99.  In arranging contingencies for a self-modification program, you should avoid setting a behavioral target that
a.  causes quick satiation.
b.  is a challenge to reach.
c.  is possible and realistic.
d.  takes effort to accomplish.

ANS: a                    Pgs: 132-133
LO: 26                    Factual

100.  A system providing for symbolic reinforcers is called a(n)
a.  extinction system.
b.  token economy.
c.  feedback loop.
d.  contingency alternative.

ANS: b                    Pg: 133
LO: 26                    Factual

101.  The reinforcement of successively closer approximations of a desired response is known as
a.  shaping.
b.  extinction.
c.  continuous reinforcement.
d.  negative reinforcement.

ANS: a                    Pg: 133
LO: 26                    Factual

102.  In controlling the antecedents of overeating, the core of the strategy is to overcome temptation by
a.  avoiding it altogether.
b.  strengthening one's will power.
c.  purposely overeating until nauseated.
d.  always having another person with you.

ANS: a                    Pg: 134
LO: 27                    Conceptual

103. To use punishment effectively in a self-modification program, you should
a. continue it until an emotional response occurs.
b. eliminate its aversive qualities.
c. ensure that the punishment is very strong.
d. use it in conjunction with positive reinforcement.

**ANS: d**         **Pg: 134**
**LO: 27**        **Conceptual**

104. The use of a behavioral contract in a behavior modification program
a. is generally not of much use.
b. will ensure that you follow your plan.
c. should be supervised by an attorney.
d. can strengthen your motivation to stick to your plan.

**ANS: d**         **Pg: 135**
**LO: 28**        **Conceptual**

105. A successful self-modification program may end spontaneously when
a. one experiences a traumatic event.
b. one's self-esteem is threatened.
c. the target behavior suddenly reappears.
d. the new behavior becomes habitual.

**ANS: d**         **Pg: 135**
**LO: 28**        **Conceptual**


## MULTIPLE CHOICE QUESTIONS FROM STUDY GUIDE

1. If you look for the good in what is happening in a stressful situation, you are using which of the following coping strategies?
a. denial
b. planning
c. restraint coping
d. positive reinterpretation

**ANS: d**         **Pg: 118**
**LO: 13**        **Conceptual**

2. Passive behavior produced by exposure to unavoidable aversive events is called
a. catharsis.
b. aggression.
c. learned helplessness.
d. irrational self-talk.

**ANS: c**         **Pg: 107**
**LO: 3**        **Conceptual**

3.  Which of the following conclusions about research on the cathartic value of aggressive behavior is most accurate?
a.  Aggression reliably produces a cathartic effect.
b.  The adaptive value of aggressive behavior tends to be minimal.
c.  Aggression generally results in learned helplessness rather than catharsis.
d.  Aggression can be cathartic as long as it is directed at a stranger.

**ANS: b**          **Pg: 109**
**LO: 4**           **Conceptual**

4.  Which of the following is <u>least</u> closely associated with the use of defense mechanisms as a coping strategy?
a.  denial
b.  reality
c.  normal
d.  deception

**ANS: b**          **Pgs: 111-112**
**LO: 7**           **Conceptual**

5.  To use constructive coping effectively, a person must
a.  confront problems directly.
b.  make a realistic appraisal of one's coping resources.
c.  inhibit potentially disruptive emotional reactions.
d.  do all of these.

**ANS: d**          **Pgs: 113-114**
**LO: 9**           **Factual**

6.  To use constructive coping effectively, a person must
a.  confront problems directly.
b.  make a realistic appraisal of one's coping resources.
c.  inhibit potentially disruptive emotional reactions.
d.  do all of these.

**ANS: d**          **Pg: 114**
**LO: 10**          **Conceptual**

7.  Improving one's self-control is an example of which of the following constructive coping tactics?
a.  appraisal-focused coping
b.  problem-focused coping
c.  emotion-focused coping
d.  defense-focused coping

**ANS: b**          **Pg: 114**
**LO: 11**          **Factual**

8. Which of the following statements is likely to be considered an irrational assumption?
a. It's okay if I don't win all the time.
b. Other people are not always considerate.
c. Things will not always go the way I want them to.
d. I must have love and affection from people who are close to me.

**ANS: d**      **Pg: 116**
**LO: 12**      **Conceptual**


9. Which of the following has been offered as an explanation for the stress-reducing effects of humor?
a. Humor increases the experience of positive emotions.
b. Humor positively affects the appraisals of stressful events.
c. A good sense of humor promotes social support, which can buffer the effects of stress.
d. All of these have been offered as explanations.

**ANS: d**      **Pg: 117**
**LO: 13**      **Conceptual**


10. In generating alternative courses of action to solve a problem, it's a good idea to
a. go with the first alternative that comes to mind.
b. use a process like brainstorming to generate alternatives.
c. focus on the negative feelings associated with the problem.
d. think of the possible courses of action as alternative *solutions.*

**ANS: b**      **Pg: 119**
**LO: 14**      **Conceptual**


11. Which of the following statements about procrastination is not accurate?
a. Personality factors often contribute to procrastination.
b. Procrastinators tend to have fewer health problems than non-procrastinators.
c. Procrastination tends to have a negative impact on the quality of task performance.
d. All of these statements are accurate.

**ANS: b**      **Pg: 122**
**LO: 17**      **Conceptual**

12. Experts maintain that the key to better time management is increased
a. efficiency.
b. effectiveness.
c. emphasis on achieving perfection.
d. willingness to assume responsibility.

**ANS: b          Pg: 122**
**LO: 18          Conceptual**

13. Herbert Benson concluded that the beneficial aspects of meditation come from the
a. state of relaxation that it produces in the individual.
b. heightened spirituality of the person who learns how to meditate.
c. subtle blending of religion and psychology that brings on the relaxed state.
d. trance-like state that encourages the person to think of new solutions to personal problems.

**ANS: c          Pgs: 129-130**
**LO: 23          Conceptual**

14. Advocates of behavior modification assume that
a. what is learned can be unlearned.
b. our behavior is the product of learning.
c. some behavior patterns are more desirable than others.
d. all of these.

**ANS: d          Pg: 131**
**LO: 24          Factual**

15. Having specified a target behavior, the next step in a behavior modification program is to
a. gather baseline data.
b. design the program.
c. select a reinforcer.
d. set behavioral goals.

**ANS: a          Pg: 131**
**LO: 27          Conceptual**


## MULTIPLE CHOICE QUESTIONS ON WEB SITE

1. Learned helplessness results when humans are subjected to aversive events that
a. are unavoidable.
b. negatively reinforce aggressiveness.
c. positively reinforce aggressiveness.
d. are high in control, but low in predictability.

**ANS: a          Pg: 107**
**LO: 3          Conceptual**

2.	Experimental research indicates that aggressive behavior
a.	is basically uncontrollable.
b.	does not reliably lead to catharsis.
c.	is often adaptive in interpersonal relationships.
d.	is an instinctual approach for dealing with frustration.

**ANS: b**		**Pg: 109**
**LO: 4**		**Conceptual**

3.	Albert Ellis believes that problematic emotional reactions to stress are caused by
a.	unpleasant events.
b.	catastrophic thinking.
c.	excessively logical thinking.
d.	the over-reliance on defense mechanisms.

**ANS: b**		**Pg: 111**
**LO: 6**		**Factual**

4.	Defense mechanisms can operate at
a.	the unconscious level only.
b.	the conscious level only.
c.	the preconscious level only.
d.	both the conscious and unconscious levels.

**ANS: d**		**Pg: 112**
**LO: 7**		**Conceptual**

5.	Constructive coping involves
a.	confronting problems directly.
b.	realistically appraising stress.
c.	learning to manage some emotional reactions to stress.
d.	all of these.

**ANS: d**		**Pgs: 113-114**
**LO: 10**		**Conceptual**

6.	According to Albert Ellis, our emotional reactions to life events result mainly from
a.	our activation level at the time.
b.	our appraisals of the events.
c.	the consequences of the events.
d.	congruence between events and expectations.

**ANS: b**		**Pg: 115**
**LO: 11**		**Conceptual**

7. Which of the following is an example of positive reinterpretation?
a. cutting your losses
b. learning the hard way
c. comparing yourself to those who are better off
d. looking for something good in a bad experience

**ANS: d**          **Pg: 118**
**LO: 13**          **Conceptual**

8. According to D'Zurilla and Sheedy, the first step in systematic problem solving is
a. taking action.
b. clarifying the problem.
c. selecting a course of action.
d. generating alternative courses of action.

**ANS: b**          **Pgs: 118-119**
**LO: 14**          **Factual**

*9. Systematic problem solving involves
a. generating alternative courses of action.
b. listing only plausible resolutions.
c. focusing on guaranteed solutions.
d. focusing on emotional outcomes.

**ANS: a**          **Pg: 119**
**LO: 14**          **Factual**

10. In order to achieve increased effectiveness, one must learn to _____ important tasks.
a. control the number of
b. enjoy
c. allocate appropriate time to
d. monitor the occurrence of

**ANS: c**          **Pg: 123**
**LO: 18**          **Factual**

*11. Research suggests that forgiving is an effective _____-focused coping strategy.
a. emotion
b. problem
c. solution
d. interpersonal

**ANS: a**          **Pg: 127**
**LO: 21**          **Factual**

12.     The physiological changes often seen in meditation
a.      are unique to religion-based techniques.
b.      are best considered a type of catharsis.
c.      often result in elevated levels of arousal.
d.      can also be seen with other relaxation training procedures.

**ANS: d**          **Pg: 129**
**LO: 22**          **Conceptual**

*13.    Which of the following would NOT be a good target behavior for a self-modification
        program?
a.      smoking
b.      yelling at one's children
c.      eating junk food
d.      getting embarrassed

**ANS: d**          **Pg: 131**
**LO: 24**          **Conceptual**

14.     A system providing for symbolic reinforcers is called a(n)
a.      extinction system.
b.      token economy.
c.      feedback loop.
d.      contingency alternative.

**ANS: b**          **Pg: 133**
**LO: 26**          **Factual**

15.     A successful self-modification program may end spontaneously when
a.      one experiences a traumatic event.
b.      one's self-esteem is threatened.
c.      the target behavior suddenly reappears.
d.      the new behavior becomes habitual.

**ANS: d**          **Pg: 135**
**LO: 28**          **Conceptual**


**\*TRUE/FALSE QUESTIONS**

1.      Giving up as a coping strategy can be adaptive in some circumstances.

**ANS: true**       **Pg: 108**
**LO: 3**           **Factual**

2.       Research suggests that Internet addiction is primarily limited to shy, male computer whizzes.

**ANS: false**         **Pg: 110**
**LO: 5**           **Factual**

3.       Studies of individuals diagnosed with AIDS show that those with unrealistically optimistic expectations of the likely course of their disease actually experience a **more rapid** course of illness.

**ANS: false**         **Pg: 113**
**LO: 8**           **Factual**

4.       IQ scores are highly correlated with the use of constructive coping strategies.

**ANS: false**         **Pg: 113**
**LO: 10**         **Factual**

5.       One strategy for using time more effectively is to complete routine tasks before tackling larger, more difficult tasks.

**ANS: false**         **Pg: 121**
**LO: 16**         **Factual**

6.       The practice of creating self-imposed deadlines to help reduce procrastination can be helpful, but self-imposed deadlines are not as effective as externally-imposed deadlines.

**ANS: true**          **Pg: 122**
**LO: 17**         **Factual**

7.       Emotional disclosure is associated with enhanced immune functioning.

**ANS: true**          **Pg: 127**
**LO: 20**         **Conceptual**

8.       Research has shown that forgiveness is positively related to measures of well-being and negatively related to measures of anxiety and depression.

**ANS: true**          **Pg: 128**
**LO: 21**         **Factual**

9.       In order to get the full benefit from relaxation response, it only needs to be practiced 3-4 days per week.

**ANS: false**         **Pg: 130**
**LO: 23**         **Factual**

10.    When designing a self-modification program, making yourself earn rewards that you used to take for granted, like drinking soda with dinner, is often a useful strategy.

**ANS: true**          **Pg: 132**
**LO: 26**              **Factual**


## SHORT-ANSWER ESSAY QUESTIONS

1.    Briefly explain how coping strategies can be helpful or destructive.

**Pgs: 106-107**
**LO: 2**

2.    Discuss the evidence supporting and refuting the notion that physical aggression leads to catharsis.

**Pgs: 108-109**
**LO: 4**

3.    Summarize the evidence on the adaptive value of personal illusions.

**Pgs: 112-113**
**LO: 8**

4.    Discuss several reasons why constructive coping is considered healthy.

.
**Pgs: 113-114**
**LO: 10**

5.    Describe Albert Ellis's suggestions for reducing unrealistic appraisals of stress.

**Pgs: 115-117**
**LO: 12**

6.    Explain how humor moderates the impact of stress.

**Pg: 117**
**LO: 13**

7.    Briefly describe some of the factors that contribute to procrastination.

**Pg: 122**
**LO: 17**

8.    Distinguish between "efficiency" and "effectiveness" as they apply to time management techniques.

**Pgs: 122-123**
**LO: 18**

9. Briefly explain the role of antecedents in devising a behavior modification program.

**Pg: 132**
**LO: 25**

10. Describe the role of a behavioral contract in a self-modification program.

**Pg: 135**
**LO: 28**

# Chapter 5
# THE SELF

## LEARNING OBJECTIVES

1. Describe some key aspects of the self-concept.
2. Cite two types of self-discrepancies and describe their effects.
3. Describe two ways of coping with self-discrepancies.
4. Discuss important factors that help form the self-concept.
5. Discuss how individualism and collectivism influence self-concept.
6. Describe some implications of self-concept confusion and self-esteem instability.
7. Discuss how low and high self-esteem are related to adjustment.
8. Distinguish between high self-esteem and narcissism, and discuss narcissism and aggression.
9. Discuss some key influences in the development of self-esteem.
10. Summarize the findings on ethnicity and gender regarding self-esteem.
11. Distinguish between automatic and controlled processing.
12. Define self-attributions and identify the key dimensions of attributions.
13. Explain how optimistic and pessimistic explanatory styles are related to adjustment.
14. Discuss four motives that guide self-understanding.
15. Describe four strategies people use to maintain positive feelings about the self.
16. Define self-regulation and explain the ego-depletion model of self-regulation.
17. Explain why self-efficacy is important to psychological adjustment.
18. Describe how individuals develop self-efficacy.
19. Describe the three categories of self-defeating behavior.
20. Explain why and when individuals engage in impression management.
21. Cite some strategies people use to make positive impressions on others.
22. Describe how high self-monitors are different from low self-monitors.
23. Explain when it is inadvisable to increase self-esteem, and why this is so.
24. Describe seven ways to build self-esteem.

## MULTIPLE CHOICE QUESTIONS

1.      An organized set of beliefs about one's personal qualities and typical behavior constitute one's
a.      self-ideal.
b.      public self.
c.      self-concept.
d.      self-actualization.

**ANS: c**          **Pg: 140**
**LO: 1**           **Factual**

2.      Another term for self-concept is
a.      self-ideal.
b.      public self.
c.      self-actualization.
d.      self-schema.

**ANS: d**          **Pg: 140**
**LO: 1**           **Factual**

3.      The self-concept that you have in mind at a given time is referred to as a _____ self-concept.
a.      recent
b.      working
c.      public
d.      possible

**ANS: b**          **Pg: 140**
**LO: 1**           **Factual**

4.      Which of the following is **not** one of the factors that help shape our vision of our possible selves?
a.      past experiences
b.      biology
c.      current behavior
d.      future expectations

**ANS: b**          **Pg: 140**
**LO: 1**           **Factual**

5.      According to your textbook, people are motivated to maintain a(n) _____ view of the self.
a.      accurate
b.      positive
c.      creative
d.      consistent

**ANS: d**          **Pg: 141**
**LO: 1**           **Factual**

6. Hazel Markus uses the term _____ selves to refer to one's conceptions about the kind of person one might become in the future.
a. possible
b. timeless
c. potential
d. expected

**ANS: a**      **Pg: 141**
**LO: 1**      **Factual**

7. Some researchers believe that self-concept is most likely to change when a person
a. reaches puberty.
b. moves to a new city.
c. has his or her first sexual encounter.
d. is faced with an approach-approach conflict.

**ANS: b**      **Pg: 141**
**LO: 1**      **Conceptual**

8. The self-schema that you use to process information relevant to your self-concept depends heavily on
a. your potential.
b. your personality.
c. your age.
d. your situation.

**ANS: d**      **Pg: 141**
**LO: 1**      **Conceptual**

9. Social roles, abilities and values help to foster an individual's
a. self-esteem.
b. self-concept.
c. coping ability.
d. psychological adjustment.

**ANS: b**      **Pg: 141**
**LO: 1**      **Factual**

10. A mismatching of self-perceptions is termed
a. ideal self.
b. self-discrepancy.
c. self-complexity.
d. self-awareness.

**ANS: b**      **Pg: 141**
**LO: 2**      **Factual**

11.  According to E. Tory Higgins, which of the following is **not** one of the three types of self-perceptions that people have?
a.  unrealistic
b.  actual
c.  ideal
d.  ought

**ANS: a**          **Pg: 141**
**LO: 2**           **Factual**

12.  According to E. Tory Higgins, a discrepancy between the actual self and the ideal self is most likely to trigger which of the following emotions?
a.  dejection
b.  agitation
c.  apprehension
d.  ambivalence

**ANS: a**          **Pg: 141**
**LO: 2**           **Conceptual**

13.  A woman who describes herself as "frank and honest" but who in fact lies frequently is manifesting her
a.  self-concept.
b.  self-conflict.
c.  self-discrepancy.
d.  self-ambivalence.

**ANS: c**          **Pg: 141**
**LO: 2**           **Conceptual**

14.  If you are feeling anxious because you know that you should have visited your sick great aunt in the convalescent home over the holidays, you are experiencing a discrepancy between your actual self and your _____ self.
a.  ideal
b.  possible
c.  ought
d.  working

**ANS: c**          **Pgs: 141-142**
**LO: 2**           **Conceptual**

15.  Matt is slightly overweight and out of shape but would like to be lean and athletic. His most probable emotional reaction to this type of self-discrepancy would be
a.  anger.
b.  irritability.
c.  guilt.
d.  dejection.

**ANS: d**          **Pg: 141**
**LO: 2**           **Conceptual**

*16.    As actual-ideal discrepancies outnumber actual-ideal congruencies, cheerfulness
       decreases and
a.     sadness increases.
b.     sadness decreases.
c.     anxiety increases.
d.     anxiety decreases.

**ANS: a**          **Pg: 141**
**LO: 2**           **Factual**

17.    Sarah knows that she should be studying hard for the LSATs if she wants to attend law
       school. Her most probable emotional reaction to this type of self-discrepancy would be
a.     anxiety.
b.     irritability.
c.     rage.
d.     dissatisfaction.

**ANS: a**          **Pg: 142**
**LO: 2**           **Conceptual**

*18.    Self-guide preferences appear to be rooted in
a.     parent-child interactions and individual's temperament.
b.     culture and parenting style.
c.     individual's self-esteem and self-concept.
d.     individual's intelligence and self-observation .

**ANS: a**          **Pg: 142**
**LO: 2**           **Factual**

19.    Which of the following factors is **not** important in determining how likely it is that a self-
       discrepancy will damage a person's self-esteem?
a.     a person's awareness of the discrepancy
b.     how important the discrepancy is to a person
c.     the number of other self-discrepancies the person experiences
d.     the amount of discrepancy the person experiences

**ANS: c**          **Pg: 142**
**LO: 2**           **Conceptual**

20.    Which of the following is **not** a coping technique used to deal with self-discrepancies?
a.     consuming alcohol
b.     increasing size of reference group
c.     avoiding situations that increase self-awareness
d.     changing behaviors to be more in line with personal standards

**ANS: b**          **Pg: 142**
**LO: 3**           **Conceptual**

21. Substance use in response to feelings of self-discrepancy is an example of a type of coping technique known as
a. social comparison.
b. blunting self-awareness.
c. changing one's behavior.
d. expanding the possible self.

**ANS: b**        **Pg: 142**
**LO: 3**        **Conceptual**

22. Taking tennis lessons in response to a self-discrepancy in the area of athleticism is an example of a coping technique called
a. improving self-awareness.
b. blunting self-awareness.
c. expanding the possible self.
d. changing one's behavior.

**ANS: d**        **Pg: 142**
**LO: 3**        **Conceptual**

23. Which of the following researchers proposed social comparison theory?
a. Albert Bandura
b. E. Tory Higgins
c. Leon Festinger
d. Martin Seligman

**ANS: c**        **Pg: 143**
**LO: 4**        **Factual**

24. The term "reference group" refers to
a. your library study partners.
b. behavioral qualities of your ideal self.
c. a set of people against whom you compare yourself.
d. the group to which your ideal self might belong.

**ANS: c**        **Pg: 143**
**LO: 4**        **Factual**

25. The most likely reference group for a first year medical student would be
a. first year medical students.
b. medical interns.
c. first year medical residents.
d. newly board-certified doctors in the specialty that interests that student.

**ANS: a**        **Pg: 143**
**LO: 4**        **Factual**

26. According to social comparison theory, we tend to compare ourselves with a reference group comprised of people whom we perceive as
a. better than us.
b. inferior to us.
c. similar to us.
d. Any of these may apply depending on the situations.

**ANS: d**          **Pg: 143**
**LO: 4**           **Conceptual**

27. Jim is a freshman pledge who is seeking admission this fall to a prestigious and exclusive fraternity on his campus. His reference group(s) during this time most likely include(s)
   1. other freshmen
   2. other pledges
   3. the fraternity brothers

a. 1 only
b. 1 and 2 only
c. 2 and 3 only
d. 1, 2, and 3

**ANS: d**          **Pg: 143**
**LO: 4**           **Conceptual**

28. The findings of Morse and Gergen's Mr. Clean/Mr. Dirty study provided support for which of the following theories?
a. psychoanalysis
b. self-perception
c. cognitive dissonance
d. social comparison

**ANS: d**          **Pg: 143**
**LO: 4**           **Conceptual**

29. People may distort their self-concepts
a. in negative directions only.
b. in positive directions only.
c. in both positive and negative directions.
d. people usually don't distort their own self-concepts.

**ANS: c**          **Pg: 143**
**LO: 4**           **Factual**

30.    Research has shown that children's self-perceptions are more strongly related to their
       _____ than to their parents' attitudes toward them.
a.    friends' attitudes toward them
b.    siblings' attitudes toward them
c.    perceptions of their physical appearance
d.    perceptions of their parents' attitudes toward them

**ANS: d**          **Pg: 144**
**LO: 4**           **Factual**

31.    Feedback from others tends to carry less weight in formulation of one's self-concept
       when
a.    self-esteem is high.
b.    objective evidence is available.
c.    self-discrepancy is low.
d.    cultural influences are limited.

**ANS: b**          **Pg: 144**
**LO: 4**           **Factual**

*32.   There is evidence that a close partner's support and affirmation can bring the loved one's
       actual self-views and behavior more in line with his/her ideal self.  Researchers refer to
       this as the
a.    Michelangelo phenomenon.
b.    stage-manage phenomenon.
c.    significant-construct experience.
d.    exceptional person experience.

**ANS: a**          **Pg: 145**
**LO: 4**           **Factual**

33.    _____ involves putting personal goals ahead of group goals and defining one's identity
       in terms of personal attributes rather than group memberships.
a.    Individualism
b.    Behaviorism
c.    Collectivism
d.    Humanism

**ANS: a**          **Pg: 145**
**LO: 5**           **Factual**

34.    Mainstream American culture would most accurately be described as
a.    Collectivist.
b.    Humanist.
c.    Individualistic.
d.    Behaviorist.

**ANS: c**          **Pg: 145**
**LO: 5**           **Factual**

35. Individuals reared in individualistic cultures are less likely than individuals from collectivist cultures to perceive themselves as
a. unique.
b. self-contained.
c. distinct from others.
d. responsible for others.

**ANS: d**        **Pg: 145**
**LO: 5**        **Conceptual**

36. "Look out for number one" is an attitude that is most likely associated with an individual
a. from an individualistic culture.
b. with an interdependent view.
c. with a shared sense of responsibility.
d. from a collectivistic culture.

**ANS: a**        **Pg: 145**
**LO: 5**        **Conceptual**

37. Individuals from a collectivistic culture are less likely that individuals from individualistic cultures to have which of the following traits?
a. an interdependent view of self
b. adjust themselves to needs of the group
c. strive for self-satisfaction
d. sense of shared responsibility

**ANS: c**        **Pg: 145**
**LO: 5**        **Conceptual**

38. Your friend Tyra has decided to postpone starting business school for two years in order to help her family operate their small hardware store during her dad's illness. She is exhibiting a characteristic behavior of persons from a(n) _____ culture
a. individualistic
b. collectivistic
c. behavioristic
d. humanistic

**ANS: b**        **Pg: 145**
**LO: 5**        **Conceptual**

*39. Which of the following is the best description of the way that men and women tend to get their social needs met?
a. Both men and women display relational interdependence.
b. Both men and women display collective interdependence.
c. Men are more likely to display collective interdependence and women are more likely to display relational interdependence.
d. Women are more likely to display collective interdependence and men are more likely to display relational interdependence.

ANS: c          Pg: 146
LO: 5          Conceptual

40. Research suggests that increases in a culture's affluence and social mobility tend to be accompanied by increases in
a. collectivism.
b. individualism.
c. stereotyping.
d. obedience.

ANS: b          Pg: 146
LO: 5          Conceptual

41. The evaluative component of self-concept is
a. authentic self.
b. public self.
c. self-esteem.
d. self-ideal.

ANS: c          Pg: 146
LO: 6          Factual

42. Which of the following is **not** true of research on self-esteem?
a. Most of the data are correlational.
b. Self-esteem may be both a cause and an effect.
c. Information is usually derived from self-reports.
d. The validity of self-esteem measures is unquestionable.

ANS: d          Pgs: 146-147
LO: 6          Conceptual

43. Which of the following must be kept in mind when one interprets the results of research on self-esteem?
a. Self-esteem is only a fair predictor of happiness.
b. One cannot draw causal conclusions regarding self-esteem based on the research.
c. It is a fascinating topic related to psychological adjustment.
d. Self-esteem is a popular concept in psychology.

ANS: b          Pg: 147
LO: 6          Conceptual

44.    Which of the following is **not** true of self-esteem according to the research?
a.    Self-esteem is generally stable over time.
b.    People vary in the degree to which they experience self-esteem as stable.
c.    Self-esteem may fluctuate in the short term in response to situational factors.
d.    All of these are true according to the research.

**ANS: d**          **Pg: 147**
**LO: 6**           **Conceptual**

45.    Investigation of self-esteem is hampered by the fact that it is difficult to
a.    measure reliably.
b.    sort out cause and effect.
c.    find enough people with low self-esteem.
d.    find links between behaviors and self-esteem.

**ANS: b**          **Pg: 147**
**LO: 6**           **Conceptual**

46.    The self-views of those who appear to have low self-esteem are _____ than those of people with high self-esteem.
a.    more confused
b.    more negative
c.    less accurate
d.    less culturally based

**ANS: a**          **Pg: 146**
**LO: 6**           **Conceptual**

*47.   Which of the following is NOT consistent with empirical data?
a.    Self-esteem is strongly related to happiness.
b.    High self-esteem has not been shown to be a reliable cause of improvement in academic performance.
c.    Self-esteem does not appear to be related to how quickly love relationships end.
d.    Objective data gathered from peers indicates that people with high self-esteem are more likeable and make better impressions than those with low self-esteem.

**ANS: d**          **Pg: 147**
**LO: 7**           **Conceptual**

*48.   Sociometer theory suggests that self-esteem is
a.    an objective measure of one's worth and competence.
b.    a subjective measure of one's interpersonal popularity and success.
c.    an unstable measure of one's worth and accomplishments.
d.    a stable measure of one's strengths and weaknesses.

**ANS: b**          **Pg: 148**
**LO: 7**           **Factual**

49. Both low and high self-esteem may be maintained in part by the power of
a. expectations.
b. cultural norms.
c. individualism.
d. repression.

**ANS: a**      **Pg: 148**
**LO: 7**      **Factual**

50. _____ is a sense of grandiose self-importance.
a. Self-esteem
b. Narcissism
c. Individualism
d. Self-efficacy

**ANS: b**      **Pg: 148**
**LO: 8**      **Factual**

51. Baumeister's research suggests that a narcissist who experiences an ego threat is likely to
a. work hard to counter the threat.
b. become aggressive or violent.
c. quit trying.
d. use indirect strategies to avoid the threat.

**ANS: b**      **Pgs: 148-149**
**LO: 8**      **Factual**

52. Research on narcissism may have practical use for professionals who are trying to rehabilitate
a. those who engage in domestic violence.
b. drug addicts.
c. women with eating disorders.
d. college professors.

**ANS: a**      **Pgs: 148-149**
**LO: 8**      **Factual**

53. Maccoby and Martin's research suggests that parental _____ and _____ are major determinants of a child's self esteem.
a. income; employment
b. health; happiness
c. narcissism; self-esteem
d. acceptance; control

**ANS: d**      **Pg: 149**
**LO: 9**      **Factual**

54. Affectionate, accepting, involved, and democratic parents may well produce offspring who tend to be
a. high in self-esteem.
b. sensation seekers.
c. high self-monitors.
d. emotionally dependent.

**ANS: a**      **Pg: 149**
**LO: 9**      **Factual**

55. Ted's mother wears a t-shirt that says "Because I'm your mom, that's why!" She is usually critical of her son and his friends, and only rarely allows him to give his opinion in family decision-making. Ted's mom is exhibiting the traits associated with the _____ parenting style.
a. permissive
b. authoritative
c. authoritarian
d. neglectful

**ANS: c**      **Pg: 149**
**LO: 9**      **Factual**

56. Which of the following is likely to be the most influential determinant of self-esteem for college age individuals?
a. views of peers
b. parental feedback
c. stereotypes presented in the media
d. comparisons to national statistics for one's age group

**ANS: a**      **Pg: 151**
**LO: 9**      **Conceptual**

*57. According to Baumrind's parental classification system, authoritative parents display
a. high acceptance and high control.
b. high acceptance and low control.
c. low acceptance and low control.
d. low acceptance and high control.

**ANS: a**      **Pg: 148**
**LO: 9**      **Conceptual**

*58. Which of the following best describes the correlation of parenting style with self-esteem from highest to lowest?
a. authoritarian > permissive > authoritative > neglectful
b. authoritative > authoritarian > permissive > neglectful
c. permissive > authoritative > neglectful > authoritarian
d. authoritative > permissive > neglectful > authoritarian

**ANS: b**      **Pg: 149**
**LO: 9**      **Conceptual**

\*59.	Research done by numerous investigators suggests that for individuals with similar talents _____ plays a critical role in the development of self-esteem.
a.	cultural norms
b.	sibling assessment
c.	self-assessment
d.	social comparison

**ANS: d**　　　　　**Pg: 151**
**LO: 9**　　　　　**Conceptual**

\*60.	Which of the following is MOST consistent with the research data?
a.	Self-esteem of whites is higher than that of blacks.
b.	White females have higher self-esteem than white males.
c.	Minority females have lower self-esteem than minority males.
d.	Blacks have higher self-esteem than Asians.

**ANS: d**　　　　　**Pg: 151**
**LO: 10**　　　　　**Factual**

\*61.	The largest gender differences in self-esteem have been found for
a.	10-12 year olds.
b.	15-18 year olds.
c.	20-25 year olds.
d.	25-29 year olds.

**ANS: b**　　　　　**Pg: 151**
**LO: 10**　　　　　**Conceptual**

62.	Driving a car to work in normal conditions of traffic is an example of a cognitive task that is done mainly by
a.	instinct
b.	controlled processing
c.	automatic processing
d.	mindful processing

**ANS: c**　　　　　**Pg: 152**
**LO: 11**　　　　　**Factual**

\*63.	_____ helps to explain the ability to pick out our name in a room full of chattering people.
a.	Selective attention
b.	Automatic processing
c.	Mindfulness
d.	Narrow attention

**ANS: a**　　　　　**Pg: 152**
**LO: 11**　　　　　**Factual**

64.  Which of the following theorists was the first to suggest that people tend to attribute behavior to either internal or external causes?
a.  Fritz Heider
b.  Albert Bandura
c.  Erik Erikson
d.  Sigmund Freud

ANS: a          Pg: 152
LO: 12          Factual

65.  _____ are the inferences that people make about what causes their behavior.
a.  Automatic processes
b.  Controlled processes
c.  Self-attributions
d.  Explanatory styles

ANS: c          Pg: 152
LO: 12          Factual

66.  Internal attributions ascribe causes of behavior to _____ factors.
a.  situational
b.  personal
c.  interpersonal
d.  environmental

ANS: b          Pg: 152
LO: 12          Conceptual

67.  Research suggests that people who attribute their failures to internal causes while discounting external causes may be more prone to _____ than people who display opposite tendencies.
a.  shyness
b.  depression
c.  cognitive dissonance
d.  the fundamental attribution error

ANS: b          Pg: 152
LO: 12          Conceptual

68.  Which of the following would be considered an example of an internal-stable factor in attribution?
a.  one's effort at the task
b.  one's feelings about one's boss
c.  one's health at the time of the task
d.  one's ability for the task in question

ANS: d          Pgs: 152-153
LO: 12          Conceptual

69. Which of the following is an example of an external-unstable factor in attribution?
a. bad luck
b. one's self-esteem
c. lack of ability
d. the nature of the task

**ANS: a**        **Pgs: 152-153**
**LO: 12**        **Factual**

70. All of the following are dimensions of the attributional process **except**
a. internal versus external.
b. automatic versus controlled.
c. stable versus unstable.
d. controllable versus uncontrollable.

**ANS: b**        **Pgs: 152-153**
**LO: 12**        **Factual**

71. The tendency to use similar causal explanations for a wide variety of events in one's life is known as
a. self-attribution.
b. explanatory style.
c. self-categorization.
d. homogeneity of attribution.

**ANS: b**        **Pg: 153**
**LO: 13**        **Conceptual**

72. Lisa thinks that the reason she didn't get the job was that the interviewer was prejudiced against people from the Midwest. This is an example of
a. pessimistic explanatory style.
b. optimistic explanatory style.
c. lack of explanatory style.
d. the fundamental attribution error.

**ANS: b**        **Pg: 153**
**LO: 13**        **Conceptual**

73. People who attribute their setbacks to internal, stable, and global factors are exhibiting a(n) _____ explanatory style.
a. irrational
b. coherent
c. pessimistic
d. optimistic

**ANS: c**        **Pgs: 153-154**
**LO: 13**        **Conceptual**

74. People who tend to attribute their setbacks to external, unstable, specific factors are exhibiting
a. an optimistic explanatory style.
b. a pessimistic attributional style.
c. poor self-image and low self-esteem.
d. the fundamental attribution error.

**ANS: a**          **Pgs: 153-154**
**LO: 13**          **Factual**

*75. Research indicates that people with negative self-views preferred partners who viewed them _____.
a. positively
b. negatively
c. realistically
d. unrealistically

**ANS: b**          **Pg: 154**
**LO: 14**          **Factual**

*76. Advertisers of personal care products are tapping into the _____ motive.
a. self-enhancement
b. self-improvement
c. self-assessment
d. self-verification

**ANS: b**          **Pg: 155**
**LO: 14**          **Conceptual**

*77. Illusions of control and the "better than average effect" are examples of
a. self-enhancement.
b. self-improvement.
c. self-assessment.
d. self-verification.

**ANS: a**          **Pg: 155**
**LO: 14**          **Conceptual**

*78. Who of the following does NOT provide an illustration of self-enhancement?
a. Juan asserts that he has above average intelligence.
b. June prefers to be with partners who hold a similar view of her as she does of herself.
c. Jimmy picks his own lottery numbers.
d. Janey predicts that she will have below average problems in her future.

**ANS: b**          **Pg: 155**
**LO: 14**          **Conceptual**

79. The notion that people prefer to receive feedback from others that is consistent with their own self-views is called
a. self-enhancement.
b. self-verification .
c. self-serving bias.
d. downward social comparison.

**ANS: b**      **Pgs: 154-155**
**LO: 14**      **Factual**

*80. In a series of studies that pitted self-assessment, self-verification, and self-enhancement against each other, the _____ motive was found to be the strongest.
a. assessment
b. verification
c. enhancement
d. None of these; they were found to be equally strong.

**ANS: c**      **Pg: 155**
**LO: 14**      **Conceptual**

81. The tendency to use various strategies to maintain a positive view of the self is called
a. self-verification.
b. self-serving bias.
c. self-enhancement.
d. fundamental attribution error.

**ANS: c**      **Pg: 155**
**LO: 14**      **Conceptual**

82. An individual who recently had preventive bypass surgery might think, "At least I didn't have a serious heart attack like my older brother did." This thinking exemplifies the strategy known as
a. self-serving bias.
b. pessimistic explanatory style.
c. downward social comparison.
d. basking in reflected glory.

**ANS: c**      **Pgs: 155-156**
**LO: 15**      **Conceptual**

83. Self-serving bias is the tendency to take credit for our _____ and disavow responsibility for _____.
a. failures; our successes
b. successes; our failures
c. own successes; our friends' successes
d. own successes; the successes of those we don't like

**ANS: b**      **Pg: 156**
**LO: 15**      **Factual**

84. The notion of "basking in reflected glory" was proposed by
a. Albert Bandura.
b. Robert Cialdini.
c. Roy Baumeister.
d. Martin Seligman.

**ANS: b**          **Pgs: 156-157**
**LO: 15**          **Factual**

85. The tendency to sabotage one's performance to provide an excuse for possible failure is called
a. self-centered bias.
b. self-serving bias.
c. self-handicapping.
d. basking in reflected failure.

**ANS: c**          **Pg: 157**
**LO: 15**          **Conceptual**

*86. Which of the following is consistent with the self-serving bias?
a. the tendency to attribute one's successes to situational factors
b the tendency to attribute one's successes to the ease of the task
c. the tendency to attribute one's failures to situational factors
d. the tendency to attribute one's failures to dispositional factors

**ANS: c**          **Pg: 156**
**LO: 15**          **Factual**

*87. In contrast to Americans, Japanese are likely to exhibit a _____ in explaining successes.
a. self-serving bias
b. self-effacing bias
c. self-efficacious bias
d. self-enhancing bias

**ANS: b**          **Pg: 156**
**LO: 15**          **Factual**

88. Someone who says, "I probably won't do well on the exam because I was up all night with a sick friend," is using the strategy of
a. projection.
b. reaction formation.
c. self-handicapping.
d. basking in reflected glory.

**ANS: c**          **Pg: 157**
**LO: 15**          **Conceptual**

*89. Even though she never met him, Jane told all of her friends that the new mayor of their town was her second cousin. Jane was using the method of self-enhancement known as
a. downward social comparison.
b. upward social comparison.
c. basking in reflected glory.
d. "CORFing".

**ANS: c**        **Pgs: 156-157**
**LO: 15**       **Conceptual**

*90. Self-regulation refers to
a. directing and controlling one's behavior.
b. maintaining a positive self-esteem in the face of adversity.
c. consistently using internal attributions in an effort to take personal responsibility.
d. using time saving devices that promote self-efficiency.

**ANS: a**        **Pg: 158**
**LO: 16**       **Factual**

*91. If you use self-control resources by resisting temptation in a given situation
a. you are more likely to resist temptation in the future.
b. you may have a hard time resisting the next temptation.
c. you are more likely to be able to persist at a new and difficult task.
d. you may have difficulty showing empathy for those who exhibit poor self-control.

**ANS: b**        **Pg: 158**
**LO: 16**       **Conceptual**

*92. Unlike her coworkers, Susan resisted the temptation to overeat at the company retreat potluck. Following the potluck the coworkers were put into groups and asked to tackle some difficult work-related tasks. The likelihood that Susan would give up more quickly than her coworkers is consistent with
a. ego depletion model of self-regulation.
b. ego integrity model of self-efficacy.
c. self-handicapping.
d. self-sandbagging.

**ANS: a**        **Pg: 158**
**LO: 16**       **Conceptual**

93. Research indicates that self-efficacy is related to all of the following **except**
a. career choice.
b. responses to stress.
c. performance on tasks.
d. intelligence.

**ANS: d**        **Pgs: 158-159**
**LO: 17**       **Factual**

94. Sources of self-efficacy include all of the following **except**
a. mastery experiences.
b. vicarious experiences.
c. denial of emotional arousal.
d. persuasion and encouragement.

**ANS: c**        **Pg: 159**
**LO: 17**        **Conceptual**

*95. Self-efficacy is most associated with
a. skill level.
b. beliefs.
c. intelligence.
d. encouragement.

**ANS: b**        **Pg: 159**
**LO: 17**        **Conceptual**

*96. Which of the following is NOT a source of self-efficacy?
a. mastering new skills
b. watching others perform a skill one wants to learn
c. soliciting encouragement and advice from others
d. comparing one's self to others who are less fortunate

**ANS: d**        **Pgs: 159-160**
**LO: 18**        **Conceptual**

*97. The best way for parents, teachers, and coaches to instill high self-efficacy in children is to
a. set low, attainable goals to increase the probability of frequent success.
b. set high, attainable goals and encourage children to persevere until they succeed and learn from their mistakes.
c. set high, unattainable goals that teach children to persevere even when they cannot succeed.
d. set high, unattainable goals that teach children how to accept defeat.

**ANS: b**        **Pgs: 159-160**
**LO: 18**        **Conceptual**

98. The habitual use of misguided or ineffective strategies for achieving desirable outcomes is called
a. deliberate self-destruction.
b. tradeoff.
c. ingratiation.
d. counterproductive.

**ANS: d**        **Pg: 160**
**LO: 19**        **Conceptual**

*99. Which of the following does NOT typically underlie most self-defeating tradeoffs?
a. poor judgment
b. emotional distress
c. intentional self-harm
d. high self-awareness

ANS: c          Pgs: 160-161
LO: 19          Conceptual

*100. People engage in counterproductive strategies because
a. they are intent on self-defeat.
b. they believe they will eventually be successful.
c. they are masochistic.
d. they are experiencing only minimal emotional arousal.

ANS: b          Pgs: 160-161
LO: 19          Conceptual

101. Most of us have
a. no public self.
b. one public self.
c. a number of public selves.
d. a public self for family and friends, and another for strangers.

ANS: c          Pgs: 161-162
LO: 20          Conceptual

102. Trying to present oneself to others in a positive way is called
a ingratiation.
b. self-monitoring.
c. false consensus.
d. impression management.

ANS: d          Pg: 162
LO: 20          Factual

103. Which of the following is not considered a self-presentation strategy?
a. ingratiation
b. intimidation
c. identification
d. exemplification

ANS: c          Pg: 163
LO: 21          Factual

104.    Presenting yourself in a way that you think will cause others to respect you is most
        consistent with which of the following self-presentation strategies?
a.      ingratiation
b.      self-promotion
c.      intimidation
d.      exemplification

**ANS: b**              **Pg: 163**
**LO: 21**              **Conceptual**

105.    With the self-presentation strategy of _____, people try to present themselves as weak
        and dependent in order to get favors from others.
a.      ingratiation
b.      self-promotion
c.      intimidation
d.      supplication

**ANS: d**              **Pgs: 163-164**
**LO: 21**              **Conceptual**

*106.   Which of the following is NOT an example of ingratiation?
a.      Theo gives a sincere compliment to his psychology instructor.
b.      Ted does a favor for a neighbor.
c.      Theresa plays up her strong points to her boss.
d.      Terry goes along with some new friends to a movie that he doesn't really want to see.

**ANS: c**              **Pg: 163**
**LO: 21**              **Conceptual**

107.    Jerry is very careful to dress for events in a manner that fits the style of those with whom
        he will be socializing, and he spends a great deal of time familiarizing himself with the
        interests of his companions. Jerry would best be classified as a
a.      high approval seeker.
b.      low approval seeker.
c.      high self-monitor.
d.      low self-monitor.

**ANS: c**              **Pg: 164**
**LO: 22**              **Factual**

*108.   Which of the following is NOT consistent with the research on high self-monitors?  High
        self-monitors
a.      control their emotions poorly.
b.      are talented at self-presentation.
c.      deliberately regulate nonverbal signals.
d.      perceive themselves as flexible.

**ANS: a**              **Pg: 164**
**LO: 22**              **Factual**

*109.	Which of the following is NOT one of the seven guidelines described in the textbook for building self-esteem?
a.	Recognize that you do not control your self-image.
b.	Learn more about yourself.
c.	Don't let others set your goals.
d.	Emphasize your strengths.

**ANS: a**	**Pgs: 165-167**
**LO: 24**	**Factual**


## MULTIPLE CHOICE QUESTIONS FROM STUDY GUIDE

1.	Which of the following is not one of the main types of self-perceptions, according to E. Tory Higgins?
a.	ideal self
b.	other self
c.	actual self
d.	ought self

**ANS: b**	**Pg: 141**
**LO: 2**	**Factual**

2.	Which of the following sources influence the development of one's self-concept?
a.	one's own observations
b.	feedback from others
c.	cultural guidelines
d.	all of these

**ANS: d**	**Pgs: 143-145**
**LO: 4**	**Factual**

3.	People with an independent view of the self are most likely to engage in which of the following behaviors?
a.	see themselves as responsible for group failures
b.	place great importance on social duties and obligations
c.	claim more than their share of credit for group successes
d.	adjust themselves to the needs of the groups to which they belong

**ANS: c**	**Pg: 145**
**LO: 5**	**Conceptual**

4.	The critical childhood determinant of self-esteem appears to be the parents'
a.	genetic makeup.
b.	use of disciplinary techniques.
c.	unconditional love for the child.
d.	sincere interest in their children.

**ANS: d**	**Pg: 149**
**LO: 9**	**Factual**

148

5.  The "cocktail party effect" (the ability to pick out one's name in a room full of chattering people) illustrates the concept of
a.  internal attribution.
b.  external attribution.
c.  selective attention.
d.  controlled processing.

**ANS: c**        **Pg: 152**
**LO: 11**        **Factual**

6.  According to Martin Seligman, people with a pessimistic explanatory style tend to attribute their setbacks to which of the following combinations of factors?
a.  internal, stable, and global
b.  internal, unstable, and specific
c.  external, stable, and global
d.  external, unstable, and specific

**ANS: a**        **Pgs: 153-154**
**LO: 13**        **Conceptual**

7.  The tendency to maintain positive feelings about the self is called
a.  self-complexity.
b.  self-attribution.
c.  self-enhancement.
d.  self-verification.

**ANS: c**        **Pg: 155**
**LO: 15**        **Factual**

8.  Psychologists have found that when people are threatened, they frequently choose to compare themselves to someone who is
a.  in similar circumstances.
b.  worse off than they are.
c.  better off than they are.
d.  a member of their immediate family.

**ANS: b**        **Pgs: 155-156**
**LO: 15**        **Conceptual**

9.  The self-serving bias is the tendency to attribute one's successes to _____ factors and one's failures to _____ factors.
a.  external; stable
b.  stable; unstable
c.  situational; personal
d.  personal; situational

**ANS: d**        **Pg: 156**
**LO: 15**        **Factual**

10.  The notion of "basking in reflected glory" is most closely associated with which of the following researchers?
a.   Robert Cialdini
b.   Albert Bandura
c.   Erik Erikson
d.   Roy Baumeister

**ANS: a**          **Pgs: 156-157**
**LO: 15**          **Factual**

11.  A person who says, "I probably won't play very well because my ankle hurts," just before the beginning of a tennis match is engaging in
a.   ingratiation.
b.   self-monitoring.
c.   self-handicapping.
d.   basking in reflected glory.

**ANS: c**          **Pg: 157**
**LO: 15**          **Conceptual**

12.  Research has demonstrated that self-efficacy is related to all but which of the following?
a.   career choice
b.   health habits
c.   responses to stress
d.   marital satisfaction

**ANS: d**          **Pg: 159**
**LO: 17**          **Factual**

13.  Which of the following statements concerning the presentation of a public self is **not** true?
a.   Everyone presents a public self.
b.   Your public self is based on how you see yourself.
c.   It is perfectly normal to present a public self.
d.   Typically, individuals have a number of public selves.

**ANS: b**          **Pg: 162**
**LO: 20**          **Conceptual**

14.  Doing favors for others in order to get them to like you is a form of
a.   ingratiation.
b.   self-monitoring.
c.   self-handicapping.
d.   basking in reflected glory.

**ANS: a**          **Pg: 163**
**LO: 21**          **Conceptual**

15. Which of the following is **not** good advice for building self-esteem?
a. Emphasize your strengths.
b. Don't let others set your goals.
c. Always compare yourself to the best.
d. Recognize and eliminate negative self-talk.

**ANS: c**          **Pgs: 165-167**
**LO: 24**          **Conceptual**


## MULTIPLE CHOICE QUESTIONS ON WEB SITE

1. The self-concept that you have in mind at a given time is referred to as a _____ self-concept.
a. recent
b. working
c. public
d. possible

**ANS: b**          **Pg: 140**
**LO: 1**           **Factual**

2. According to E. Tory Higgins, a discrepancy between the actual self and the ideal self is most likely to trigger which of the following emotions?
a. dejection
b. agitation
c. apprehension
d. ambivalence

**ANS: a**          **Pg: 141**
**LO: 2**           **Conceptual**

*3. Self-guide preferences appear to be rooted in
a. parent-child interactions and individual's temperament.
b. culture and parenting style.
c. individual's self-esteem and self-concept.
d. individual's intelligence and self-observation .

**ANS: a**          **Pg: 142**
**LO: 2**           **Factual**

4. Which of the following researchers proposed social comparison theory?
a. Albert Bandura
b. E. Tory Higgins
c. Leon Festinger
d. Martin Seligman

**ANS: c**          **Pg: 143**
**LO: 4**           **Factual**

5. The findings of Morse and Gergen's Mr. Clean/Mr. Dirty study provided support for which of the following theories?
a. psychoanalysis
b. self-perception
c. cognitive dissonance
d. social comparison

**ANS: d**       **Pg: 143**
**LO: 4**       **Conceptual**

6. _____ involves putting personal goals ahead of group goals and defining one's identity in terms of personal attributes rather than group memberships.
a. Individualism
b. Behaviorism
c. Collectivism
d. Humanism

**ANS: a**       **Pg: 145**
**LO: 5**       **Factual**

7. Your friend Tyra has decided to postpone starting business school for two years in order to help her family operate their small hardware store during her dad's illness. She is exhibiting a characteristic behavior of persons from a(n) _____ culture
a. individualistic
b. collectivistic
c. behavioristic
d. humanistic

**ANS: b**       **Pg: 145**
**LO: 5**       **Conceptual**

8. Which of the following must be kept in mind when one interprets the results of research on self-esteem?
a. Self-esteem is only a fair predictor of happiness.
b. One cannot draw causal conclusions regarding self-esteem based on the research.
c. It is a fascinating topic related to psychological adjustment.
d. Self-esteem is a popular concept in psychology.

**ANS: b**       **Pg: 147**
**LO: 6**       **Conceptual**

*9. Sociometer theory suggests that self-esteem is
a. an objective measure of one's worth and competence.
b. a subjective measure of one's interpersonal popularity and success.
c. an unstable measure of one's worth and accomplishments.
d. a stable measure of one's strengths and weaknesses.

**ANS: b**       **Pg: 148**
**LO: 7**       **Factual**

10. Ted's mother wears a t-shirt that says "Because I'm your mom, that's why!" She is usually critical of her son and his friends, and only rarely allows him to give his opinion in family decision-making. Ted's mom is exhibiting the traits associated with the _____ parenting style.
a.  permissive
b.  authoritative
c.  authoritarian
d.  neglectful

ANS: c          Pg: 149
LO: 9           Factual

11. _____ are the inferences that people make about what causes their behavior.
a.  Automatic processes
b.  Controlled processes
c.  Self-attributions
d.  Explanatory styles

ANS: c          Pg: 152
LO: 12          Factual

12. People who attribute their setbacks to internal, stable, and global factors are exhibiting a(n) _____ explanatory style.
a.  irrational
b.  coherent
c.  pessimistic
d.  optimistic

ANS: c          Pgs: 153-154
LO: 13          Conceptual

*13. Advertisers of personal care products are tapping into the _____ motive.
a.  self-enhancement
b.  self-improvement
c.  self-assessment
d.  self-verification

ANS: b          Pg: 155
LO: 14          Conceptual

*14. Which of the following is consistent with the self-serving bias?
a.  the tendency to attribute one's successes to situational factors
b   the tendency to attribute one's successes to the ease of the task
c.  the tendency to attribute one's failures to situational factors
d.  the tendency to attribute one's failures to dispositional factors

ANS: c          Pg: 156
LO: 15          Factual

*15.     Which of the following is NOT a source of self-efficacy?
a.       mastering new skills
b.       watching others perform a skill one wants to learn
c.       soliciting encouragement and advice from others
d.       comparing one's self to others who are less fortunate

**ANS: d**              **Pgs: 159-160**
**LO: 18**              **Conceptual**


## TRUE/FALSE QUESTIONS

1.      It has been found that, for individuals who have experienced traumatic events, psychological adjustment is best among those who are able to envision a variety of positive selves.

**ANS: true**           **Pg: 141**
**LO: 1**               **Conceptual**

2.      Research suggests that a preference for an "ought self-guide" is strongly associated with a positive temperament and parental warm, while a preference for the "ideal self-guide" is strongly associated with a negative temperament and parental rejection.

**ANS: false**          **Pg: 142**
**LO: 2**               **Conceptual**

3.      It has been found that alcoholics who have high self-awareness are who experience negative or painful life events relapse more quickly and completely than alcoholics with low self-awareness.

**ANS: true**           **Pg: 142**
**LO: 3**               **Conceptual**

4.      In describing himself, a person living in an individualistic culture might respond, "I am generous," whereas someone from a collectivist culture might respond, "My family thinks that I am generous."

**ANS: true**           **Pg: 145**
**LO: 5**               **Factual**

5. Ethnic differences in self-esteem are likely rooted in how the different groups view themselves, based on cultural messages.

**ANS: true**          **Pg: 151**
**LO: 10**             **Factual**

6. Individuals who have high self-esteem are LESS prone to self-enhancement than others.

**ANS: false**         **Pg: 155**
**LO: 14**             **Conceptual**

7. Self-handicapping is considered a "win-win" strategy.

**ANS: false**         **Pg: 157**
**LO: 15**             **Conceptual**

8. Self-regulation seems to develop early and remain relatively stable.

**ANS: true**          **Pg: 158**
**LO: 16**             **Factual**

9. People who see themselves as being similar across different social roles (e.g., with friends, at work, at school, with parents) are better adjusted than those who perceive less integration in their self-views across these roles.

**ANS: true**          **Pg: 162**
**LO: 20**             **Conceptual**

10. Research indicates that people strive to make positive impressions when they interact with friends and family but shift toward modesty when they interact with strangers.

**ANS: false**         **Pg: 164**
**LO: 21**             **Factual**


**SHORT-ANSWER ESSAY QUESTIONS**


1. Describe the role of social comparisons and feedback from others in developing the self-concept.

**Pgs: 143-145**
**LO: 4**

2. Describe several obstacles to conducting research on self-esteem.

**Pgs: 146-147**
**LO: 6**

3.      Describe the kinds of things parents can do to help their children develop healthy self-esteem.

**Pgs: 149-150**
**LO: 9**

4.      Describe how a person might explain poor performance on a test by using each of the four combinations of internal/external and stable/unstable attributions.

**Pgs: 152-154**
**LO: 12**

5.      Explain how downward comparisons are used to maintain positive feelings about one's self.

**Pgs: 155-156**
**LO: 15**

6.      Use examples to illustrate the concepts of basking in reflected glory and self-handicapping.

**Pgs: 156-157**
**LO: 15**

7.      Briefly explain the relationship between self-regulation and self-efficacy.

**Pgs: 158-159**
**LO: 16**

8.      Briefly describe the three categories of self-defeating behavior and give an example of each.

**Pgs: 160-161**
**LO: 19**

9.      Briefly describe some basic behavioral differences between high self-monitors and low self-monitors.

**Pgs: 164-165**
**LO: 22**

10.     Discuss the role of self-knowledge in building and maintaining good self-esteem.

**Pgs: 165-166**
**LO: 24**

# Chapter 6
# SOCIAL THINKING AND SOCIAL INFLUENCE

## LEARNING OBJECTIVES

1. Cite the five sources of information people use to form impressions of others.
2. Describe the key differences between snap judgments and systematic judgments.
3. Define attributions and explain when people are likely to make them.
4. Describe two expectancies that can distort observers' perceptions.
5. Describe four important cognitive distortions and how they operate.
6. Describe some ways in which perceptions of others are efficient, selective, and consistent.
7. Explain how "old-fashioned" and modern discrimination differ.
8. Describe some of the key determinants of prejudice and explain how they work.
9. Describe the operation of several strategies for reducing prejudice.
10. Cite the key elements in the persuasion process.
11. Describe several source factors that influence persuasion.
12. Discuss the evidence on one-sided versus two-sided messages, and the value of arousing fear or positive feelings in persuasion.
13. Describe several receiver factors that influence persuasion.
14. Explain how the two cognitive routes to persuasion operate.
15. Summarize what Asch discovered about conformity.
16. Discuss the difference between normative and informational influence.
17. Describe some conformity pressures in everyday life and how people can resist them.
18. Describe some situational and personality factors involved in obedience to authority.
19. Cite an important factor in resisting inappropriate demands of authority figures.
20. Describe how culture can affect people's responses to social influence.
21. Describe two compliance strategies based on the principles of commitment and consistency.
22. Describe several compliance strategies based on the principle of reciprocity.
23. Discuss how the principle of scarcity can increase a person's desire for something.

## MULTIPLE CHOICE QUESTIONS

1.     All but which of the following are key sources of information In the process of person perception?
a.     appearance
b.     actions
c.     nonverbal messages
d.     material possessions

**ANS: d**              **Pg: 172**
**LO: 1**               **Factual**

*2.    Person perception is
a.     the process of forming impressions of others.
b.     the act of reading someone else's mind.
c.     using behavioral cues to categorize personality.
d.     a level of sensory acuity.

**ANS: a**              **Pg: 172**
**LO: 1**               **Factual**

3.     _____ are assessments of others that are made quickly and on the basis of only a few bits of information.
a.     Attributions
b.     Snap judgments
c.     Systematic judgments
d.     Recency judgments

**ANS: b**              **Pg: 172**
**LO: 2**               **Factual**

4.     An assessment of a _____ is most likely to be made using a snap judgment.
a.     waiter
b.     boss
c.     friend
d.     potential mate

**ANS: a**              **Pg: 172-173**
**LO: 2**               **Conceptual**

5.     An attribution is
a.     a defense mechanism used in social situations.
b.     an inference about the causes of behavior.
c.     always negative in tone.
d.     all of these.

**ANS: b**              **Pg: 173**
**LO: 3**               **Factual**

6.    The attribution process refers to the inferences we make about the
a.    causes of behavior.
b.    consequences of behavior.
c.    nature of our self-concept.
d.    likelihood of failure on a given task.

**ANS: a        Pg: 173**
**LO: 3          Factual**

7.    Internal attributions ascribe causes of behavior to
a.    situational factors.
b.    interpersonal factors.
c.    environmental factors.
d.    personal dispositions.

**ANS: d        Pg: 173**
**LO: 3          Factual**

8.    External attributions ascribe causes of behavior to
a.    extraneous factors.
b.    dispositional factors.
c.    situational factors.
d.    personal factors.

**ANS: c        Pg: 173**
**LO: 3          Factual**

9.    If you think that someone's behavior was caused by situational factors, you're making a(n)
a.    internal attribution.
b.    external attribution.
c.    defensive attribution.
d.    fundamental attribution.

**ANS: b        Pg: 173**
**LO: 3          Conceptual**

10.   Explaining your friend's poor performance on a test by suggesting that the test was unfair exemplifies which of the following type of attribution?
a.    internal
b.    external
c.    rational
d.    fundamental

**ANS: b        Pg: 173**
**LO: 3          Conceptual**

11. People are most likely to make attributions when
    1. events are not personally relevant
    2. events are unusual
    3. others behave in unexpected ways
    4. others' motives arouse suspicion

a. 1 only
b. 1 and 2 only
c. 1, 2, and 3 only
d. 2, 3, and 4 only

**ANS: d**         **Pg: 174**
**LO: 3**         **Conceptual**

12. You make a new acquaintance at a football game, and you ask him only questions about sports and athletics. This is an example of probable
a. external attribution.
b. confirmation bias.
c. self-serving bias.
d. fundamental bias.

**ANS: b**         **Pg: 174**
**LO: 4**         **Conceptual**

*13. All of the following terms are used to describe expectations about a person that cause the person to behave in ways that confirm the expectations, **except**
a. Pygmalion effect.
b. behavioral confirmation.
c. Michelangelo effect.
d. self-fulfilling prophecy.

**ANS: c**         **Pg: 174-175**
**LO: 14**         **Factual**

14. The process whereby expectations about a person cause the person to behave in ways that confirm the expectations is called
a. the self-fulfilling prophecy.
b. the fundamental attribution error.
c. self-regulatory attribution.
d. confirmation bias.

**ANS: a**         **Pg: 175**
**LO: 4**         **Factual**

15. Which of the following individuals coined the term "self-fulfilling prophecy"?
a.  Sigmund Freud
b.  Robert Merton
c.  Stanley Milgram
d.  Robert Cialdini

**ANS: b**          **Pg: 175**
**LO: 4**           **Factual**

16. The best-known experiments on the self-fulfilling prophecy have been conducted in which of the following settings?
a.  classrooms
b.  bus stations
c.  summer camps
d.  basketball games

**ANS: a**          **Pg: 175**
**LO: 4**           **Factual**

17. According to the research on expectations and self-fulfilling prophecy,
    1.  perceivers behave towards targets according to expectations
    2.  targets adjust behaviors to fit perceiver expectations
    3.  expectations of authority figures, such as teachers, influence subordinates' performance
a.  1 and 2 only
b.  1 and 3 only
c.  2 and 3 only
d.  1, 2, and 3

**ANS: d**          **Pgs: 175-176**
**LO: 4**           **Conceptual**

*18. Diagnostic questions provide people with information about
a.  the internal attributions of people's behavior.
b.  the external attributions of people's behavior.
c.  the accuracy of their expectations.
d.  the impressions that others have of them.

**ANS: c**          **Pg: 175**
**LO: 4**           **Factual**

19. Which of the following is **not** among the consequences of categorizing people according to race, sex, age, sexual orientation, and so forth?
a. We tend to have more favorable attitudes toward in-group members than toward out-group members.
b. We usually see out-group members as being more similar to each other than they really are.
c. Categorizing heightens the visibility of out-group members when there are only a few of them in a larger group.
d. We tend to make excuses for the shortcomings we observe in out-group members.

ANS: d          Pg: 176
LO: 5           Conceptual

20. Explaining the behavior of out-group members on the basis of the characteristic that sets them apart is known as the
a. fundamental attribution error.
b. self-fulfilling prophecy.
c. out-group homogeneity effect.
d. out-group heterogeneity effect.

ANS: c          Pg: 176
LO: 5           Conceptual

21. After reading about a rape that occurred in the neighborhood, Jane says that "all men are violent, sex-crazed, and dangerous." This is an example of the
a. fundamental attribution error.
b. self-fulfilling prophecy.
c. out-group heterogeneity effect.
d. out-group homogeneity effect.

ANS: c          Pg: 176
LO: 5           Conceptual

22. The tendency of humans to categorize allows for _____ of cognitive processing, but also contributes to the creation of _____.
a. accuracy; impressions
b. efficiency; stereotypes
c. homogeneity; attributions
d. clarity; expectations

ANS: b          Pg: 176
LO: 5           Conceptual

23. Categorizing leads to heightened visibility, which means that
a. in-group members may strive to become more visible so they don't simply "blend in" with others of a group.
b. the visibility of out-group members is greater when there are only a few of them in a group.
c. we tend to attribute the behavior of out-group members to the characteristic that sets them apart.
d. we are more likely to notice in-group members as opposed to out-group members.

**ANS: b**          **Pg: 176**
**LO: 5**          **Conceptual**

24. _____ are widely held beliefs that people have certain characteristics because of their membership in a particular group.
a. Attributions
b. Stereotypes
c. Person perceptions
d. Self-fulfilling prophecies

**ANS: b**          **Pg: 176**
**LO: 5**          **Factual**

*25. Which of the following was NOT given as a reason why stereotypes persist?
a. cognitive functionality
b. confirmation bias
c. self-fulfilling prophecy
d. systematic judgments

**ANS: d**          **Pgs: 176-177**
**LO: 5**          **Factual**

*26. Which of the following is NOT consistent with the "what-is-beautiful-is-good" stereotype?
a. Attractive people do have an advantage in the social arena.
b. Cross cultural studies indicate that attractive individuals in Western and Eastern cultures are judged as more assertive than unattractive individuals.
c. Attractive individuals are perceived in a more favorable light than is actually the case.
d. The tendency to associate attractiveness with positive qualities occurs outside the United States.

**ANS: b**          **Pg: 176**
**LO: 5**          **Factual**

27. Which of the following is **not** among the most prevalent stereotypes in America?
a. age
b. gender
c. ethnicity
d. intelligence

ANS: d          Pgs: 176-177
LO: 5          Factual

28. Compared to those who are less attractive, physically attractive people are likely to
a. be more competent.
b. be more assertive.
c. have better social skills.
d. have better mental health.

ANS: c          Pg: 176
LO: 5          Conceptual

29. In explaining the causes of behavior, the fundamental attribution error refers to the
_____ overestimation of the role of _____ factors.
a. actor's; personal
b. actor's; situational
c. observer's; personal
d. observer's; situational

ANS: c          Pg: 177
LO: 5          Conceptual

30. An observer's bias in favor of internal attributions of another person's behavior is called
a. defensive attribution.
b. the fundamental attribution error.
c. the motivational error.
d. self-fulfilling prophecy.

ANS: b          Pg: 177
LO: 5          Conceptual

*31. East Asian mentality, characterized by attention focused on the field surrounding an object and causality understood to reside in the relationship between the object and its field, is referred to as
a. analytic.
b. dynamic.
c. holistic.
d. diagnostic.

ANS: c          Pg: 178
LO: 5          Factual

*32.    Of the following people, who is MOST likely to be prone to the fundamental attribution error?
a.    a Chinese farmer
b.    an American accountant
c.    a Hindu high school student
d.    a Japanese businessman

**ANS: b**         **Pg: 178**
**LO: 5**          **Conceptual**

33.    _____ is a tendency to blame victims for their misfortune, so that one feels less likely to be victimized in a similar way.
a.    Defensive attribution
b.    Fundamental attribution
c.    Person perception
d.    Environmental attribution

**ANS: a**         **Pg: 178**
**LO: 5**          **Factual**

34.    Which of the following reactions to a news account of a rape illustrates a defensive attribution on the part of a female?
a.    Most men are animals.
b.    Policemen don't consider rape to be serious.
c.    The victim probably asked for it.
d.    Women need training in self-defense.

**ANS: c**         **Pg: 178**
**LO: 5**          **Conceptual**

*35.    Defensive attributions help people maintain a belief in a
a.    "just world".
b.    "imperfect society".
c.    distorted sense of cultural identity.
d.    synchronized society.

**ANS: a**         **Pg: 178**
**LO: 5**          **Factual**

36.    The tendency for people to see what they expect to see helps to perpetuate
a.    individualism.
b.    out-group heterogeneity effects.
c.    external attributions.
d.    stereotypes.

**ANS: d**         **Pg: 177**
**LO: 5**          **Conceptual**

37. Since individualistic cultures like America's tend to view people as responsible for their own actions, Americans are probably more likely to
a. demonstrate confirmation bias.
b. be influenced by the primacy effect.
c. commit the fundamental attribution error.
d. fall prey to the out-group homogeneity effect.

**ANS: c**          **Pg: 178**
**LO: 5**           **Conceptual**

38. Melissa grew up in the South and is prejudiced against New Yorkers. She sees a TV program about a kind-hearted but clumsy New Yorker and afterward she talks about how the program made the New Yorker appear to be bumbling, stupid, and ignorant. Melissa's behavior best illustrates which of the following?
a. self-serving bias
b. the selectivity of person perception
c. defensive attribution
d. the fundamental attribution error

**ANS: b**          **Pg: 180**
**LO: 6**           **Conceptual**

39. _____ is **not** a key theme in person perception.
a. Selectivity
b. Defensiveness
c. Efficiency
d. Consistency

**ANS: b**          **Pgs: 179-180**
**LO: 6**           **Conceptual**

40. The fact that first impressions have a powerful influence on our perceptions of others is most consistent with which of the following concepts?
a. recency effect
b. primacy effect
c. categorizing
d. defensive attribution

**ANS: b**          **Pg: 180**
**LO: 6**           **Conceptual**

*41. Which of the following BEST describes the process of person perception?
a. People prefer to exert as little cognitive effort as necessary.
b. People are likely to remember traits about people that are inconsistent with their expectations, because these traits "catch their eye."
c. First impressions are easily changed, because people are well aware that these may be distorted.
d. Recent studies indicate that the accuracy of Web-based impressions are not comparable to the accuracy of face-to-face impressions.

**ANS: a**         **Pgs: 179-180**
**LO: 6**         **Factual**

42. An unrealistically negative attitude that is held toward a particular group of people is referred to as
a. perceptionism.
b. prejudice.
c. discrimination.
d. defensive attribution.

**ANS: b**         **Pg: 181**
**LO: 7**         **Factual**

43. Prejudice is defined as
a. an effort to subjugate a racial group.
b. a negative attitude toward some group.
c. behaving differently toward someone because of their race.
d. all of these.

**ANS: b**         **Pg: 181**
**LO: 7**         **Factual**

44. In general, prejudice is _____ and discrimination is _____.
a. an attitude; a behavior
b. a behavior; an attitude
c. a behavior; an attribution
d. an attitude; an attribution

**ANS: a**         **Pg: 181**
**LO: 7**         **Conceptual**

45. Treating Asian people differently just because they're Asian constitutes
a. racism.
b. racial prejudice.
c. racial discrimination.
d. all of these.

**ANS: c**         **Pg: 181**
**LO: 7**         **Conceptual**

46.     Over the past 40 years, prejudice and discrimination against minority groups have
a.      diminished.
b.      increased.
c.      stayed about the same.
d.      become more blatant.

**ANS: a**              **Pg: 181**
**LO: 7**               **Factual**

47.     Joshua says that women should be treated as men's equals. He thinks that women don't
        need the ERA or sexual harassment laws anymore and opposes such governmental
        actions. Joshua's attitudes are examples of
a.      "old-fashioned" discrimination.
b.      modern discrimination.
c.      situational prejudice.
d.      out-group prejudice.

**ANS: b**              **Pg: 181**
**LO: 7**               **Factual**

*48.    The beatings and subsequent murders of James Byrd and Matthew Shepard in 1998 are
        examples of
a.      "old-fashioned" discrimination.
b.      modern discrimination.
c.      defensive discrimination.
d.      perceptual discrimination.

**ANS: a**              **Pg: 181**
**LO: 7**               **Conceptual**

49.     Blaming racial minorities for their plight by saying they should be able to "pull
        themselves up by their own bootstraps" discounts the importance of situational factors.
        This illustrates
a.      the primacy effect.
b.      the recency effect.
c.      the fundamental attribution error.
d.      defensive attribution.

**ANS: c**              **Pg: 183**
**LO: 8**               **Conceptual**

50.     Which of the following is generally **not** considered as a contributor to racial prejudice?
a.      egocentrism
b.      stereotyping
c.      defensive attribution
d.      the fundamental attribution error

**ANS: a**              **Pg: 183**
**LO: 8**               **Conceptual**

51.    Which of the following statements is true?
a.    Derogatory stereotypes no longer exist in modern society.
b.    People tend to selectively recall instances that counteract their stereotypes.
c.    People tend to see what they expect to see when they encounter minorities they view with prejudice.
d.    Although prejudice toward minorities still exists in America, discrimination has all but disappeared.

**ANS: c**          **Pgs: 182-183**
**LO: 8**           **Conceptual**

52.    Which of the following personality types is most likely to be associated with prejudice?
a.    defensive
b.    right-wing authoritarian
c.    conscientious
d.    open to experience

**ANS: b**          **Pg: 182**
**LO: 8**           **Conceptual**

53.    Which of the following is the most common response to threats to collective self-esteem?
a.    in-group favoritism
b.    "old-fashioned" discrimination
c.    cooperative interdependence
d.    diffusion of responsibility

**ANS: a**          **Pg: 184**
**LO: 8**           **Conceptual**

*54.    Right-wing authoritarianism is characterized by all of the following **except**
a.    authoritarian submission.
b.    authoritarian aggression.
c.    conventionalism.
d.    deconstruction.

**ANS: d**          **Pg: 182**
**LO: 8**           **Conceptual**

*55.    The classic Robbers' Cave State Park study illustrates the correlation between prejudice and
a.    competition.
b.    threats to social identity.
c.    cognitive distortions.
d.    right-wing authoritarianism.

**ANS: a**          **Pg: 183**
**LO: 8**           **Conceptual**

56.    Which of the following researchers conducted the classic study of group competition at Robbers' Cave State Park in Oklahoma?
a.    Albert Bandura
b.    Muzafer Sherif
c.    Robert Cialdini
d.    Mark Snyder

ANS: b          Pg: 183
LO: 8           Factual

*57.   Threats to personal and social identity motivate individuals to restore
a.    social order.
b.    self-esteem.
c.    "old-fashioned" discrimination.
d.    cooperation.

ANS: b          Pg: 184
LO: 8           Conceptual

58.    Research supports the theory that a shift from _____ to _____ can reduce stereotyping and prejudice.
a.    automatic processing; controlled processing
b.    "old-fashioned" discrimination; symbolic racism
c.    cooperative interdependence; inter-group competition
d.    defensive attribution; diffusion of responsibility

ANS: a          Pg: 184
LO: 9           Factual

59.    Which of the following is **not** considered an essential element of reducing inter-group hostility through cooperative interdependence?
a.    working together for a common goal
b.    successful outcomes to cooperative efforts
c.    ensuring that everyone has equal status
d.    assigning specific titles or names to each group

ANS: d          Pgs: 184-185
LO: 9           Conceptual

*60.   An example of applying intergroup contact as a means for reducing prejudice is the
a.    "jigsaw classroom".
b.    "network classroom".
c.    "superordinate worksite".
d.    "connection worksite".

ANS: a          Pg: 185
LO: 9           Factual

61. Persuasion involves the communication of arguments and information intended to change another person's
a. attitudes.
b. personality.
c. perceptions.
d. attributions.

**ANS: a**          **Pg: 185**
**LO: 10**          **Factual**

62. Which of the following is **not** considered a basic element of the persuasion process?
a. source
b. signal
c. message
d. receiver

**ANS: b**          **Pg: 186**
**LO: 10**          **Factual**

63. Which of the following characteristics of the source is **least** likely to help make persuasion successful?
a. credibility
b. likeability
c. similarity to the audience
d. having a stake in the issue at hand

**ANS: d**          **Pgs: 186-187**
**LO: 11**          **Conceptual**

64. Vicki is a persuasive, successful salesperson. It is most likely that she possesses which of the following sets of characteristics?
a. attractiveness and affluence
b. sense of humor and verbal skills
c. knowledge and charm
d. credibility and likeability

**ANS: d**          **Pgs: 186-187**
**LO: 11**          **Conceptual**

65. Persuasion is most likely to be successful when the source of the persuasive communication is
a. perceived as trustworthy.
b. perceived as ingratiating.
c. dissimilar to the receiver.
d. likely to benefit from changing the receiver's attitudes.

**ANS: a**          **Pgs: 186-187**
**LO: 11**          **Conceptual**

66. Research shows that a key consideration in likability of a persuasive source is
a. gender.
b. tone of voice.
c. physical attractiveness.
d. authoritative presence.

**ANS: c**      **Pg: 187**
**LO: 11**      **Factual**

67. You are dealing with an audience that is uneducated on the issue you're speaking about. The facts are clearly in your favor, so you have strong facts to present. Your best strategy is to present a message that
a. is one-sided.
b. is two-sided.
c. arouses fear in the audience.
d. draws conclusions for your audience.

**ANS: a**      **Pg: 187**
**LO: 12**      **Conceptual**

68. Fear arousal is likely to be an effective persuasive tactic
a. as long as the level of fear is sufficiently high.
b. with an audience that is relatively ignorant of the issues.
c. as long as the receiver thinks the source's advice is reasonable, and the level of fear is extremely high.
d. if the negative consequences are unpleasant, e.g., fairly probable if the receivers don't follow the source's advice, and avoidable if they do.

**ANS: d**      **Pg: 187**
**LO: 12**      **Conceptual**

69. Persuasion tends to work best when there is _____ discrepancy between a receiver's initial position on an issue and the position advocated by the source.
a. an extreme
b. a moderate
c. little or no
d. an indeterminate

**ANS: b**      **Pg: 187**
**LO: 13**      **Conceptual**

70. The notion that people are usually willing to consider alternative views on an issue if the views aren't too different from their own is based on which of the following theories?
a. social judgment
b. social comparison
c. cognitive dissonance
d. elaboration likelihood model

**ANS: a**      **Pg: 188**
**LO: 13**      **Conceptual**

71. How much discrepancy between the receiver's initial position on an issue and the position advocated by the source is ideal for persuasion?
a. a small discrepancy
b. a large discrepancy
c. a small discrepancy, as long as it is within the latitude of acceptance
d. a large discrepancy, as long as it is within the latitude of acceptance

ANS: d          Pg: 188
LO: 13          Conceptual

72. Which of the following statements about the routes of persuasive messages is true?
a. Persuasion usually occurs via the central route.
b. Attitudes formed via the central route are longer lasting than those formed via the peripheral route.
c. Attitudes formed via the peripheral route are better predictors of behavior than those formed via the central route.
d. Attitudes formed via the central route are longer lasting, but those formed via the peripheral route are more resistant to challenge.

ANS: b          Pgs: 188-189
LO: 14          Conceptual

73. Conformity occurs when people change their behavior
a. as a result of punishment.
b. as a result of positive reinforcement.
c. in response to real or imagined social pressure.
d. after observing a model being reinforced for a particular response.

ANS: c          Pg: 190
LO: 15          Factual

74. In Asch's studies of conformity, participants
a. were ordered to deliver painful electric shocks to a stranger.
b. were the recipients of painful electric shocks delivered by an accomplice.
c. indicated which of three lines matched a standard line in length.
d. were ordered to give consistently wrong answers to simple questions.

ANS: c          Pg: 190
LO: 15          Factual

75. How did Asch induce conformity in his studies involving judgments of line length?
a. An authority figure urged participants to select a certain line.
b. Participants discussed the problem and came to a group consensus.
c. An attractive confederate of the opposite sex persuaded the participants.
d. Several accomplices gave incorrect answers before the true participant answered.

ANS: d          Pg: 190
LO: 15          Conceptual

76. In Asch's studies, _____ and _____ were found to be key determinants of conformity.
a. task difficulty; group size
b. group size; group unanimity
c. group size; the participants' intelligence
d. the group leader's personality; group unanimity

**ANS: b**      **Pg: 190**
**LO: 15**      **Factual**

77. Asch found that group size had little influence on group conformity if
a. the task was ambiguous.
b. the experimenter ridiculed the group's wrong answers.
c. just one accomplice failed to go along with the rest of the group.
d. at least several accomplices failed to go along with the rest of the group.

**ANS: c**      **Pg: 190**
**LO: 15**      **Factual**

78. In follow-ups of Asch's studies of conformity, participants who made their responses anonymously
a. conformed significantly less than those who made their responses publicly.
b. conformed significantly more than those who made their responses publicly.
c. conformed about as often as those who made their responses publicly.
d. failed to conform under any conditions.

**ANS: a**      **Pg: 190**
**LO: 15**      **Conceptual**

79. In follow-ups of Asch's studies of conformity, the behavior of participants who responded anonymously implies that
a. no conformity actually took place.
b. the participants who responded publicly truly changed their beliefs.
c. the extent of conformity in the real world is probably very limited.
d. the participants in the earlier studies complied with social pressure without actually changing their private beliefs.

**ANS: d**      **Pg: 190**
**LO: 15**      **Conceptual**

80. In follow-ups of Asch's line judgment studies, participants responding anonymously conformed less than those who gave answers publicly. Thus Asch's original participants actually _____ rather than conformed.
a. complied
b. yielded
c. obeyed
d. capitulated

**ANS: a**      **Pg: 190**
**LO: 15**      **Conceptual**

*81.    Normative influence operates when people conform to social norms because of
a.      hope of positive social consequences.
b.      fear of violent consequences.
c.      fear of negative social consequences.
d.      hope of monetary gain.

**ANS: c**          **Pg: 191**
**LO: 16**          **Factual**

*82.    Which of the following is the best example of normative influence?
a.      a child goes along with his peers in bullying a new student out of fear of being bullied
        himself
b.      a man goes along with the investment choices of his roommates because of the belief that
        "they can't all be wrong"
c.      a woman complies with traditional feminine roles in order to win the favor of her
        traditional relatives
d.      an individual joins a gang to look cool in front of his friends

**ANS: a**          **Pg: 191**
**LO: 16**          **Conceptual**

83.     Conformity is promoted by all of the following **except**
a.      normative influence.
b.      ambiguity of situation.
c.      weak group identification.
d.      bystander effect.

**ANS: c**          **Pg: 191**
**LO: 17**          **Conceptual**

84.     Obedience is a form of compliance in which people change their behavior in response to
a.      direct commands.
b.      implied pressure.
c.      requests from others.
d.      persuasive communications.

**ANS: a**          **Pg: 192**
**LO: 18**          **Factual**

85.     Mike served in the Army for four years and now is especially prone to follow direct
        orders from authority figures.  Mike shows a high degree of
a.      dependency.
b.      obedience.
c.      conformity.
d.      prejudice.

**ANS: b**          **Pg: 192**
**LO: 18**          **Conceptual**

86. In Milgram's studies of obedience, participants were
a. ordered to deliver "painful electric shocks" to a stranger.
b. asked to select one of three lines that matched a standard line in length.
c. ordered to give consistently wrong answers to simple questions.
d. the recipients of painful electric shocks delivered by an experimental accomplice.

ANS: a          Pgs: 192-193
LO: 18          Factual

87. In Milgram's study, what percentage of the participants fully obeyed the experimenter and administered the maximum level of shock?
a. 5%
b. 35%
c. 65%
d. 95%

ANS: c          Pg: 193
LO: 18          Factual

88. The results of Milgram's study imply that
a. many people will obey an authority figure, even if innocent people get hurt.
b. in the real world, most people will refuse to follow orders to inflict harm on a stranger.
c. most people are willing to give obviously wrong answers when ordered to do so.
d. most people adhere to their own beliefs, even when group members unanimously disagree.

ANS: a          Pgs: 193-194
LO: 18          Conceptual

89. The important conclusion from Milgram's study of obedience is that
a. people apparently like to shock other people
b. people will yield to imagined pressure
c. people who appear to be good may be inherently bad
d. situational pressures can cause good people to do bad things

ANS: d          Pg: 194
LO: 18          Conceptual

90. The main criticism of Milgram's obedience experiment focuses on which of the following issues?
a. the unusual levels of shock that were used
b. the generalizability of the results to real life
c. ethical considerations such as inducing stress in participants
d. the reliability of the findings across other studies

ANS: c          Pg: 194
LO: 18          Conceptual

91. Which of the following is **not** considered a factor in prompting individuals to resist pressure from authority figures?
a. The person must view the problem as important.
b. Social support is important.
c. Refusal to see oneself as helpless is important.
d. The rewards for ethical resistance must be sufficient.

**ANS: d**         **Pg: 194**
**LO: 19**        **Conceptual**

92. In 1996 Dr. Jeffrey Wigand, a former tobacco company scientist, shared information with the press and judiciary systems concerning systematic corporate deception of the public regarding the dangers of smoking. This is an example of
a. informational influence.
b. the reciprocity norm.
c. ethical resistance.
d. insider trading.

**ANS: c**         **Pg: 194**
**LO: 19**        **Conceptual**

93. Which of the following statements regarding the influence of culture on responses to social pressure is true?
a. Of the cultures studied, Americans are least likely to obey an authority figure.
b. People from Western Europe are more likely to conform than Americans are.
c. Individuals in Asian countries view conformity more positively than Americans do.
d. Researchers have found cultural differences in attitudes toward social pressure, but not in behaviors.

**ANS: c**         **Pg: 194**
**LO: 20**        **Conceptual**

94. Which of the following researchers was the first to investigate the foot-in-the-door technique?
a. Albert Bandura
b. Roy Baumeister
c. Robert Cialdini
d. Jonathon Freedman

**ANS: d**         **Pg: 195**
**LO: 21**        **Factual**

95. Researchers think that the reason the foot-in-the-door technique is effective is that people have a tendency to
a. please others.
b. behave consistently.
c. use the reciprocity norm.
d. engage in fundamental attribution.

**ANS: b**        **Pgs: 195-96**
**LO: 21**        **Conceptual**

96. The _____ technique involves making a large request that will probably be refused to increase the chances of being granted a smaller request later.
a. foot-in-the-door
b. through-the-backdoor
c. door-in-the-face
d. door-to-door

**ANS: c**        **Pg: 197**
**LO: 21**        **Factual**

*97. Reaserch indicates that the door-in-the-face technique is less likely to be effective under all of the following conditions **except**
a. the second request follows very quickly on the heels of the first request.
b. the requester is not likeable.
c. the initial request is too trivial to register.
d. the second request is so large it is unreasonable.

**ANS: b**        **Pg: 197**
**LO: 21**        **Conceptual**

98. The local animal shelter sends you cute return address labels with cuddly kittens on them. They are hoping that you will send a donation based on the effects of
a. compliance.
b. the lowball technique.
c. the reciprocity norm.
d. the foot in the door technique.

**ANS: c**        **Pg: 196**
**LO: 22**        **Conceptual**

99. _____ has written extensively about how the reciprocity norm is used in social influence efforts.
a. Robert Cialdini
b. Stanley Milgram
c. Muzafer Sherif
d. Martin Seligman

**ANS: a**        **Pg: 196**
**LO: 22**        **Factual**

100. If Harold intends to use the reciprocity norm to influence Ramon, a potential customer, to buy his product, Harold might
a. offer Ramon a great bargain, revealing hidden costs later.
b. take Ramon to dinner at a nice restaurant.
c. try to convince Ramon of the scarcity of his product.
d. try to stimulate a reactance response in Ramon.

ANS: b          Pg: 196
LO: 22          Conceptual

101. Providing customers with free samples best illustrates which of the following compliance tactics?
a. the door-in-the-face technique
b. the foot-in-the-door technique
c. the reciprocity norm
d. the lowball technique

ANS: c          Pg: 196
LO: 22          Conceptual

102. Shakira decides to buy a new car after seeing a good deal advertised on television. Now she's committed to buying the car, but the dealer tells her about a number of hidden costs that will be added on. Shakira is a victim of the
a. reciprocity norm.
b. feigned scarcity technique.
c. overeager buyer syndrome.
d. lowball technique.

ANS: d          Pg: 196
LO: 21          Conceptual

103. The lowball technique involves
a. playing on potential customers' guilt.
b. engendering cognitive dissonance in potential customers.
c. getting someone to commit to an attractive deal before revealing its hidden costs.
d. making a large request that will probably be refused to increase the chances of being granted a smaller request later.

ANS: c          Pg: 196
LO: 21          Conceptual

104. The advertising phrase, "Get them while they last!" makes use of which of the following compliance tactics?
a. reactance
b. feigned scarcity
c. the reciprocity norm
d. both reactance and feigned scarcity

ANS: d          Pg: 197
LO: 23          Conceptual

105. Two potential buyers made appointments to see Theresa's house, which is for sale. Theresa scheduled the appointments so that they overlap and the two buyers will see each other. Theresa is using which of the following compliance tactics?
a.    reciprocity
b.    low-balling
c.    scarcity
d.    fundamental attribution

**ANS: c          Pg: 197**
**LO: 23          Conceptual**

106. _____ occurs when someone's number of choices has been restricted and he or she pursues the choices that have been denied.
a.    Reactance
b.    Compliance
c.    Reciprocity
d.    Ethical resistance

**ANS: a          Pg: 197**
**LO: 23          Factual**

107. One fraternity has only 3 openings, but during pledge week the number of pledges increases from 4 to 9. Another fraternity has 8 openings but only 2 pledges by the end of the week. This discrepancy was likely influenced by
1.    the scarcity principle
2.    the compliance norm
3.    reactance

a.    1 only
b.    1 and 3 only
c.    2 only
d.    1, 2, and 3

**ANS: b          Pg: 197**
**LO: 23          Factual**

108. A significant benefit that comes from understanding techniques of persuasion and compliance is that such understanding can help you to _____ them.
a.    resist
b.    control
c.    avoid
d.    give in to

**ANS: a          Pg: 197**
**LO: 20-24          Conceptual**

# MULTIPLE CHOICE QUESTIONS FROM STUDY GUIDE

1.  Which of the following is **not** one of the key sources of information about other people used in the process of person perception?
a.  appearance
b.  verbal statements
c.  nonverbal messages
d.  All of these are key sources.

**ANS: d**          **Pg: 172**
**LO: 1**           **Conceptual**

2.  In forming impressions of those who can affect their welfare and happiness, people tend to make _____ judgments.
a.  snap
b.  primacy
c.  systematic
d.  attributional

**ANS: c**          **Pg: 172**
**LO: 2**           **Conceptual**

3.  Which of the following statements about the attribution process is accurate?
a.  Our perceptions of others tend to be bias-free.
b.  We make attributions about everyone we meet.
c.  The process is sometimes illogical and unsystematic.
d.  The types of attributions we make don't have much impact on our everyday social interactions.

**ANS: c**          **Pg: 174**
**LO: 3**           **Conceptual**

4.  The best-known experiments on self-fulfilling prophecy have been conducted in which of the following settings?
a.  subway
b.  classroom
c.  laboratory
d.  fast-food restaurant

**ANS: b**          **Pg: 175**
**LO: 4**           **Factual**

5.  Attractive people are most likely to have an advantage in which of the following types of situations?
a.  social
b.  academic
c.  work-related
d.  sports-related

**ANS: a**          **Pg: 176**
**LO: 5**           **Conceptual**

6. The fundamental attribution error is the tendency to explain other people's behavior as the result of _____ rather than _____ factors.
a. external; fundamental
b. fundamental; personal
c. personal; situational
d. situational; personal

ANS: c         Pg: 177
LO: 5         **Factual**

7. The term "defensive attribution" is synonymous with which of the following?
a. modern racism
b. blaming the victim
c. the self-fulfilling prophecy
d. the fundamental attribution error

ANS: b         Pg: 178
LO: 5         **Conceptual**

8. Which of the following is **not** one of the recurrent themes in the process of person perception?
a. stability
b. efficiency
c. ambiguity
d. selectivity

ANS: c         Pgs: 179-180
LO: 6         **Conceptual**

9. In general, first impressions of other people tend to be particularly potent. This finding is most closely associated with which of the following effects?
a. primacy
b. stereotype
c. group homogeneity
d. self-fulfilling prophecy

ANS: a         Pg: 180
LO: 6         **Conceptual**

10. Which of the following statements about prejudice and discrimination is false?
a. Prejudice can occur without discrimination.
b. Discrimination can occur without prejudice.
c. Over the past 40 years, prejudice and discrimination against minority groups have diminished.
d. The distinction between blatant and subtle discrimination is a uniquely American phenomenon.

ANS: d         Pg: 181
LO: 7         **Conceptual**

11. Which of the following characteristics of a source of a persuasive message is least likely to be effective?
a. likable
b. credible
c. trustworthy
d. controversial

**ANS: d**          **Pgs: 186-187**
**LO: 11**          **Conceptual**

12. A one-sided argument is most likely to be effective when the audience is
a. mostly college students.
b. just returning from lunch.
c. relatively uneducated about the issue.
d. very curious about the message.

**ANS: c**          **Pg: 187**
**LO: 12**          **Conceptual**

13. Employees often follow their boss's instructions even when they believe the instructions don't make sense. This example illustrates the concept of
a. conformity.
b. compliance.
c. obedience.
d. attribution.

**ANS: c**          **Pg: 192**
**LO: 16**          **Conceptual**

14. The foot-in-the-door technique involves getting people to agree to a _____ request to increase the chances that they will agree to a _____ request later.
a. large; larger
b. large; smaller
c. small; smaller
d. small; larger

**ANS: d**          **Pg: 195**
**LO: 21**          **Conceptual**

15. A fast-food restaurant that advertises its "Mammoth Burger" as being available for a "limited time only" is making use of which of the following social influence tactics?
a. scarcity
b. reciprocity
c. the lowball technique
d. observational learning

**ANS: a**          **Pg: 197**
**LO: 23**          **Conceptual**

# MULTIPLE CHOICE QUESTIONS ON WEB SITE

1.      An attribution is
a.      a defense mechanism used in social situations.
b.      an inference about the causes of behavior.
c.      always negative in tone.
d.      all of these.

**ANS: b**          **Pg: 173**
**LO: 3**           **Factual**

2.      Explaining your friend's poor performance on a test by suggesting that the test was unfair
        exemplifies which of the following type of attribution?
a.      internal
b.      external
c.      rational
d.      fundamental

**ANS: b**          **Pg: 173**
**LO: 3**           **Conceptual**

3.      The best-known experiments on the self-fulfilling prophecy have been conducted in
        which of the following settings?
a.      classrooms
b.      bus stations
c.      summer camps
d.      basketball games

**ANS: a**          **Pg: 175**
**LO: 4**           **Factual**

*4.     Which of the following was NOT given as a reason why stereotypes persist?
a.      cognitive functionality
b.      confirmation bias
c.      self-fulfilling prophecy
d.      systematic judgments

**ANS: d**          **Pgs: 176-177**
**LO: 5**           **Factual**

5.      The tendency for people to see what they expect to see helps to perpetuate
a.      individualism.
b.      out-group heterogeneity effects.
c.      external attributions.
d.      stereotypes.

**ANS: d**          **Pg: 177**
**LO: 5**           **Conceptual**

6. The fact that first impressions have a powerful influence on our perceptions of others is most consistent with which of the following concepts?
a. recency effect
b. primacy effect
c. categorizing
d. defensive attribution

**ANS: b**       **Pg: 180**
**LO: 6**       **Conceptual**

7. Prejudice is defined as
a. an effort to subjugate a racial group.
b. a negative attitude toward some group.
c. behaving differently toward someone because of their race.
d. all of these.

**ANS: b**       **Pg: 181**
**LO: 7**       **Factual**

8. Which of the following is generally **not** considered as a contributor to racial prejudice?
a. egocentrism
b. stereotyping
c. defensive attribution
d. the fundamental attribution error

**ANS: a**       **Pg: 183**
**LO: 8**       **Conceptual**

*9. An example of applying intergroup contact as a means for reducing prejudice is the
a. "jigsaw classroom".
b. "network classroom".
c. "superordinate worksite".
d. "connection worksite".

**ANS: a**       **Pg: 185**
**LO: 9**       **Factual**

10. Persuasion is most likely to be successful when the source of the persuasive communication is
a. perceived as trustworthy.
b. perceived as ingratiating.
c. dissimilar to the receiver.
d. likely to benefit from changing the receiver's attitudes.

**ANS: a**       **Pgs: 186-187**
**LO: 11**       **Conceptual**

11. Conformity occurs when people change their behavior
a. as a result of punishment.
b. as a result of positive reinforcement.
c. in response to real or imagined social pressure.
d. after observing a model being reinforced for a particular response.

**ANS: c**        **Pg: 190**
**LO: 15**        **Factual**

12. Asch found that group size had little influence on group conformity if
a. the task was ambiguous.
b. the experimenter ridiculed the group's wrong answers.
c. just one accomplice failed to go along with the rest of the group.
d. at least several accomplices failed to go along with the rest of the group.

**ANS: c**        **Pg: 190**
**LO: 15**        **Factual**

13. The important conclusion from Milgram's study of obedience is that
a. people apparently like to shock other people
b. people will yield to imagined pressure
c. people who appear to be good may be inherently bad
d. situational pressures can cause good people to do bad things

**ANS: d**        **Pg: 194**
**LO: 18**        **Conceptual**

14. Researchers think that the reason the foot-in-the-door technique is effective is that people have a tendency to
a. please others.
b. behave consistently.
c. use the reciprocity norm.
d. engage in fundamental attribution.

**ANS: b**        **Pgs: 195-96**
**LO: 21**        **Conceptual**

15. The lowball technique involves
a. playing on potential customers' guilt.
b. engendering cognitive dissonance in potential customers.
c. getting someone to commit to an attractive deal before revealing its hidden costs.
d. making a large request that will probably be refused to increase the chances of being granted a smaller request later.

**ANS: c**        **Pg: 196**
**LO: 21**        **Conceptual**

## TRUE/FALSE QUESTIONS

1.  Research suggests that people are likely to make attributions about most people they met.

**ANS: false**       **Pg: 174**
**LO: 3**             **Factual**

2.  Self-fulfilling prophecies are less likely to operate if target individuals are NOT aware of another's beliefs and these beliefs do NOT contradict their self views.

**ANS: false**       **Pg: 175**
**LO: 4**             **Factual**

3.  Research indicates that Koreans are less prone to the fundamental attribution error than Americans.

**ANS: true**        **Pg: 178**
**LO: 5**             **Factual**

4.  It is possible for prejudice to occur without discrimination, but it is NOT possible for discrimination to occur without prejudice.

**ANS: false**       **Pg: 181**
**LO: 7**             **Conceptual**

5.  The perception of threats is more likely to cause hostility between groups than are actual threats to an ingroup.

**ANS: true**        **Pg: 182**
**LO: 8**             **Factual**

6.  Most discrimination is rooted in "ingroup love" as opposed to "outgroup hate."

**ANS: true**        **Pg: 184**
**LO: 8**             **Factual**

7.  Informational influence was at work when Susan looked to her classmates to decide how to behave when the alarm sounded.

**ANS: true**        **Pg: 191**
**LO: 8**             **Conceptual**

8.  In general, we are more likely to get help in an emergency when there is only one witness.

**ANS: true**        **Pg: 192**
**LO: 17**           **Factual**

9.      Japanese and Koreans are less conforming than Americans.

**ANS: false**          **Pg: 194**
**LO: 20**              **Factual**

10.     For the door-in-the-face to work, there must be no delay between the two requests.

**ANS: true**           **Pg: 197**
**LO: 22**              **Factual**

## SHORT-ANSWER ESSAY QUESTIONS

1.      Compare and contrast the roles that verbal and nonverbal messages play in the process of impression formation.

**Pgs: 172**
**LO: 1**

2.      Briefly describe a situation in which we are more likely to make a systematic judgment, as opposed to a snap judgment, of another person.

**Pgs: 172-173**
**LO: 2**

3.      Briefly describe the conditions under which we are most likely to make attributions of other people and describe the role that "confirmation bias" plays in our attributions.

**Pgs: 173-175**
**LO: 4**

4.      Identify and briefly describe the three steps involved in the self-fulfilling prophecy and how the effects of expectations influence the classroom environment.

**Pgs: 175-176**
**LO: 4**

5.      Distinguish between prejudice and discrimination, and give an example of each.

**Pg: 181**
**LO: 7**

6.      Describe the four conditions necessary for reducing inter-group hostility.

**Pg: 185**
**LO: 9**

7.    List and describe some of the source factors that influence the persuasion process and explain how forewarning affects the persuasiveness of an argument.

**Pgs: 186-187**
**LO: 11**

8.    Using examples from Asch's studies, distinguish between compliance and conformity.

**Pgs: 190-191**
**LO: 15**

9.    Discuss some of the specific aspects of Milgram's experiment on obedience to authority that have led to questions about the ethics of the procedure.

**Pgs: 192-194**
**LO: 18**

10.   Briefly describe the factors that determine whether people will resist social pressure.

**Pg: 194**
**LO: 19**

# Chapter 7
# INTERPERSONAL COMMUNICATION

## LEARNING OBJECTIVES

1.    List and explain the six components of the communication process.
2.    List several important differences between face-to-face and computer-mediated communication.
3.    Discuss how interpersonal communication is important to adjustment.
4.    List five general principles of nonverbal communication.
5.    Define proxemics and discuss personal space.
6.    Discuss display rules and what can be discerned from facial cues.
7.    Summarize the characteristics associated with effective eye contact.
8.    Describe the roles of body movement, posture, and gestures in communication.
9.    Summarize the research findings on touching and paralanguage.
10.   Discuss the difficulty of detecting deception and the nonverbal cues linked to deception.
11.   Explain what polygraphs do and cite some problems with their use.
12.   Describe the significance of nonverbal messages in interpersonal interactions.
13.   List five suggestions for creating a positive interpersonal climate.
14.   Give five steps involved in making small talk.
15.   Cite some ways to reduce the risks of self-disclosure.
16.   Describe the role of self-disclosure in relationship development.
17.   Discuss cultural and gender differences in self-disclosure.
18.   Cite four points good listeners need to keep in mind.
19.   Discuss four responses to communication apprehension.
20.   Describe five barriers to effective communication.
21.   Cite some positive outcomes associated with constructive interpersonal conflict.
22.   Describe five personal styles of dealing with interpersonal conflict.
23.   List six tips for coping effectively with interpersonal conflict.
24.   Explain why Deborah Tannen characterizes America as "the argument culture."
25.   Describe some reasons for increased social contentiousness today.
26.   Describe what individuals and social institutions can do to reduce the level of public conflict.
27.   Differentiate assertive communication from submissive and aggressive communication.
28.   Describe five steps that lead to more assertive communication.

# MULTIPLE CHOICE QUESTIONS

1.  Which of the following statements about interpersonal communication is **not** true?
a.  Interpersonal communication is a process.
b.  Interpersonal communication depends heavily on the sender's social identity.
c.  Participants send as well as receive messages when they're interacting.
d.  For communication to be considered interpersonal, at least two people must be involved.

**ANS: b**          **Pg: 202**
**LO: 1**           **Conceptual**

2.  Elements in the communication process include all of the following **except**
a.  sender.
b.  message.
c.  personal space.
d.  distorting noise.

**ANS: c**          **Pg: 202**
**LO: 1**           **Factual**

3.  In interpersonal communication, the person who originates a message is called the
a.  channel.
b.  sender.
c.  context.
d.  speaker.

**ANS: b**          **Pg: 202**
**LO: 1**           **Factual**

4.  In interpersonal communication the information that is transmitted from one person to another is called the
a.  code.
b.  noise.
c.  message.
d.  context.

**ANS: c**          **Pg: 202**
**LO: 1**           **Factual**

5.  In interpersonal communication, speaker is to encode as receiver is to
a.  noise.
b.  decode.
c.  verbalize.
d.  detect.

**ANS: b**          **Pg: 202**
**LO: 1**           **Factual**

6. When your friend calls you at home to make plans for the weekend, the _____ of communication is sound.
a. sender
b. channel
c. message
d. stimulus

**ANS: b**        **Pgs: 202-203**
**LO: 1**        **Factual**

7. When your friend silently makes faces at you during a class lecture, the channel of communication is primarily
a. gestures.
b. verbal.
c. fluent.
d. encoded.

**ANS: a**        **Pg: 203**
**LO: 1**        **Factual**

8. Bill's use of the word "broad" in conversation when referring to women offends Betty and makes it hard for her to follow his meaning. This type of miscommunication is called
a. noise.
b. context.
c. background.
d. a display rule.

**ANS: a**        **Pg: 203**
**LO: 1**        **Factual**

9. The context of interpersonal communication includes
1. mood
2. cultural background
3. physical place

a. 1 and 3 only
b. 2 only
c. 2 and 3 only
d. 1, 2, and 3

**ANS: d**        **Pg: 203**
**LO: 1**        **Factual**

*10.   Which of the following was NOT listed as a basic guideline for cell phone use in public?
a.   Put your cell phone on vibrate mode.
b.   Keep calls short.
c.   Use a catchy tune as a ring tone.
d.   Make and receive calls out of earshot from others.

**ANS: c**         **Pg: 203**
**LO: 2**          **Conceptual**

11.   Numerous studies have shown that good communication is most likely to be related to which of the following?
a.   satisfaction in relationships
b.   employee absenteeism
c.   reduced risk for cancer
d.   recovery from posttraumatic stress disorder

**ANS: a**         **Pg: 205**
**LO: 3**          **Conceptual**

12.   When you and your friend make faces at each other during a class lecture it is an example of
a.   miscommunication.
b.   verbal communication.
c.   nonverbal communication.
d.   encoded communication.

**ANS: c**         **Pg: 205**
**LO: 4**          **Factual**

13.   Nonverbal communication
a.   is frequently used to express feelings or emotions.
b.   is not influenced by culture.
c.   usually occurs in a single channel.
d.   is consistent with verbal messages.

**ANS: a**         **Pg: 206**
**LO: 4**          **Conceptual**

14.   Nonverbal communication is most informative when it is
a.   multichanneled.
b.   typical of the majority culture.
c.   occurring in a single channel only.
d.   accompanied by verbal messages.

**ANS: d**         **Pg: 206**
**LO: 4**          **Conceptual**

15. The study of people's use of interpersonal space is called
a. proxemics.
b. territoriality.
c. paralanguage.
d. distance analysis.

**ANS: a          Pg: 207**
**LO: 5          Factual**

16. The size of an individual's personal space is related to which of the following?
a. age
b. gender
c. cultural background
d. all of these

**ANS: d          Pgs: 206-207**
**LO: 5          Conceptual**

17. The anthropologist who described interpersonal distance zones was
a. Sidney Jourard.
b. Edward Hall.
c. Albert Mehrabian.
d. Daryl Bem.

**ANS: b          Pg: 207**
**LO: 5          Factual**

18. According to Edward Hall, people who interact at distances of 12 feet and beyond are considered to be in the _____ distance zone.
a. public
b. social
c. intimate
d. personal

**ANS: a          Pg: 207**
**LO: 5          Factual**

19. According to proxemics research, the personal-space zones of women appear to be _____ than those of men.
a. more fluid
b. more social
c. smaller
d. friendlier

**ANS: c          Pg: 207**
**LO: 5          Conceptual**

20.     _____ and his colleagues have identified six primary emotions that have distinctive facial expressions.
a.     Paul Ekman
b.     Eric Berne
c.     Edward Hall
d.     Erving Goffman

**ANS: a          Pg: 207**
**LO: 6          Factual**

21.     The "primary" emotions are designated as such because
a.     they are present from birth in nearly all mammalian species.
b.     they are the emotions that people feel most readily in a variety of situations.
c.     the facial expressions associated with them are recognized across world cultures.
d.     Freud designated these emotions as generated by the Id from birth.

**ANS: c          Pgs: 207-208**
**LO: 6          Factual**

22.     According to Paul Ekman and his colleagues, _____ is **not** associated with a specific facial expression
a.     fear
b.     surprise
c.     frustration
d.     happiness

**ANS: c          Pgs: 207-208**
**LO: 6          Conceptual**

23.     _____ are norms governing the appropriate display of emotions.
a.     Manners
b.     Proxemics
c.     Display rules
d.     Principles of facial display

**ANS: c          Pg: 208**
**LO: 6          Factual**

24.     We're better at sending deceptive messages with our _____ than with other body parts.
a.     faces
b.     mouths
c.     hands
d.     lower bodies

**ANS: a          Pg: 208**
**LO: 6          Conceptual**

25. Among the display rules for men in many world cultures is found
a. the use of the face to show anger.
b. the pressure to smile at others even when uncomfortable or frustrated.
c. the pressure to deceive others by use of eye contact.
d. the pressure to inhibit facial displays of emotion.

**ANS: d**          **Pg: 208**
**LO: 6**          **Conceptual**

26. Which of the following is considered the most meaningful aspect of eye contact?
a. size of pupillary opening
b. duration of eye contact
c. gender of the persons involved
d. relationship between the persons involved

**ANS: b**          **Pg: 208**
**LO: 7**          **Factual**

27. People who engage in high levels of eye contact are usually judged as more _____ than those who maintain less eye contact.
a. attentive
b. attractive
c. intelligent
d. trustworthy

**ANS: a**          **Pgs: 208-209**
**LO: 7**          **Conceptual**

28. Gender patterns in eye contact are most likely to be confounded by which of the following?
a. age
b. status
c. height
d. culture

**ANS: b**          **Pg: 209**
**LO: 7**          **Conceptual**

29. Which of the following is **poor** advice for avoiding "road rage"?
a. Don't use obscene gestures.
b. Signal before switching lanes.
c. Don't drive when you're angry or upset.
d. Try making eye contact with hostile motorists.

**ANS: d**          **Pg: 209**
**LO: 7**          **Conceptual**

30. Various confounding factors can lead to misinterpretation of eye contact between individuals. This may cause such nonverbal communication to become a form of _____ in interpersonal communication.
a. encoding
b. mutual gaze
c. noise
d. signal

**ANS: c**          **Pg: 209**
**LO: 7**           **Conceptual**

31. The study of communication through body movement is called
a. kinesics.
b. musculature.
c. paralanguage.
d. proxemics.

**ANS: a**          **Pg: 210**
**LO: 8**           **Factual**

32. Which of the following can most readily be determined about a person from the study of kinesics?
    1. attitude
    2. social status
    3. level of tension
    4. attraction patterns

a. 1 and 2 only
b. 1, 2, and 3 only
c. 2 and 4 only
d. 1, 2, 3, and 4

**ANS: b**          **Pg: 210**
**LO: 8**           **Conceptual**

33. Jamal is leaning back with open arms as he talks to the other members of his study group. He is most likely feeling _____ his peers.
a. anxious with
b. relaxed with
c. amused by
d. admired by

**ANS: b**          **Pg: 210**
**LO: 8**           **Conceptual**

34. In terms of postural cues, a forward lean is most likely to indicate which of the following?
a. low status
b. high status
c. interest
d. anxiety

**ANS: c**            **Pg: 210**
**LO: 8**            **Conceptual**

35. Which of the following statements about interpersonal touching is **not** true?
a. Touch can convey messages of status and power.
b. Women generally respond more favorably to touching than men do.
c. Touching is more frequent between male-male pairs than between female-female pairs.
d. As people age, men tend to touch women less, and women tend to touch men more.

**ANS: c**            **Pg: 210**
**LO: 8**            **Conceptual**

36. At the mall, Sara and Fred are talking intently and occasionally touch each other during the conversation. He is more prone to perceive the touching as signifying _____ while she will more likely view it as a sign of _____.
a. deception; friendship
b. friendship; discomfort
c. sexual interest; support
d. status difference; sexual interest

**ANS: c**            **Pg: 210**
**LO: 8**            **Conceptual**

37. _____ includes all vocal cues other than the content of the verbal message itself.
a. Kinesics
b. Proxemics
c. Sublanguage
d. Paralanguage

**ANS: d**            **Pgs: 210-211**
**LO: 9**            **Factual**

38. Which of the following is **not** considered an aspect of paralanguage?
a. loudness of speech
b. speed of talking
c. content of message
d. rhythm of speech

**ANS: c**            **Pgs: 210-211**
**LO: 9**            **Factual**

39. Loud vocalization is most likely to convey which of the following?
a. anger
b. anxiety
c. uncertainty
d. happiness

**ANS: a**      **Pg: 211**
**LO: 9**      **Conceptual**

40. Anna is speaking rapidly to Steve as she asks him out to lunch. Her paralanguage most likely conveys _____ in this situation.
a. frustration
b. anxiety
c. uncertainty
d. sadness

**ANS: b**      **Pg: 211**
**LO: 9**      **Conceptual**

41. Martin speaks slowly as he gives his answers in an oral examination for a master's degree in psychology. His paralanguage most likely conveys _____ in this situation.
a. anger
b. sadness
c. uncertainty
d. frustration

**ANS: c**      **Pg: 211**
**LO: 9**      **Conceptual**

42. Conventions for conveying emotion in email communication include
     1. use of "emoticons"
     2. use of capitalized letters to indicate emphasis
     3. interpretation of capitalized letters as shouting

a. 1 only
b. 1 and 2 only
c. 2 only
d. 1, 2, and 3

**ANS: d**      **Pg: 211**
**LO: 9**      **Factual**

43. Which of the following is **not** associated with lying?
a. higher pitch
b. pupil dilation
c. relatively short responses
d. excessive shifting of posture

**ANS: d**      **Pgs: 211-212**
**LO: 10**      **Conceptual**

44. Deception on the part of another person may be signaled by
a. pauses before speaking.
b. slowness in speech patterns.
c. giving short answers.
d. shifts in body posture.

**ANS: c**      **Pg: 212**
**LO: 10**      **Conceptual**

45. Which of the following is **not** monitored by a polygraph?
a. perspiration
b. heart rate
c. blood pressure
d. neural activity in the brain

**ANS: d**      **Pg: 212**
**LO: 11**      **Factual**

*46. Which of the following is the most accurate description of the polygraph machine?
a. emotion detector
b. facial expression detector
c. lie detector
d. criminal behavior detector

**ANS: a**      **Pg: 212**
**LO: 11**      **Conceptual**

47. Some problems that arise in interpreting the results of a polygraph test are related to the fact that
1. some people experience emotional arousal when telling the truth
2. some people can lie without experiencing emotional arousal
3. polygraph results are subject to a high degree of observer bias

a. 1 only
b. 1 and 2
c. 2 and 3 only
d. 1, 2, and 3

**ANS: b**      **Pg: 212**
**LO: 11**      **Factual**

48. Research suggests that people who have negative self-concepts tend to
a. ignore positive nonverbal messages and attend to negative verbal ones.
b. ignore negative verbal messages and attend to positive nonverbal ones.
c. ignore negative verbal messages and attend to positive verbal ones.
d. ignore negative nonverbal messages and attend to positive verbal ones.

**ANS: d**      **Pg: 213**
**LO: 12**      **Factual**

49.     Adopting another person's frame of reference so you can understand his or her point of
        view is called
a.      empathy.
b.      sympathy.
c.      attribution.
d.      self-disclosure.

**ANS: a            Pg: 214**
**LO: 13            Factual**

50.     Keisha's friends like to talk with her about their personal concerns because she seems to
        understand how they feel, and she never puts them down for their feelings. Keisha's
        behavior exemplifies which of the following?
a.      empathy
b.      sympathy
c.      attribution
d.      self-disclosure

**ANS: a            Pg: 214**
**LO: 13            Conceptual**

51.     Which of the following is **not** a good suggestion for creating a positive interpersonal
        climate?
a.      Strive for honesty.
b.      Practice withholding judgment.
c.      Learn to feel and communicate empathy.
d.      Express your opinions in a direct, non-tentative manner.

**ANS: d            Pg: 215**
**LO: 13            Conceptual**

52.     Which of the following communication behaviors does **not** tend to produce a positive
        interpersonal climate?
a.      empathizing with others
b.      treating others as equals
c.      expressing inflexible opinions
d.      expressing opinions tentatively

**ANS: c            Pg: 215**
**LO: 13            Factual**

53.     Expressing your opinions tentatively indicates that
a.      you really don't have firm opinions.
b.      you probably have a low level of self-esteem.
c.      your attitudes are flexible and subject to revision.
d.      you need to be more courageous in communicating.

**ANS: c            Pg: 215**
**LO: 13            Conceptual**

54. Which of the following types of opening lines is likely to be **least** effective in initiating a conversation with an other-gender stranger?
a. direct
b. cute/flippant
c. innocuous
d. complimentary

**ANS: b**       **Pg: 215**
**LO: 14**       **Conceptual**

\*55. Which of the following opening lines is likely to be **least** effective in initiating a conversation with an other-gender stranger?
a. "Is it okay if I sit next to you?"
b. "I'm Jake. I work at the Starbucks just down the street."
c. "If I said you had a beautiful body, would you hold it against me?"
d. "That's a cool tattoo. I'd like to get one, but can't decide what to get."

**ANS: c**       **Pg: 215**
**LO: 14**       **Conceptual**

56. Steps for making effective small talk include:
    1. talk about a subject in which you are especially interested
    2. introduce yourself
    3. comment on the surroundings
    4. keep the conversation ball rolling

a. 1 and 3 only
b. 1, 3, and 4 only
c. 2, 3, and 4 only
d. 1, 2, 3, and 4

**ANS: d**       **Pg: 215**
**LO: 14**       **Conceptual**

57. The voluntary act of verbally communicating your personal information to another person is called
a. empathy.
b. clarification.
c. self-disclosure.
d. self-actualization.

**ANS: c**       **Pg: 215**
**LO: 15**       **Factual**

58.    Rather than high self-disclosure, the critical factor that helps couples avoid stress may be
a.    equity in self-disclosure.
b.    honesty in self-disclosure.
c.    the duration of self-disclosure.
d.    the disattribution of self-disclosure.

**ANS: a**          **Pgs: 215-216**
**LO: 15**          **Factual**

59.    Which of the following would be considered the best strategy for reducing the risks of
       engaging in self-disclosure?
a.    You should discuss a variety of superficial topics.
b.    You should move gradually when using self-disclosure.
c.    You should emphasize the number of personal problems you have.
d.    You should avoid revealing truthful information until you know you can trust the other
person.

**ANS: b**          **Pg: 216**
**LO: 15**          **Conceptual**

60.    Which of the following types of self-disclosure is most likely to lead to feelings of
       intimacy between individuals?
a.    factual
b.    conceptual
c.    emotional
d.    attributional

**ANS: c**          **Pg: 216**
**LO: 15**          **Conceptual**

61.    Self-disclosure can aid adjustment by
a.    improving one's self-esteem.
b.    enhancing one's sexual attractiveness.
c.    reducing one's stress.
d.    controlling one's anxiety.

**ANS: c**          **Pgs: 216-217**
**LO: 15**          **Conceptual**

62.    Once relationships are well established, self-disclosure tends to
a.    taper off.
b.    become more reciprocal.
c.    increase in breadth, but not depth.
d.    increase in depth, but not breadth.

**ANS: a**          **Pg: 217**
**LO: 16**          **Conceptual**

63. Which of the following statements about self-disclosure is **not** true?
a. Japanese men tend to disclose more than American men.
b. In the United States, females tend to self-disclose more than males.
c. Females disclose more about positive emotions, and men disclose more about negative emotions.
d. Women disclose more personal information, and men disclose more non-personal information.

**ANS: c**      **Pg: 217**
**LO: 17**      **Factual**

64. In the beginning stages of a relationship with a person of the opposite sex,
a. women typically disclose more than men.
b. men often disclose more than women.
c. there is very little reciprocal self-disclosure.
d. men tend to disclose more about negative emotions.

**ANS: b**      **Pg: 217**
**LO: 17**      **Factual**

65. Which of the following is **not** likely to promote effective listening?
a. paraphrasing the speaker's message
b. asking the other person for clarification
c. attending to the other person's nonverbal signals
d. assuming a body posture with arms and legs crossed

**ANS: d**      **Pg: 218**
**LO: 18**      **Conceptual**

66. Active listening consists of
    1. paying careful attention to what is being said
    2. asking for clarifications
    3. mindful processing of what is said

a. 1 only
b. 1 and 2 only
c. 2 and 3 only
d. 1, 2, and 3

**ANS: d**      **Pg: 218**
**LO: 18**      **Factual**

67. Anxiety caused by having to talk with others is called communication
a. aversion.
b. disruption.
c. avoidance.
d. apprehension.

**ANS: d**      **Pg: 219**
**LO: 19**      **Factual**

68. Which of the following responses to communication apprehension is the most common?
a. excessive communication
b. communication avoidance
c. communication disruption
d. communication withdrawal

**ANS: b**        **Pg: 219**
**LO: 19**        **Conceptual**

69. Which of the following is **not** considered a possible response to communication apprehension?
a. excessive communication
b. communication avoidance
c. communication disruption
d. communication attribution

**ANS: d**        **Pg: 220**
**LO: 19**        **Conceptual**

70. The root of communication apprehension is thought to be
a. the context in which the communication is to take place.
b. the strength of one's physiological reactions to communication.
c. the interpretation of one's own physiological reactions.
d. the audience to whom one is going to communicate.

**ANS: c**        **Pg: 220**
**LO: 19**        **Conceptual**

71. Researchers suggest that avoidance and withdrawal tactics are effective strategies for coping with communication apprehension, but only
a. in the short-term.
b. in intimate relationships.
c. when used consistently.
d. when used in same-gender relationships.

**ANS: a**        **Pg: 220**
**LO: 19**        **Conceptual**

72. Effective strategies for managing communication apprehension include:
1. use of anti-anxiety medications
2. cognitive restructuring techniques
3. systematic desensitization

a. 1 only
b. 1 and 3 only
c. 2 and 3 only
d. 1, 2, and 3

**ANS: c**        **Pg: 220**
**LO: 19**        **Conceptual**

73.    Which of the following is **not** considered one of the common barriers to effective communication?
a.    defensiveness
b.    game playing
c.    cognitive restructuring
d.    motivational distortion

**ANS: c**          **Pgs: 220-221**
**LO: 20**          **Conceptual**

74.    Engaging in selective attention is an example of which of the following barriers to effective communication?
a.    collusion
b.    game playing
c.    defensiveness
d.    motivational distortion

**ANS: d**          **Pg: 220**
**LO: 20**          **Conceptual**

75.    Thomas likes to talk about himself a great deal. It is often quite hard to move the topic of conversation away from his interests, achievements, and activities. The barrier to effective communication with Tom is
a.    working self-concept.
b.    self-defensiveness.
c.    self-preoccupation.
d.    motivational distortion.

**ANS: c**          **Pgs: 220-221**
**LO: 20**          **Conceptual**

76.    Eric Berne defines _____ as manipulative interactions with predictable outcomes, in which people conceal their real motivations.
a.    games
b.    communications
c.    self-preoccupations
d.    interpersonal conflicts

**ANS: a**          **Pg: 221**
**LO: 20**          **Factual**

*77.    Which of the following topics is LEAST likely to produce motivational distortion?
a.    gardening
b.    politics
c.    religion
d.    sexuality

**ANS: a**          **Pg: 220**
**LO: 20**          **Conceptual**

78.        _____ exists whenever two or more people disagree.
a.    Communication distortion
b.    Interpersonal conflict
c.    Game playing
d.    Collusion

**ANS: b**              **Pg: 221**
**LO: 21**              **Factual**

79.    Interpersonal conflict
a.    is inherently a good thing.
b.    is inherently bad for relationships.
c.    should be suppressed if at all possible.
d.    can lead to a variety of good outcomes.

**ANS: d**              **Pg: 224**
**LO: 21**              **Conceptual**

80.    Individualistic cultures tend to _____ as a conflict management strategy.
a.    promote conflict avoidance
b.    encourage direct confrontations
c.    encourage indirect confrontations
d.    downplay the importance of conflicts

**ANS: b**              **Pg: 225**
**LO: 21**              **Conceptual**

81.    Which of the following is the best advice for minimizing value-based conflicts?
a.    Change the conflict to one focused on content.
b.    Bring your values in line with those of the other person.
c.    Match up with a person who has similar values as yours.
d.    Recognize that value-based conflict is actually false conflict.

**ANS: c**              **Pg: 222**
**LO: 21**              **Conceptual**

82.    Which of the following types of conflict is the most difficult to manage?
a.    pseudoconflict
b.    ego conflict
c.    value conflict
d.    fact conflict

**ANS: b**              **Pgs: 222-223**
**LO: 21**              **Factual**

83.     Bernie and Lisa cannot agree about the date of the final exam in their psychology course. This is an example of a
a.      pseudoconflict.
b.      policy conflict.
c.      value-based conflict.
d.      fact-based conflict.

**ANS: b**              **Pg: 222**
**LO: 21**              **Factual**

*84.    Game playing is one type of
a.      values conflict.
b.      policy conflict.
c.      pseudoconflict.
d.      ego conflict.

**ANS: c**              **Pg: 222**
**LO: 21**              **Factual**

85.     Which of the following styles of managing conflict is characterized by low concern for self and others?
a.      avoidance
b.      competition
c.      compromise
d.      accommodation

**ANS: a**              **Pg: 223**
**LO: 22**              **Conceptual**

86.     Lauren hates it when Eric leaves the cap off the toothpaste, but she's never told him this, because she doesn't want to "make a scene."  Besides, she hopes he'll get better on his own.  Lauren's behavior exemplifies which of the following styles of managing conflict?
a.      competition
b.      compromise
c.      avoidance
d.      collaboration

**ANS: c**              **Pg: 223**
**LO: 22**              **Conceptual**

87.     In which style of dealing with conflict does a person readily give in?
a.      avoidance
b.      compromise
c.      collaboration
d.      accommodation

**ANS: d**              **Pg: 223**
**LO: 22**              **Conceptual**

88. Carmen hates it when Manuel leaves the cap off the toothpaste. She confronted him with her feelings about it, but when he argued that it was a trivial matter, she gave in quickly, not wanting Manuel to be angry with her. Carmen's behavior exemplifies which of the following styles of managing conflict?
a. compromise
b. competition
c. avoidance
d. accommodation

**ANS: d**         **Pg: 223**
**LO: 22**         **Conceptual**

89. Which style of managing conflict tends to become a black-and-white, win-or-lose confrontation?
a. avoidance
b. accommodation
c. competition
d. compromise

**ANS: c**         **Pgs: 223-224**
**LO: 22**         **Conceptual**

90. When disagreements arise over chores and other household obligations, Jane and her two roommates hold an evening meeting to discuss fair ways to manage the issue. These students are exhibiting a _____ strategy for handling conflicts.
a. collusive
b. competitive
c. defensive
d. collaborative

**ANS: d**         **Pg: 224**
**LO: 22**         **Conceptual**

91. Which of the following styles of managing conflict involves a sincere effort to maximize the satisfaction of both parties?
a. accommodation
b. competition
c. compromise
d. collaboration

**ANS: d**         **Pg: 224**
**LO: 22**         **Conceptual**

92. You're the boss. You have a relatively minor conflict with a subordinate. An effective way to manage this situation is to
a. try to set this difference aside.
b. use your power to help settle the conflict.
c. give the other person credit for his or her status.
d. demonstrate that other subordinates are in agreement with you.

**ANS: a**          **Pg: 224**
**LO: 23**         **Conceptual**

93. In order to deal constructively with an interpersonal conflict, one should
a. monitor one's use of manipulation.
b. limit complaints to the present situation.
c. assume some responsibility for the other person's feelings.
d. use general statements about the other person's personality.

**ANS: b**          **Pg: 224**
**LO: 23**         **Conceptual**

94. Which of the following is **not** good advice for promoting constructive conflict resolution?
a. Make communication honest and open.
b. Limit complaints to the present situation.
c. Assume responsibility for your own feelings and preferences.
d. Use general statements about the other person's personality.

**ANS: d**          **Pg: 224**
**LO: 23**         **Conceptual**

95. Which of the following researchers is known for describing America as "the argument culture"?
a. Paul Ekman
b. Deborah Tannen
c. James McCroskey
d. Roy Baumeister

**ANS: b**          **Pg: 225**
**LO: 24**         **Factual**

*96. Which of the following is NOT one of the factors contributing to social contentiousness in the United States?
a. a nondualistic view of nature
b. the decline of face-to-face interactions
c. an individualistic culture
d. excessive exposure to aggressive acts

**ANS: a**          **Pg: 225**
**LO: 25**         **Factual**

97. Strategies for restoring productive public communication include:
   1. paying attention to nonverbal signals
   2. practicing conflict management skills
   3. confronting others whenever conflict arises

a. 1 only
b. 1 and 2 only
c. 3 only
d. 1, 2, and 3

**ANS: b**          **Pgs: 226-227**
**LO: 26**          **Conceptual**

*98. Which of the following is an accurate statement reflecting cultural attitudes toward assertiveness?
a. Israelis distain assertiveness.
b. Some Native American tribes have a confrontational interactional style whereby vigorous debate is expected.
c. Collectivist societies place a higher value on interpersonal harmony than assertiveness.
d. All of these are true.

**ANS: c**          **Pgs: 227-228**
**LO: 27**          **Factual**

99. _____ is acting in your own best interests by expressing your thoughts and feelings directly and honestly.
a. Aggression
b. Assertiveness
c. Attribution
d. Egocentrism

**ANS: b**          **Pg: 227**
**LO: 27**          **Factual**

*100. Which of the following is FALSE regarding interpersonal communication?
a. Aggressive people tend to ignore the rights of others.
b. Assertive people sacrifice their own rights.
c. Assertiveness varies from situation to situation, that is, one may be assertive in one situation and timid in another.
d. It is wise to use role playing to practice assertive behavior.

**ANS: b**          **Pgs: 227-228**
**LO: 28**          **Factual**

# MULTIPLE CHOICE QUESTIONS FROM STUDY GUIDE

1.     In nonverbal communication, meaning is transmitted from one person to another
a.    using coded words that have private meanings.
b.    with the aid of computers or other devices.
c.    without anyone else being aware of it.
d.    through means or symbols other than words.

**ANS: d**         **Pgs: 205-206**
**LO: 4**         **Factual**

2.     Which of the following statements regarding nonverbal communication is **not** true?
a.    Nonverbal communication is multi-channeled.
b.    Nonverbal messages may contradict verbal messages.
c.    Nonverbal communication frequently conveys emotions.
d.    Nonverbal messages tend to be clearer than spoken words.

**ANS: d**         **Pg: 206**
**LO: 4**         **Conceptual**

3.     Norms that govern the appropriate display of emotions are called
a.    proxemics.
b.    display rules.
c.    nonverbal indicators.
d.    attribution features.

**ANS: b**         **Pg: 208**
**LO: 6**         **Factual**

4.     Which of the following aspects of eye contact is generally considered the most meaningful?
a.    its duration
b.    its intensity
c.    the gender of the initiator
d.    the accompanying body language

**ANS: a**         **Pgs: 208-209**
**LO: 7**         **Factual**

5.     Men are most likely to view touch as a way to
a.    show support.
b.    signify affection.
c.    assert power.
d.    express hostility.

**ANS: c**         **Pg: 210**
**LO: 8**         **Factual**

6. As an indicator of lying, lack of eye contact is
a. a fairly reliable signal.
b. not a reliable signal.
c. the best available signal.
d. a more reliable signal when one is dealing with people of lower status.

**ANS: b**       **Pgs: 211-212**
**LO: 10**       **Conceptual**

7. Which of the following is NOT monitored by a polygraph?
a. heart rate
b. brain waves
c. perspiration
d. blood pressure

**ANS: b**       **Pg: 212**
**LO: 11**       **Factual**

8. Adopting another's frame of reference to understand his or her point of view is called
a. empathy.
b. intimacy.
c. withholding judgment.
d. positive paralanguage.

**ANS: a**       **Pg: 214**
**LO: 13**       **Factual**

9. Research findings show that self-disclosure in romantic relationships
a. is positively correlated with relationship satisfaction.
b. is an indication that there may be communication problems.
c. appears to be unrelated to how partners actually feel about each other.
d. may actually be detrimental to the development of feelings of empathy.

**ANS: a**       **Pg: 216**
**LO: 16 Factual**

10. Research findings on gender and self-disclosure indicate that
a. females consistently disclose more than males.
b. when dealing with strangers, men may be more prone to self-disclosure than women.
c. men generally disclose more personal information and feelings than women do.
d. the gender disparity in self-disclosure is consistent across cultures.

**ANS: b**       **Pg: 217**
**LO: 17**       **Factual**

11. Which of the following is the most common response to communication apprehension?
a. communication avoidance
b. communication withdrawal
c. communication disruption
d. excessive communication

**ANS: a**      **Pg: 219**
**LO: 19**      **Factual**

12. Perhaps the most basic barrier to effective communication is
a. game playing.
b. defensiveness.
c. self-preoccupation.
d. attribution distortion.

**ANS: b**      **Pg: 220**
**LO: 20**      **Conceptual**

13. Which of the following is **not** one of the positive outcomes associated with constructive confrontation?
a. It may lead to new insights.
b. It helps bring problems out into the open.
c. It decreases the likelihood of future conflict.
d. It may put an end to chronic sources of discontent.

**ANS: c**      **Pg: 224**
**LO: 21**      **Conceptual**

14. A pseudoconflict is a
a. situation in which the conflict is invented or created by one of the involved parties.
b. conflict based on trivial differences in beliefs or values.
c. conflict in which people disagree about issues of a factual nature.
d. conflict in which one of the people is an authority figure.

**ANS: a**      **Pg: 222**
**LO: 22**      **Factual**

15. Which of the following is **not** good advice for dealing constructively with conflict?
a. Avoid "loaded" words.
b. Focus complaints on past behavior.
c. Assume responsibility for your own feelings.
d. Make communication open and honest.

**ANS: b**      **Pg: 224**
**LO: 23**      **Conceptual**

# MULTIPLE CHOICE QUESTIONS ON WEB SITE

1.  In interpersonal communication, speaker is to encode as receiver is to
a.  noise.
b.  decode.
c.  verbalize.
d.  detect.

**ANS: b**        **Pg: 202**
**LO: 1**        **Factual**

2.  When you and your friend make faces at each other during a class lecture it is an example of
a.  miscommunication.
b.  verbal communication.
c.  nonverbal communication.
d.  encoded communication.

**ANS: c**        **Pg: 205**
**LO: 4**        **Factual**

3.  According to Edward Hall, people who interact at distances of 12 feet and beyond are considered to be in the _____ distance zone.
a.  public
b.  social
c.  intimate
d.  personal

**ANS: a**        **Pg: 207**
**LO: 5**        **Factual**

4.  The "primary" emotions are designated as such because
a.  they are present from birth in nearly all mammalian species.
b.  they are the emotions that people feel most readily in a variety of situations.
c.  the facial expressions associated with them are recognized across world cultures.
d.  Freud designated these emotions as generated by the Id from birth.

**ANS: c**        **Pgs: 207-208**
**LO: 6**        **Factual**

5.  Gender patterns in eye contact are most likely to be confounded by which of the following?
a.  age
b.  status
c.  height
d.  culture

**ANS: b**        **Pg: 209**
**LO: 7**        **Conceptual**

6.      The study of communication through body movement is called
a.      kinesics.
b.      musculature.
c.      paralanguage.
d.      proxemics.

**ANS: a**            **Pg: 210**
**LO: 8**             **Factual**

7.      Anna is speaking rapidly to Steve as she asks him out to lunch. Her paralanguage most
        likely conveys _____ in this situation.
a.      frustration
b.      anxiety
c.      uncertainty
d.      sadness

**ANS: b**            **Pg: 211**
**LO: 9**             **Conceptual**

*8.     Which of the following is the most accurate description of the polygraph machine?
a.      emotion detector
b.      facial expression detector
c.      lie detector
d.      criminal bchavior detector

**ANS: a**            **Pg: 212**
**LO: 11**            **Conceptual**

9.      The voluntary act of verbally communicating your personal information to another
        person is called
a.      empathy.
b.      clarification.
c.      self-disclosure.
d.      self-actualization.

**ANS: c**            **Pg: 215**
**LO: 15**            **Factual**

10.     Which of the following responses to communication apprehension is the most common?
a.      excessive communication
b.      communication avoidance
c.      communication disruption
d.      communication withdrawal

**ANS: b**            **Pg: 219**
**LO: 19**            **Conceptual**

11. Which of the following types of conflict is the most difficult to manage?
a. pseudoconflict
b. ego conflict
c. value conflict
d. fact conflict

**ANS: b**        **Pgs: 222-223**
**LO: 21**        **Factual**

12. Lauren hates it when Eric leaves the cap off the toothpaste, but she's never told him this, because she doesn't want to "make a scene." Besides, she hopes he'll get better on his own. Lauren's behavior exemplifies which of the following styles of managing conflict?
a. competition
b. compromise
c. avoidance
d. collaboration

**ANS: c**        **Pg: 223**
**LO: 22**        **Conceptual**

13. Which style of managing conflict tends to become a black-and-white, win-or-lose confrontation?
a. avoidance
b. accommodation
c. competition
d. compromise

**ANS: c**        **Pgs: 223-224**
**LO: 22**        **Conceptual**

14. You're the boss. You have a relatively minor conflict with a subordinate. An effective way to manage this situation is to
a. try to set this difference aside.
b. use your power to help settle the conflict.
c. give the other person credit for his or her status.
d. demonstrate that other subordinates are in agreement with you.

**ANS: a**        **Pg: 224**
**LO: 23**        **Conceptual**

*15. Which of the following is an accurate statement reflecting cultural attitudes toward assertiveness?
a. Israelis distain assertiveness.
b. Some Native American tribes have a confrontational interactional style whereby vigorous debate is expected.
c. Collectivist societies place a higher value on interpersonal harmony than assertiveness.
d. All of these are true.

**ANS: c**        **Pgs: 227-228**
**LO: 27**        **Factual**

## TRUE/FALSE QUESTIONS

1.  People of similar status tend to stand closer together than people of unequal status.

**ANS: true**          **Pgs: 206-207**
**LO: 5**              **Factual**

2.  Low self-monitors are better than high self-monitors at managing facial expressions.

**ANS: false**         **Pg: 208**
**LO: 6**              **Conceptual**

3.  Even when women are in high-power positions they show the visual pattern of eye contact of lower-status people.

**ANS: false**         **Pg: 209**
**LO: 7**              **Conceptual**

4.  Using all capital letters in an e-mail is generally considered rude.

**ANS: true**          **Pg: 211**
**LO: 9**              **Factual**

5.  The polygraph experts' claim that lie detector tests are 85-90% accurate is clearly supported by empirical evidence.

**ANS: false**         **Pg: 212**
**LO: 11**             **Factual**

6.  One reason listeners sometimes become bored with speakers is that listeners process speech much more rapidly than people speak.

**ANS: true**          **Pg: 218**
**LO: 18**             **Conceptual**

7.  Sometimes avoidance IS the best way to handle a conflict.

**ANS: true**          **Pg: 221**
**LO: 21**             **Conceptual**

8.  Exposure to television violence is positively correlated with viewing the world as a dangerous place.

**ANS: true**          **Pgs: 226-227**
**LO: 25**             **Conceptual**

9.  It is a good idea for parents who watch violent television programming with their kids to say nothing about the aggressive content.

**ANS: false**         **Pgs: 226-227**
**LO: 26**             **Conceptual**

10. Telling a store clerk that he overcharged you for an item is an example of aggressive behavior.

**ANS: false**     **Pg: 227**
**LO: 27**     **Conceptual**


## SHORT-ANSWER ESSAY QUESTIONS

1. Briefly explain why nonverbal communication is generally more ambiguous than verbal communication.

**Pg: 206**
**LO: 4**

2. Distinguish between the positive and negative messages associated with high levels of eye contact.

**Pgs: 208-209**
**LO: 7**

3. Discuss some of the cultural influences on patterns of eye contact.

**Pg: 209**
**LO: 7**

4. Summarize the research on gender differences in touching as a form of communication.

**Pg: 210**
**LO: 8**

5. Briefly describe some of the nonverbal cues that are associated with actual deception.

**Pgs: 211-212**
**LO: 10**

6. Briefly explain the role of nonverbal communication in being an effective listener.

**Pg: 214**
**LO: 18**

7. Briefly describe several positive outcomes that may occur as a result of interpersonal conflict.

**Pg: 224**
**LO: 23**

8.     Briefly explain why collaboration is a preferred strategy for managing interpersonal conflict.

**Pg: 224**
**LO: 22**

9.     Briefly explain how our individualistic culture plays a role in Americans' tendency to be adversarial.

**Pgs: 225-226**
**LO: 25**

10.     Briefly describe the techniques for fostering assertiveness in everyday communication.

**Pgs: 228-230**
**LO: 28**

# Chapter 8
# FRIENDSHIP AND LOVE

## LEARNING OBJECTIVES

1. Define close relationships and give some examples.
2. Describe how members from individualistic cultures and collectivist cultures view love and marriage.
3. Describe the differences between Internet and face-to-face interactions and how the Internet affects relationship development.
4. Discuss the roles of proximity and familiarity in initial attraction.
5. Summarize the findings on physical attractiveness in initial attraction.
6. Discuss the role of reciprocal liking and similarity in getting acquainted.
7. Describe the personality qualities that people like in others.
8. Give some commonly used relationship maintenance strategies and explain what is meant by "minding" relationships.
9. Define the elements of interdependence theory and explain how rewards, costs, and investments influence relationship satisfaction and commitment.
10. Summarize the research on what makes a good friend.
11. Describe some key gender differences in friendships.
12. Summarize the research findings on the experience of love in gay and straight couples.
13. Discuss some gender differences regarding love.
14. Define passion, intimacy, and commitment, and describe Sternberg's eight types of love.
15. Discuss adult attachment styles, including their correlates and stability.
16. Discuss the course of romantic love over time.
17. Explain why relationships fail and what couples can do to help relationships last.
18. Describe various types of loneliness.
19. Discuss the prevalence of loneliness.
20. Explain how early experiences and current social trends contribute to loneliness.
21. Describe how shyness, poor social skills, and self-defeating attributions contribute to loneliness.
22. Summarize the suggestions for conquering loneliness.

# MULTIPLE CHOICE QUESTIONS

1.    Which of the following is **not** necessarily true about close relationships?
a.    They are important.
b.    They are long lasting.
c.    They are interdependent.
d.    They are emotionally intimate.

**ANS: d**          **Pg: 236**
**LO: 1**           **Conceptual**

2.    A majority of college students identified which of the following as the person to whom they felt the closest?
a.    friend
b.    co-worker
c.    family member
d.    romantic partner

**ANS: d**          **Pg: 236**
**LO: 1**           **Factual**

3.    The notion that love is a prerequisite for marriage
a.    is a uniquely American tradition.
b.    is a universal cultural phenomenon.
c.    is a product of 18th century Western culture.
d.    can be traced to Asian cultures of over 3000 years ago.

**ANS: c**          **Pg: 236**
**LO: 2**           **Factual**

4.    Which of the following is probably **not** a true difference between arranged marriages and marriages based on romantic love?
a.    Romantic love is valued in individualistic cultures.
b.    Marriages based on love are happier than those that are arranged.
c.    Love as a basis for marriage when placed in a historical context, is a relatively recent idea.
d.    None of these statements is a true difference.

**ANS: b**          **Pgs: 236-237**
**LO: 2**           **Conceptual**

*5.    Cultural views of love and marriage are linked to a culture's values and its
a.    mortality rates.
b.    economic health.
c.    population.
d.    divorce rates.

**ANS: b**          **Pgs: 236-237**
**LO: 2**           **Conceptual**

6.	The great popularity of the Internet as an arena for socializing
a.	has caused psychologists to re-evaluate the importance of proximity and attractiveness in relationship development.
b.	is interpreted by psychologists as one more sign of social isolation and alienation.
c.	has caused researchers to suspect that self-disclosure is less important in relationship development than previously believed.
d.	has been predicted to decline as this decade progresses.

**ANS: a**		**Pgs: 237-238**
**LO: 3**		**Factual**

7.	One factor that may contribute to the success of online relationships is
a.	the "absence makes the heart grow fonder" effect.
b.	that similarity of interests and values may play a greater role than initial attraction.
c.	the excitement of the idea of forming a "dangerous liaison" with a stranger.
d.	that the lack of emphasis on self-disclosure has a protective effect in online relationships.

**ANS: b**		**Pgs: 237-238**
**LO: 3**		**Conceptual**

8.	Factors influencing the nature of initial encounters between two people include which of the following?
	1.	proximity
	2.	familiarity
	3.	resource exchange
	4.	physical attractiveness

a.	1 only
b.	1 and 4 only
c.	1, 2, and 4 only
d.	1, 2, 3, and 4

**ANS: c**		**Pg: 239**
**LO: 4**		**Conceptual**

9.	_____ refers to geographic, residential, and other forms of spatial closeness.
a.	Proximity
b.	Familiarity
c.	Similarity
d.	Personal space

**ANS: a**		**Pg: 239**
**LO: 4**		**Factual**

10.     The mere exposure effect is most closely associated with which of the following factors in initial attraction?
a.     proximity
b.     familiarity
c.     similarity
d.     personal space

**ANS: b**          **Pg: 240**
**LO: 4**           **Conceptual**

11.     If your initial reaction to a person is negative,
a.     mere exposure will help you to gradually overcome that impression.
b.     mere exposure will help you to rapidly overcome that impression.
c.     mere exposure will most likely increase the intensity of that impression.
d.     mere exposure will lead gradually to a tolerant indifference to that person.

**ANS: c**          **Pg: 240**
**LO: 4**           **Conceptual**

12.     Physical attractiveness
        1.     is a key factor in dating
        2.     influences our choice of friends
        3.     influences the dating choices of men and women in roughly the same degree

a.     1 only
b.     1 and 2 only
c.     1 and 3 only
d.     1, 2, and 3

**ANS: d**          **Pg: 240**
**LO: 5**           **Conceptual**

13.     Which of the following statements about physical attractiveness is **not** true?
a.     Attractiveness is an important factor in dating.
b.     Males in particular reportedly prefer attractiveness in their same- and other-gender friends.
c.     When it comes to their behavior, women are as influenced by physical attractiveness as men.
d.     Homosexuals place more importance on the physical attractiveness of their dating partners than do heterosexuals.

**ANS: d**          **Pg: 240**
**LO: 5**           **Conceptual**

14. One should be cautious in interpreting the results of surveys on the importance of physical attractiveness in romantic relationships because
a. the research results are several decades old and therefore may not be relevant to current relationship concerns.
b. people's verbal reports often do not match their true attitudes and behaviors.
c. the definition of physical attractiveness varies significantly from person to person.
d. studies of attractiveness are concerned only with the role of physique in attraction.

**ANS: b**       **Pg: 240**
**LO: 5**       **Conceptual**

15. Which of the following physical characteristics of males is **least** likely to be seen as physically attractive?
a. slim waists
b. thick legs
c. small buttocks
d. broad shoulders

**ANS: b**       **Pgs: 240-241**
**LO: 5**       **Factual**

16. In a cross-cultural study of characteristics commonly sought in a mate, David Buss found all of the following **except**:
a. Intelligence was rated equally by males and females.
b. Females rated good earning capacity higher than males did.
c. Males ranked physical attractiveness higher than females did.
d. Both males and females rated physical attractiveness higher than kindness and understanding.

**ANS: d**       **Pg: 241**
**LO: 5**       **Factual**

17. Which of the following facial features is **not** associated with physical attractiveness in women?
a. large eyes
b. small nose
c. narrow smile
d. prominent cheekbones

**ANS: c**       **Pgs: 240-241**
**LO: 5**       **Factual**

18. Across ethnic groups, nationalities, and genders there is general agreement
a. that attractive facial features are important.
b. that body build is not so important.
c. that there is an overemphasis on thinness for women.
d. that looks really don't count for much in the early phase of a relationship.

**ANS: a**       **Pgs: 240-241**
**LO: 5**       **Factual**

19.    Which of the following facial features is most likely to be seen as attractive in men?
a.    large eyes
b.    broad jaw
c.    small nose
d.    prominent cheekbones

**ANS: b**         **Pg: 241**
**LO: 5**          **Factual**

20.    The matching hypothesis suggests that people of similar _____ gravitate toward each other.
a.    intellectual ability
b.    personal warmth
c.    physical attractiveness
d.    academic accomplishment

**ANS: c**         **Pg: 242**
**LO: 5**          **Factual**

21.    The fact that dating and married couples tend to be similar to each other in physical attractiveness supports
a.    social exchange theory.
b.    the matching hypothesis.
c.    the reciprocity principle.
d.    cognitive dissonance theory.

**ANS: b**         **Pg: 242**
**LO: 5**          **Conceptual**

22.    The matching hypothesis appears to apply to all of the following **except**
a.    male-male friendships.
b.    female-female friendships.
c.    dating heterosexual couples.
d.    married heterosexual couples.

**ANS: b**         **Pg: 242**
**LO: 5**          **Conceptual**

23.    The finding that women rate "good financial prospects" in a potential mate as more important than men do is explained by evolutionary psychologists in terms of gender differences in inherited
a.    intelligence.
b.    resource potential.
c.    strength differences.
d.    reproductive strategies.

**ANS: d**         **Pgs: 242-243**
**LO: 5**          **Conceptual**

24. According to evolutionary psychologists, men seeking a prospective mate are likely to display the most interest in characteristics that denote a woman's
a. intelligence.
b. financial prospects.
c. reproductive capacity.
d. capacity for resource acquisition.

**ANS: c**        **Pg: 242-243**
**LO: 5**        **Factual**

25. According to evolutionary psychologists, women seeking a prospective mate are likely to display the most interest in characteristics that denote a man's
a. intelligence.
b. financial prospects.
c. reproductive capacity.
d. capacity for resource acquisition.

**ANS: d**        **Pgs: 242-243**
**LO: 5**        **Factual**

26. Evolutionary explanations for dating and mating habits include
    1. resource exchange theory
    2. the matching hypothesis
    3. parental investment theory

a. 1 only
b. 1 and 3 only
c. 2 and 3 only
d. 1, 2, and 3

**ANS: b**        **Pgs: 242-243**
**LO: 5**        **Factual**

*27. Heterosexual women's preferences for a physically attractive man
a. are not influenced by her economic power.
b. appear to increase along with her economic power.
c. appear to decrease along with her career opportunities.
d. are determined by biological factors.

**ANS: b**        **Pg: 222**
**LO: 5**        **Conceptual**

28. Which of the following refers to the fact that we tend to like others who like us?
a. proximity
b. reciprocity
c. matching hypothesis
d. social exchange theory

**ANS: b**        **Pg: 244**
**LO: 6**        **Factual**

29.     Researchers have suggested that the _____ can be used to explain the notion of reciprocal liking.
a.      matching hypothesis
b.      self-fulfilling prophecy
c.      fundamental attribution error
d.      theory of cognitive dissonance

**ANS: b**                    **Pg: 244**
**LO: 6**                     **Conceptual**

*30.    Which of the following adages has the most empirical support?
a.      "Birds of a feather flock together."
b.      "Opposites attract."
c.      "Similarity breeds contempt."
d.      All of these have equally high support.

**ANS: a**                    **Pgs: 244-245**
**LO: 7**                     **Conceptual**

31.     Which of the following sets of characteristics is most likely to enhance one's desirability as a potential date?
a.      exciting, easygoing, friendly
b.      rebellious, exciting, unstable
c.      emotionally stable, sensitive, shy
d.      understanding, shy, down-to-earth

**ANS: a**                    **Pg: 245**
**LO: 7**                     **Conceptual**

32.     In married couples, the relationship between personality similarity and marital happiness is
a.      negative.
b.      positive.
c.      inconsistent.
d.      confounded by physical attractiveness.

**ANS: b**                    **Pgs: 244-245**
**LO: 7**                     **Conceptual**

33.     The "similarity principle" tends to be found most frequently in
a.      heterosexual couples.
b.      homosexual couples.
c.      friendships.
d.      all of these.

**ANS: d**                    **Pgs: 244-245**
**LO: 7**                     **Conceptual**

34.  Heterosexual couples tend to be similar in
    1.   intelligence
    2.   physical attractiveness
    3.   socioeconomic status

a.   1 only
b.   1 and 3 only
c.   2 and 3 only
d.   1, 2, and 3

**ANS: d**          **Pg: 245**
**LO: 7**            **Conceptual**

35.  _____ involves the actions one takes to sustain the desirable qualities of a relationship.
a.   Social exchange
b.   Relationship maintenance
c.   Reciprocity
d.   Attribution

**ANS: b**          **Pg: 246**
**LO: 8**            **Factual**

36.  _____ is an active relationship maintenance process that includes knowledge of the partner's opinions and making positive attributions regarding the partner's behaviors.
a.   Reciprocity
b.   Fundamental attribution error
c.   Social exchange
d.   Minding

**ANS: d**          **Pg: 246**
**LO: 8**            **Factual**

37.  The idea that interpersonal relationships are governed by perceptions of rewards and costs is a key premise in
a.   social exchange theory.
b.   the matching hypothesis.
c.   social comparison theory.
d.   the theory of cognitive dissonance.

**ANS: a**          **Pg: 247**
**LO: 9**            **Factual**

38.     Kelly thinks she works hard to make sure that her relationship with her boyfriend
        Michael is fulfilling and fun.  However, lately she has begun to think that Michael doesn't
        appreciate her efforts.  According to _____, this relationship might not last.
a.      social learning theory
b.      social exchange theory
c.      the matching hypothesis
d.      the notion of reciprocal liking

**ANS: b**          **Pg: 247**
**LO: 9**           **Conceptual**


39.     In social exchange theory, the _____ refers to one's personal standard of what
        constitutes an acceptable balance of rewards and costs in a relationship.
a.      romantic ideal
b.      cost/benefit ratio
c.      comparison level
d.      reciprocity standard

**ANS: c**          **Pg: 247**
**LO: 9**           **Factual**


40.     Eight-year-old Cindy has to decide whether to be best friends with Jillian, who has lots of
        toys to play with, or with Kaitlin, whose family gets the Disney channel on their TV.
        According to social exchange theory, Cindy's choice will most likely be influenced by
        her consideration of which of the following?
a.      comparison level for alternatives
b.      evaluation of the matching hypothesis
c.      relative proximity of the two possible friends
d.      the socioeconomic status of the girls' families

**ANS: a**          **Pg: 247**
**LO: 9**           **Conceptual**


41.     Some people resist social exchange theory's approach to understanding close
        relationships, primarily because
a.      of the notion that self-interest is so important in relationships.
b.      people are inherently altruistic in their interactions with others.
c.      they believe that its principles apply only to romantic relationships.
d.      it implies that people are irrational in dealing with close relationships.

**ANS: a**          **Pgs: 247-248**
**LO: 9**           **Conceptual**

42. According to Clark and Mills, social exchange principles usually apply to _____ relationships, but these principles don't operate as consistently in _____ relationships.
a. sexual; close
b. close; business
c. communal; romantic
d. exchange; communal

**ANS: d**           **Pgs: 247-248**
**LO: 9**           **Factual**

43. Social exchange theory seems to be less applicable
a. in individualistic cultures.
b. in the theory of the "interpersonal marketplace".
c. in collectivistic cultures.
d. in taking an economic perspective on the nature of relationships.

**ANS: c**           **Pgs: 247-248**
**LO: 9**           **Factual**

*44. The "problematic qualities" in friends
a. may be as significant as the presence of positive qualities.
b. is less significant than the presence of positive qualities.
c. is more significant than the presence of positive qualities.
d. has not been researched.

**ANS: a**           **Pg: 248**
**LO: 10**          **Conceptual**

*45. Which of the following is NOT one of the common themes underlying friendships?
a. expressing affection and support
b. participating in mutually shared activities
c. providing intellectual stimulation
d. social compatibility

**ANS: c**           **Pg: 249**
**LO: 10**          **Conceptual**

*46. Several lines of research indicate that the most important element of friendship is
a. emotional support.
b. intellectual stimulation.
c. access to financial resources.
d. physical contact.

**ANS: a**           **Pg: 249**
**LO: 10**          **Conceptual**

47. Cross-cultural research identified _____ as the common thread running through the informal "rules" of friendship.
a. honesty in self-disclosure
b. providing emotional and social support
c. dealing with others in a considerate manner
d. sharing both positive and negative experiences

**ANS: b**          **Pg: 249**
**LO: 10**          **Conceptual**

48. In general, women's friendships are more likely to focus on _____, whereas men's friendships tend to be based on _____.
a. shared interests; family events
b. family events; emotional intimacy
c. shared interests; financial matters
d. emotional intimacy; shared interests

**ANS: d**          **Pg: 249**
**LO: 11**          **Conceptual**

49. Friendships between which of the following pairs of individuals are most likely to include discussions about personal problems and people?
a. two men
b. two women
c. a man and a woman
d. a man and his teenage daughter

**ANS: b**          **Pg: 249**
**LO: 11**          **Conceptual**

50. Friendships between men tend to be regulated by
a. hormones.
b. social roles.
c. their spouses.
d. the need for intimacy.

**ANS: b**          **Pg: 249**
**LO: 11**          **Conceptual**

*51. Which of the following is the most accurate statement regarding gender and e-mail communications?
a. Men and women are equally likely to discuss personal issues via e-mail.
b. Men and women are equally likely to focus on activities via e-mail as opposed to personal issues.
c. The gender differences associated with other forms of communication also appear in research on e-mail communication patterns.
d. Men are more likely to focus on personal problems and women are more likely to focus on activities in their communication via e-mail.

ANS: c          Pg: 249
LO: 11          Factual

52. Which of the following has **not** been offered as an explanation for gender differences in same-gender friendships?
a. Men are more aggressive than women.
b. Men may have less need for intimacy than women do.
c. Fear of homosexuality is greater in men than in women.
d. Men and women seem to have different pathways to intimacy.

ANS: a          Pgs: 249-250
LO: 11          Conceptual

53. Which of the following is **not** true about men's same-gender friendships?
a. Men's friendships tend to center around shared activities.
b. Men's friendships are influenced by the tendency for men to see themselves as competitors.
c. Men are socialized to be "strong and silent" and this interferes with the process of self-disclosure.
d. In all world cultures, men's friendships tend not to be emotionally intimate.

ANS: d          Pgs: 249-250
LO: 11          Conceptual

54. Confusion about a romantic relationship is
a. a common experience.
b. an indication of trouble in the relationship.
c. rare early in the relationship, but more common later on.
d. desirable because it leads one to examine the relationship carefully.

ANS: a          Pg: 250
LO: 12          Conceptual

55.    Most homosexual women prefer to call themselves
a.    gay.
b.    lesbians.
c.    bisexuals.
d.    homosexuals.

**ANS: b**          **Pg: 250**
**LO: 12**          **Factual**

56.    Harry assumes that all individuals and relationships are heterosexual until he is told
       otherwise. His attitude reflects
a.    his sexism.
b.    his heterosexism.
c.    the reciprocity principle.
d.    the fundamental attribution error.

**ANS: b**          **Pg: 250**
**LO: 12**          **Conceptual**

57.    One possible problem with generalizing the results of research on romantic love and
       relationships is that
a.    researchers tend to assume that subjects are heterosexual.
b.    homosexuals don't volunteer enough for laboratory studies.
c.    homosexuals tend to misrepresent their sexual orientation on surveys.
d.    funding is only available for research on heterosexual relationships.

**ANS: a**          **Pg: 250**
**LO: 12**          **Conceptual**

58.    Research findings suggest that _____ are more romantic, and _____ are more sensitive
       to problems that occur in relationships.
a.    men; men
b.    women; women
c.    men; women
d.    women; men

**ANS: c**          **Pg: 251**
**LO: 13**          **Conceptual**

59.    Research findings suggest that as a woman's _____ increases, so does her
       interest in men's physical attractiveness.
a.    physical attractiveness
b.    age
c.    hormone production
d.    economic power

**ANS: d**          **Pg: 251**
**LO: 13**          **Conceptual**

60.  Research findings indicate that _____ are more romantic with regard to expressions of love, and _____ hold more romantic beliefs.
a.  men; men
b.  women; women
c.  men; women
d.  women; men

**ANS: d**          **Pg: 251**
**LO: 13**          **Conceptual**

*61.  The parental investment model helps to explain why
a.  men are more "picky" in selecting a mate.
b.  women are more "picky" in selecting a mate.
c.  women fall in love more easily than men.
d.  women hold more romantic beliefs than men.

**ANS: b**          **Pg: 251**
**LO: 13**          **Conceptual**

62.  Susan and Manny's relationship is characterized by warmth, closeness, and sharing. Their relationship would be considered high in which of the following?
a.  sharing
b.  passion
c.  intimacy
d.  commitment

**ANS: c**          **Pgs: 251-252**
**LO: 14**          **Conceptual**

63.  Which of the following is **not** one of the components in Robert Sternberg's triangular theory of love?
a.  passion
b.  support
c.  intimacy
d.  commitment

**ANS: b**          **Pgs: 251-252**
**LO: 14**          **Factual**

64.  In addition to sexual desire, passion may include needs for
a.  self-esteem.
b.  dominance.
c.  self-actualization.
d.  all of these.

**ANS: d**          **Pg: 252**
**LO: 14**          **Conceptual**

65.     Alicia and Michael have thought seriously about splitting up on several occasions. The fact that they're still together indicates a high level of _____ in their relationship.
a.      passivity
b.      irrationality
c.      commitment
d.      stubbornness

ANS: c          Pg: 252
LO: 14          Conceptual


66.     According to Sternberg's triangular theory of love, when passion, intimacy, and commitment are all present in a relationship, then _____ is said to exist.
a.      liking
b.      infatuation
c.      fatuous love
d.      consummate love

ANS: d          Pgs: 251-252
LO: 14          Conceptual


67.     According to Sternberg's triangular theory of love, companionate love can be divided into which of the following components?
a.      friendship and passion
b.      intimacy and infatuation
c.      commitment and intimacy
d.      sexuality and commitment

ANS: c          Pgs: 251-252
LO: 14          Conceptual


*68.    Measures of _____ were the best predictors of whether dating couples continued their relationships.
a.      commitment and intimacy
b.      commitment and passion
c.      intimacy and passion
d.      financial security and sexual compatibility

ANS: a          Pgs: 251-252
LO: 14          Factual


*69.    Stevie and Pat's relationship is marked by a high level of commitment but low passion and low intimacy. According to Sternberg, their relationship is best characterized as
a.      fatuous love.
b.      infatuation.
c.      companionate.
d.      empty love.

ANS: d          Pgs: 251-252
LO: 14          Conceptual

70.    Romantic love as attachment is a relationship mode that is based on the work of
a.    Freud.
b.    Sternberg.
c.    Berscheid & Hatfield.
d.    Bowlby & Ainsworth.

**ANS: d**          **Pg: 252**
**LO: 15**          **Factual**

71.    According to Hazan and Shaver, common elements in infant attachment and adult love
       include all but which of the following?
a.    distress at separation
b.    efforts to stay close to the other
c.    sexual passion
d.    intense fascination with the other person

**ANS: c**          **Pg: 252**
**LO: 15**          **Factual**

72.    According to Hazan and Shaver,
a.    adult romantic relationships are similar to attachment relationships in infancy.
b.    those who had ambivalent attachments in infancy will probably never fall in love as
       adults.
c.    those who had avoidant relationships in infancy often overcompensate by becoming
       excessively intimate in their adult love relationships.
d.    all of these.

**ANS: a**          **Pg: 252**
**LO: 15**          **Factual**

73.    Hazan and Shaver found that, like infants in their attachment relationships, adults fall into
       the following three categories in their love relationships:
a.    secure, insecure, volatile
b.    ambitious, authentic, altruistic
c.    avoidant, anxious-ambivalent, secure
d.    intimate, approach-avoidant, secure

**ANS: c**          **Pgs: 252-253**
**LO: 15**          **Factual**

74.    According to Hazan and Shaver, the largest proportion of adults falls into which of the
       following categories?
a.    secure
b.    avoidant
c.    inconsistent
d.    anxious-ambivalent

**ANS: a**          **Pgs: 252-253**
**LO: 15**          **Factual**

75.     Adults who are obsessed and preoccupied with their relationships would be considered as belonging to which of the following categories?
a.      secure
b.      avoidant
c.      inconsistent
d.      anxious-ambivalent

**ANS: d**          **Pgs: 253-254**
**LO: 15**          **Conceptual**

76.     Kim Bartholomew's model of adult attachment identifies four attachment styles based on combinations of which of the following two dimensions?
a.      image of self, image of other
b.      infant self-image, adult self-image
c.      positive self-image, negative self-image
d.      positive other-image, negative other-image

**ANS: a**          **Pg: 254**
**LO: 15**          **Factual**

77.     The main difference between the Bartholomew and the Hazan/Shaver models of adult attachment styles is that Bartholomew's model
a.      considers only positive relationships.
b.      delineates two avoidant attachment styles.
c.      is based on one's notion of the "ideal" other.
d.      includes homosexual as well as heterosexual relationships.

**ANS: b**          **Pg: 254**
**LO: 15**          **Factual**

*78.    Jennifer can be described as having a fearful avoidant attachment style, thus it is likely that she
a.      needs others to bolster her self-validation.
b.      suffers extreme jealousy in her relationships.
c.      wants more relationship closeness than her partner does.
d.      has a positive self view.

**ANS: a**          **Pg: 254**
**LO: 15**          **Conceptual**

*79.    Research comparing the distribution and correlates of attachment styles indicates
a.      significant differences in cross-cultural studies, specifically those done in Israel.
b.      males are more likely to be avoidant and females are more likely to be anxious.
c.      proportions of gay men and lesbians in the different styles match those of heterosexual men and women.
d.      securely attached individuals are likely to be attracted to other securely attached individuals; avoidants are likely to be attracted to other avoidants; and ambivalents are likely to be attracted to others who are ambivalent.

**ANS: c**          **Pg: 254**
**LO: 15**          **Conceptual**

80. Researchers have found that adult attachment styles are correlated with all but which of the following?
a. intelligence
b. gender roles
c. religious beliefs
d. job satisfaction

**ANS: a**          **Pg: 254**
**LO: 15**          **Conceptual**

81. Researchers have found that insecure attachment styles appear to be associated with
    1. loneliness
    2. aggression
    3. anxiety
    4. depression

a. 1 only
b. 1, 2, and 4 only
c. 1, 3, and 4 only
d. 1, 2, 3, and 4

**ANS: d**          **Pgs: 254-255**
**LO: 15**          **Conceptual**

*82. Which of the following best summarizes the stability of attachment style?
a. Secure attachment is extremely stable over the course of development.
b. Across adulthood, style stability appears to increase to some degree.
c. The avoidant style appears to be the most stable attachment style.
d. Studies indicate that it is common for attachment style to change several times throughout the lifespan.

**ANS: b**          **Pg: 256**
**LO: 15**          **Factual**

83. According to Sternberg, which of the following components of a love relationship is most likely to peak early in the relationship and then decline in intensity as time progresses?
a. respect
b. passion
c. intimacy
d. commitment

**ANS: b**          **Pgs: 256-257**
**LO: 16**          **Factual**

*84. Which of the following is NOT considered one of the major factors explaining why passion fades in romantic relationships?
a. fantasy
b. novelty
c. arousal
d. age

**ANS: d**        **Pg: 257**
**LO: 16**       **Factual**

85. Which of the following is **not** considered a prominent factor contributing to the breakup of a romantic relationship?
a. premature commitment
b. incompatible attachment styles
c. ineffective conflict management skills
d. availability of a more attractive relationship

**ANS: b**        **Pgs: 257-258**
**LO: 17**       **Factual**

86. Research based on Sternberg's theory of love found which of the following to be the best predictor of whether dating couples' relationships would continue?
a. compatibility of attachment styles
b. duration of high levels of passion
c. levels of intimacy and commitment
d. compatibility of communication styles

**ANS: c**        **Pgs: 258-259**
**LO: 17**       **Conceptual**

*87. Studies indicate that the proportion of seriously dating couples who split up over the course of a two-three year period is typically around
a. 10%.
b. 25%.
c. 50%.
d. 80%.

**ANS: d**        **Pg: 257**
**LO: 17**       **Conceptual**

*88. The tendency for a member of a couple to chronically blame the spouse for problems and not take responsibility when he/she should illustrates the common attributional error referred to as
a. primary attribution error.
b. secondary attribution error.
c. actor-observer effect.
d. audience effect.

**ANS: c**        **Pgs: 258-259**
**LO: 17**       **Conceptual**

89. Carla wants to discuss their disagreement about vacation plans as soon as possible but Henry keeps stalling and finding excuses not to talk to her about this matter. This is an example of
a. the defensive attribution process.
b. the inequity dynamic.
c. a demand-withdraw pattern.
d. a Mars-Venus impasse.

**ANS: c**          **Pg: 259**
**LO: 17**         **Conceptual**

90. The "demand-withdraw" pattern of interaction common to dissatisfied couples typically involves
a. the man pressing the woman to discuss a problem and the woman avoiding the interaction.
b. the woman pressing the man to discuss a problem and the man avoiding the interaction.
c. the tendency for long-term relationships to be characterized by approach-avoidance conflicts.
d. the man's perception that the woman spends too much time with their children and not enough time with him.

**ANS: b**          **Pg: 259**
**LO: 17**         **Conceptual**

91. _____ occurs when one has fewer interpersonal relationships than desired, or when relationships are less satisfying than desired.
a. Shyness
b. Moodiness
c. Loneliness
d. Depression

**ANS: c**          **Pg: 260**
**LO: 18**         **Factual**

92. Which of the following is generally **not** considered a major social trend contributing to loneliness?
a. reduced social interactions at home
b. superficiality of social interactions
c. increased time spent at computer terminals
d. decreased ability to communicate verbally

**ANS: d**          **Pgs: 260-261**
**LO: 18**         **Factual**

*93.   Ten-year-old Jimmy is very popular at school, excelling in academics as well as in sports; however, since his parent's divorce, he rarely sees his father and his mother spends most of her time with her new boyfriend. It is likely that Jimmy will experience
a.   social loneliness.
b.   emotional loneliness.
c.   intellectual loneliness.
d.   performance loneliness.

**ANS: b**          **Pgs: 260-261**
**LO: 18**          **Conceptual**

*94.   In college students, social loneliness is most influenced by the _____ of friendship.
a.   quality
b.   quantity
c.   duration
d.   context

**ANS: b**          **Pg: 261**
**LO: 18**          **Factual**

*95.   For older individuals, social loneliness is most influenced by the _____ of friendship.
a.   quality
b.   quantity
c.   duration
d.   context

**ANS: a**          **Pg: 263**
**LO: 18**          **Factual**

*96.   Jenny and her partner recently moved so that Jenny could take advantage of a job opportunity. It has been difficult for them to leave all of their friends. It is likely that they are currently experiencing
a.   transient loneliness.
b.   emotional loneliness.
c.   transitional loneliness.
d.   acute loneliness.

**ANS: c**          **Pg: 261**
**LO: 18**          **Conceptual**

*97.   Which of the following is the most accurate statement regarding the association between loneliness and age?
a.   Loneliness increases with age.
b.   Loneliness decreases with age.
c.   Loneliness remains stable across the lifespan.
d.   Loneliness decreases with age until about age 45, at which time it begins to increase.

**ANS: b**          **Pg: 261**
**LO: 19**          **Conceptual**

*98. Who of the following 25-year-olds is statistically more likely to suffer from loneliness?
a. Courtney, whose parents divorced when she was 7 years old
b. Bailey, whose parents divorced when she was 16 years old
c. Alexandrea, whose mother died when she was 7 years old
d. Paula, whose mother died when she was 16 years old

ANS: a          Pg: 261
LO: 19          Conceptual

*99. A key problem regarding chronic loneliness is that negative social behaviors in childhood lead to
a. aggression in peers.
b. competition with adults.
c. rejection by peers.
d. overdependence on peers.

ANS: c          Pg: 262
LO: 20          Conceptual

*100. Research on adult attachment and loneliness indicates the following order from most to least amounts of loneliness:
a. anxious-ambivalent >> avoidant >> secure
b. avoidant >> secure >> anxious-ambivalent
c. avoidant >> anxious-ambivalent >> secure
d. secure >> avoidant >> anxious-ambivalent

ANS: a          Pg: 262
LO: 20          Factual

101. Which of the following is generally **not** considered a personal quality associated with loneliness?
a. shyness
b. self-defeating attributional style
c. interdependence
d. anxiety about social skills

ANS: c          Pgs: 263-264
LO: 21          Factual

*102. Shy people tend to be
a. timid about expressing themselves.
b. embarrassed easily.
c. not easily aroused.
d. overly self-conscious.

ANS: c          Pg: 263
LO: 21          Factual

*103.  Which of the following is NOT a common finding regarding the comparison of lonely people with nonlonely people?
a.  Lonely people are more responsive to conversational partners.
b.  Lonely people are more self-focused.
c.  Lonely people disclose less about themselves.
d.  Lonely people spend less time speaking.

ANS: a          Pg: 263
LO: 21          Factual

*104.  Individuals who suffer from chronic loneliness are likely to have a self-defeating attributional style characterized by attributing their loneliness to
a.  stable, internal causes.
b.  stable, external causes.
c.  unstable, internal causes.
d.  unstable, external causes.

ANS: a          Pg: 264
LO: 21          Conceptual

*105.  Which of the following was offered as the LEAST helpful strategy for coping with loneliness?
a.  use the internet
b.  read a book
c.  challenge irrational beliefs
d.  work on developing social skills

ANS: b          Pgs: 264-265
LO: 22          Conceptual


## MULTIPLE CHOICE QUESTIONS ON STUDY GUIDE

1.  Love as the basis for marriage is
a.  a universal phenomenon
b.  most common in collectivist cultures
c.  an 18th-century invention of Western culture
d.  becoming increasingly uncommon across cultures

ANS: c          Pgs: 237-238
LO: 2          Factual

2.      Which of the following statements about the role of physical attractiveness in relationships is **not** true?
a.      Good looks play a role in friendships.
b.      All studies show that attractiveness is an important factor in dating.
c.      Women are more likely to report that physical attractiveness is unimportant to them than men are.
d.      Both genders rate physical attractiveness of a potential mate higher than personal qualities such as kindness and warmth.

**ANS: d**          **Pg: 240**
**LO: 5**            **Conceptual**

3.      According to the matching hypothesis,
a.      people seek potential mates who match their attractiveness ideal.
b.      people of similar levels of physical attractiveness gravitate toward each other.
c.      people tend to gravitate toward those with the same sexual orientation.
d.      physically attractive people have an easier time finding a partner than those who are less attractive.

**ANS: b**          **Pg: 242**
**LO: 5**            **Factual**

4.      The research on similarity seems to show that married and dating couples
a.      tend to be similar on most important attributes.
b.      are often far apart on many important attributes.
c.      show no significant relationships on important attributes.
d.      who are too similar soon look for a way out of the relationship.

**ANS: a**          **Pgs: 244-245**
**LO: 6**            **Factual**

5.      If you want to *have* a friend, *be* a friend. This statement is most consistent with which of the following concepts?
a.      proximity
b.      reciprocity
c.      matching hypothesis
d.      mere exposure effect

**ANS: b**          **Pg: 244**
**LO: 6**            **Conceptual**

6.      Encouraging your partner to disclose his or her thoughts and feelings to you illustrates which of the following relationship maintenance strategies?
a.      positivity
b.      assurances
c.      openness
d.      social networking

**ANS: c**          **Pg: 246**
**LO: 8**            **Conceptual**

7.   According to interdependence theory, what constitutes an acceptable balance of rewards and costs in a relationship is
a.   referred to as mutuality.
b.   determined by Skinner's principle of reinforcement.
c.   based on outcomes one has experienced in past relationships.
d.   determined largely by what one's parents found acceptable.

**ANS: b**          **Pg: 247**
**LO: 9**           **Conceptual**

8.   Studies indicate that the most important element of friendship is
a.   generosity.
b.   emotional support.
c.   physical attractiveness.
d.   similar religious attitudes.

**ANS: a**          **Pgs: 248-249**
**LO: 10**          **Factual**

9.   Women's friendships tend to focus on
a.   talking and emotional intimacy.
b.   the significant men in their lives.
c.   shared interests and doing things together.
d.   personal issues as opposed to global ones.

**ANS: a**          **Pg: 249**
**LO: 11**          **Factual**

10.  Research evidence suggests that
a.   women are more romantic than men.
b.   men are more romantic than women.
c.   men and women are equally romantic.
d.   there is no relationship between gender and romanticism.

**ANS: b**          **Pg: 251**
**LO: 13**          **Factual**

11.  Which of the following is **not** one of the components in Robert Sternberg's triangular theory of love?
a.   passion
b.   intimacy
c.   sexuality
d.   commitment

**ANS: c**          **Pgs: 251-252**
**LO: 14**          **Factual**

12. According to Sternberg's triangular theory of love, the combination of intimacy and passion produces
a. liking.
b. infatuation.
c. romantic love.
d. companionate love.

ANS: c          Pgs: 251-252
LO: 14          Factual

13. Cindy Hazan and Phillip Shaver suggested that patterns of adult romantic love are related to
a. levels of affiliation motive.
b. psychosexual stages in childhood.
c. attachment relationships in infancy.
d. same-gender bonds in adolescence.

ANS: c          Pg: 252
LO: 15          Factual

14. The tendency to attribute one's own behavior to situational factors and others' behavior to personal factors is called
a. negative attribution.
b. the actor-observer effect.
c. disruptive social reasoning.
d. downward social comparison.

ANS: b          Pg: 258
LO: 16          Factual

15. Which of the following is a personal consequence associated with chronic loneliness?
a. hostility
b. depression
c. alcoholism
d. all of these

ANS: d          Pg: 264
LO: 22          Factual

# MULTIPLE CHOICE QUESTIONS FROM WEB SITE

*1.    Cultural views of love and marriage are linked to a culture's values and its
a.    mortality rates.
b.    economic health.
c.    population.
d.    divorce rates.

ANS: b            Pgs: 236-237
LO: 2            Conceptual


2.    _____ refers to geographic, residential, and other forms of spatial closeness.
a.    Proximity
b.    Familiarity
c.    Similarity
d.    Personal space

ANS: a            Pg: 239
LO: 4            Factual


3.    One should be cautious in interpreting the results of surveys on the importance of
       physical attractiveness in romantic relationships because
a.    the research results are several decades old and therefore may not be relevant to current
       relationship concerns.
b.    people's verbal reports often do not match their true attitudes and behaviors.
c.    the definition of physical attractiveness varies significantly from person to person.
d.    studies of attractiveness are concerned only with the role of physique in attraction.

ANS: b            Pg: 240
LO: 5            Conceptual


4.    Which of the following facial features is most likely to be seen as attractive in men?
a.    large eyes
b.    broad jaw
c.    small nose
d.    prominent cheekbones

ANS: b            Pg: 241
LO: 5            Factual


5.    According to evolutionary psychologists, women seeking a prospective mate are likely to
       display the most interest in characteristics that denote a man's
a.    intelligence.
b.    financial prospects.
c.    reproductive capacity.
d.    capacity for resource acquisition.

ANS: d            Pgs: 242-243
LO: 5            Factual

6.    The "similarity principle" tends to be found most frequently in
a.    heterosexual couples.
b.    homosexual couples.
c.    friendships.
d.    all of these.

**ANS: d**           **Pgs: 244-245**
**LO: 7**            **Conceptual**

7.    The idea that interpersonal relationships are governed by perceptions of rewards and
      costs is a key premise in
a.    social exchange theory.
b.    the matching hypothesis.
c.    social comparison theory.
d.    the theory of cognitive dissonance.

**ANS: a**           **Pg: 247**
**LO: 9**            **Factual**

8.    In general, women's friendships are more likely to focus on _____, whereas men's
      friendships tend to be based on _____.
a.    shared interests; family events
b.    family events; emotional intimacy
c.    shared interests; financial matters
d.    emotional intimacy; shared interests

**ANS: d**           **Pg: 249**
**LO: 11**           **Conceptual**
9.    Most homosexual women prefer to call themselves
a.    gay.
b.    lesbians.
c.    bisexuals.
d.    homosexuals.

**ANS: b**           **Pg: 250**
**LO: 12**           **Factual**

10.   Susan and Manny's relationship is characterized by warmth, closeness, and sharing.
      Their relationship would be considered high in which of the following?
a.    sharing
b.    passion
c.    intimacy
d.    commitment

**ANS: c**           **Pgs: 251-252**
**LO: 14**           **Conceptual**

11.	According to Sternberg's triangular theory of love, companionate love can be divided into which of the following components?
a.	friendship and passion
b.	intimacy and infatuation
c.	commitment and intimacy
d.	sexuality and commitment

**ANS: c**	**Pgs: 251-252**
**LO: 14**	**Conceptual**

12.	Hazan and Shaver found that, like infants in their attachment relationships, adults fall into the following three categories in their love relationships:
a.	secure, insecure, volatile
b.	ambitious, authentic, altruistic
c.	avoidant, anxious-ambivalent, secure
d.	intimate, approach-avoidant, secure

**ANS: c**	**Pgs: 252-253**
**LO: 15**	**Factual**

13.	Which of the following is **not** considered a prominent factor contributing to the breakup of a romantic relationship?
a.	premature commitment
b.	incompatible attachment styles
c.	ineffective conflict management skills
d.	availability of a more attractive relationship

**ANS: b**	**Pgs: 257-258**
**LO: 17**	**Factual**

*14.	For older individuals, social loneliness is most influenced by the _____ of friendship.
a.	quality
b.	quantity
c.	duration
d.	context

**ANS: a**	**Pg: 263**
**LO: 18**	**Factual**

*15.	Individuals who suffer from chronic loneliness are likely to have a self-defeating attributional style characterized by attributing their loneliness to
a.	stable, internal causes.
b.	stable, external causes.
c.	unstable, internal causes.
d.	unstable, external causes.

**ANS: a**	**Pg: 264**
**LO: 21**	**Conceptual**

# *TRUE/FALSE QUESTIONS

1.  People who have marriages based on romantic love reported greater marital satisfaction than those who are in an arranged marriage.

**ANS: false**       **Pg: 237**
**LO: 2**         **Factual**

2.  In general, the Internet has had a negative impact on people's social relationships.

**ANS: false**       **Pg: 237**
**LO: 3**         **Factual**

3.  Americans are becoming more and more health conscious as evident by the increased number of organic foods sold in stores and the decreased rate of cosmetic surgery.

**ANS: false**       **Pg: 241**
**LO: 5**         **Factual**

4.  Interdependent theory is based on B.F. Skinner's principle of reinforcement.

**ANS: true**       **Pg: 247**
**LO: 9**         **Factual**

5.  Relationship differences between heterosexual and gay couples seem to be rooted in gender rather than sexual orientation.

**ANS: true**       **Pg: 251**
**LO: 12**        **Factual**

6.  Psychotherapy may be a helpful option for those with attachment difficulties.

**ANS: true**       **Pg: 256**
**LO: 15**        **Factual**

7.  The elderly are the loneliest age group.

**ANS: false**       **Pgs: 260-261**
**LO: 18**        **Factual**

8.  All forms of loneliness can be treated and thus improved using the same methods.

**ANS: false**       **Pg: 261**
**LO: 18**        **Conceptual**

9.  The majority of shy people indicate that this is an enduring and pervasive problem thus affecting most areas of their lives.

**ANS: false**       **Pg: 263**
**LO: 21**        **Conceptual**

10. Internet use is associated with social deficits and increases in feelings of loneliness.

**ANS: false**       **Pg: 264**
**LO: 2  2**         **Factual**


## SHORT-ANSWER ESSAY QUESTIONS

1. Briefly describe the role of the mere exposure effect in initial attraction between two people.

**Pg: 240**
**LO: 4**

2. Discuss how relationships that form through use of the Internet compare to those that begin through face-to-face interactions.

**Pgs: 237-238**
**LO: 3**

3. Briefly describe several physical features in both males and females that tend to be associated with high attractiveness ratings.

**Pgs: 240-241**
**LO: 5**

4. Discuss some of the ways in which views of romance and marriage vary across cultures.

**Pgs: 236-237**
**LO: 2**

5. Briefly explain the role of the matching hypothesis in physical attraction.

**Pgs: 242**
**LO: 5**

6. Discuss how evolutionary psychologists would explain the finding that more attractive women are more likely to demand high status in their prospective dates than less attractive women.

**Pgs: 242-244**
**LO: 5**

7. Explain why the reciprocity principle is considered to be at odds with the dating strategy of "playing hard to get."

**Pg: 244**
**LO: 6**

8.    Describe an example that illustrates how interdependence theory might work in an interpersonal relationship.

**Pgs: 247-248**
**LO: 9**

9.    Compare and contrast women's same-gender friendships with men's same-gender friendships.

**Pgs: 249-250**
**LO: 11**

10.   Research evidence indicates that men are more romantic than women, but that women tend to be more romantic with regard to expressions of love. Briefly explain this apparent contradiction.

**Pg: 251**
**LO: 13**

*11.   Discuss two prominent factors that contribute to romantic breakups and two strategies that may increase the likelihood that relationships will last.

**Pgs: 257-259**
**LO: 17**

12.   Describe several specific techniques that a counselor might use to help a person overcome his or her loneliness.

**Pgs: 264-265**
**LO: 22**

# Chapter 9
# MARRIAGE AND INTIMATE RELATIONSHIPS

## LEARNING OBJECTIVES

1. Discuss recent trends relating to the acceptance of singlehood and cohabitation.
2. Discuss changing views on the permanence of marriage and gender roles.
3. Explain how increased childlessness and the decline of the nuclear family have affected the institution of marriage.
4. Discuss several factors influencing the selection of a mate.
5. Outline Murstein's stage theory of mate selection.
6. Summarize evidence on predictors of marital success.
7. Explain what the family life cycle is.
8. Discuss the factors couples weigh in deciding to have children.
9. Analyze the dynamics of the transition to parenthood.
10. Identify common problems that surface as a family's children reach adolescence.
11. Discuss the transitions that occur in the later stages of the family life cycle.
12. Discuss how gaps in role expectations may affect marital adjustment.
13. Summarize how spouses' work affects their marital satisfaction and their children.
14. Discuss how financial issues are related to marital adjustment.
15. Summarize evidence on the relationship between communication quality and marital adjustment.
16. Describe the evidence on changing divorce rates.
17. Discuss how men and women tend to adjust to divorce.
18. Analyze the evidence on the effects of divorce on children.
19. Summarize data on the frequency and success of remarriage and its impact on children.
20. Describe stereotypes of single life and summarize evidence on the adjustment of single people.
21. Discuss the prevalence of cohabitation and whether it improves the probability of marital success.
22. Discuss the stability and dynamics of intimate relationships among homosexual couples.
23. Outline some misconceptions about gay couples.
24. Discuss the incidence and consequences of date rape.
25. Explain factors that contribute to date rape.
26. Discuss the incidence of partner abuse and the characteristics of batterers.
27. Discuss why women stay in abusive relationships.

**MULTIPLE CHOICE QUESTIONS**

1.      Which statement most accurately reflects the current state of marriage in modern Western society?
a.      It is a cherished but dying tradition.
b.      It remains popular but appears to be under assault from changes in society.
c.      It is being largely replaced by cohabitation and serial monogamy.
d.      It is beset by tragic interpersonal violence in all segments of society.

**ANS: b**          **Pg: 270**
**LO: 2**            **Conceptual**

2.      Which of the following statements is true regarding the commonly held stereotype of single people?
a.      The previously negative stereotype is vanishing.
b.      The previously positive stereotype is vanishing.
c.      The stereotype is changing from positive to negative.
d.      The stereotype is changing from negative to positive.

**ANS: a**          **Pg: 270**
**LO: 1**            **Conceptual**

3.      Living together in a sexually intimate relationship without actually being married is called
a.      endogamy.
b.      cohabitation.
c.      pseudo-marriage.
d.      common law marriage.

**ANS: b**          **Pg: 270**
**LO: 1**            **Factual**

*4.     Approximately what percentage of marriages will result in separation or divorce?
a.      25
b.      50
c.      75
d.      83

**ANS: b**          **Pg: 270**
**LO: 2**            **Factual**

*5.     Juan and Dori recently got married. If current demographics continue, what is the likelihood they will get divorced or separated?
a.      25
b.      50
c.      75
d.      83

**ANS: b**          **Pg: 270**
**LO: 2**            **Applied**

*6. What percentage of Americans will marry at least once?
a. 50
b. 75
c. 90
d. 98

**ANS: c**       **Pg: 272**
**LO: 2**       **Factual**

7. Changing gender roles have affected the traditional model of marriage by
a. reducing the social stigma associated with divorce.
b. establishing clearer standards for behavior in a marriage.
c. creating new potential for conflict between marital partners.
d. resurrecting old-fashioned views of what men and women bring to a marriage.

**ANS: c**       **Pg: 271**
**LO: 3**       **Conceptual**

8. An increasing number of married couples are deciding
a. not to have children.
b. to have only one child.
c. to have larger families than in the past.
d. to have children earlier in the marriage.

**ANS: a**       **Pg: 271**
**LO: 2**       **Factual**

9. The traditional model of marriage has been challenged by a number of social trends, including
a. changing gender roles.
b. declining popularity of cohabitation.
c. increased premium on permanence.
d. decreased acceptability of singlehood.

**ANS: a**       **Pgs: 270-271**
**LO: 3**       **Conceptual**

10. Endogamy refers to the tendency
a. of people to marry within their social group.
b. for women to marry "up" in socioeconomic status.
c. for men to marry a woman who is much younger.
d. to marry others who have similar personal characteristics.

**ANS: a**       **Pg: 272**
**LO: 4**       **Factual**

*11. John and Jenny are an interracial couple. When Jenny looked into statistics to see how unusual they, were she likely found
a. the number of interracial couples has decreased since 1980.
b. the number of interracial couples has barely increased since 1980.
c. the number of interracial couples has barely increased, but the number of children they have has not increased.
d. the number of interracial couples has nearly doubled since 1980.

**ANS: d**          **Pg: 272**
**LO: 4**           **Applied**

*12. The popular view in Western Culture is that people marry because of
a. love.
b. parental pressure.
c. economic needs.
d. a multitude of pressures.

**ANS: a**          **Pg: 272**
**LO: 4**           **Factual**

13. Homogamy represents an example of _____ effects in action.
a. similarity
b. ingratiation
c. actor-observer
d. complementarity

**ANS: a**          **Pg: 272**
**LO: 4**           **Conceptual**

14. In terms of what they look for in a marital partner, women place a higher value than men on which of the following?
a. youthfulness
b. socioeconomic status
c. physical attractiveness
d. interest in raising a family

**ANS: b**          **Pg: 273**
**LO: 4**           **Conceptual**

15. Which of the following characteristics of potential mates is **not** valued equally by both sexes?
a. ambition
b. emotional stability
c. amiable disposition
d. dependability

**ANS: a**          **Pg: 273**
**LO: 4**           **Conceptual**

*16.    In terms of what they look for in a marital partner, men place a higher value than women on which of the following?
a.      ambition
b.      intelligence
c.      financial prospects
d.      youthfulness

**ANS: d**              **Pg: 273**
**LO: 4**               **Conceptual**

*17.    Sara is marrying Bill, a man three years older than her, who has completed college. Sara has not completed college. In relation to the text's discussion of deviations from homogamy, this couple would be considered
a.      unusual.
b.      typical.
c.      typical for age, but not education.
d.      typical for education, but not age.

**ANS: b**              **Pg: 272**
**LO: 4**               **Applied**

*18.    The validity of evolutionary concepts in psychology rests on the assumption that
a.      environment can affect genes.
b.      people contemplate what would be best for their "genes" in the long run.
c.      genes are adaptive.
d.      genes are a cause of psychological behaviors.

**ANS: d**              **Pgs: 273-274**
**LO: 4**               **Factual**

*19.    Jerry is seeking a mate based on evolutionary theory. His most primary, underlying concern will be to look for a female that is
a.      likely to be successful at having children.
b.      likely to provide him love.
c.      likely to be intelligent.
d.      likely to be stronger than average.

**ANS: a**              **Pg: 274**
**LO: 4**               **Applied**

*20.    Jean is seeking a mate based on evolutionary theory. Her most primary, underlying concern will be to look for a male that is
a.      likely to be devious.
b.      likely to provide her love.
c.      likely to be attractive.
d.      likely to provide well for her children.

**ANS: d**              **Pg: 274**
**LO: 4**               **Applied**

21.    The theory that couples experience a three-stage process of mate selection is also known as the
a.    evolutionary theory.
b.    meeting-chasing-catching theory.
c.    stimulus-value-role theory.
d.    find'em-fool'em-forget'em theory.

**ANS: c**          **Pg: 274**
**LO: 5**           **Factual**

22.    According to stimulus-value-role theory, during the first stage in mate selection, attraction depends mainly on
a.    parents' attitudes.
b.    compatibility in values.
c.    performance of role obligations.
d.    superficial, easily identifiable characteristics.

**ANS: d**          **Pg: 274**
**LO: 5**           **Factual**

23.    In the first stage of his theory, Murstein borrows heavily from
a.    Freudian theory.
b.    Behaviorism.
c.    Social Exchange theory.
d.    Social Learning theory.

**ANS: c**          **Pg: 274**
**LO: 5**           **Factual**

24.    In which of Murstein's stages of mate selection does evaluation of the other in the role of intimate companion occur?
a.    role
b.    value
c.    stimulus
d.    response

**ANS: a**          **Pg: 274**
**LO: 5**           **Factual**

*25.    Rosa and Garrett have started evaluating each other on their likelihood of making a good companion.  They are likely in which of Murstein's stages?
a.    response
b.    value
c.    stimulus
d.    role

**ANS: d**          **Pg: 274**
**LO: 5**           **Applied**

*26.    Kyra and Thomas have started evaluating each other on their attitudes about sex politics
        and religion.  They are likely in which of Murstein's stages?
a.      response
b.      value
c.      stimulus
d.      role

**ANS: b**                  **Pg: 274**
**LO: 5**                   **Applied**

27.     The main problem with research on marital success is that
a.      few researchers are interested in the topic.
b.      marital quality is hard to measure.
c.      most people don't like to reveal such information to researchers.
d.      all of these.

**ANS: b**                  **Pg: 274**
**LO: 6**                   **Conceptual**

28.     Which of the following is associated with a higher probability of marital success?
a.      younger age
b.      shorter courtship
c.      having happily married parents
d.      all of the above

**ANS: c**                  **Pg: 274**
**LO: 6**                   **Conceptual**

29.     Which of the following factors is most likely to contribute to higher divorce rates among
        those who marry at an older-than-average age?
a.      partners are more "set in their ways"
b.      greater likelihood of differences in many areas
c.      jealousy about spouse's previous close relationships
d.      failure to experience the excitement of young romance

**ANS: b**                  **Pg: 274**
**LO: 6**                   **Conceptual**

30.     Which of the following is associated with a higher probability of marital success?
a.      conscientiousness
b.      having divorced parents
c.      perfectionism
d.      insecurity

**ANS: a**                  **Pg: 275**
**LO: 6**                   **Factual**

*31. Which of the following personality traits is most likely to be associated with marital problems?
a. conscientiousness
b. surgency
c. perfectionism
d. b and c

**ANS: c** **Pg: 275**
**LO: 6** **Conceptual**

*32. Bonita's mother pointed out that Bonita and Ahmad tended to be negative and slightly sarcastic to each other and that this was going to cause problems in the future if they got married. Bonita, an attentive psychology student, said:
a. research shows that commutation tends to improve after marriage.
b. research shows that commutation is not that important.
c. research did not support her mother's statement.
d. research support her mother's statement.

**ANS: d** **Pg: 275**
**LO: 6** **Applied**

33. An orderly sequence of stages through which families progress is called
a. family development.
b. the family life cycle.
c. group dynamics.
d. serial monogamy.

**ANS: b** **Pg: 275**
**LO: 7** **Factual**

34. The course of marital satisfaction over the family life cycle, if drawn on a graph, would be most likely to resemble
a. a straight line.
b. an ascending line.
c. a descending line.
d. the letter "U".

**ANS: d** **Pgs: 276-279**
**LO: 7** **Conceptual**

35. In which stage of the family life cycle is marital satisfaction likely to be the lowest?
a. beginning families
b. families with school-aged children
c. families in the middle years
d. aging families

**ANS: b** **Pgs: 277**
**LO: 7** **Conceptual**

36.     The term "marital bliss" would be most characteristic of which of the following stages of the family life cycle?
a.      beginning families
b.      families with preschool children
c.      families with teenagers
d.      families in the middle years

**ANS: a**          **Pg: 276**
**LO: 7**           **Conceptual**

*37.    Since 1980, the percentage of childless couples has
a.      barely increased.
b.      doubled.
c.      tripled.
d.      none of these

**ANS: b**          **Pg: 277**
**LO: 8**           **Factual**

38.     Which of the following reasons do couples give for remaining childless?
a.      the cost of raising children
c.      less time to spend with each other
b.      loss of independence
d.      all of these

**ANS: d**          **Pg: 277**
**LO: 8**           **Factual**

39.     If you asked newly married couples why they want to have children, they will most likely cite
a.      pressure from their parents.
b.      the joy of watching children grow up.
c.      needing someone to care for them in old age.
d.      all of these.

**ANS: b**          **Pg: 277**
**LO: 8**           **Conceptual**

*40.    Crisis during the transition to first parenthood is more likely for
a.      males.
b.      females.
c.      Males and females are equally likely to experience crisis.
d.      Research does not support a major transition to adulthood.

**ANS: b**          **Pg: 277**
**LO: 9**           **Conceptual**

41. The text states that the stress that accompanies the transition to parenthood is likely to be greatest when
a. the newborn child wasn't planned.
b. the new parents are relatively young.
c. parenting costs and benefits are not realistic.
d. the father is unlikely to be heavily involved in child care.

**ANS: c**          **Pg: 277**
**LO: 9**           **Conceptual**

42. Which of the following is most likely to be a source of conflict between adolescents and their parents?
a. drug use
b. career plans
c. style of dress
d. educational goals

**ANS: c**          **Pg: 278**
**LO: 10**          **Conceptual**

43. Which of the following statements about couples' care of their elderly parents is true?
a. Today's average married couple has more parents than children.
b. An increasing number of adults provide care to their aging parents.
c. Women tend to assume most of the responsibility for elderly relatives.
d. All of these statements are true.

**ANS: d**          **Pg: 278**
**LO: 11**          **Factual**

44. The expression "sandwich generation" refers to
a. adolescents because of the prevalence of fast food in their diets.
b. young adults because they feel pressured by teachers and parents to achieve independence as quickly as possible.
c. middle-aged adults who must take care of children and aging parents.
d. elderly adults who feel "sandwiched" between two different technological eras.

**ANS: c**          **Pg: 278**
**LO: 11**          **Factual**

45. In the post-parental period, marital satisfaction tends to
a. decrease.
b. increase.
c. level off.
d. decrease sharply, then gradually increase.

**ANS: b**          **Pg: 279**
**LO: 11**          **Conceptual**

46.     According to the text, mismatched expectations about marriage roles are especially likely among today's husbands and wives because
a.      gender roles are changing rapidly.
b.      people are getting married at a younger age today.
c.      in childhood, boys and girls get different messages about marriage.
d.      of the abundance of unhealthy marriages portrayed in the mass media.

**ANS: a**          **Pg: 280**
**LO: 12**          **Conceptual**

47.     Gender equality in marital chores is
a.      notably increased.
b.      fairly common.
c.      idealistic and probably not really desirable.
d.      fairly rare.

**ANS: a**          **Pgs: 280-281**
**LO: 12**          **Factual**

*48.    Wives account for _____ percent of the housework.
a.      50
b.      65
c.      75
d.      85

**ANS: b**          **Pgs: 280**
**LO: 12**          **Factual**

*49.    Betty has the attitudes of a typical married woman. She likely does _____ housework than her husband and _____ consider it unfair.
a.      more; does
b.      less; does not
c.      more; does not
d.      less; does

**ANS: c**          **Pg: 280**
**LO: 12**          **Conceptual**

50.     What does research tell us about the relationship between women's employment status and the quality of infant-mother emotional attachment?
a.      Full-time mothers are more likely to have securely attached children.
b.      Part-time working mothers have more securely attached children than full-time mothers or women employed full-time.
c.      Mothers who work full-time can have securely attached children, but only if the husband shares child-rearing responsibilities.
d.      There appears to be no relationship.

**ANS: d**          **Pg: 282**
**LO: 13**          **Factual**

*51.    While Fatima is very busy as a mother, wife, and employee, research has shown an advantage of these multiple roles is that
a.      she and her husband are more satisfied with the wife's role.
b.      her husband can still be the primary breadwinner.
c.      time away from children is a good stress relief.
d.      she receives extra social support and success.

**ANS: d          Pg: 282**
**LO: 13          Applied**

52.     When financial resources are plentiful in a marriage, arguments about money
a.      simply don't occur.
b.      may still be a problem.
c.      generally don't threaten marital satisfaction.
d.      tend to occur if the wife doesn't work outside the home.

**ANS: b          Pg: 283**
**LO: 14          Conceptual**

53.     How do happily married couples and those who get divorced differ in their handling of money?
a.      Happy couples engage in more joint decision making on finances.
b.      Eventually-divorced couples have more arguments about how much money each partner earns.
c.      Among couples who get divorced, one spouse provides a regular allowance for the other.
d.      Among happy couples, typically there is agreement about who is primarily responsible for financial matters.

**ANS: a          Pg: 283**
**LO: 14          Conceptual**

*54.    Satistified and non-satisfied couples can almost always be differentiated by _____ in the relationship.
a.      jealousy
b.      sexual infidelity
c.      communication
d.      in-law problems

**ANS: c          Pg: 283**
**LO: 15          Conceptual**

55.     In order to develop his theory of the role of marital communication and risk factors for divorce, Gottman
a.      analyzed his own marital experiences and those of three close friends.
b.      did an Internet survey of 500 couples.
c.      observed couples at 20 shopping malls in the United States over a period of two months.
d.      studied over 50 couples using a combination of interview and observational techniques.

**ANS: d          Pgs: 283-285**
**LO: 15          Factual**

56.      Gottman asserts that
a.       conflict and anger in marital interaction are not normal.
b.       jealousy is by far the greatest of all threats to marital stability.
c.       the style of communication is the key issue in predicting marital dissolution.
d.       there are eight communication patterns that are predictive of marital dissolution.

**ANS: c**          **Pg: 285**
**LO: 15**          **Factual**

57.      Which of the following is **not** one of the communication styles identified by Gottman as
         a risk factor for divorce?
a.       contempt
b.       criticism
c.       belligerence
d.       complaining

**ANS: d**          **Pg: 285**
**LO: 15**          **Factual**

*58.     At their peak, divorce rates were about _____%; the risk of divorce today is about
         _____%.
a.       60; 50
b.       60; 40
c.       50; 60
d.       50; 40

**ANS: d**          **Pg: 285**
**LO: 16**          **Factual**

59.      Which of the following is **not** one of the social trends contributing to increasing divorce
         rates?
a.       Marriage has lost some of its sacred quality.
b.       The stigma attached to divorce has gradually eroded.
c.       Counselors are increasingly recommending divorce for troubled couples.
d.       Working wives are less financially dependent on the continuation of their marriage.

**ANS: c**          **Pg: 286**
**LO: 16**          **Conceptual**

60.      The decision to divorce is usually **not**
a.       a process rather than a discrete event.
b.       postponed repeatedly.
c.       barely traumatic now that divorce is more common.
d.       made with a great deal of agonizing forethought.

**ANS: c**          **Pg: 288**
**LO: 16**          **Conceptual**

*61.    _____ percent of children do not show emotional or psychological problems 2-3 years after their parents divorce.
a.    25
b.    50
c.    75
d.    90

ANS: c          Pg: 289
LO: 18          Conceptual

62.    Available evidence indicates that remaining in an unhappy marriage tends to
a.    be best for the children.
b.    be better than getting a divorce.
c.    be detrimental to one's adjustment.
d.    make the marriage stronger in the end.

ANS: c          Pg: 288
LO: 16          Conceptual

63.    Which of the following has been found in adults whose parents divorced when they were children?
a.    marital instability
b.    antisocial behavior
c.    lower educational attainments
d.    all of the above

ANS: d          Pg: 289
LO: 18          Factual

64.    According to Furstenberg and Kiernan, most researchers
a.    are coming closer to establishing the truth about the lasting effects of divorce on children.
b.    are now able to define the specific factors that lead to better adjustment of children of divorce.
c.    are becoming more wary about making blanket statements about a complex phenomenon such as divorce.
d.    no longer wish to do research on divorce because of serious ethical and practical concerns.

ANS: c          Pg: 289
LO: 18          Conceptual

*65.    Early research showed children's adjustment after divorce was _____ ; more recent research is more _____.
a.    poor; optimistic
b.    good; pessimistic
c.    strictly based on gender; strictly based on education level
d.    none of these

ANS: d          Pgs: 288-289
LO: 18          Conceptual

66. Which of the following statements about adjusting to divorce is **not** true?
a. Fathers tend to increase their contact with their children.
b. Women are more likely to assume the responsibility of raising the children.
c. Women file for a larger percentage of divorce than men.
d. Divorced women are less likely to have adequate income than divorced men.

**ANS: a**      **Pg: 288**
**LO: 18**      **Conceptual**

67. About _____ of divorced people eventually remarry.
a. one-fourth
b. one-half
c. one-third
d. three-fourths

**ANS: d**      **Pg: 289**
**LO: 19**      **Factual**

68. Divorce rates for second marriages are
a. higher than those for first marriages.
b. lower than those for first marriages.
c. the same as those for first marriages.
d. different depending on the wife's age at the time of the second marriage.

**ANS: a**      **Pg: 289**
**LO: 19**      **Factual**

69. Which of the following is **not** true regarding the adjustment of stepchildren?
a. They experience the stepfamily as less cohesive and warm than their original family.
b. Their psychological adjustment is similar to that of children from single parent homes.
c. The differences between child adjustment in stepfamilies and intact families is substantial.
d. All of these are true of stepchildren.

**ANS: d**      **Pgs: 289-290**
**LO: 19**      **Conceptual**

70. The proportion of young adults who choose to remain single
a. is increasing.
b. is decreasing.
c. has remained stable.
d. is increasing for men, but decreasing for women.

**ANS: a**      **Pg: 290**
**LO: 20**      **Factual**

71.    Which of the following has caused much of the increase in the proportion of single
       adults?
a.     loss of faith in the institution of marriage
b.     people marrying at a higher median age
c.     society's positive view toward cohabitation
d.     fewer young people willing to assume the financial burdens associated with marriage

**ANS: b**          **Pg: 291**
**LO: 20**          **Conceptual**

72.    Compared to married people, sexual relations among single people can be characterized
       as
a.     more frequent and more satisfying.
b.     less frequent, but more satisfying.
c.     more frequent, but less satisfying.
d.     less frequent and less satisfying.

**ANS: d**          **Pg: 291**
**LO: 20**          **Factual**

*73.   The strength of the relationship between mental and physical health and marriage is
a.     very weak.
b.     weak.
c.     modest.
d.     strong.

**ANS: c**          **Pg: 291**
**LO: 20**          **Conceptual**

*74.   The strength of the relationship between mental and physical health and marriage is
       _____ for males than females.
a.     less important
b.     equally important
c.     more important
d.     Gender is unrelated to marriage and health.

**ANS: c**          **Pg: 291**
**LO: 20**          **Conceptual**

75.    People who remain single are
a.     mostly frustrated, lonely losers.
b.     mostly carefree, suave swingers.
c.     generally happier than their married counterparts.
d.     not easily fit into stereotypes.

**ANS: d**          **Pg: 291**
**LO: 20**          **Factual**

76. Research on satisfaction with one's life among single people indicates that single
a. men are more satisfied than single women.
b. women are more satisfied than single men.
c. people are happier than married people.
d. people are more satisfied with their sex lives.

**ANS: b**       **Pg: 291**
**LO: 20**       **Factual**

77. The greater happiness of married people could be attributed to which of the following?
a. social support
b. physical health
c. financial well-being
d. all of the above

**ANS: d**       **Pg: 291**
**LO: 20**       **Conceptual**

78. In the 1990s, a little over _____ percent of people getting married for the first time had cohabited prior to their marriage.
a. 10
b. 25
c. 50
d. 75

**ANS: c**       **Pg: 291**
**LO: 21**       **Factual**

79. Which of the following is **not** a prominent characteristic among people who choose cohabitation?
a. lower economic status
b. well-educated
c. liberal in values
d. nontraditional about intimate relationships

**ANS: b**       **Pg: 292**
**LO: 21**       **Factual**

80. Most theorists see cohabitation as
a. a threat to the institution of marriage.
b. a new stage in the courtship process.
c. a fad that will level off in the next several decades.
d. an indication of young people's preference for alternative lifestyles.

**ANS: b**       **Pg: 292**
**LO: 21**       **Factual**

81. Which of the following statements about cohabiting couples is **not** true?
a. Most cohabitants expect to marry their current partner.
b. Cohabiting relationships tend to be more stable than marital relationships.
c. Cohabiting couples are more likely to stay together if they have a child together.
d. Cohabitants report that they are less satisfied with their relationships than married couples.

**ANS: b**　　　　　**Pg: 292**
**LO: 21**　　　　　**Conceptual**

*82. Bill is a gay male who was once married to a woman. Among his gay male friends, he finds about _____ percent of them share his former marriage status.
a. 10%
b. 25%
c. 50%
d. 75%

**ANS: b**　　　　　**Pg: 295**
**LO: 22**　　　　　**Applied**

83. People involved in gay relationships and those involved in marital relationships report similar levels of
a. sexual satisfaction.
b. overall satisfaction with their relationships.
c. love and commitment in their relationships.
d. all of these.

**ANS: d**　　　　　**Pg: 294**
**LO: 22**　　　　　**Factual**

84. Compared to heterosexual couples, homosexual couples tend to be _____ in their views about role expectations.
a. more flexible
b. less flexible
c. about the same
d. more egocentric

**ANS: a**　　　　　**Pg: 294**
**LO: 23**　　　　　**Conceptual**

85. Research on homosexual couples suggests that
a. they rarely have long-term relationships.
b. one partner generally adopts a cross-gender role.
c. gays of both genders tend to be highly promiscuous.
d. gay couples show a more equitable balance of power in their relationships.

**ANS: d**　　　　　**Pg: 294**
**LO: 23**　　　　　**Factual**

86. Which of the following statements about sexual activity among lesbians is true?
a. Lesbians tend to prefer bisexual relationships.
b. Lesbian relationships are generally sexually exclusive.
c. Lesbians tend to engage in casual sex with many partners.
d. Lesbians tend to emphasize the importance of sexual pleasure and conquest.

**ANS: b**      **Pg: 295**
**LO: 23**      **Conceptual**

87. There has been an increase in the number of homosexuals opting to have children in the context of their gay relationships. Preliminary evidence suggests that
a. their children tend to become homosexuals.
b. their children show signs of being maladjusted.
c. gay parents are similar to their heterosexual counterparts.
d. lesbian mothers exhibit less maternal behavior than heterosexual mothers.

**ANS: c**      **Pg: 295**
**LO: 23**      **Factual**

*88. About _____ of women are victimized sexually in a dating situation.
a. 80%
b. 60%
c. 40%
d. 20%

**ANS: d**      **Pg: 296**
**LO: 24**      **Factual**

89. Which of the following is most likely to be involved in a sexually aggressive incident?
a. alcohol
b. strangers
c. a "date rape drug"
d. an authority figure

**ANS: a**      **Pg: 296**
**LO: 25**      **Conceptual**

90. Which of the following statements about violent pornography is **not** true?
a. Violent pornography directly induces men to commit rape.
b. Men who view sexually violent films report greater acceptance of rape myths.
c. Violent pornography elevates some men's tendency to behave aggressively toward women.
d. None of these are true.

**ANS: a**      **Pgs: 296-297**
**LO: 24**      **Conceptual**

*91. The belief that sexual aggressors have that women don't tell the truth about their romantic feelings
a.   contributes to date rape.
b.   is nonexistent among sexual aggressors.
c.   is called the social exchange effect.
d.   none of these.

**ANS: a**          **Pg: 297**
**LO: 25**          **Conceptual**

92.  Which of the following is generally **not** considered a common characteristic of batterers?
a.   possessive
b.   unemployed
c.   drinking and drug problems
d.   All of these are common characteristics of batterers.

**ANS: d**          **Pg: 298**
**LO: 26**          **Factual**


## MULTIPLE CHOICE QUESTIONS FROM STUDY GUIDE

1.   Role expectations for husbands and wives are becoming
a.   less varied and flexible.
b.   more specific and stable.
c.   less of a concern to married couples.
d.   more varied and flexible.

**ANS: d**          **Pg: 271**
**LO: 2**           **Factual**

2.   Which of the following is the main reason most people get married?
a.   the financial security that comes from having dual incomes
b.   to ensure that their children are considered "legitimate" by society
c.   the desire to participate in a socially sanctioned, mutually rewarding, intimate relationship
d.   to avoid the risk of sexually transmitted diseases that is associated with multiple sexual partners

**ANS: c**          **Pg: 272**
**LO: 2**           **Factual**

3.   Endogamy refers to the tendency of people to marry someone who
a.   has similar personality characteristics.
b.   is older.
c.   comes from one's own social group.
d.   is younger.

**ANS: c**          **Pg: 272**
**LO: 4**           **Factual**

4. In assessing a potential mate, women place a higher value than men on all but which of the following?
a. intelligence
b. youthfulness
c. socioeconomic status
d. financial prospects

**ANS: b**      **Pg: 273**
**LO: 4**      **Factual**

5. On reaching Murstein's second stage of mate selection (the "value" stage), couples begin to
a. explore each other's attitudes about such things as religion, politics, and gender role.
b. focus on the more intimate aspects of a relationship.
c. evaluate the other's physical attractiveness, age, and education.
d. apply the principles of social exchange theory.

**ANS: a**      **Pg: 274**
**LO: 5**      **Factual**

6. Couples who have high levels of intimacy, closeness, and commitment prior to the birth of the first child
a. usually exhibit low levels of satisfaction after the child arrives.
b. find the transition to parenthood a difficult experience.
c. may see the newborn as an intruder into their life.
d. maintain a high level of satisfaction after the birth of a child.

**ANS: d**      **Pg: 277**
**LO: 6**      **Factual**

7. Parents overwhelmingly rate _____ as the most difficult stage of parenting.
a. infancy
b. middle childhood
c. adolescence
d. early adulthood

**ANS: c**      **Pg: 278**
**LO: 10**      **Factual**

8. Conflict between adolescent children and their parents is most likely to involve which of the following issues?
a. the adolescent's career plans
b. the kinds of clothes the adolescent wears
c. whether or not the adolescent plans to attend college
d. whether or not the adolescent will engage in sexual relations

**ANS: b**      **Pg: 278**
**LO: 10**      **Factual**

9. Research on maternal employment indicates that
a. it is not harmful to the children.
b. it is harmful to the children.
c. children are not harmed when they are younger but are when they are older.
d. there is no conclusive evidence about its effect on children.

ANS: a          Pg: 282
LO: 13          Factual

10. After a divorce, children are likely to exhibit all but which of the following?
a. aggression
b. reduced physical health
c. improved academic performance
d. precocious sexual behavior

ANS: c          Pg: 289
LO: 18          Factual

11. Which of the following statements about remarriage is **not** true?
a. Adaption to remarriage can be difficult for children.
b. Divorce rates are lower for second than for first marriages.
c. Roughly three-quarters of divorced people eventually remarry.
d. The average length of time between divorce and remarriage is slightly less than four years.

ANS: b          Pg: 289
LO: 19          Factual

12. In comparison to married people, single people
a. have sex more frequently.
b. rate themselves as happier.
c. exhibit poorer physical and mental health.
d. are more likely to develop post-traumatic stress disorder.

ANS: c          Pg: 291
LO: 20          Factual

13. Which the following statements about cohabitation is true?
a. Premarital cohabitation increases the likelihood of subsequent marital success.
b. Cohabitants tend to repudiate marriage as a viable alternative for them.
c. The majority of cohabitants plan to marry eventually.
d. Cohabitants are generally people who shy away from responsibility.

ANS: c          Pg: 292
LO: 21          Factual

14. The majority of homosexual men and women prefer
a. a stable, long-term relationship.
b. to engage in casual sex with a variety of partners.
c. to adopt a masculine or feminine role in their relationships.
d. a heterosexual relationship if the opportunity presents itself.

**ANS: a**          **Pg: 294**
**LO: 22**         **Factual**

15. Which of the following is considered a "date rape drug"?
a. caffeine
b. ecstasy
c. marijuana
d. rohypnol

**ANS: d**          **Pg: 296**
**LO: 24**         **Factual**

## MULTIPLE CHOICE QUESTIONS ON WEB SITE

*1. Juan and Dori recently got married. If current demographics continue, what is the likelihood they will get divorced or separated?
a. 25
b. 50
c. 75
d. 83

**ANS: b**          **Pg: 270**
**LO: 2**         **Applied**

2. Endogamy refers to the tendency
a. of people to marry within their social group.
b. for women to marry "up" in socioeconomic status.
c. for men to marry a woman who is much younger.
d. to marry others who have similar personal characteristics.

**ANS: a**          **Pg: 272**
**LO: 4**         **Factual**

3. Which of the following characteristics of potential mates is **not** valued equally by both sexes?
a. ambition
b. emotional stability
c. amiable disposition
d. dependability

**ANS: a**          **Pg: 273**
**LO: 4**         **Conceptual**

*4.    Jean is seeking a mate based on evolutionary theory.  Her most primary, underlying concern will be to look for a male that is
a.    likely to be devious.
b.    likely to provide her love.
c.    likely to be attractive.
d.    likely to provide well for her children.

ANS: d            Pg: 74
LO: 4             Applied

*5.    Rosa and Garrett have started evaluating each other on their likelihood of making a good companion.  They are likely in which of Murstein's stages?
a.    response
b.    value
c.    stimulus
d.    role

ANS: d            Pg: 274
LO: 5             Applied

6.    Which of the following is associated with a higher probability of marital success?
a.    conscientiousness
b.    having divorced parents
c.    perfectionism
d.    insecurity

ANS: a            Pgs: 275
LO: 6             Factual

7.    In which stage of the family life cycle is marital satisfaction likely to be the lowest?
a.    beginning families
b.    families with school-aged children
c.    families in the middle years
d.    aging families

ANS: b            Pgs: 277
LO: 7             Conceptual

*8.    Crisis during the transition to first parenthood is more likely for
a.    males.
b.    females.
c.    Males and females are equally likely to experience crisis.
d.    Research does not support a major transition to adulthood.

ANS: b            Pg: 277
LO: 9             Conceptual

9. Gender equality in marital chores is
a. notably increased.
b. fairly common.
c. idealistic and probably not really desirable.
d. fairly rare.

**ANS: a**          **Pgs: 280**
**LO: 12**          **Factual**

10. In order to develop his theory of the role of marital communication and risk factors for divorce, Gottman
a. analyzed his own marital experiences and those of three close friends.
b. did an Internet survey of 500 couples.
c. observed couples at 20 shopping malls in the United States over a period of two months.
d. studied over 50 couples using a combination of interview and observational techniques.

**ANS: d**          **Pg: 283**
**LO: 15**          **Factual**

11. Available evidence indicates that remaining in an unhappy marriage tends to
a. be best for the children.
b. be better than getting a divorce.
c. be detrimental to one's adjustment.
d. make the marriage stronger in the end.

**ANS: c**          **Pg: 288**
**LO: 16**          **Conceptual**

12. Compared to married people, sexual relations among single people can be characterized as
a. more frequent and more satisfying.
b. less frequent, but more satisfying.
c. more frequent, but less satisfying.
d. less frequent and less satisfying.

**ANS: d**          **Pg: 291**
**LO: 20**          **Factual**

13. Research on satisfaction with one's life among single people indicates that single
a. men are more satisfied than single women.
b. women are more satisfied than single men.
c. people are happier than married people.
d. people are more satisfied with their sex lives.

**ANS: b**          **Pg: 291**
**LO: 20**          **Factual**

*14.    Bill is a gay male who was once married to a woman.  Among his gay male friends, he finds about _____ percent of them share his former marriage status.
a.    10%
b.    25%
c.    50%
d.    75%

**ANS: b**          **Pg. 295**
**LO: 22**          **Applied**

15.    Which of the following is most likely to be involved in a sexually aggressive incident?
a.    alcohol
b.    strangers
c.    a "date rape drug"
d.    an authority figure

**ANS: a**          **Pg: 296**
**LO: 25**          **Conceptual**


**TRUE/FALSE QUESTIONS**

1.    Endogamy is living together in an intimate relationship.

**ANS: false**          **Pg: 271**
**LO: 4**          **Factual**

2.    Females are more likely than males to value intelligence in a potential mate.

**ANS: true**          **Pg: 273**
**LO: 4**          **Factual**

3.    Youthfulness is a characteristic both genders look for in a mate.

**ANS: false**          **Pg: 273**
**LO: 4**          **Factual**

4.    The family life cycle is a theorized set of stages families progress through.

**ANS: true**          **Pg: 275**
**LO: 7**          **Factual**

5.    According to the text, gender roles tend to be inflexible because of their biological component.

**ANS: false**          **Pg: 279-280**
**LO: 12**          **Factual**

6.      About 50% of marriages end in divorce.

**ANS: true**          **Pg: 285**
**LO: 16**             **Factual**

7.      Divorce rates for second marriages are lower than for first marriages.

**ANS: false**         **Pg: 289**
**LO: 19**             **Factual**

8.      People marrying later in life seem to be largely responsible for the increase of single people in our society.

**ANS: true**          **Pg: 291**
**LO: 20**             **Factual**

9.      Date rape drugs are the most common factor in date rapes.

**ANS: false**         **Pg: 296**
**LO: 25**             **Factual**

10.     Unemployment seems to be an important factor in spouse battery.

**ANS: true**          **Pg: 298**
**LO: 26**             **Factual**


## SHORT-ANSWER ESSAY QUESTIONS

1.      List three factors contributing to the decline of the traditional nuclear family in the United States.

**Pg: 271**

2.      Briefly describe the main gender differences in mate selection preferences and their relationship to evolutionary theory.

**Pg: 273**

*3.     Discuss the effects of cohabitation on long-term relationships and marriage.

**Pgs: 291-292**

*4.     Discuss several ways people select a mate that are similar to themselves.

**Pg: 272**

*5.     How do males and females differ in their mate selection preferences?

**Pgs: 273-274**

6.      Briefly explain the U-shaped relationship found between stages of family life cycle and spouses' marital satisfaction.

**Pgs: 276-278**

7.      Briefly describe the kinds of issues that are most likely to result in conflict between parents and their adolescent children.

**Pg: 278**

*8.     Discuss men's contribution to household chores.

**Pg: 280**

9.      List several explanations for the rise in marital satisfaction that occurs after children leave home.

**Pgs: 278-279**

10.     Summarize the research findings indicating that maternal employment can have positive effects on children.

**Pg: 282**

11.     List some of the characteristics of communication patterns in unhappily married spouses.

**Pgs: 283-285**

*12.    Discuss the effects of divorce on children.

**Pgs: 288-289**

13.     Briefly explain the finding that premarital cohabitation is associated with higher divorce rates in some countries, including the United States.

**Pg: 292**

14.     List several similarities between gay relationships and marital relationships.

**Pgs: 293-294**

15.     Discuss the factors that contribute to the occurrence of date or acquaintance rape.

**Pgs: 296-297**

16.     Discuss the factors that contribute to a battered woman staying in the abusive relationship.

**Pg: 299**

# Chapter 10
# GENDER AND BEHAVIOR

## LEARNING OBJECTIVES

1.  Explain the nature of gender stereotypes and the connection with instrumentality and expressiveness.
2.  Discuss four important points about gender stereotypes.
3.  Summarize the research findings on gender similarities and differences in verbal, mathematical, and spatial abilities.
4.  Summarize the research on gender differences in personality and social behavior.
5.  Summarize the research on gender and psychological disorders.
6.  Summarize the situation regarding overall behavioral differences between males and females.
7.  Give two explanations for why gender differences appear to be larger than they actually are.
8.  Summarize evolutionary explanations for gender differences.
9.  Review the evidence linking gender differences in cognitive abilities to brain organization.
10. Review the evidence relating hormones to gender differences.
11. Define socialization and gender roles, and describe Margaret Mead's findings on the variability of gender roles and their implications.
12. Explain how reinforcement and punishment, observational learning, and self-socialization operate in gender-role socialization.
13. Describe how parents and peers influence gender-role socialization.
14. Describe how schools and the media influence gender-role socialization.
15. List five elements of the traditional male role and contrast these with the modern male role.
16. Describe three common problems associated with the traditional male role.
17. List three major expectations of the traditional female role.
18. Describe three common problems associated with the traditional female role.
19. Describe two ways in which women are victimized by sexism.
20. Explain the basis for traditional gender roles and why they are changing.
21. Define gender-role identity and discuss two alternatives to traditional gender roles.
22. Describe how the different socialization experiences of males and females contribute to communication problems between men and women.
23. Describe expressive and instrumental styles of communication.
24. Describe some common mixed-gender communication problems.

# MULTIPLE CHOICE QUESTIONS

1.       Which of the following terms refers to the state of being male or female?
a.     sex
b.     gender
c.     gender identity
d.     sexual orientation

**ANS: b**         **Pg: 303**
**LO: 1**         **Factual**

*2.     If Bruce is a stereotypical male, he will generally be _____.
a.     instructive
b.     expressive
c.     intrinsic
d.     instrumental

**ANS: d**         **Pg: 305**
**LO: 1**         **Applied**

*3.     An _____ orientation is an orientation toward emotion and relationships.
a.     instructive
b.     expressive
c.     intrinsic
d.     instrumental

**ANS: b**         **Pg: 305**
**LO: 1**         **Factual**

4.     _____ are widely shared beliefs about males' and females' abilities, personality traits, and social behavior.
a.     Gender roles
b.     Gender differences
c.     Sexual orientations
d.     Gender stereotypes

**ANS: d**         **Pg: 304**
**LO: 2**         **Factual**

5.     Which of the following is generally **not** considered an element of the traditional gender stereotype associated with masculinity?
a.     ambitious
b.     persistent
c.     emotional
d.     self-confident

**ANS: c**         **Pg: 305**
**LO: 2**         **Factual**

*6.     The boundaries between how the typical male and the typical female are expected to
        behave is becoming
a.      more defined.
b.      non-existent.
c.      stagnate.
d.      more flexible.

**ANS d**              **Pg: 305**
**LO: 2**              **Conceptual**


7.      The fact that gender stereotypes view male behavior as normal reflects an _____ bias.
a.      egocentric
b.      ethnocentric
c.      androcentric
d.      androgynous

**ANS: c**             **Pg: 305**
**LO: 2**              **Coceptual**


8.      The androcentric bias in gender stereotypes refers to
a.      the fact that a greater number of traits are attributed to men than to women.
b.      the fact that a greater number of traits are attributed to women than to men.
c.      the belief that traits associated with males represent the norm.
d.      the belief that traits associated with females represent the norm.

**ANS: c**             **Pg: 305**
**LO: 2**              **Conceptual**


9.      An important point about gender stereotypes is that since the 1980s, they
a.      have become more pronounced.
b.      seem to have become less rigid.
c.      have nearly reversed themselves.
d.      have become more universal across cultures.

**ANS: b**             **Pg: 305**
**LO: 2**              **Factual**


10.     A research technique used to evaluate the results of many studies on the same question is
        called a
a.      meta-analysis.
b.      factor analysis.
c.      quasi-experiment.
d.      correlational analysis.

**ANS: a**             **Pg: 306**
**LO: 3**              **Factual**

11.    In gender research, the meta-analysis has allowed researchers to
a.    obtain larger samples.
b.    determine causal relationships.
c.    better assess the size and consistency of gender differences.
d.    examine perceptions of gender stereotypes.

**ANS: c**          **Pg: 306**
**LO: 3**           **Factual**

*12.    As a child, Pat started speaking early and had a large vocabulary. It is likely that Pat is
a.    female.
b.    male.
c.    better than normal at math.
d.    an only child.

**ANS: a**          **Pg: 306**
**LO: 3**           **Applied**

13.    Research on gender differences in cognitive abilities indicates that there exists
a.    a slight advantage for males due to larger brain size.
b.    a slight advantage for females due to overall better physical health.
c.    a male advantage on verbal skills and a female advantage on math skills.
d.    no substantial differences in overall intelligence.

**ANS: d**          **Pg: 306**
**LO: 3**           **Factual**

14.    Research on gender differences in mathematical ability indicates that
a.    girls are more precocious than boys in mathematics.
b.    boys generally do better than girls on mathematical analogies.
c.    girls outperform boys at the high end of the mathematical ability distribution.
d.    boys outperform girls in mathematical problem-solving when they reach high school.

**ANS: d**          **Pgs: 306-307**
**LO: 3**           **Factual**

*15.    Research on gender differences in verbal ability indicates that
a.    girls are more verbally fluent.
b.    girls generally do better than boys on verbal analogies.
c.    a and b.
d.    none of the these.

**ANS: a**          **Pg: 306**
**LO: 3**           **Factual**

16. Jerry and Jane are 10-year-old twins. They have performed about the same in all school subjects up to the present time. It would be reasonably safe to predict that
a. Jerry has a higher IQ than Jane and will shortly begin to outperform Jane in all middle and high school subjects.
b. starting in high school, Jane will begin to outperform Jerry in all subjects that require intensive memorization.
c. Jane will fail miserably at any task involving spatial skills, starting in 10th grade.
d. Jerry will outperform Jane slightly in mathematical problem-solving starting in high school.

**ANS: d**          **Pg: 306**
**LO: 3**          **Factual**

17. A meta-analysis showed that males clearly outperform females in one type of spatial ability:
a. mental rotation.
b. body orientation.
c. spatial analogies.
d. cognitive mapping.

**ANS: a**          **Pg: 307**
**LO: 3**          **Factual**

18. For which of the following has a clear and consistent gender difference never been found?
a. verbal ability
b. spatial ability
c. self-esteem
d. talkativeness in mixed-sex groups

**ANS: c**          **Pg: 307**
**LO: 4**          **Conceptual**

*19. Casey and Caleb are a set of female/male twins. When tested for self-esteem they scored virtually the same. They are most likely
a. Caucasian and in the upper-class.
b. non-Caucasian and in the upper-class.
c. non-Caucasian and in a lower-class.
d. Caucasian and in a lower-class.

**ANS: b**          **Pg: 307**
**LO: 4**          **Applied**

20.     It appears that boys engage in more _____ aggression and girls engage in more _____
        aggression.
a.      verbal; physical
b.      physical; relational
c.      physical; antisocial
d.      relational; antisocial

ANS: b              Pg: 308
LO: 4               Factual

21.     A young girl is more likely than a young boy to engage in which of the following
        behaviors?
a.      hitting another child
b.      pushing another child
c.      threatening another child
d.      spreading rumors about another child

ANS: d              Pg: 308
LO: 4               Conceptual

*22.    The type of aggression shown in boys and girls
a.      changes according to the culture.
b.      does not change according to culture.
c.      Girls are more physically aggressive in non-Western cultures.
d.      Boys are more indirectly aggressive in non-Western cultures.

ANS: b              Pgs: 308
LO: 4               Conceptual

23.     One explanation for women's apparent tendency to conform more readily to social
        pressure is that
a.      women typically hold lower social status in most groups.
b.      women are genetically inclined to conform.
c.      women in general are more gullible than men are.
d.      women are biologically programmed to manipulate rather than demand.

ANS: a              Pg: 308
LO: 4               Factual

24.     Research suggests that the major emotional difference between men and women is
a.      women are more emotional than men.
b.      women are more expressive than men.
c.      women don't get angry as easily as men.
d.      men don't fall in love very often.

ANS: b              Pgs: 308-309
LO: 4               Conceptual

*25.    Regarding gender differences in sexuality,
a.      men are more interested in sex than women.
b.      the connection of sex and intimacy is more important for women.
c.      aggression is more often linked to sex for men.
d.      All of the these are true.

**ANS: d**          **Pg: 308**
**LO: 4**           **Factual**


*26.    Regarding gender differences in sexuality, which is NOT true?
a.      Men are more interested in sex than women.
b.      The connection of sex an intimacy is more important for women.
c.      Aggression more often linked to sex for men.
d.      It is natural for a women to not enjoy sex.

**ANS: d**          **Pg: 308**
**LO: 4**           **Factual**


27.     Regarding overall incidence of mental disorders, men and women are _____; regarding
        the disorders men and women tend to develop, they're _____.
a.      similar; different
b.      different; similar
c.      similar; also very similar
d.      different; also very different

**ANS: a**          **Pg: 309**
**LO: 5**           **Conceptual**


28.     Research indicates that about _____ will develop a psychological disorder at one time or
        another.
a.      a third of all men
b.      20% of all women
c.      half of all people
d.      one out of every three people

**ANS: d**          **Pg: 309**
**LO: 5**           **Factual**


29.     Judy has been diagnosed with a psychological disorder.  Which of the following disorders
        is she most likely to have?
a.      alcoholism
b.      depression
c.      antisocial behavior
d.      multiple-personality disorder

**ANS: b**          **Pg: 309**
**LO: 5**           **Conceptual**

30.  Which of the following is a reason that has been proposed for gender differences in the occurrence of psychological disorders?
a.  Sex hormones may be linked to different mental illnesses in males and females.
b.  Females are genetically more prone to depression and hysteria than are men.
c.  The disorders and their symptoms reflect the dynamics enforced by traditional gender roles.
d.  Brain differences between men and women may account for these differences.

**ANS: c**      **Pgs: 309-310**
**LO: 5**       **Conceptual**

31.  Genuine, documented gender differences in behavior
a.  tell us nothing about specific individuals.
b.  tell us a great deal about specific individuals.
c.  permit very accurate predictions about individuals.
d.  permit only very general predictions about individuals.

**ANS: a**      **Pg: 310**
**LO: 6**       **Conceptual**

32.  Which of the following researchers proposed social role theory?
a.  Alice Eagly
b.  Diane Halpern
c.  Deborah Tannen
d.  Janet Shibley Hyde

**ANS: a**      **Pg: 310**
**LO: 7**       **Factual**

33.  Social role theory suggests that
a.  we tend to explain role-related behaviors in term of situational factors.
b.  we construct our own reality on the basis of our individual social experiences.
c.  large gender differences in behavior tend to be downplayed by inconsistent social roles.
d.  minor gender differences are exaggerated by the social roles men and women occupy.

**ANS: d**      **Pg: 310**
**LO: 7**       **Factual**

34.  "Gender differences are in the eye of the beholder" is a statement of the explanation for these differences put forth by
a.  social role theorists.
b.  social constructionists.
c.  social learning theorists.
d.  visual gender determinists.

**ANS: b**      **Pg: 310**
**LO: 7**       **Factual**

35. According to _____, the tendency to look for gender differences, as well as our specific beliefs about gender, are rooted in the "gendered" messages and conditioning that are common in our socialization experiences.
a. evolutionary psychology
b. social learning theory
c. social constructionism
d. the theory of cognitive dissonance

ANS: c          Pg: 310
LO: 7           Conceptual

36. Which of the following possible influences on gender differences in behavior is most likely to be emphasized by an evolutionary psychologist?
a. economic constraints
b. patterns of socialization
c. natural selection pressures
d. environmental pressures such as the media

ANS: c          Pg: 311
LO: 8           Factual

37. Dr. Pliocene believes that males are more aggressive in virtually all world cultures because aggressiveness has a partial genetic cause and leads to social dominance and greater access to material resources. Dr. Pliocene holds a _____ view of gender differences.
a. social
b. clinical
c. evolutionary
d. physiological

ANS: c          Pg: 311
LO: 8           Factual

38. To support their assertions, evolutionary psychologists look for gender differences
a. in spatial ability only.
b. that are consistent across cultures.
c. that are specific to particular cultures.
d. in behaviors that are consistent with gender stereotypes.

ANS: b          Pg: 311
LO: 8           Conceptual

39. The two major divisions of the largest portion of the brain are the
a. frontal lobes.
b. parietal lobes.
c. cerebral hemispheres.
d. verbal brain and the spatial brain.

ANS: c          Pg: 312
LO: 9           Factual

40. It appears that the left hemisphere is more actively involved in _____ and mathematical processing, while the right hemisphere is specialized to handle _____ processing.
a. nonverbal; verbal
b. verbal; visual-spatial
c. visual-spatial; verbal
d. nonverbal; visual-spatial

**ANS: b**          **Pg: 312**
**LO: 9**           **Factual**

41. Which of the following has not been found in studies on hemispheric specialization?
a. Females tend to have a larger corpus callosum.
b. Males exhibit more cerebral specialization than females.
c. The cerebral cortex is more convoluted in males than in females.
d. The right and left hemispheres are specialized to handle different cognitive tasks.

**ANS: c**          **Pg: 312**
**LO: 9**           **Factual**

42. The notion that cerebral specialization is linked to gender differences in mental abilities
a. is still under debate.
b. has no basis in scientific fact.
c. is based primarily on anecdotal evidence.
d. has been consistently supported by research.

**ANS: a**          **Pg: 312**
**LO: 9**           **Factual**

43. Chemical substances released into the bloodstream by the endocrine glands are called
a. gonads.
b. enzymes.
c. hormones.
d. neurotransmitters.

**ANS: c**          **Pg: 312**
**LO: 10**          **Factual**

44. Research on females exposed to high levels of androgens prenatally suggests that
a. androgen is basically a "female hormone".
b. prenatal hormones may contribute to gender differences.
c. the female embryo is highly resistant to the effects of such hormones.
d. none of the these.

**ANS: b**          **Pg: 313**
**LO: 10**          **Factual**

*45.    Claudia has been diagnosed with low testosterone; she is likely to
a.      experience high sexual desire.
b.      experience low sexual desire.
c.      show traits of "super-femininity".
d.      be relatively unaffected.

**ANS: b**          **Pg: 313**
**LO: 10**          **Applied**

46.     The overall evidence suggests that biological factors play a relatively minor role in
        gender differences, creating pre-dispositions that are largely shaped by
a.      experience.
b.      prepubescent hormones.
c.      unconscious sexual desires.
d.      the desire for self-actualization.

**ANS: a**          **Pg: 313**
**LO: 10**          **Conceptual**

47.     Which of the following statements regarding the origin of gender differences is most
        accurate?
a.      Most of the variation is due to hormonal differences.
b.      Most of the variation is due to differences in brain organization.
c.      Gender differences occur mainly as a function of classical conditioning.
d.      Any explanation must take into account biological and environmental factors.

**ANS: d**          **Pgs: 313-314**
**LO: 10**          **Conceptual**

48.     _____ is the acquisition of the norms and roles expected of people in a particular
        society.
a.      Socialization
b.      Social learning
c.      Social attribution
d.      Sexual orientation

**ANS: a**          **Pg: 313**
**LO: 11**          **Factual**

49.     Cultural expectations about what is appropriate for each gender are called
a.      display rules.
b.      gender roles.
c.      primary sex characteristics.
d.      secondary sex characteristics.

**ANS: b**          **Pg: 313**
**LO: 11**          **Factual**

50. In part, gender roles are shaped by the power of rewards and punishment—the key processes in
a. operant conditioning.
b. classical conditioning.
c. observational learning.
d. social constructionism.

**ANS: a**          **Pg: 314**
**LO: 12**          **Factual**

51. Which of the following is likely to be a typical reaction by a father to gender inappropriate behavior in his son?
a. ridicule
b. physical punishment
c. negative reinforcement
d. positive reinforcement

**ANS: a**          **Pg: 314**
**LO: 12**          **Conceptual**

52. All but which of the following has been shown to influence gender-role socialization?
a. imitation
b. reinforcement
c. self-socialization
d. sexual motivation

**ANS: d**          **Pgs: 314-315**
**LO: 12**          **Conceptual**

53. Gender-role socialization involves
a. imitation.
b. punishment.
c. reinforcement.
d. all of the these.

**ANS: d**          **Pg: 314**
**LO: 12**          **Factual**

54. The fact that children tend to imitate the behavior of same-gender models is most consistent with which of the following?
a. self-attribution
b. self-socialization
c. social learning theory
d. the theory of cognitive dissonance

**ANS: c**          **Pg: 314**
**LO: 12**          **Conceptual**

55.     Which of the following contributes to traditional gender roles?
a.      Parents dress boys and girls in similar colors.
b.      Parents purchase gender-appropriate toys for their children.
c.      Parents encourage similar leisure activities for boys and girls.
d.      Children are assigned household chores without regard to their gender.

ANS: b          Pgs: 314-315
LO: 13          Conceptual

*56.    Men seem to be experiencing a "masculinity-crisis" due to
a.      females, not males, seem to be experiencing the crisis.
b.      shifting male gender roles.
c.      economic displacement.
d.      female infringement on traditional male roles.

ANS: b          Pg: 319
LO: 15          Conceptual

*57.    Which of these is NOT part of the "modern male role"?
a.      organizational power
b.      emotional expressivity toward women
c.      emotional sensitivity toward women
d.      economic inexpressiveness

ANS: d          Pg: 319
LO: 15          Conceptual

58.     Gender bias in school is most likely to show up in which of the following?
a.      teachers' behaviors
b.      the books that are used
c.      academic and career counseling
d.      all of the these

ANS: d          Pg: 317
LO: 14          Factual

59.     Which of the following statements best reflects the effect that television has on gender role socialization?
a.      It contributes to traditional stereotypes.
b.      It tends to combat traditional stereotypes.
c.      It reinforces traditional stereotypes for girls more than for boys.
d.      Regular programming has no effect, but commercials reinforce stereotypes.

ANS: a          Pg: 317
LO: 14          Conceptual

60. Who tends to hold more stereotyped beliefs about gender?
a. only boys who watch television frequently
b. only girls who watch television frequently
c. all children who watch television frequently
d. all children who watch television infrequently

ANS: c          Pg: 318
LO: 14          Factual

61. Sources of gender-role socialization include
a. family.
b. schools.
c. the media.
d. all of the these.

ANS: d          Pg: 315
LO: 13          Factual

62. Which of the following is not considered a key element of the traditional male role?
a. the sexual element
b. the dependent element
c. the aggressive element
d. the anti-feminine element

ANS: b          Pgs: 318-319
LO: 15          Factual

63. Remaining cool and calm under pressure is characteristic of which of the following elements of the traditional male role?
a. the sexual element
b. the success element
c. the aggressive element
d. the self-reliant element

ANS: d          Pg: 319
LO: 15          Conceptual

64. According to Joseph Pleck, which of the following characteristics is most closely associated with the "modern male role"?
a. aggressiveness
b. physical strength
c. economic achievement
d. emotional inexpressiveness

ANS: c          Pg: 319
LO: 15          Factual

65. Which of the following would not be considered a cost associated with the male gender role in our culture?
a. pressure to succeed
b. the fatherhood mandate
c. inability to express feelings
d. obsession with sexual performance

**ANS: b**       **Pgs: 319-320**
**LO: 16**       **Conceptual**

66. Difficulties in expressing emotions are most likely to occur in
a. men with traditional attitudes.
b. men with nontraditional attitudes.
c. women with traditional attitudes.
d. women with nontraditional attitudes.

**ANS: a**       **Pg: 320**
**LO: 16**       **Factual**

67. Male gender role socialization may lead to
a. pressure that inhibits sexual performance.
b. an emphasis on intimacy rather than sex.
c. greater satisfaction in sexual encounters.
d. a lack of concern for one's sexual performance.

**ANS: a**       **Pg: 320**
**LO: 16**       **Factual**

68. An intense fear and intolerance of homosexuality is called
a. sexism.
b. homophobia.
c. heterophobia.
d. cross-gender typing.

**ANS: b**       **Pg: 320**
**LO: 16**       **Factual**

69. The traditional female role consists of two major mandates: the _____ mandate, and the _____ mandate.
a. success; marriage
b. success; motherhood
c. marriage; nurturance
d. marriage; motherhood

**ANS: d**       **Pg: 320**
**LO: 17**       **Factual**

70. The marriage and motherhood mandates fuel women's intense focus on _____; that is, learning how to attract and interest males as prospective mates.
a. sexual orientation
b. heterosexual success
c. reproductive fitness
d. the self-reliant mandate

**ANS: b**        **Pg: 321**
**LO: 17**        **Conceptual**

71. In general, higher intelligence and grades are associated with higher career aspirations, but this is less likely to hold true for girls than for boys. This finding illustrates which of the following concepts?
a. reproductive fitness
b. heterosexual success
c. economic discrimination
d. the ability-achievement gap

**ANS: d**        **Pg: 323**
**LO: 18**        **Conceptual**

72. Today, about _____ percent of married women with children under the age of six work outside the home.
a. 25%
b. 40%
c. 60%
d. 80%

**ANS: c**        **Pg: 323**
**LO: 18**        **Factual**

73. Women's sexual problems are likely to focus on which of the following?
a. impotence
b. difficulty enjoying sex
c. obsession with performance
d. the maternal urge to reproduce

**ANS: b**        **Pg: 323**
**LO: 18**        **Factual**

74. Discrimination against people on the basis of their gender is called
a. sexism.
b. androcentrism.
c. gender stereotyping.
d. gender identification.

**ANS: a**        **Pg: 324**
**LO: 19**        **Factual**

*75.    In 2003, about _____ percent of physicians were women.
a.    10
b.    30
c.    50
d.    75

ANS: b          Pg: 324
LO: 19          Factual

76.    Economic discrimination against women is most likely to involve which of the following?
a.    lack of appropriate training
b.    differential treatment on the job
c.    stricter guidelines regarding appropriate attire
d.    none of the these

ANS: b          Pgs: 324-325
LO: 19          Factual

77.    Women are most likely to hold which of the following jobs?
a.    clergy
b.    physician
c.    college teacher
d.    kindergarten teacher

ANS: d          Pg: 324
LO: 19          Factual

78.    Which of the following is generally not considered a form of aggression toward girls and women?
a.    rape
b.    sexual harassment
c.    violent pornography
d.    All of the these are considered aggression toward females.

ANS: d          Pg: 325
LO: 19          Factual

79.    In earlier societies, gender roles
a.    were nonexistent.
b.    were largely androgynous.
c.    constituted an economic division of labor.
d.    were the opposite of modern roles.

ANS: c          Pg: 326
LO: 20          Factual

*80.    Who is more likely to embrace the success ethic as part of masculinity?
a.      only males older than 58
b.      all males older than 38
c.      only males 18-37
d.      Males of all ages embrace the success ethic equally.

ANS: b          Pg: 326
LO: 20          Conceptual

81.     Gender roles are changing mainly because of
a.      political changes.
b.      economic changes.
c.      changes in religious beliefs.
d.      changes that are essentially temporary fads.

ANS: b          Pg: 326
LO: 20          Factual

82.     A person's identification with the traits regarded as masculine or feminine is called
a.      sexual orientation.
b.      gender stereotype.
c.      gender-role identity.
d.      gender-role transcendence.

ANS: c          Pg: 327
LO: 21          Factual

83.     A personality pattern in which one scores high on measures of both masculinity and
        femininity is called
a.      bisexual.
b.      androgynous.
c.      androcentrism.
d.      gender-role undifferentiated.

ANS: b          Pg: 327
LO: 21          Factual

84.     When Pat takes a personality inventory, the resulting scores on the subscales that measure
        masculinity and femininity are both low. This pattern of scoring is called
a.      bisexual.
b.      androgyny.
c.      androcentrism.
d.      gender-role undifferentiated.

ANS: d          Pg: 327
LO: 21          Factual

85. The idea that being androgynous is psychologically healthier than being gender-typed was proposed by
a. Phyllis Chesler.
b. Sandra Bem.
c. Daryl Bem.
d. Margaret Mead.

**ANS: b**          **Pg: 328**
**LO: 21**          **Factual**

86. According to research findings, people who display which of the following types of traits are likely to be the healthiest, psychologically?
a. androgyny
b. traditionally feminine
c. traditionally masculine
d. gender-role undifferentiated

**ANS: c**          **Pg: 328**
**LO: 21**          **Factual**

87. The concept of gender role transcendence challenges the assumption that
a. gender roles are a source of difficulty in modern societies.
b. the male role is more complimentary than the female role.
c. gender roles are necessary for an equitable division of labor.
d. some traits are inherently masculine and others are feminine.

**ANS: d**          **Pg: 328**
**LO: 21**          **Conceptual**

88. According to Deborah Tannen, _____ are likely to learn a language of "status and independence" and _____ are likely to learn a language of "connection and intimacy."
a. females; males
b. males; females
c. adults; children
d. children; adults

**ANS: b**          **Pg: 330**
**LO: 22**          **Factual**

89. According to Deborah Tannen, communication between males and females is most similar to communication between which of the following?
a. different cultures
b. adolescents and parents
c. children and older siblings
d. employees and supervisors

**ANS: a**          **Pg: 330**
**LO: 22**          **Conceptual**

90. In general, girls achieve high status in their groups through
a. sharing.
c. popularity.
b. dominant behavior.
d. verbal aggression.

**ANS: b**        **Pg: 330**
**LO: 22**        **Factual**

91. Male athletes are popular in high school in part because their peers view them as
a. sharing.
b. dominant.
c. aggressive.
d. humorous.

**ANS: b**        **Pg: 330**
**LO: 22**        **Conceptual**

92. An _____ style of communication focuses on reaching practical goals and finding solutions to problems.
a. operant
b. expressive
c. instrumental
d. androgynous

**ANS: c**        **Pg: 331**
**LO: 23**        **Factual**

93. An _____ style of communication is characterized by the ability to express tender emotions easily and being sensitive to the feelings of others.
a. operant
b. expressive
c. instrumental
d. androgynous

**ANS: b**        **Pg: 331**
**LO: 23**        **Factual**

94. Men are more likely to use a(n) _____ style of communication, and women are more likely to use a(n) _____ style.
a. aggressive; nurturing
b. nurturing; aggressive
c. instrumental; expressive
d. expressive; instrumental

**ANS: c**        **Pg: 331**
**LO: 23**        **Factual**

95.     A large number of studies indicate that women are more skilled than men in _____
        communication.
a.      sexual
b.      nonverbal
c.      persuasive
d.      instrumental

**ANS: b**          **Pg: 331**
**LO: 23**          **Factual**

96.     Barb wants Bob to sympathize with her; Bob thinks Barb wants him to help her to solve a
        problem. This couple's difficulty exemplifies the mixed-sex communication problem
        known as
a.      report talk.
b.      rapport talk.
c.      a mismatch.
d.      lecturing and listening.

**ANS: c**          **Pg: 331**
**LO: 24**          **Applied**

97.     Tannen suggests that many frustrations could be avoided if
a.      men used instrumental communication styles more than they do.
b.      women made greater use of instrumental communication.
c.      men and women were more aware of gender-based differences in communication style.
d.      men and women were less conscious of their differences and learned to relax in their
        relationships.

**ANS: c**          **Pgs: 332-333**
**LO: 24**          **Conceptual**

# MULTIPLE CHOICE QUESTIONS FROM STUDY GUIDE

1. Which of the following statements regarding gender differences in verbal abilities is accurate?
a. Boys have larger vocabularies than girls.
b. Girls usually start speaking earlier than boys.
c. Girls seem to fare better on verbal analogies.
d. Girls are more likely than boys to be stutterers.

**ANS: b**            **Pg: 306**
**LO: 3**             **Conceptual**

2. Research findings indicate that with respect to aggressive behavior,
a. females are slightly more aggressive than males.
b. males engage in more physical aggression.
c. males are more aggressive, but only when they are provoked.
d. males are more aggressive than females, but the difference disappears by about 10 years of age.

**ANS: b**            **Pg: 308**
**LO: 4**             **Conceptual**

3. Regarding gender differences in communication, it has been found that
a. women talk more than men.
b. women tend to speak more tentatively.
c. men are more sensitive to nonverbal cues.
d. men tend to interrupt women less than women interrupt men.

**ANS: b**            **Pg: 309**
**LO: 4**             **Factual**

4. The overall incidence of mental disorders indicates that
a. it is roughly the same for both genders.
b. they are more likely to occur in women than men.
c. they are more likely to occur in men than women.
d. gender differences are unclear because many disorders are unreported.

**ANS: a**            **Pg: 309**
**LO: 5**             **Factual**

5. Which of the following disorders is more common in men than in women?
a. depression.
b. eating disorders.
c. anxiety disorders.
d. alcoholism.

**ANS: d**            **Pg: 309**
**LO: 5**             **Factual**

6. Evolutionary psychologists explain social behaviors such as aggression and mating patterns in terms of different _____ pressures operating on the genders over the course of human history.
a. economic
b. hormonal
c. environmental
d. natural selection

**ANS: d**          **Pg: 311**
**LO: 8**           **Conceptual**

7. The notion that cerebral specialization is linked to gender differences in mental abilities
a. is still under debate.
b. has been rejected by researchers.
c. has been consistently supported by empirical evidence.
d. was popular 50 years ago, and has recently resurfaced.

**ANS: a**          **Pg: 312**
**LO: 9**           **Conceptual**

8. Gender-role socialization occurs through
a. self-socialization.
b. observational learning.
c. reinforcement and punishment.
d. All of the these play a part in the acquisition of gender roles.

**ANS: a**          **Pg: 315**
**LO: 12**          **Factual**

9. Between the ages of four and six, children tend to separate into
a. same-gender groups.
b. opposite-gender groups.
c. groups based on their level of socialization.
d. small groups that are formed on the basis of socioeconomic status.

**ANS: a**          **Pg: 316**
**LO: 13**          **Factual**

10. The intense fear and intolerance of homosexuality is
a. termed homophobia.
b. more common in women than in men.
c. the root cause of anxiety disorders in many men.
d. virtually nonexistent in Western cultures.

**ANS: a**          **Pg: 320**
**LO: 16**          **Factual**

11. Heterosexual success refers to
a. the efforts of men to be a good husband and parent.
b. males' level of sexual activity during late adolescence.
c. homosexuals' efforts to gain success in a heterosexual world.
d. women learning how to attract and interest males as prospective mates.

**ANS: d**       **Pg: 321**
**LO: 17**      **Factual**

12. An androgynous person is one who
a. is said to be gender-typed.
b. scores above average on measures of both masculinity and femininity.
c. scores low on measures of both masculinity and femininity.
d. is said to be gender-role undifferentiated.

**ANS: b**       **Pg: 327**
**LO: 21**      **Factual**

13. Sandra Bem suggests that androgynous people are
a. less flexible in their behavior.
b. psychologically healthier than those who are gender-typed.
c. becoming the norm in modern society.
d. more likely to engage in homosexual behavior.

**ANS: b**       **Pg: 328**
**LO: 21**      **Conceptual**

14. When Deborah Tannen says that males and females are socialized in different "cultures," she means that
a. males are influenced by their fathers and females by their mothers.
b. males learn status and independence, while females learn connection and intimacy.
c. males tend to have only male friends, whereas females have friends of both genders.
d. more attention is paid to female children throughout their early childhood.

**ANS: b**       **Pg: 330**
**LO: 22**      **Conceptual**

15. Tannen suggests that many frustrations could be avoided if
a. men used instrumental communication styles more than they do.
b. women made greater use of instrumental communication.
c. men and women were more aware of gender-based differences in communication style.
d. men and women could learn to relax in their relationships with each other.

**ANS: c**       **Pg: 332-333**
**LO: 24**      **Factual**

1.  The fact that gender stereotypes view male behavior as normal reflects an _____ bias.
    a.  egocentric
    b.  ethnocentric
    c.  androcentric
    d.  androgynous

    **ANS: c**          **Pg: 305**
    **LO: 2**           **Conceptual**

2.  Research on gender differences in mathematical ability indicates that
    a.  girls are more precocious than boys in mathematics.
    b.  boys generally do better than girls on mathematical analogies.
    c.  girls outperform boys at the high end of the mathematical ability distribution.
    d.  boys outperform girls in mathematical problem-solving when they reach high school.

    **ANS: d**          **Pg: 305**
    **LO: 3**           **Factual**

3.  A young girl is more likely than a young boy to engage in which of the following behaviors?
    a.  hitting another child
    b.  pushing another child
    c.  threatening another child
    d.  spreading rumors about another child

    **ANS: d**          **Pg: 308**
    **LO: 4**           **Conceptual**

4.  Research indicates that about _____ will develop a psychological disorder at one time or another.
    a.  a third of all men
    b.  20% of all women
    c.  half of all people
    d.  one out of every three people

    **ANS: d**          **Pg: 309**
    **LO: 5**           **Factual**

5.  According to _____, the tendency to look for gender differences, as well as our specific beliefs about gender, are rooted in the "gendered" messages and conditioning that are common in our socialization experiences.
    a.  evolutionary psychology
    b.  social learning theory
    c.  social constructionism
    d.  the theory of cognitive dissonance

    **ANS: c**          **Pg: 310**
    **LO: 7**           **Conceptual**

6. The notion that cerebral specialization is linked to gender differences in mental abilities
a. is still under debate.
b. has no basis in scientific fact.
c. is based primarily on anecdotal evidence.
d. has been consistently supported by research.

**ANS: a**     **Pg: 312**
**LO: 9**      **Factual**

7. Cultural expectations about what is appropriate for each gender are called
a. display rules.
b. gender roles.
c. primary sex characteristics.
d. secondary sex characteristics.

**ANS: b**     **Pg: 313-314**
**LO: 11**     **Factual**

*8. Men seem to be experiencing a "masculinity-crisis" due to
a. Females not males seem to be experiencing the crisis.
b. shifting male gender roles.
c. economic displacement.
d. female infringement on traditional male roles.

**ANS: b**     **Pg: 319**
**LO: 15**     **Conceptual**

9. Remaining cool and calm under pressure is characteristic of which of the following elements of the traditional male role?
a. the sexual element
b. the success element
c. the aggressive element
d. the self-reliant element

**ANS: d**     **Pg: 318-319**
**LO: 15**     **Conceptual**

10. The marriage and motherhood mandates fuel women's intense focus on _____, that is, learning how to attract and interest males as prospective mates.
a. sexual orientation
b. heterosexual success
c. reproductive fitness
d. the self-reliant mandate

**ANS: b**     **Pg: 321**
**LO: 17**     **Conceptual**

11. Women are most likely to hold which of the following jobs?
a. clergy
b. physician
c. college teacher
d. kindergarten teacher

**ANS: d**       **Pg: 324**
**LO: 19**      **Factual**

12. When Pat takes a personality inventory, the resulting scores on the subscales that measure masculinity and femininity are both low. This pattern of scoring is called
a. bisexual.
b. androgyny.
c. androcentrism.
d. gender-role undifferentiated.

**ANS: d**       **Pg: 327**
**LO: 21**      **Factual**

13. According to Deborah Tannen, communication between males and females is most similar to communication between which of the following?
a. different cultures
b. adolescents and parents
c. children and older siblings
d. employees and supervisors

**ANS: a**       **Pg: 330**
**LO: 22**      **Conceptual**

14. An _____ style of communication focuses on reaching practical goals and finding solutions to problems.
a. operant
b. expressive
c. instrumental
d. androgynous

**ANS: c**       **Pg: 331**
**LO: 23**      **Factual**

15. Men are more likely to use a(n) _____ style of communication, and women are more likely to use a(n) _____ style.
a. aggressive; nurturing
b. nurturing; aggressive
c. instrumental; expressive
d. expressive; instrumental

**ANS: c**       **Pg: 331**
**LO: 23**      **Factual**

# TRUE/FALSE QUESTIONS

1. Gender is defined in psychology as biologically determined.

**ANS: false**      **Pg: 303**
**LO: 1**           **Factual**

2. Female babies tend to speak sooner than male babies.

**ANS: true**       **Pg: 306**
**LO: 3**           **Factual**

3. Males consistently outperform females in mental rotation.

**ANS: true**       **Pg: 307**
**LO: 3**           **Factual**

4. Females conform in ways that are typical of low-status members of a group

**ANS: true**       **Pg: 308**
**LO: 4**           **Factual**

5. Social role theories' main principle is that biologically determined behaviors are primarily responsible for gender differences.

**ANS: false**      **Pg: 310**
**LO: 7**           **Factual**

6. Hormones are chemical substances released in the bloodstream.

**ANS: true**       **Pg: 312**
**LO: 10**          **Factual**

7. Gender roles are cognitive structures that guide processing of gender-relevant information.

**ANS: false**     **Pg: 313**
**LO: 10**          **Factual**

8. Gender-role identity is a person's identification with masculinity of femininity.

**ANS:  true**      **Pg: 327**
**LO: 21**          **Factual**

9. Bisexuality is indicated by high scores on both masculine and feminine scales.

**ANS: false**      **Pg: 327**
**LO: 21**          **Factual**

10. Tannen theorizes that male and female communication styles are as different as the styles between different cultures.

**ANS: true**　　　**Pg: 330**
**LO: 24**　　　**Factual**


## SHORT-ANSWER ESSAY QUESTIONS

1. Briefly explain the distinction between the terms "sex" and "gender."

**Pgs: 303-304**

2. Briefly explain how meta-analysis is used in research on gender and some of the findings this technique has clarified.

**Pg: 306**

*3. Summarize the research findings on gender differences in verbal ability.

**Pg: 306**

*4. Summarize the research findings on gender in mathematical ability.

**Pgs: 306-307**

*5. Summarize the research findings on gender differences in aggressive behavior.

**Pg: 308**

6. Summarize the research findings on gender differences in verbal and nonverbal communication.

**Pg: 309**

7. Identify several psychological disorders that tend to be associated with each gender.

**Pgs: 309-310**

8. Identify and briefly discuss the four primary sources of gender role socialization and compare and contrast play behavior among same-gender peers in boys and girls.

**Pgs: 315-318**

9. Briefly explain how the traditional male role can create sexual problems for males.

**Pg: 320**

10. Distinguish between the "marriage mandate" and the "motherhood mandate" as they apply to the traditional female role.

**Pg: 320**

11.     Explain why socio-linguist Deborah Tannen characterizes mixed-gender communication as a clash of two "cultures."

**Pg: 330**

# Chapter 11
# DEVELOPMENT IN ADOLESCENCE AND ADULTHOOD

## LEARNING OBJECTIVES

1. Define and discuss pubescence and secondary sex characteristics.
2. Define and discuss puberty and primary sex characteristics.
3. Summarize the findings on early and late maturation in boys and girls.
4. Describe the cognitive changes that occur during adolescence.
5. Explain Erikson's psychosocial crisis of adolescence and Marcia's four identity statuses.
6. Discuss whether adolescence is a period of turmoil and recent trends in adolescent suicide.
7. Summarize the key developmental transitions in early adulthood, including Erikson's views.
8. Summarize the key developmental transitions in middle adulthood, including Erikson's views.
9. Summarize the key developmental transitions in late adulthood, including Erikson's views.
10. Discuss age-related changes in appearance and their psychological significance.
11. Describe the sensory, neurological, and endocrine changes that accompany aging.
12. Discuss health changes associated with aging and two things people can do to maintain their health.
13. Describe age-related changes in intelligence, information processing, and memory.
14. Summarize evidence on personality change and stability in adulthood.
15. Discuss cultural and individual attitudes about death.
16. Describe Kübler-Ross's five stages of dying and research findings about the dying process.
17. Describe cultural variations in mourning practices and discuss the grieving process.
18. Discuss different types of loss and what helps people cope with bereavement.
19. Describe Ainsworth's three attachment styles and how caregivers can promote secure attachment in their infants.
20. Summarize the research on the effects of day care on infants and children.
21. Discuss Baumrind's parenting styles and their effects on children's development.
22. Discuss issues related to the effective parenting of adolescents.
23. List five suggestions for more effective parenting.
24. List five suggestions for the effective use of punishment.

**MULTIPLE CHOICE QUESTIONS**

1.    Pubescence is a term used to describe the
a.    onset of adolescence.
b.    two-year span preceding puberty.
c.    first occurrence of menstruation in girls.
d.    two-year span immediately following puberty.

**ANS: b**              **Pg: 338**
**LO: 1**               **Factual**

2.    Secondary sex characteristics include all but which of the following?
a.    facial hair in males
b.    voice changes in males
c.    breast growth in females
d.    maturation of reproductive structures

**ANS: d**              **Pg: 338**
**LO: 1**               **Factual**

3.    Which of the following would **not** be considered a secondary sex characteristic?
a.    appearance of pubic hair
b.    sperm production in males
c.    deepened voice in males
d.    breast development in females

**ANS: b**              **Pg: 338**
**LO: 1**               **Factual**

4.    Puberty is the stage during which _____ develop fully.
a.    master glands
b.    gender stereotypes
c.    primary sex characteristics
d.    secondary sex characteristics

**ANS: c**              **Pg: 338**
**LO: 2**               **Factual**

5.    The structures necessary for reproduction, which are developed fully during puberty, are
      called
a.    gonads.
b.    master glands.
c.    primary sex characteristics.
d.    secondary sex characteristics.

**ANS: c**              **Pg: 338**
**LO: 2**               **Factual**

*6.     Lizzy is beginning to develop breasts and grow pubic hair.  She is most likely in which
        stage?
a.      middle childhood
b.      pubescence
c.      adolescence
d.      teenesence

**ANS: b**              **Pg: 338**
**LO: 1**               **Applied**

7.      The onset of puberty in females is signalled by
a.      menarche.
b.      breast development.
c.      presence of pubic hair.
d.      widening of pelvic bones.

**ANS: a**              **Pg: 339**
**LO: 2**               **Factual**

8.      Which of the following constitutes an index of sexual maturity in males?
a.      deepening of the voice
b.      the appearance of facial hair
c.      the capacity to ejaculate sperm
d.      an increase in height and weight

**ANS: c**              **Pg: 339**
**LO: 2**               **Factual**

9.      Which of the following statements about puberty is accurate?
a.      In girls, it officially ends with menarche.
b.      It ends by age 11 in both boys and girls.
c.      It arrives about the same time in boys and girls.
d.      It arrives about two years later in boys than in girls.

**ANS: d**              **Pg: 339**
**LO: 2**               **Factual**

*10.    Spermarchy is
a.      when the testes gain the ability to produce sperm.
b.      when females are first capable of being inseminated.
c.      the first ejaculation.
d.      a nocturnal emission.

**ANS: c**              **Pg: 339**
**LO: 2**               **Conceptual**

11.    Girls who mature _____ and boys who mature _____ seem to feel particularly anxious
       and self-conscious about their changing bodies.
a.     early; early
b.     early; late
c.     late; early
d.     late; late

**ANS: b**          **Pg: 340**
**LO: 3**           **Conceptual**

12.    Which of the following groups is likely to have the easiest time dealing with puberty?
a.     girls who mature late
b.     girls who mature early
c.     boys who mature late
d.     boys who mature early

**ANS: d**          **Pg: 340**
**LO: 3**           **Conceptual**

13.    Compared to those who are younger, adolescents can think
a.     abstractly.
b.     concretely.
c.     egotistically.
d.     empathetically.

**ANS: a**          **Pg: 340**
**LO: 4**           **Factual**

*14.   In early adolescence, major changes take place in thinking and problem solving for
       whom?
a.     females
b.     males
c.     males and females
d.     Major changes do not take place until middle adolescence.

**ANS: c**          **Pg: 340**
**LO: 4**           **Conceptual**

*15.   Kelso, 17 years old, is constantly doing activities like climbing mountains and riding a
       motorcycle without a helmet.  Kelso probably
a.     knows the risks.
b.     does not know the risks.
c.     can't abstractly consider the consequences.
d.     none of these.

**ANS: a**          **Pg: 341**
**LO: 4**           **Factual**

16. Which of the researchers is best known for his work on the development of identity?
a. Carl Jung
b. Erik Erikson
c. Alfred Adler
d. Albert Ellis

**ANS: b** **Pg: 342**
**LO: 5** **Factual**

17. _____ refers to a relatively clear and stable sense of who you are in the larger society.
a. Self-image
b. Identity
c. Self-concept
d. Authentic self

**ANS: b** **Pg: 342**
**LO: 5** **Factual**

18. Erikson saw _____ as the most crucial period for identity development.
a. early childhood
b. adolescence
c. early adulthood
d. middle age

**ANS: b** **Pg: 342**
**LO: 5** **Factual**

*19. Erikson believed an "identity crisis" occurrs during
a. pubescence.
b. adolescence.
c. early adulthood.
d. middle adulthood.

**ANS: a** **Pg: 342**
**LO: 5** **Conceptual**

20. For Erikson, the search for identity is a(n)
a. experience that occurs when no role model is present.
b. normal developmental process.
c. unlikely to occur in the normal person.
d. failed attempt at identity development.

**ANS: b** **Pg: 342**
**LO: 5** **Conceptual**

21.     An identity crisis usually results in
a.      a period of moratorium or recovery.
b.      disillusionment about one's self-concept.
c.      reluctance to continue the search for identity.
d.      commitment to career and personal value system.

**ANS: d**          **Pg: 342**
**LO: 5**            **Conceptual**

22.     According to Marcia, the two factors of _____ and _____ combine in various ways to
        produce four different identity statuses.
a.      parental influence; peer influence
b.      genetics; environment
c.      crisis; commitment
d.      personality; life circumstances

**ANS: c**          **Pg: 342**
**LO: 5**            **Conceptual**

23.     Rachel says she is studying to be an accountant because her dad is an accountant. Her
        identity status is most likely to be
a.      moratorium.
b.      identity diffusion.
c.      identity achievement.
d.      identity foreclosure.

**ANS: d**          **Pg: 343**
**LO: 5**            **Applied**

24.     Harry has gone to college off and on for the past several years, dropping out and working
        at odd jobs for a semester at a time. He is probably employing which pattern of identity
        formation?
a.      foreclosure
b.      moratorium
c.      identity diffusion
d.      identity achievement

**ANS: b**          **Pg: 343**
**LO: 5**            **Applied**
25.     A person in the identity status called "identity diffusion"
a.      is likely to engage in identity "experiments".
b.      has adopted the commitments of others.
c.      has passed through an identity crisis and can make a commitment.
d.      may experience much self-doubt and cannot commit to an identity.

**ANS: d**          **Pg: 343**
**LO: 5**            **Conceptual**

26. Fifteen-year-old Marta has had a relatively smooth adolescent period and, at the urging of her parents, has already decided on a college and a career. If Marta is simply playing a passive role in carrying out her parents' wishes, she is probably in which of the following identity statuses?
a. foreclosure
b. moratorium
c. identity diffusion
d. identity postponement

ANS: a   Pg: 343
LO: 5   Applied

27. Which of the following is **not** considered a stage of adult development in Erikson's theory?
a. autonomy vs. doubt
b. intimacy vs. isolation
c. generativity vs. stagnation
d. actualization vs. confusion

ANS: d   Pg: 342
LO: 5   Factual

28. According to Erik Erikson, the primary challenge of adolescence is developing
a. a clear sense of identity.
b. a relationship of tolerance for one's parents.
c. an understanding of one's career aspirations.
d. a close social relationship with a member of the other gender.

ANS: a   Pg: 342
LO: 5   Factual

29. Sixteen-year-old Bill wants to spend a few years experimenting with different lifestyles and careers before he settles on who and what he wants to be. Bill is in the identity status known as
a. foreclosure.
b. moratorium.
c. identity diffusion.
d. identity achievement.

ANS: b   Pg: 343
LO: 5   Conceptual

30. The adolescent who has arrived at a sense of self and direction after some consideration
of alternative possibilities is in the identity phase called
a. foreclosure.
b. moratorium.
c. identity diffusion.
d. identity achievement.

**ANS: d**       **Pg: 343**
**LO: 5**       **Conceptual**

31. Which of the following contributes to the intensity of the struggle that many people
experience during adolescence?
a. the pressure to contemplate occupational choices
b. the changes in cognitive abilities that promote self-reflection
c. the rapid physical changes that stimulate thoughts about self-image
d. all of these

**ANS: d**       **Pg: 342**
**LO: 6**       **Conceptual**

32. Evidence supports that a majority of teenagers make it through adolescence
a. without any difficulties.
b. with an appreciation for the efforts of their parents.
c. with fairly severe emotional scars as a result of parent-adolescent conflict.
d. with only little more turmoil than one is likely to encounter in other life stages.

**ANS: d**       **Pg: 343**
**LO: 6**       **Conceptual**

33. You are talking to the parents of a 12-year-old. Based on research cited in your textbook,
which of the following is the most accurate statement you can make to them?
a. Adolescence tends to be marked by change and upheaval.
b. Adolescence is the single most turbulent period in the life span.
c. The number of adolescents with serious problems is fairly large.
d. The majority of adolescents have difficulty coping with the transition to adulthood.

**ANS: a**       **Pg: 343**
**LO: 6**       **Conceptual**

*34. _____ percent of homosexual youth have attempted suicide as compared to _____
percent of heterosexual youth?
a. 13; 13
b. 33; 33
c. 13; 33
d. 33; 13

**ANS: d**       **Pg: 344**
**LO: 6**       **Factual**

35.     Which of the following statements regarding adolescent suicide is accurate?
a.      The suicide rate for adolescents has increased dramatically since 1960.
b.      The ratio of attempted to completed suicides among adolescents is about
        5 to 1.
c.      The suicide rate for the 15-24 age group is higher than that for any older age group.
d.      All of these statements are accurate.

**ANS: a**          **Pg: 344**
**LO: 6**           **Conceptual**

36.     _____ is a person's notion of a developmental schedule that specifies what he or she
        should have accomplished by certain points in life.
a.      The social clock
b.      An identity status
c.      A social agenda
d.      Psychosocial stage

**ANS: a**          **Pg: 345**
**LO: 7**           **Factual**

*37.    Kimme is a typical lesbian.  She likely recognizes her sexual orientation around _____
        years old
a.      10
b.      25
c.      35
d.      45

**ANS: b**          **Pg: 346**
**LO: 7**           **Applied**

*38.    Homosexuals typically recognize their sexual orientation _____ heterosexuals.
a.      earlier than
b.      around the same time as
c.      later than
d.      after an average of 1.7 failed marriages

**ANS: c**          **Pg: 346**
**LO: 7**           **Conceptual**

39.     In early adulthood, the psychosocial crisis centers on establishing close personal
        relationships with others.  This stage is known as
a.      identity vs. diffusion.
b.      integrity vs. despair.
c.      intimacy vs. isolation.
d.      generativity vs. stagnation.

**ANS: c**          **Pg: 346**
**LO: 7**           **Factual**

40.	An individual who is concerned with opening up to others and committing to others is probably in which of the following psychosocial stages?
a.	identity vs. diffusion
b.	integrity vs. despair
c.	intimacy vs. isolation
d.	generativity vs. stagnation

**ANS: c**	**Pg: 346**
**LO: 7**	**Conceptual**

41.	According to Erikson, the intimacy vs. isolation stage of psychosocial development focuses on all but which of the following?
a.	truly commit to others
b.	learning to open up to others
c.	need to find a marriage partner
d.	ability to give of oneself unselfishly

**ANS: c**	**Pg: 346**
**LO: 7**	**Conceptual**

42.	Men and women who are capable of forming open and close relationships with both male and female friends would be classified as belonging to which of the following intimacy statuses?
a.	intimate
b.	preintimate
c.	stereotyped
d.	pseudointimate

**ANS: a**	**Pg: 346**
**LO: 7**	**Conceptual**

43.	Men and women who have relationships that are manipulative and superficial would be classified as belonging to which of the following intimacy statuses?
a.	intimate
b.	preintimate
c.	stereotyped
d.	pseudointimate

**ANS: c**	**Pg: 346**
**LO: 7**	**Conceptual**

44.	According to Erikson, the ability to establish and maintain intimate relationships depends on
a.	having effective parental role models.
b.	finding an appropriate opposite sex partner.
c.	successfully weathering the identity crises of adolescence.
d.	resolving the conflict between generativity and stagnation.

**ANS: c**	**Pg: 346**
**LO: 7**	**Conceptual**

*45.    Research on gender differences in identity development found that _____ women seem to resolve _____ issues first.
a.      non-career oriented; intimacy
b.      non-career oriented; identity
c.      career oriented; intimacy
d.      No gender difference has been found on this issue.

**ANS: a**              **Pg: 347**
**LO: 7**               **Conceptual**

46.     According to Erikson, the adult who provides unselfish guidance to younger people because of concern about the welfare of future generations has successfully resolved the crisis of
a.      integrity vs. despair.
b.      intimacy vs. isolation.
c.      industry vs. inferiority.
d.      generativity vs. stagnation.

**ANS: d**              **Pg: 348**
**LO: 8**               **Conceptual**

47.     According to Erikson, middle-aged adults face which of these crises?
a.      identity vs. diffusion
b.      integrity vs. despair
c.      intimacy vs. isolation
d.      generativity vs. stagnation

**ANS: d**              **Pg: 348**
**LO: 8**               **Factual**

48.     Linda is a 50-year-old college professor who spends a great deal of her time advising students about career options.  Linda is probably in which of the following stages?
a.      integrity vs. despair
b.      identity vs. diffusion
c.      industry vs. inferiority
d.      generativity vs. stagnation

**ANS: d**              **Pg: 348**
**LO: 8**               **Applied**

49.     Chief among the challenges of middle adulthood is
a.      facing the inevitable midlife crisis.
b.      establishing a stable career pattern.
c.      coming to terms with the aging process.
d.      dealing with the declining influence over one's children.

**ANS: c**              **Pg: 348**
**LO: 8**               **Conceptual**

50. Transitions in the parenting role during middle adulthood typically include all but which of the following?
a. "emptying of the nest"
b. learning the grandparent role
c. strained parent/adolescent relationships
d. learning how to cope with blended families

**ANS: d**          **Pg: 349**
**LO: 8**            **Conceptual**

51. Parents overwhelmingly rate _____ as the most difficult stage of child-rearing.
a. infancy
b. preschool
c. pubescence
d. adolescence

**ANS: d**          **Pg: 349**
**LO: 8**            **Factual**

52. Middle-aged workers who earn more money and wield more influence than their younger co-workers are likely to be following which of the following patterns?
a. stable career
b. changing careers
c. stereotyped career
d. transitional career

**ANS: a**          **Pg: 349**
**LO: 8**            **Conceptual**

*53. Carmello recently returned to live with his parents because of a divorce. The impact on _____ is likely to be _____.
a. his career; positive
b. his career; negative
c. his relationship with his parents; positive
d. his relationship with his parents; negative

**ANS: d**          **Pg: 349**
**LO: 8**            **Applied**

54. Which of the following statements regarding the midlife crisis is accurate?
a. The midlife crisis is not universal, and it probably isn't even typical.
b. Both men and women tend to go through some form of midlife crisis.
c. Most men go through a midlife crisis, but only a small minority of women do.
d. The midlife crisis is occurring at an earlier age today than it did in previous generations.

**ANS: a**          **Pg: 350**
**LO: 8**            **Conceptual**

55. Ralph is 75 years old, lives in a nursing home, and is bitter. He looks back on his life with regret about mistakes and missed opportunities. He expects to die soon. Ralph has not resolved the psychosocial crisis of
a. integrity vs. despair.
b. intimacy vs. isolation.
c. industry vs. inferiority.
d. generativity vs. stagnation.

**ANS: a**        **Pg: 350**
**LO: 9**        **Applied**

*56. Fred, 72 years old and recently retired, is likely to depend on _____ for his social support network.
a. family members
b. friends
c. parents
d. none of these

**ANS: b**        **Pg: 351**
**LO: 9**        **Applied**

*57. The elderly have _____ friends and they are _____ satisfied with them than younger people.
a. less; more
b. less; less
c. more; less
d. more; more

**ANS: a**        **Pg: 351**
**LO: 9**        **Factual**

58. For elderly African Americans, certain neighbours or peers acquire the status of a close family member and render mutual aid and support. These relationships are based on the concept of
a. ritual kin.
b. shared attribution.
c. the double standard.
d. fundamental attribution.

**ANS: a**        **Pgs: 351-352**
**LO: 9**        **Factual**

59.     Research findings indicate that attractiveness ratings decline in age when the subject is a
        woman, but not when the subject is a man. These findings provide support for the notion
        of
a.      ageism.
b.      menopausal crisis.
c.      egocentrism.
d.      a "double standard" of aging.

**ANS: d**          **Pg: 352**
**LO: 10**          **Conceptual**

60.     From about age 30 to the mid-60s, most people
a.      see no change in visual acuity.
b.      become increasingly farsighted.
c.      become increasingly nearsighted.
d.      have a difficult time changing focus.

**ANS: b**          **Pg: 352**
**LO: 11**          **Factual**

61.     Which of the following is a common visual problem in older people?
a.      reduced peripheral vision
b.      poor recovery from glare
c.      difficulty adapting to darkness
d.      all of these

**ANS: d**          **Pg: 352**
**LO: 11**          **Factual**

62.     Individual cells that receive, integrate, and transmit information are called
a.      axons.
b.      neurons.
c.      dendrites.
d.      neurotransmitters.

**ANS: b**          **Pg: 353**
**LO: 11**          **Factual**

63.     As neurons die, the brain decreases in both weight and volume, especially after age 50.
        This process
a.      is a normal part of the aging process.
b.      has been found to be associated with senility.
c.      appears to contribute to age-related dementia.
d.      inevitably results in the development of Alzheimer's disease.

**ANS: a**          **Pg: 353**
**LO: 11**          **Factual**

64.        _____ is the correct term for an abnormal condition marked by multiple cognitive deficits that include memory impairment.
a.     Senility
b.     Dementia
c.     Parkinson's disease
d.     Alzheimer's disease

**ANS: b**                    **Pg: 353**
**LO: 11**                    **Factual**

65.     Which of the following is thought to be a cause of dementia?
a.     AIDS
b.     Parkinson's disease
c.     Alzheimer's disease
d.     all of these

**ANS: d**                    **Pg: 353**
**LO: 11**                    **Factual**

66.     Which of the following statements about Alzheimer's disease is **not** accurate?
a.     It is often difficult to detect the beginnings of the disease.
b.     Although the causes are well known, there is not yet a cure.
c.     It can strike during middle age (40-65), or later in life (after 65).
d.     The disease is one of progressive deterioration, ending in death.

**ANS: b**                    **Pg: 353**
**LO: 11**                    **Conceptual**

67.     The significant endocrine changes that occur in older men
a.     are the basis for the loss of interest in sex.
b.     occur rapidly, beginning around the age of 65.
c.     frequently result in the onset of mood disorders, such as depression.
d.     are gradual and are largely unrelated to physical or psychological distress.

**ANS: d**                    **Pg: 354**
**LO: 12**                    **Factual**

68.     Distress related to the onset of menopause is often related to
a.     loss of fertility.
b.     loss of physical attractiveness.
c.     loss of bone density.
d.     Alzheimer's disease.

**ANS: b**                    **Pg: 354**
**LO: 12**                    **Conceptual**

69. What is the probable reason for decreased sexual activity among older people?
a. physical incapability of engaging in sex
b. age-related changes in hormone levels
c. social norms that sex in the elderly is "inappropriate"
d. prevalence of physical illnesses that preclude sexual relations

**ANS: c**      **Pg: 354**
**LO: 12**      **Conceptual**

70. Which of the following groups of older Americans is likely to have the most health problems?
a. whites
b. Hispanics
c. Native Americans
d. African Americans

**ANS: c**      **Pg: 354**
**LO: 12**      **Factual**

71. Regular exercise in adulthood has been shown to do which of the following?
a. protect against heart disease
b. reduce the chance of injuries
c. reduce anxiety and mild depression
d. all of these

**ANS: d**      **Pg: 355**
**LO: 12**      **Factual**

72. The idea that older people have vivid memories of events in the distant past
a. is not supported by evidence.
b. has not been examined empirically.
c. has been consistently supported by research.
d. has been supported for some cultures, but not for others.

**ANS: a**      **Pg: 358**
**LO: 13**      **Factual**

73. Which of the following declines somewhat over the adult years?
a. success in problem solving when time is limited
b. speed in retrieving memories
c. ability to filter out irrelevant stimuli
d. all of these

**ANS: d**      **Pg: 356**
**LO: 13**      **Factual**

74.     Research on lifelong patterns of productivity indicates that
a.      productivity is often stable into the 70s.
b.      masterpieces are just as likely to occur at any age.
c.      in most professions, the 40s decade is most productive.
d.      all of these.

**ANS: d**          **Pg: 356**
**LO: 13**          **Factual**

75.     Which of the following statements regarding personality changes in adulthood is
        accurate?
        1.  There is evidence for long-term stability in personality.
        2.  Personality is characterized by both stability and change.
        3.  There is evidence that substantial personality changes occur throughout life.

a.      1 only
b.      2 only
c.      3 only
d.      1, 2, and 3

**ANS: d**          **Pg: 358**
**LO: 14**          **Conceptual**

76.     Which of the following personality traits is most likely to change as people grow older?
a.      femininity
b.      extraversion
c.      assertiveness
d.      emotional stability

**ANS: a**          **Pg: 358**
**LO: 14**          **Conceptual**

77.     Conflicting evidence on the stability of personality is best explained by the likelihood
        that
a.      personality measures are ambiguous.
b.      current theories of personality are deficient.
c.      some personality traits are more consistent than others.
d.      most of the research on personality has been seriously flawed.

**ANS: c**          **Pg: 358**
**LO: 14**          **Conceptual**

78.     The collection of rituals and procedures used by a culture to handle death is called
a.      bereavement.
b.      a death system.
c.      the stages of dying.
d.      the grieving process.

**ANS: b**          **Pgs: 358-359**
**LO: 15**          **Factual**

79. In our culture, the most common strategy for dealing with death is
a. avoidance.
b. bargaining.
c. celebration.
d. preoccupation.

**ANS: a**      **Pg: 358**
**LO: 15**      **Conceptual**

80. Negativism and avoidance as strategies for dealing with death
a. appear to be universal attitudes.
b. are not found in all cultures' death systems.
c. are inconsistent with our culture's attitudes.
d. lead to viewing death as a natural transition.

**ANS: b**      **Pgs: 326-359**
**LO: 15**      **Conceptual**

81. Which of the following groups is likely to exhibit the most anxiety about death?
a. confirmed atheists
b. devout Christians
c. people with ambivalent religious views
d. people with a well-formulated philosophy of death

**ANS: c**      **Pg: 359**
**LO: 15**      **Conceptual**

*82. Dr. Klein believes that death anxiety is a result of the conflict between human's self-preservation instinct and the awareness of the inevitability of death. What type of theorist is Dr. Klein?
a. learning
b social instinct
c. evolutionary
d. terror-management

**ANS: d**      **Pg: 359**
**LO: 15**      **Conceptual**

*83. Research shows that death anxiety is highest in terminally ill children when their parents
a. avoid telling them about their condition.
b. tell the child about the condition.
c. avoid for males, but tell for females.
d. none of these.

**ANS: a**      **Pg: 359**
**LO: 15**      **Conceptual**

84.     Which of the following individuals pioneered research on the experience of dying?
a.      Jean Piaget
b.      Erik Erikson
c.      Diana Baumrind
d.      Elisabeth Kübler-Ross

ANS: d          Pg: 359
LO: 16          Factual

85.     Esther knows she is dying.  In her prayers she asks God to keep her alive until Christmas, so she can see all of her family.  In return, she promises to try harder to be kind and patient with others.  Esther is probably in which of the following stages of dying?
a.      denial
b.      resistance
c.      bargaining
d.      acceptance

ANS: c          Pg: 359
LO: 16          Conceptual

86.     The strongest objections to Kübler-Ross's views on dying have focused on which of the following?
a.      her reliance on the reports of family members
b.      her belief that the dying process is stage-based
c.      the notion that most people come to accept death
d.      the fact that she ignored gender differences in attitudes toward death

ANS: b          Pg: 359
LO: 16          Factual

87.     The painful loss of a loved one through death is called
a.      grief.
b.      mourning.
c.      bereavement.
d.      a death system.

ANS: c          Pg: 360
LO: 17          Factual

88.     The formal practices of an individual and a community in response to death are termed
a.      grief.
b.      mourning.
c.      bereavement.
d.      a death system.

ANS: b          Pg: 360
LO: 17          Factual

89. Accepting the loss of a loved one, which often brings feelings of helplessness and depression, is characteristic of which of the following stages of the grieving process?
a. numbness
b. yearning
c. disorganization and despair
d. reorganization

ANS: c          Pg: 360
LO: 18          Conceptual

90. According to studies that examined the amount of distress widows experienced both one month after the death of their husbands and a year or two later, the most common pattern of grief was
a. chronic.
b. absent.
c. normal.
d. delayed.

ANS: b          Pg: 361
LO: 18          Factual

91. In the first few months of life, infants rely on _____ to maintain contact with caregivers.
a. their parents' innate love for them
b. culturally sanctioned parental roles
c. parents' instinct for care of offspring
d. built-in behaviours such as cooing, crying, and smiling

ANS: d          Pg: 363
LO: 19          Factual

92. At the age of 10 months, baby Sara seems to ignore her mother. According to Ainsworth, Sara would be classified as having a(n) _____ attachment style.
a. avoidant
b. unattached
c. securely attached
d. anxious-ambivalent

ANS: a          Pg: 363
LO: 19          Applied

93. Thirteen-month-old Juan raises his arms for his mother to pick him up, but when she does, he squirms to get away from her. According to Ainsworth, Juan would be classified as having a(n) _____ attachment style.
a. securely attached
b. insecurely attached
c. anxious and avoidant
d. anxious and ambivalent

ANS: d          Pg: 363
LO: 19          Conceptual

94.     Most infants experience a secure attachment relationship, which seems to
a.      have positive effects that last for a year or two.
b.      be reflected in a smooth transition through adolescence.
c.      ensure that their cognitive development proceeds normally.
d.      provide a basis for successful social relationships later in life.

**ANS: d**          **Pg: 363**
**LO: 19**          **Conceptual**

95.     According to census data, about what percent of mothers who have infants less than 12
        months of age work outside the home?
a.      35%
b.      45%
c.      55%
d.      65%

**ANS: c**          **Pg: 363**
**LO: 20**          **Factual**

96.     According to Diana Baumrind, four different parenting styles result from the interactions
        of which of the following dimensions?
a.      parental acceptance; parental control
b.      educational level; religious commitment
c.      use of punishment; use of reinforcement
d.      communicative openness; conditions of worth

**ANS: a**          **Pg: 364**
**LO: 21**          **Factual**

97.     Which of the following is **not** one of the parenting styles identified by Baumrind?
a.      permissive
b.      conditional
c.      authoritarian
d.      authoritative

**ANS: b**          **Pg: 364**
**LO: 21**          **Factual**

98.     Adolescents raised by _____ parents tend to show the highest competence and
        adjustment.
a.      neglectful
b.      permissive
c.      authoritarian
d.      authoritative

**ANS: d**          **Pg: 364**
**LO: 22**          **Conceptual**

99. Adolescents raised by _____ parents tend to show the lowest competence and adjustment.
a.   neglectful
b.   permissive
c.   authoritarian
d.   authoritative

**ANS: a**          **Pg: 364**
**LO: 22**          **Conceptual**

*100.   This is a good replacement for punishment.
a.   specified nagging
b.   negative reinforcement
c.   negative punishment
d.   positive instigation

**ANS: b**          **Pg: 369**
**LO: 24**          **Conceptual**


## MULTIPLE CHOICE QUESTIONS FROM STUDY GUIDE

1.   The two-year span preceding puberty is
a.   called the latency period.
b.   referred to as pubescence.
c.   when growth slows down.
d.   usually considered a time of turmoil.

**ANS: b**          **Pg: 338**
**LO: 1**           **Factual**

2.   Today's girls begin puberty _____, and complete it more _____ than their counterparts in earlier generations.
a.   earlier; slowly
b.   earlier; rapidly
c.   later; slowly
d.   later; rapidly

**ANS: b**          **Pg: 339**
**LO: 2**           **Conceptual**

3.   Optimal adjustment for girls is associated with puberty arriving _____, and optimal adjustment for boys is related to puberty arriving _____.
a.   early; on time
b.   early; late
c.   on time; early
d.   late; on time

**ANS: c**          **Pg: 340**
**LO: 3**           **Conceptual**

4.  During adolescence, a sense of identity usually develops
a.  earlier in boys than in girls.
b.  as a result of the first sexual experience.
c.  quickly, during the final stages of puberty.
d.  gradually, following a period of personal questioning.

**ANS: d**          **Pg: 342**
**LO: 5**            **Conceptual**

5.  Which of the following statements regarding the notion of adolescence as a time of turmoil is <u>not</u> accurate?
a.  Conflicts with parents increase during adolescence.
b.  Adolescence is inherently fraught with chaos and pain.
c.  Adolescents tend to engage in increased risk behavior (e.g., substance abuse).
d.  Adolescents experience more volatile emotions and extremes of mood than adults do.

**ANS: b**          **Pg: 343**
**LO: 6**            **Factual**

6.  A person's notion of a developmental schedule that specifies what he or she should have accomplished by certain points in life is called a(n)
a.  social clock.
b.  psychosocial focus.
c.  egocentric timetable.
d.  developmental stopwatch.

**ANS: a**          **Pg: 345**
**LO: 7**            **Factual**

7.  Which of the following statements regarding early adulthood is <u>not</u> true?
a.  Most people get married in their 20s.
b.  Most married couples are in dual-worker relationships.
c.  The majority of married couples are now choosing not to have children.
d.   Marital satisfaction typically declines after the arrival of children

**ANS: c**          **Pgs: 347-348**
**LO: 7**            **Conceptual**

8.  Researchers relying on objective measures of emotional stability have found signs of midlife crises in
a.  most men, but few women.
b.  the majority of men and women.
c.  only a small minority of individuals.
d.  people who are contemplating retirement.

**ANS: c**          **Pg: 350**
**LO: 8**            **Factual**

9. Although 65 is the age typically associated with retirement, individuals today
a. are leaving the workplace earlier.
b. tend to keep working well into their 70s.
c. retire at about age 70 and then stay busy with part-time work.
d. tend to remain actively involved at work until health problems force them to retire.

**ANS: a**          **Pg: 350**
**LO: 9**           **Factual**

10. Dementia
a. is part of the normal aging process.
b. is the main cause of Alzheimer's disease.
c. is an abnormal condition marked by multiple cognitive deficits.
d. is a function of the progressive neuronal loss associated with aging.

**ANS: c**          **Pg: 353**
**LO: 11**          **Factual**

11. Throughout the adult years the IQ
a. declines slowly but consistently beginning at about age 45.
b. is stable throughout most of adulthood, with most declines beginning after age 60.
c. shows a small but steady increase due to accumulated learning.
d. shows no predictable pattern of change.

**ANS: b**          **Pg: 355**
**LO: 13**          **Factual**

12. The memory losses associated with aging are _____ in size and _____ universal.
a. large; are
b. large; are not
c. moderate; are
d. moderate; are not

**ANS: d**          **Pg: 357**
**LO: 13**          **Conceptual**

13. Which of the following is the correct order for John Bowlby's four stages of grieving?
a. yearning; numbness; reorganization; disorganization and despair
b. numbness; reorganization; disorganization and despair; yearning
c. numbness; yearning; disorganization and despair; reorganization
d. disorganization and despair; reorganization; numbness; yearning

**ANS: c**          **Pg: 360**
**LO: 17**          **Factual**

14. According to Diana Baumrind, _____ parenting is most likely to foster social and cognitive competence in children.
a. authoritarian
b. authoritative
c. permissive
d. educated

**ANS: b**          **Pg: 364**
**LO: 21**          **Conceptual**

15. Psychologists would say that physical punishment should not be used frequently because it
a. can lead to the development of posttraumatic stress disorder.
b. seldom leads to the suppression of the undesirable behavior.
c. it is associated with a host of problematic outcomes.
d. results in overwhelming feelings of guilt in the punisher.

**ANS: c**          **Pg: 368**
**LO: 24**          **Conceptual**

## MULTIPLE CHOICE QUESTIONS ON WEB SITE

1. Which of the following statements about puberty is accurate?
a. In girls, it officially ends with menarche.
b. It ends by age 11 in both boys and girls.
c. It arrives about the same time in boys and girls.
d. It arrives about two years later in boys than in girls.

**ANS: d**          **Pg: 339**
**LO: 2**           **Factual**

*2. Spermarchy is
a. when the testes gain the ability to produce sperm.
b. when females are first capable of being inseminated.
c. the first ejaculation.
d. a nocturnal emission.

**ANS: c**          **Pg: 339**
**LO: 2**           **Conceptual**

3. For Erikson, the search for identity is a(n)
a. experience that occurs when no role model is present.
b. normal developmental process.
c. unlikely to occur in the normal person.
d. failed attempt at identity development.

**ANS: b**          **Pg: 342**
**LO: 5**           **Conceptual**

336

4.      Sixteen-year-old Bill wants to spend a few years experimenting with different lifestyles
        and careers before he settles on who and what he wants to be. Bill is in the identity status
        known as
a.      foreclosure.
b.      moratorium.
c.      identity diffusion.
d.      identity achievement.

**ANS: b**          **Pg: 343**
**LO: 5**           **Conceptual**

*5.     Homosexuals typically recognize their sexual orientation _____ heterosexuals.
a.      earlier than
b.      around the same time as
c.      later than
d.      after an average of 1.7 failed marriages

**ANS: c**          **Pg: 346**
**LO: 7**           **Conceptual**

6.      In early adulthood, the psychosocial crisis centers on establishing close personal
        relationships with others.  This stage is known as
a.      identity vs. diffusion.
b.      integrity vs. despair.
c.      intimacy vs. isolation.
d.      generativity vs. stagnation.

**ANS: c**          **Pg: 346**
**LO: 7**           **Factual**

7.      Which of the following statements regarding the midlife crisis is accurate?
a.      The midlife crisis is not universal, and it probably isn't even typical.
b.      Both men and women tend to go through some form of midlife crisis.
c.      Most men go through a midlife crisis, but only a small minority of women do.
d.      The midlife crisis is occurring at an earlier age today than it did in previous generations.

**ANS: a**          **Pg: 350**
**LO: 8**           **Conceptual**

8.      Which of the following statements about Alzheimer's disease is **not** accurate?
a.      It is often difficult to detect the beginnings of the disease.
b.      Although the causes are well known, there is not yet a cure.
c.      It can strike during middle age (40-65), or later in life (after 65).
d.      The disease is one of progressive deterioration, ending in death.

**ANS: b**          **Pg: 353**
**LO: 11**          **Conceptual**

9.    The significant endocrine changes that occur in older men
a.    are the basis for the loss of interest in sex.
b.    occur rapidly, beginning around the age of 65.
c.    frequently result in the onset of mood disorders, such as depression.
d.    are gradual and are largely unrelated to physical or psychological distress.

**ANS: d**          **Pg: 354**
**LO: 12**          **Factual**

10.    Which of the following declines somewhat over the adult years?
a.    success in problem solving when time is limited
b.    speed in retrieving memories
c.    ability to filter out irrelevant stimuli
d.    all of these

**ANS: d**          **Pg: 356**
**LO: 13**          **Factual**

11.    Conflicting evidence on the stability of personality is best explained by the likelihood
       that
a.    personality measures are ambiguous.
b.    current theories of personality are deficient.
c.    some personality traits are more consistent than others.
d.    most of the research on personality has been seriously flawed.

**ANS: c**          **Pg: 358**
**LO: 14**          **Conceptual**

12.    The collection of rituals and procedures used by a culture to handle death is called
a.    bereavement.
b.    a death system.
c.    the stages of dying.
d.    the grieving process.

**ANS: b**          **Pgs: 358-359**
**LO: 15**          **Factual**

13.    Which of the following individuals pioneered research on the experience of dying?
a.    Jean Piaget
b.    Erik Erikson
c.    Diana Baumrind
d.    Elisabeth Kübler-Ross

**ANS: d**          **Pg: 359**
**LO: 16**          **Factual**

14. Esther knows she is dying. In her prayers she asks God to keep her alive until Christmas, so she can see all of her family. In return, she promises to try harder to be kind and patient with others. Esther is probably in which of the following stages of dying?
a. denial
b. resistance
c. bargaining
d. acceptance

**ANS: c**         **Pg: 359**
**LO: 16**       **Conceptual**

15. At the age of 10 months, baby Sara seems to ignore her mother. According to Ainsworth, Sara would be classified as having a(n) _____ attachment style.
a. avoidant
b. unattached
c. securely attached
d. anxious-ambivalent

**ANS: a**         **Pg: 363**
**LO: 19**       **Applied**

## TRUE/FALSE QUESTIONS

1. Facial hair in males is a secondary sex characteristic.

**ANS: true**      **Pg: 338**
**LO: 1**        **Factual**

2. Pubescence is the onset of puberty.

**ANS: false**     **Pg: 338**
**LO: 1**        **Factual**

3. Primary sex characteristics are directly involved in reproduction.

**ANS: true**      **Pg: 338**
**LO: 2**        **Factual**

4. Moratorium is a normal period in identity development.

**ANS: true**      **Pg: 343**
**LO: 5**        **Factual**

5. Identity foreclosure is a positive step in identity formation.

**ANS: false**     **Pg: 343**
**LO: 5**        **Factual**

6.      Atheists usually have high levels of death anxiety.

**ANS: false**          **Pg: 359**
**LO: 15**              **Conceptual**

7.      Kubler-Ross theorized about the psychological stages in death acceptance.

**ANS: true**           **Pg: 359**
**LO: 16**              **Factual**

8.      Authoritarian parents have the best adjusted children.

**ANS: false**          **Pg: 364**
**LO: 21**              **Factual**

9.      Negative reinforcement is designed to increase good behaviour.

**ANS: true**           **Pg: 369**
**LO: 23**              **Factual**

10.     Punishment has the best effects when its administration is delayed.

**ANS: false**          **Pg: 369**
**LO: 24**              **Conceptual**


## SHORT-ANSWER ESSAY QUESTIONS

1.      Compare and contrast primary sex characteristics and secondary sex characteristics.

**Pg: 338**

*2.     Contrast the varying effects the timing of puberty has on males and female .

**Pg: 340**

*3.     Discuss Marcia's (1980) four categories of identity status.

**Pg: 343**

4.      Describe several factors that may lead an adolescent to attempt suicide.

**Pg: 344**

*5.     Discuss the relationship of Erikson's young adult to adolescent stage.

**Pg: 342**

6.      List and briefly describe the five different intimacy statuses, which are based on the quality of a person's relationships with others.

# Chapter 12
# CAREERS AND WORK

## LEARNING OBJECTIVES

1. Describe personal and family influences on job choice.
2. Cite several helpful sources of career information.
3. List some aspects of potential occupations that are important to know about.
4. Explain the role of occupational interest inventories in career decisions.
5. List five important considerations in choosing an occupation.
6. Summarize Holland's hexagonal model of career choice.
7. Summarize Super's five-stage model of career development.
8. Discuss women's career development.
9. List six work-related trends.
10. Describe the relationship between education and salary.
11. Summarize important demographic changes that are transforming the workforce.
12. Cite some problems that women and minorities face in today's workplace.
13. Describe some challenges presented by workforce diversity to organizations and workers.
14. List some important sources of job stress.
15. Summarize the effects of job stress on physical and mental health.
16. Describe actions organizations are taking to reduce job stress.
17. Describe the prevalence and consequences of sexual harassment.
18. Cite some ways that organizations and individuals can reduce sexual harassment.
19. Describe some causes and effects of unemployment.
20. Summarize current perspectives on workaholism.
21. Define work-family conflict and discuss the benefits of multiple roles.
22. List several types of leisure activities and summarize the benefits of them.
23. Summarize the guidelines for putting together an effective résumé.
24. Discuss strategies for targeting companies you would like to work for.
25. Describe several strategies for landing a job interview.
26. List some factors that can influence an interviewer's rating of a job candidate.
27. List the dos and don'ts of interviewing for jobs.

**MULTIPLE CHOICE QUESTIONS**

1.    _____ is the study of human behavior in the workplace.
a.    Workforce psychology
b.    Industrial/organizational psychology
c.    Career-work environment psychology
d.    Business psychology

**ANS: b**          **Pg: 373**
**LO: 1**            **Factual**

2.    Which of the following is the single best predictor type of occupation entered?
a.    years of education
b.    parents' expectations
c.    grade point average in high school
d.    score on occupational interest inventory

**ANS: a**          **Pg: 375**
**LO: 1**            **Conceptual**

*3.    Which of these is the best predictor of the likelihood of entering a particular occupation?
a.    intelligence
b.    math aptitude
c.    identity
d.    social skills

**ANS: a**          **Pg: 374**
**LO: 1**            **Conceptual**

*4.    Which is an increasingly important specific job skill?
a.    intelligence
b.    math aptitude
c.    identity
d.    social skills

**ANS: d**          **Pg: 374**
**LO: 1**            **Conceptual**

*5.    Paula's parents taught her time importance of always being to work on time and showing deference to supervisor's wishes.  Most likely Paula's parent instilled good
a.    attention level.
b.    work-related values.
c.    gender-role expectations.
d.    none of these.

**ANS: b**          **Pg: 375**
**LO: 1**            **Applied**

*6.     According to recent research cited in the text, _____ has more influence on careers than _____.
a.      gender; ethnicity
b.      ethnicity; gender
c.      socioeconomic status; ethnicity
d.      ethnicity; socioeconomic status

**ANS: c          Pgs: 375**
**LO: 1           Factual**

7.      Good sources of information about job characteristics include
a.      the Occupational Outlook Handbook.
b.      literature from professional organizations.
c.      current members of an occupation.
d.      all of these.

**ANS: d          Pg: 376**
**LO: 2           Factual**

8.      After you've read the available literature about an occupation, it's a good idea to talk to
a.      an occupational therapist.
b.      an employment counsellor.
c.      individuals working in that area.
d.      your high school guidance counselor.

**ANS: c          Pg: 376**
**LO: 2           Factual**

9.      What you can derive from a job in terms of helping people, being creative, or shouldering responsibility is most closely associated with which of the following job characteristics?
a.      potential status
b.      working conditions
c.      intrinsic job satisfaction
d.      opportunities for advancement

**ANS: c          Pg: 376**
**LO: 3           Conceptual**

*10.    Jessica recently took an occupational interest inventory. Which of these was it not likely to be?
a.      Strong Interest Survey
b.      Campbell Interest and Skill Survey
c.      Self-Directed Search
d.      Minnesota Multiphasic Interest Inventory

**ANS: d          Pg: 377**
**LO: 3           Applied**

11.     Which of the following instruments is designed to predict the career in which you might expect to find the most satisfaction?
a.      the Self-Esteem Scale
b.      the Strong Interest Inventory
c.      the Edwards Personal Preference Schedule
d.      Cattell's 16 Personality Factor Questionnaire

ANS: b              Pg: 377
LO: 4               Factual

12.     The results of an occupational interest inventory are designed to
a.      predict whether you would be successful in various jobs.
b.      focus on recommendations for the career path you should follow.
c.      indicate how similar your interests are to the typical interests of people in various jobs.
d.      indicate whether your interests are consistent with job descriptions included in the. Dictionary of Occupational Titles.

ANS: c              Pg: 377
LO: 4               Factual

13.     If you wanted to develop a new occupational interest inventory, which of the following would be the best way to begin?
a.      Find out what specific skills are needed to be successful in various jobs.
b.      Ask job seekers what appeals to them about the jobs they're considering.
c.      Examine the interests of people who enjoy their work in various occupations.
d.      Survey people about the aspects of their jobs that are most important to them.

ANS: c              Pg: 377
LO: 4               Conceptual

14.     When considering the results of an occupational interest inventory, it is important to
        remember that
a.      there is a lingering gender bias in most of them.
b.      you shouldn't let the test make career decisions for you.
c.      you may score high on some occupations you're sure you would dislike.
d.      all of these.

ANS: d              Pg: 377
LO: 4               Conceptual

15.     Critics of occupational interest inventories have claimed that
a.      several major occupational areas have been ignored.
b.      they have helped channel women into gender-typed careers.
c.      age-related bias in the instruments has increased in recent years.
d.      they are biased toward certain ethnic groups.

ANS: b              Pg: 377
LO: 4               Conceptual

16.     Which of the following statements about vocational choice is **not** accurate?
a.     There are no limits on your career options.
b.     Some career decisions are not easily undone.
c.     You have the potential for success in a variety of jobs.
d.     Vocational development will continue throughout your lifetime.

**ANS: a**          **Pg: 377**
**LO: 5**           **Conceptual**

17.     Which of the following is the most questionable piece of vocational advice someone could give?
a.     Keep looking for that one job that fits you perfectly.
b.     Be cautious about choosing a career solely on the basis of salary.
c.     Recognize that your career options will be limited to some extent by factors beyond your control.
d.     Be prepared to reevaluate your vocational decisions at various times throughout your working life.

**ANS: a**          **Pg: 377**
**LO: 5**           **Conceptual**

18.     Which of the following statements about vocational choice is **not** accurate?
a.     There are limits to your options.
b.     There is one best job for you somewhere.
c.     Career choice is a developmental process.
d.     Some career choices are not easily undone.

**ANS: b**          **Pg: 377**
**LO: 5**           **Conceptual**

19.     Experts project that
a.     many people will have 12-15 jobs over the course of their working lives.
b.     most people will stick to one career that interests them.
c.     most people never retire from their chosen career.
d.     there will be a continued need for experts to make projections about labor trends.

**ANS: a**          **Pg: 378**
**LO: 5**           **Factual**

20.     John Holland's hexagonal model of career choice is generally considered a(n) _____ approach.
a.     trait
b.     developmental
c.     problem-based
d.     aptitude-based

**ANS: a**          **Pg: 378**
**LO: 6**           **Factual**

21. According to Holland's theory of vocational choice,
a. we're unlikely to be satisfied with our first "real" job.
b. we seek a work environment that fits our personality.
c. career choice is determined primarily by our ability to adapt.
d. occupational development is a process that begins in childhood.

**ANS: b**      **Pg: 378**
**LO: 6**      **Factual**

22. Which of the following individuals would most likely be considered to have an artistic personal orientation, according to Holland's model?
a. someone who writes children's books
b. someone who's writing an article on economics
c. someone who coordinates social activities for her company
d. someone who educates his company's employees about new software

**ANS: a**      **Pg: 378**
**LO: 6**      **Conceptual**

23. Leah likes physical tasks that require lots of coordination, but not a lot of social skills. According to Holland's model of career choice, Leah would be considered _____ type.
a. a social
b. a realistic
c. an enterprising
d. a conventional

**ANS: b**      **Pg: 378**
**LO: 6**      **Applied**

24. According to Holland's hexagonal model of career choice, a philosophy professor would probably be considered _____ type.
a. an artistic
b. a realistic
c. an investigative
d. a conventional

**ANS: c**      **Pg: 378**
**LO: 6**      **Applied**

*25. Jasmine recently took a test measuring the most researched and most supported vocational psychology model. Jasmine was measured on the
a. James-Lange Model.
b. Emotional Intelligence Test.
c. Self-directed Social Skills Model.
d. Holland's Hexagonal Model.

**ANS: d**      **Pgs: 378-379**
**LO: 6**      **Applied**

26. A hospital would be an example of an environment that is preferred by _____ types.
a. social
b. realistic
c. enterprising
d. conventional

**ANS: a** Pg: 378
**LO: 6** **Conceptual**

27. According to Holland's model, people who like to use their social skills to persuade others, and who perceive themselves as self-confident, sociable, and popular, would most likely be considered as having the _____ personal orientation.
a. social
b. artistic
c. enterprising
d. conventional

**ANS: c** Pgs: 378
**LO: 6** **Conceptual**

28. Which of the following individuals proposed an influential developmental model of career choice?
a. Nancy Betz
b. Roger Gould
c. John Holland
d. Donald Super

**ANS: d** Pgs: 378-380
**LO: 7** **Factual**

29. According to Super's developmental model of career choice, decisions about work and career reflect
a. societal and parental pressure to succeed.
b. people's educational attainment prior to entering the workforce.
c. people's attempts to express their self-concept and changing views of themselves.
d. aspirations to attain lifestyles consistent with their interests.

**ANS: c** Pg: 380
**LO: 7** **Factual**

30. _____ is the critical factor in Super's model of career choice.
a. Self-esteem
b. Self-concept
c. Developmental crisis
d. Level of aspiration

**ANS: b** Pg: 380
**LO: 7** **Factual**

31.    According to Super's developmental model of career choice, the second stage in vocational development is
a.    growth.
b.    exploration.
c.    maintenance.
d.    establishment.

**ANS: b**          **Pg: 380**
**LO: 7**           **Factual**

32.    According to Super's developmental model of career choice, the second from last stage in vocational development is
a.    growth.
b.    exploration.
c.    maintenance.
d.    establishment.

**ANS: c**          **Pg: 381**
**LO: 7**           **Conceptual**

33.    Martin sometimes fantasizes that he'd like to be a policeman or a detective, though he has no idea what would be required of him to hold such a job.  According to Super's model of career choice, what is Martin's probable stage of life?
a.    growth
b.    exploration
c.    maintenance
d.    establishment

**ANS: a**          **Pg: 380**
**LO: 7**           **Applied**

34.    Because of pressure from his parents and friends, Larry is thinking more about his future career, and he has several possibilities in mind that he thinks are realistic.  According to Super's developmental model of career choice, which of the following stages is Larry probably in?
a.    growth
b.    exploration
c.    maintenance
d.    establishment

**ANS: b**          **Pg: 380**
**LO: 7**           **Applied**

35. People who worry mainly about retaining their achieved status rather than improving it are probably in which of Super's developmental stages?
a. decline
b. exploration
c. maintenance
d. establishment

**ANS: c**      **Pg: 381**
**LO: 7**      **Conceptual**

36. David is in Super's maintenance stage of vocational development. His primary concern is likely to be
a. committing to an occupation.
b. retaining the job status he's achieved.
c. how to make enough money to support his family.
d. whether he should return to school to improve his skills so he can advance.

**ANS: b**      **Pg: 381**
**LO: 7**      **Conceptual**

37. Super's decline stage involves
a. deceleration.
b. planning for retirement.
c. decreasing vocational activity.
d. all of these.

**ANS: d**      **Pg: 381**
**LO: 7**      **Factual**

38. Approximately what percentage of women are in the labor force today?
a. 20
b. 40
c. 60
d. 80

**ANS: c**      **Pg: 381**
**LO: 8**      **Factual**

39. Women's vocational development is different from men's primarily because
a. men tend to be better trained for gender-neutral jobs.
b. women are less likely to experience labor force discontinuity.
c. women often subordinate their career goals to those of their husbands.
d. women with children one year old or younger generally don't work outside the home.

**ANS: c**      **Pg: 381**
**LO: 8**      **Conceptual**

40. Leaving the labor force, even if for increasingly brief periods of time, is called
a. overemployment.
b. labor force discontinuity.
c. token employment.
d. re-employment disclamation.

**ANS: b**      **Pg: 381**
**LO: 9**      **Factual**

*41. Who is more likely to have a history of labor force discontinuity?
a. Betty, a low-status job female
b. Carmen, an academically gifted female
c. Bill, a low-status job male
d. Betty and Carmen are both more likely than Bill.

**ANS: d**      **Pg: 381**
**LO: 9**      **Applied**

42. Which of the following is **not** an important work-related trend?
a. Lifelong learning is a necessity.
b. More jobs will be in the service sector.
c. Temporary employment is decreasing.
d. Technology is changing the nature of work.

**ANS: c**      **Pgs: 382-383**
**LO: 9**      **Factual**

43. One reason for the increase in temporary employment arrangements is that
a. more women are in the workforce.
b. corporations are downsizing and restructuring to remain competitive.
c. workers are more productive when they are hired on a temporary basis.
d. none of these.

**ANS: b**      **Pgs: 382-383**
**LO: 9**      **Conceptual**

44. The United States, like many other industrialized nations, is shifting towards
a. a shorter work-day but longer work week.
b. a manufacturing or goods-producing economy.
c. a bartering economy.
d. a service-based economy.

**ANS: d**      **Pg: 383**
**LO: 9**      **Factual**

45.     The relationship between years of education and income is
a.      positive.
b.      negative.
c.      nonsignificant.
d.      shaped like an inverted U.

**ANS: a          Pg: 384**
**LO: 10          Conceptual**

*46.    What occupations are showing the greatest growth trend in the US?
a.      mechanical jobs
b.      service jobs
c.      clerical jobs
d.      manufacturing jobs

**ANS: b          Pg: 383**
**LO: 10          Conceptual**

*47.    In 2003, about _____ of married women worked.
a.      40%
b.      60%
c.      80%
d.      90%

**ANS: b          Pg: 385**
**LO: 11          Factual**

*48.    In 1970 approximately _____ % of married women worked.  While in 2003,
        approximately _____ % of married women worked.
a.      40; 60
b.      60; 40
c.      60; 80
d.      80; 60

**ANS: a          Pg: 385**
**LO: 11          Factual**

49.     Between 1975 and 1999,
a.      the number of working women with children under the age of three almost doubled.
b.      the number of workers reared below poverty level declined sharply.
c.      20% of working women left the full-time work force to raise children at home.
d.      discrimination against women and minorities in the workplace had almost completely
        ended.

**ANS: a          Pg: 385**
**LO: 11          Factual**

50. The fact that jobs are sometimes typed simultaneously by gender and race illustrates which of the following concepts?
a. job segregation
b. job discrimination
c. stereotype harassment
d. occupation identification

**ANS: a**          **Pg: 386**
**LO: 12**          **Conceptual**

51. Women and minorities are frequently passed over for promotion in favor of white men. This practice seems to be particularly problematic in which of the following kinds of jobs?
a. traditionally blue-collar jobs
b. higher levels of management
c. positions in the area of human services
d. jobs in which a graduate degree is necessary

**ANS: b**          **Pg: 386**
**LO: 12**          **Factual**

52. There appears to be a "glass ceiling" that
a. allows supervisors to evaluate the potential of their subordinates.
b. prevents white males from succeeding in traditionally female-oriented jobs.
c. prevents most women and ethnic minorities from advancing beyond middle management.
d. allows women and ethnic minorities to be trained for jobs in upper management.

**ANS: c**          **Pg: 386**
**LO: 12**          **Conceptual**

53. When there is only one woman or minority person in an office, that person becomes a symbol of all the members of that group. This scenario illustrates which of the following concepts?
a. tokenism
b. job segregation
c. sexual harassment
d. affirmative action employee

**ANS: a**          **Pg: 386**
**LO: 12**          **Conceptual**

54. One potentially negative outcome of diversity training is that
a. more under-qualified minority workers are promoted into management positions.
b. more males are tracked into traditionally female-oriented jobs.
c. white males may feel blamed for all of the discrimination that befalls minority workers.
d. human resources personnel are attacked for discriminatory practices.

**ANS: c**          **Pg: 387**
**LO: 13**          **Conceptual**

55.     Studies have demonstrated that attaching an affirmative action label to an employee results in
a.      the employee being considered a "token".
b.      the creation of a "glass ceiling" in the workplace.
c.      negative feelings directed toward the employee.
d.      feelings of jealousy among the employee's co-workers.

**ANS: c**                    **Pg: 387**
**LO: 13**                    **Conceptual**

*56.    Jason, a minority group member, feels that his co-workers see him as a _____ worker; consequently his is likely to experience more _____ pressure than the typical white male.
a.      minority; stress
b.      token; performance
c.      minority; performance
d.      token; stress

**ANS: b**                    **Pg: 386**
**LO: 14**                    **Applied**

57.     Which is not a common job stressor?
a.      perceived inequities
b.      pressure of deadlines
c.      lack of control over one's work
d.      the monotony associated with regular hours

**ANS: d**                    **Pg: 387**
**LO: 14**                    **Conceptual**

58.     According to Robert Karasek, two factors play a key role in determining occupational stress. The two factors are
a.      decision control and employee autonomy.
b.      psychological demands and decision control.
c.      employee autonomy and relationship with superior.
d.      relationship with superior and psychological demands.

**ANS: b**                    **Pg: 388**
**LO: 14**                    **Factual**

59.     According to Karasek, occupational stress is greatest when psychological demands are _____ and decision control is _____.
a.      low; low
b.      high; high
c.      high; low
d.      low; high

**ANS: c**                    **Pg: 388**
**LO: 14**                    **Factual**

*60.    Jimenez works a typical job in his country.  He was recently sick and found out the
        company offered no sick days because it was not required by law to do so.  Where does
        Jimenez live?
a.      United Stated
b.      Germany
c.      England
d.      Spain

ANS: a          Pg: 387
LO: 14          Applied

61.     In which of the following areas can job stress have negative effects?
a.      in the work arena itself
b.      workers' physical health
c.      workers' psychological health
d.      all of these

ANS: d          Pgs: 388-389
LO: 15          Conceptual

62.     In one study, Karasek found more symptoms of heart disease among men whose jobs
        were _____ in psychological demands and _____ in decision control.
a.      low; low
b.      high; high
c.      low; high
d.      high; low

ANS: d          Pg: 389
LO: 15          Factual

*63.    Billy works on an assembly line where there is constant pressure to increase his speed
        and productivity.  Psychologists would say Billy's job contains lots of
a.      physical demands.
b.      mental load.
c.      psychological demands.
d.      automatic load.

ANS: c          Pg: 388
LO: 15          Applied

*64.    Jobs with _____ and _____ are considered the most stressful.
a.      low psychological demands; high decision control
b.      high psychological demands; high decision control
c.      low psychological demands; low decision control
d.      high psychological demands; low decision control

ANS: d          Pg: 388
LO: 15          Factual

*65.    Which of these has not been shown to be an effect of high stress jobs?
a.      anxiety
b.      heart disease
c.      depression
d.      All of these have been related to depression.

**ANS: d**        **Pg: 389**
**LO: 15**        **Factual**

*66.    _____ is a psychological state characterized by exhaustion, cynicism, and poor job performance.
a.      Anxiety
b.      Burnout
c.      Low decision control
d.      Demand

**ANS: b**        **Pg: 389**
**LO: 15**        **Factual**

*67.    Marti used to enjoy her job, but recently she has been performing poorly, feeling exhausted and cynical. Marti may have
a.      anxiety.
b.      burnout.
c.      low decision control.
d.      demand.

**ANS: b**        **Pg: 389**
**LO: 15**        **Applied**

68.     A program designed to improve employees' coping skills would be considered an intervention at which of the following levels?
a.      individual
b.      organizational
c.      home-organizational interface
d.      individual-organizational interface

**ANS: a**        **Pg: 389**
**LO: 16**        **Conceptual**

69.     Jose has engaged the services of a registered nurse, an athletic trainer, and a nutritionist to develop a three-week program to raise employee awareness of the importance of self-care on and off the job. He is offering his employees a
a.      relaxation-training program.
b.      workplace wellness program.
c.      diversity awareness program.
d.      stress-management program.

**ANS: d**        **Pgs: 389-390**
**LO: 16**        **Applied**

70.    _____ occurs when a worker is subjected to unwanted sexually oriented behavior.
a.    Sexism
b.    Job segregation
c.    Sexual orientation
d.    Sexual harassment

**ANS: d**         **Pg: 391**
**LO: 17**         **Factual**

71.    When submission to unwanted sexual advances is a condition of getting a promotion, which type of harassment is being perpetrated?
a.    quid pro quo
b.    environmental
c.    job segregation
d.    employer-sponsored

**ANS: a**         **Pg: 391**
**LO: 17**         **Factual**

72.    Maria is uncomfortable in her job as a policewoman because her coworkers tell crude sexual jokes and hang centerfold pinups in the break room at the station. She is experiencing
a.    quid pro quo hostility.
b.    hostile environmental harassment.
c.    job segregation.
d.    employer-sponsored hostility.

**ANS: b**         **Pg: 391**
**LO: 17**         **Applied**

73.    Research indicates that approximately _____ percent of female workers in the United States report having been sexually harassed.
a.    20
b.    40
c.    60
d.    80

**ANS: b**         **Pg: 391**
**LO: 17**         **Factual**

74.    Physical symptoms associated with being sexually harassed include all but which of the following?
a.    weight loss
b.    heart disease
c.    inability to sleep
d.    stomach disorders

**ANS: b**         **Pg: 392**
**LO: 17**         **Factual**

75.     Individuals who are unemployed because their jobs have disappeared are called
        _____workers.
a.      token
b.      displaced
c.      segregated
d.      underemployed

**ANS: b**          **Pg: 393**
**LO: 19**          **Factual**

76.     Unemployment causes the most psychological distress for
a.      teenagers.
b.      young male adults.
c.      young female adults.
d.      middle aged adults.

**ANS: d**          **Pg: 393**
**LO: 19**          **Factual**

77.     Unemployment can cause which of the following psychological problems?
a.      anxiety
b.      depression
c.      loss of self-esteem
d.      all of these

**ANS: d**          **Pg: 393**
**LO: 19**          **Factual**

*78.    What is the leading cause of on-the-job homicides?
a.      co-worker dispute
b.      displaced workers
c.      robbery
d.      situational propensity

**ANS: c**          **Pg: 393**
**LO: 19**          **Conceptual**

79.     _____ is the term for devotion of nearly all one's time and energy to a job.
a.      Burning out
b.      Overemployment
c.      Workaholism
d.      Ambition

**ANS: c**          **Pg: 395**
**LO: 20**          **Conceptual**

80. Which of the following statements about workaholism is **not** true?
a. Psychologists are not in agreement about how harmful workaholism is.
b. It is one of the most well-researched areas in I/O psychology.
c. There are enthusiastic and non-enthusiastic workaholics.
d. There are certain organizational climate features that promote workaholism.

**ANS: b**          **Pg: 395**
**LO: 20**          **Conceptual**

81. Joshua is a high school teacher who spends 60 hours a week at work. He is up early every morning and arrives at his classroom full of energy. He participates avidly in professional development activities and works with administration to bring innovative techniques to his school. He is probably
a. underemployed.
b. burned out.
c. over-employed.
d. an enthusiastic workaholic.

**ANS: d**          **Pg: 395**
**LO: 20**          **Applied**

82. The increase in _____ is a major recent change in the U.S. work force.
a. teenaged skilled laborers
b. dual-earner households
c. part-time laborers
d. undocumented workers

**ANS: b**          **Pg: 395**
**LO: 21**          **Factual**

*83. In the United State family-friendly benefits are
a. increasing.
b. decreasing.
c. remaining level.
d. increasing for females, but decreasing for males.

**ANS: b**          **Pg: 396**
**LO: 21**          **Factual**

*84. From 1998 to 2003, the percentage of mothers with infants who are in the workforce
a. increased.
b. decreased.
c. remained level.
d. approximately halved.

**ANS: b**          **Pg: 396**
**LO: 21**          **Conceptual**

*85. Workers in Europe get approximately _____ weeks of vacation a year; whereas workers in the US average approximately _____ weeks a year.
a. three; six
b. six; three
c. two; four
d. four; two

**ANS: d**      **Pg: 397**
**LO: 21**      **Conceptual**

86. _____ refers to unpaid activities people choose to engage in because the activities are personally meaningful.
a. Leisure
b. Tokenism
c. Unemployment
d. Underemployment

**ANS: a**      **Pg: 397**
**LO: 22**      **Factual**

87. Which of the following statements is true of research testing the notion that a satisfying balance of work, relationships, and leisure activities will lead to a more rewarding and healthy life?
a. Research has generally supported this notion.
b. Paradoxically, this notion has not been supported.
c. Virtually no research has been conducted testing this proposition.
d. Findings indicate that time spent in leisure activities actually increases feelings of stress.

**ANS: a**      **Pg: 398**
**LO: 22**      **Conceptual**

*88. Which leisure activity is negatively related to perceived well-being?
a. chat-room surfing
b. competitive sports
c. non-competitive sports
d. television viewing

**ANS: d**      **Pg: 398**
**LO: 22**      **Conceptual**

89. Which of the following is the best advice for preparing an effective resumé?
a. Be sure to use complete sentences.
b. Don't give extraneous personal information.
c. The longer the resume, the more impressive it is.
d. Use colored paper that will make your resumé stand out.

**ANS: b**      **Pg: 400**
**LO: 23**      **Conceptual**

90. The purpose of a resume is
a. to tell your life story.
b. to get you a job.
c. to help you to obtain an interview.
d. to be as flashy as possible to make you stand out in the applicant pool.

**ANS: c**      **Pg: 400**
**LO: 23**      **Conceptual**

91. Which of the following is the best advice about information that should be included in a resumé?
a. Emphasize your achievements by using the words "I" and "me."
b. Include some personal information that will make you appear more "human."
c. Avoid the use of section labels, which tend to give the resume a "cluttered" look.
d. When you list your previous experience, make sure your most recent position is the one with the greatest achievements.

**ANS: d**      **Pg: 400**
**LO: 23**      **Conceptual**

92. Experts estimate that up to _____ percent of all vacancies, especially those above the entry level, are never advertised.
a. 20
b. 40
c. 60
d. 80

**ANS: d**      **Pg: 402**
**LO: 24**      **Factual**

93. Employment agencies generally handle only
a. middle management jobs.
b. jobs that are not advertised.
c. entry-level, hourly wage jobs.
d. professional positions that require advanced degrees.

**ANS: c**      **Pg: 402**
**LO: 24**      **Factual**

94. A "headhunter" is a slang term for
a. a job applicant.
b. an executive recruiter.
c. a trade newspaper.
d. an inside contact for jobs.

**ANS: b**      **Pg: 402**
**LO: 25**      **Factual**

95. Which of the following is a good strategy to adopt in tackling the interview process?
a. Take some time to learn something about the company you're interviewing with.
b. Introduce yourself (by phone or in person) directly to the person in charge of hiring and request an interview.
c. Try to identify an acquaintance that you and the person in charge have in common.
d. All of these are good strategies.

**ANS: d**         **Pgs: 402-403**
**LO: 26**         **Conceptual**

96. _____ refers to behaviors of interviewers that lead to the reinforcement of their pre-conceived notions about a job candidate.
a. Discrimination
b. Confirmation bias
c. Harassment
d. Leading questions

**ANS: b**         **Pg: 403**
**LO: 27**         **Factual**

97. Which of the following factors has been found to be associated with ratings of job interviewees?
a. attire
b. weight
c. attractiveness
d. all of these

**ANS: d**         **Pg: 403**
**LO: 27**         **Factual**

98. Which of the following is **not** good advice regarding job interviews?
a. Try to appear confident and enthusiastic.
b. Avoid being critical of anyone, including former employers.
c. Learn all you can about the organization before the interview.
d. Always ask about salary or pay range.

**ANS: d**         **Pg: 403**
**LO: 28**         **Conceptual**

*99. Which of the following is good advice regarding the interview process?
a. Try to make the interviewer laugh.
b. Be somewhat formal and reserved.
c. Be forthcoming with negative information.
d. Interrupt the interviewer occasionally to demonstrate your self-confidence.

**ANS: b**         **Pg: 403**
**LO: 28**         **Conceptual**

# MULTIPLE CHOICE QUESTIONS FROM STUDY GUIDE

1. Occupational interest inventories
a. are focused more on job satisfaction than job success.
b. are the best measures available to determine your level of job success.
c. are used by employers to gauge the interest level of prospective employees.
d. provide you with information about occupations that are related to your college major.

**ANS: a**        **Pg: 377**
**LO: 4**        **Factual**

2. Which of the following statements regarding gender bias on occupational interest inventories is accurate?
a. There is no evidence of gender bias on these inventories.
b. Gender bias existed in the past, but it has been eliminated.
c. Gender bias exists, but only for African American women.
d. Gender bias has been reduced, but it has not been eliminated.

**ANS: d**        **Pg: 377**
**LO: 4**        **Factual**

3. When making career choices, an important point to keep in mind is
a. any career decision can be easily undone.
b. your career options are practically limitless.
c. career choice is a developmental process .
d. you should be able to find a job that fits you perfectly.

**ANS: c**        **Pg: 378**
**LO: 5**        **Conceptual**

4. According to John Holland's trait measurement and matching model of career development, which of the following personal orientations would be most compatible with a job as a nurse?
a. social
b. realistic
c. enterprising
d. conventional

**ANS: a**        **Pg: 378**
**LO: 6**        **Factual**

5. According to Donald Super, the critical factor that governs career development is one's
a. self-concept.
b. need for approval.
c. occupational ideal.
d. drive for heterosexual success.

**ANS: a**        **Pg: 380**
**LO: 7**        **Factual**

6. According to Super's developmental model of career choice, which of the following stages involves making a commitment to a specific job, and demonstrating the ability to function effectively in this job?
a. growth stage
b. exploration stage
c. establishment stage
d. maintenance stage

**ANS: c**        **Pg: 380**
**LO: 7**        **Factual**

7. The career development of males and females is
a. similar because it is against the law to discriminate.
b. similar in that both appear to be influenced by the same motivational factors.
c. different, mainly due to genetic predispositions that differ for men and women.
d. different, in part, because women still subordinate their career goals to those of their husbands.

**ANS: d**        **Pg: 381**
**LO: 7**        **Factual**

8. Which of the following statements regarding diversity in the workplace is not accurate?
a. Jobs tend to be typed by gender and race.
b. Technically, job discrimination on the basis of race and gender is not illegal.
c. Women and minorities are frequently passed over for promotion in favor of white men.
d. Employees in female-dominated fields typically earn less than those in male-dominated fields.

**ANS: b**        **Pg: 385**
**LO: 12**        **Conceptual**

9. According to Robert Karasek, occupational stress is most likely to occur under which of the following conditions?
a. high psychological demands and low decision control
b. low psychological demands and high decision control
c. low psychological demands and low decision control
d. high psychological demands and high decision control

**ANS: a**        **Pg: 388**
**LO: 13**        **Factual**

10. Interventions at the _____ are the most widely used strategy for managing work-related stress.
a. individual level
b. organizational level
c. family-organizational interface
d. individual-organizational interface

**ANS: a**        **Pg: 389**
**LO: 15**        **Factual**

11. All but which of the following is a characteristic of the typical female victim of sexual harassment in the workplace?
a. young
b. married
c. is in a nonsenior position
d. works in a masculine-stereotyped field

**ANS: b**          **Pg: 391**
**LO: 16**          **Factual**

12. Which of the following is <u>not</u> one of the results of unemployment discussed in your textbook?
a. anxiety
b. depression
c. loss of self-esteem
d. All of these are possible results.

**ANS: d**          **Pg: 393**
**LO: 18**          **Factual**

13. Employees who lose their jobs because of downsizing – instead of poor job performance – are likely to believe they have been treated arbitrarily and unfairly – a situation found to be associated with an increase in
a. anxiety.
b. self-esteem.
c. aggression.
d. job-related stress.

**ANS: c**          **Pg: 393**
**LO: 18**          **Factual**

14. Research indicates that workaholism may be either constructive or problematic, depending on the
a. individual's enjoyment of the job.
b. number of hours worked per week.
c. individual's level of performance.
d. opinion of the individual's immediate supervisor.

**ANS: a**          **Pg: 395**
**LO: 19**          **Factual**

15. Which of the following is <u>not</u> good advice for creating the right impression during a job interview?
a. Avoid any attempts at humor.
b. Go easy on the after-shave lotion or perfume.
c. Elevate your perceived worth by criticizing your previous employer.
d. Try to anticipate the questions that will be asked and have some answers ready.

**ANS: c**          **Pg: 403**
**LO: 26**          **Factual**

# MULTIPLE CHOICE QUESTIONS ON WEB SITE

1.     After you've read the available literature about an occupation, it's a good idea to talk to
a.     an occupational therapist.
b.     an employment counsellor.
c.     individuals working in that area.
d.     your high school guidance counsellor.

**ANS: c**          **Pg: 376**
**LO: 2**           **Factual**

2.     Which of the following statements about vocational choice is **not** accurate?
a.     There are no limits on your career options.
b.     Some career decisions are not easily undone.
c.     You have the potential for success in a variety of jobs.
d.     Vocational development will continue throughout your lifetime.

**ANS: a**          **Pg: 377**
**LO: 5**           **Conceptual**

3.     According to Holland's hexagonal model of career choice, a philosophy professor would probably be considered _____ type.
a.     an artistic
b.     a realistic
c.     an investigative
d.     a conventional

**ANS: c**          **Pg: 378**
**LO: 6**           **Applied**

4.     According to Holland's model, people who like to use their social skills to persuade others, and who perceive themselves as self-confident, sociable, and popular, would most likely be considered as having the _____ personal orientation.
a.     social
b.     artistic
c.     enterprising
d.     conventional

**ANS: c**          **Pgs: 378**
**LO: 6**           **Conceptual**

5.     Which of the following individuals proposed an influential developmental model of career choice?
a.     Nancy Betz
b.     Roger Gould
c.     John Holland
d.     Donald Super

**ANS: d**          **Pg: 379**
**LO: 7**           **Factual**

6.	Women's vocational development is different from men's primarily because
a.	men tend to be better trained for gender-neutral jobs.
b.	women are less likely to experience labor force discontinuity.
c.	women often subordinate their career goals to those of their husbands.
d.	women with children one year old or younger generally don't work outside the home.

**ANS: c**		**Pg: 381**
**LO: 8**		**Conceptual**

7.	Leaving the labor force, even if for increasingly brief periods of time, is called
a.	overemployment.
b.	labor force discontinuity.
c.	token employment.
d.	re-employment disclamation.

**ANS: b**		**Pg: 381**
**LO: 9**		**Factual**

*8.	In 1970 approximately _____ % of married women worked.  While in 2003, approximately _____ % of married women worked.
a.	40; 60
b.	60; 40
c.	60; 80
d.	80; 60

**ANS: a**		**Pg: 385**
**LO: 11**		**Factual**

*9.	Jason, a minority group member, feels that his co-workers see him as a _____ worker; consequently his is likely to experience more _____ pressure than the typical white male.
a.	minority; stress
b.	token; performance
c.	minority; performance
d.	token; stress

**ANS: b**		**Pg: 386**
**LO: 14**		**Applied**

10.	Which is not a common job stressor?
a.	perceived inequities
b.	pressure of deadlines
c.	lack of control over one's work
d.	the monotony associated with regular hours

**ANS: d**		**Pg: 387**
**LO: 14**		**Conceptual**

*11.   Jobs with _____ and _____ are considered the most stressful.
a.   low psychological demands; high decision control
b.   high psychological demands; high decision control
c.   low psychological demands; low decision control
d.   high psychological demands; low decision control

**ANS: d**          **Pgs: 388**
**LO: 15**          **Factual**

12.   Maria is uncomfortable in her job as a policewoman because her coworkers tell crude sexual jokes and hang centerfold pinups in the break room at the station. She is experiencing
a.   quid pro quo hostility.
b.   hostile environmental harassment.
c.   job segregation.
d.   employer-sponsored hostility.

**ANS: b**          **Pg: 391**
**LO: 17**          **Applied**

13.   Which of the following statements about workaholism is **not** true?
a.   Psychologists are not in agreement about how harmful workaholism is.
b.   It is one of the most well-researched areas in I/O psychology.
c.   There are enthusiastic and non-enthusiastic workaholics.
d.   There are certain organizational climate features that promote workaholism.

**ANS: b**          **Pg: 395**
**LO: 20**          **Conceptual**

*14.   Which leisure activity is negatively related to perceived well-being?
a.   chat-room surfing
b.   competitive sports
c.   non-competitive sports
d.   television viewing

**ANS: d**          **Pg: 398**
**LO: 22**          **Conceptual**

15.   A "headhunter" is a slang term for
a.   a job applicant.
b.   an executive recruiter.
c.   a trade newspaper.
d.   an inside contact for jobs.

**ANS: b**          **Pg: 402**
**LO: 25**          **Factual**

# TRUE/FALSE QUESTIONS

1.     Business environmental psychology is the study of behavior in the workplace.

**ANS:   false              Pg: 373**
**LO:    1                  Factual**

2.     Many people will have 12-15 jobs in their lifetime.

**ANS:   true               Pg: 378**
**LO:    5                  Factual**

3.     According to Holland's model, a happy scientist is probably a conventional type.

**ANS:   false              Pgs: 378-379**
**LO:    6                  Conceptual**

4.     Underemployment is leaving the labor force for brief periods of time.

**ANS:   false              Pg: 384**
**LO:    10                 Factual**

5.     The United States has the best vacation and leave policies in the world.

**ANS:   false              Pgs: 387-388**
**LO:    21                 Conceptual**

6.     Western Europeans tend to have more vacation time than Americans.

**ANS:   true               Pg: 387**
**LO:    21                 Factual**

7.     Stress-wise, the best jobs are high in decision control.

**ANS:   true               Pg: 388**
**LO:    13                 Conceptual**

8.     Sexual harassment does not usually cause a stressful work environment.

**ANS:   false              Pg: 392**
**LO:    16                 Factual**

9.     A good resumé is at least several pages long.

**ANS:   false              Pg: 400**
**LO:    22                 Factual**

10.     In general, you should not attempt to make the interviewer laugh during a job interview in order to lighten up the situation.

**ANS:   true          Pg: 403**
**LO:     26            Conceptual**


## SHORT-ANSWER ESSAY QUESTIONS

1.      Briefly describe how family background influences career choice.

**Pg: 375**

2.      List and briefly describe the limitations of using the results of occupational interest inventories to work through the career decision-making process.

**Pgs: 377-378**

3.      Describe and compare the Holland and Super models of career choice and development.

**Pgs: 378-380**

4.      Briefly discuss the significance of the term "labor force discontinuity."

**Pg: 381**

5.      Discuss some of the current workplace trends described in the chapter and the social changes that these changes reflect.

**Pgs: 382-383**

6.      "Today's workers need to take a more active role in shaping their careers." What does this statement mean? Why is this true?

**Pg: 382**

7.      Briefly describe the factors that are responsible for the breakdown in the boundaries between work and home.

**Pg: 383**

8.      Briefly explain the apparently conflicting findings suggesting that workaholism can be either constructive or problematic.

**Pg: 395**

9.      Identify and briefly describe the major sources of occupational stress. Discuss effective ways to manage job stress.

**Pgs: 387-390**

10. List and briefly describe five strategies that you can use to maximize your chances of obtaining a satisfying job.

**Pgs: 399-401**

*11. Discuss how to write a good resume.

**Pg: 400**

*12. What important tips would you give someone going to their first job interview?

**Pgs: 402-403**

*13. Discuss several non-traditional methods of obtaining a job interview.

**Pg: 402**

# Chapter 13
# DEVELOPMENT AND EXPRESSION OF SEXUALITY

## LEARNING OBJECTIVES

1. List four key aspects of sexual identity.
2. Discuss how hormones influence sexual differentiation and sexual behavior.
3. Discuss how families, peers, schools, and the media shape sexual attitudes and behavior.
4. Discuss gender differences in sexual socialization and how they affect individuals.
5. Summarize current thinking on the origins of sexual orientation and attitudes toward homosexuality.
6. Discuss the identity development and adjustment of lesbians and gay males.
7. List some common sexual motives.
8. Describe four common barriers in communicating about sex.
9. Describe the four phases of the human sexual response cycle.
10. Discuss gender differences in patterns of orgasm and some reasons for them.
11. Discuss fantasy as well as kissing and touching as aspects of sexual expression.
12. Discuss the prevalence of self-stimulation and attitudes about it.
13. Discuss oral and anal sex as forms of sexual expression.
14. Discuss intercourse and the preferred sexual activities of gay males and lesbians.
15. Describe how the fear of contracting AIDS has influenced sexual attitudes and practices.
16. Summarize attitudes toward and prevalence of early sexual experiences.
17. Summarize the findings on sex in dating couples and marital sex.
18. Compare and contrast sexual behavior in married versus committed homosexual couples.
19. Summarize the evidence on infidelity in committed relationships.
20. Describe constraints on effective contraception and discuss the merits of hormone-based contraceptives and condoms.
21. Describe the various types of STDs and discuss their prevalence and means of transmission.
22. List some suggestions for safer sexual practices.
23. List six general suggestions for enhancing sexual relationships.
24. Discuss the nature, prevalence, and causes of common sexual dysfunctions.
25. Describe the strategies for coping with erectile difficulties, premature ejaculation, orgasmic difficulties, and hypoactive sexual desire.

## MULTIPLE CHOICE QUESTIONS

1.      The fact that sex research is typically done using volunteer subjects causes problems with
a.      obtaining sufficient funds for sex research.
b.      getting representative samples.
c.      doing observational studies.
d.      the reliability of self-report measures.

**ANS: b**          **Pg: 407**
**LO: 1**           **Conceptual**

*2.     Dr. Feinstein is setting up a laboratory to research the human sexual response.  Her
        biggest research problem is likely to be
a.      the reliability of the subjects' responses.
b.      ethical problems with the methodology.
c.      the need to develop physiological equipment.
d.      getting representative samples of subjects.

**ANS: d**          **Pg: 407**
**LO: 1**           **Applied**

3.      _____ is comprised of the personal qualities, self-perceptions, attitudes, values, and
        preferences that guide an individual's sexual behavior.
a.      Eroticism
b.      Body image
c.      Sexual identity
d.      Sexual orientation

**ANS: c**          **Pg: 408**
**LO: 1**           **Factual**

4.      _____ seek emotional-sexual relationships with members of the same gender.
a.      Asexual people
b.      Bisexuals
c.      Homosexuals
d.      Heterosexuals

**ANS: c**          **Pg: 408**
**LO: 1**           **Factual**

5.      _____ seek emotional-sexual relationships with members of both genders.
a.      Asexual people
b.      Bisexuals
c.      Homosexuals
d.      Heterosexuals

**ANS: b**          **Pg: 408**
**LO: 1**           **Factual**

*6.    Jane seeks out and enjoys relationships with males. She is likely a(n)
a.    asexual.
b.    bisexual.
c.    homosexual.
d.    heterosexual.

ANS: d            Pg: 408
LO: 1             Factual

7.    Your _____ is how you see yourself physically.
a.    body image
b.    erotic identity
c.    sexual identity
d.    sexual orientation

ANS: a            Pg: 408
LO: 1             Factual

8.    _____ are the principal class of female sex hormones; _____ are the principal class of male sex hormones.
a.    Estrogens; androgens
b.    Androgens; estrogens
c.    Pheromones; androgens
d.    Androgens; pheromones

ANS: a            Pg: 408
LO: 2             Factual

9.    Adolescents attain reproductive capability as hormonal changes lead to the full development of the
a.    gonads.
b.    primary sex characteristics.
c.    secondary sex characteristics.
d.    pubescent sex characteristics.

ANS: b            Pg: 409
LO: 2             Factual

*10.   Juanita, 11 years old, is developing breasts. She is experiencing the growth of
a.    primary sex characteristics.
b.    secondary sex characteristics.
c.    gonadal trophisms.
d.    none of these.

ANS: b            Pg: 409
LO: 2             Conceptual

11. Which of the following statements about the role of hormones in sexual behavior is **not** accurate?
a. Estrogen levels among women correlate with sexual interest.
b. Androgen seems to be related to sexual motivation in both men and women.
c. High levels of testosterone in male and female subjects are related to higher rates of sexual activity.
d. The effects of androgens on sexual behavior are stronger in men than in women.

ANS: a          Pg: 409
LO: 2           Conceptual

12. Which of the following is **not** considered one of the principal psychosocial influences on sexual identity?
a. church
b. family
c. school
d. media

ANS: a          Pg: 409
LO: 3           Conceptual

13. Children may come to believe that sex is "dirty" because
a. they receive reinforcement for such beliefs.
b. it is portrayed as such by television and other media.
c. parents frequently punish innocent, exploratory sex play.
d. this is consistent with the way peers convey information about sex.

ANS: c          Pg: 409
LO: 3           Conceptual

14. Open communication between parents and their children about sexual topics correlates with
a. lower rates of teen pregnancy.
b. lower rates of STDs among teenagers.
c. less sexual activity in adolescence.
d. more promiscuity among high school students.

ANS: c          Pg: 410
LO: 3           Factual

15. Which of the following statements regarding adolescents who receive most of their sex education from a parent is accurate?
a. They are less likely to be sexually active.
b. They are more likely to use contraceptives if they are sexually active.
c. They wait longer before having sex.
d. All of these statements are accurate.

ANS: d          Pgs: 409-410
LO: 3           Conceptual

*16.    What percent of adolescents report that they learned "a lot" about sex from their parents?
a.      17
b.      37
c.      57
d.      77

**ANS: b**            **Pg: 409**
**LO: 3**             **Factual**

*17.    John's parents were very open about sex when he was a teenager. They went to great efforts to make sure John learned more about sex than "the street" or even school could teach him. It is likely that in his teenage years,
a.      John will have less partners, but be more sexually active than average.
b.      John will have more partners, and be more sexually active than average.
c.      John will have less partners, and be less sexually active than average.
d.      Not enough information is given.

**ANS: c**            **Pg: 410**
**LO: 3**             **Applied**

18.     Research findings indicate that exposure to erotic materials
a.      encourages pro-rape attitudes in both men and women.
b.      elevates permissive attitudes about sexual behavior.
c.      increases the likelihood that a male viewer will commit a sex crime.
d.      may lead to the development of conservative attitudes about sexual behavior.

**ANS: b**            **Pg: 411**
**LO: 3**             **Conceptual**

19.     Which of the following groups is most likely to emphasize "sex for fun" in casual relationships and reserve "sex with love" for committed relationships?
a.      men
b.      women
c.      lesbians
d.      bisexuals

**ANS: a**            **Pg: 411**
**LO: 4**             **Conceptual**

20.     In American culture, adolescent girls are usually taught to
a.      experiment sexually.
b.      enjoy sex without emotional involvement.
c.      view sex in the context of a loving relationship.
d.      use sex to validate their social status with males.

**ANS: c**            **Pg: 411**
**LO: 4**             **Factual**

21.     Gender differences in sexual socialization increase the likelihood
a.      that conflict about sexual matters will occur in heterosexual couples.
b.      that communication will be essential for mutually satisfying sexual relationships.
c.      that women will have to accept men's extramarital relationships.
d.      that the male and female approaches to sex will be complimentary.

**ANS: b**          **Pg: 413**
**LO: 4**            **Conceptual**

22.     Which of the following statements regarding gender differences in sexual socialization is
        accurate?
a.      Gay men tend to develop emotional relationships out of sexual ones.
b.      Lesbians typically feel emotional attraction to their partners before experiencing sexual
        feelings.
c.      Homosexual couples are less likely than heterosexual couples to have "compatibility
        problems."
d.      All of these statements are accurate.

**ANS: d**          **Pg: 413**
**LO: 4**            **Conceptual**

23.     _____ is the researcher who designed a seven-point scale to characterize sexual
        orientation.
a.      Alfred Kinsey
b.      Albert Bandura
c.      William Masters
d.      Virginia Johnson

**ANS: a**          **Pg: 413**
**LO: 5**            **Factual**

*24.    Modern research shows that about ___ % of the population could be characterized as
        homosexual.
a.      2
b.      7
c.      10
d.      13

**ANS: b**          **Pg: 413**
**LO: 5**            **Conceptual**

*25.    Jenna and Katie are lesbians raising a son.  The likelihood he will be a homosexual is
        _____ over heterosexual parents?
a.      lowered
b.      raised
c.      about the same as
d.      substantially lowered

**ANS: c**          **Pg: 414**
**LO: 5**            **Applied**

*26. Research has shown that masculine behavior in female children and feminine behavior in male children is related to later homosexuality. This is
a.    true for males, but not true for females.
b.    true for both males and females.
c.    not true for males, but true for females.
d.    true for bisexuality, but not homosexuality in both sexes.

**ANS: b**          **Pg: 414**
**LO: 5**           **Factual**

*27. Many homosexuals
a.    can trace their leanings back to childhood.
b.    can remember a specific instance of being forced to perform homosexual behavior in childhood.
c.    had homosexual parents.
d.    were raised in very permissive environments.

**ANS: a**          **Pg: 414**
**LO: 5**           **Conceptual**

*28. Research has shown that _____ % of subjects who had a gay identical twin were gay.
a.    less than 10
b.    22
c.    32
d.    52

**ANS: d**          **Pg: 414**
**LO: 5**           **Factual**

*29. Research has shown that _____ % of subjects who had a gay identical twin were gay while _____% with a gay fraternal twin were gay.
a.    22; 22
b.    22; 52
c.    52; 52
d.    52; 22

**ANS: d**          **Pg: 414**
**LO: 5**           **Factual**

30. Jay is clearly uncomfortable whenever he is introduced to a gay man. He frequently makes disparaging remarks about homosexuals and states that he would "punch out" any man who came on to him. Jay shows signs of
a.    bisexuality.
b.    homophobia.
c.    heterophobia.
d.    sensate focus.

**ANS: b**          **Pg: 415**
**LO: 5**           **Conceptual**

31. The pioneering research of _____ and others rejected the view that homosexuality is a psychological disorder.
a. Alfred Kinsey
b. Evelyn Hooker
c. William Masters
d. Virginia Johnson

**ANS: b          Pg: 417**
**LO: 6          Factual**

32. One important reason why people may **not** communicate their sexual preferences to their partners is that
a. they may actually not know what their preferences are.
b. they feel comfortable with the status quo in the sexual aspects of the relationship.
c. they enjoy the "game" of figuring these things out together.
d. they worry that their partner may cease to respect and love them.

**ANS: d          Pg: 419**
**LO: 8          Conceptual**

*33. _____ is when a homosexual comes out as much as possible, but hides his or her sexual identity when necessary to prevent discrimination.
a. Rational outness
b. Partial outness
c. Rational prevention
d. Partial symbolic sharing

**ANS: a          Pg: 416**
**LO: 6          Conceptual**

*34. _____ homosexuals show adjustment problems than heterosexual.
a. More
b. Fewer
c. About the same number of
d. No research is available on the subject.

**ANS: c          Pg: 417**
**LO: 6          Factual**

35. _____ conducted groundbreaking research on the physiology   of the human sexual response.
a. Alfred Kinsey
b. Albert Bandura
c. Carl Jung and Sigmund Freud
d. William Masters and Virginia Johnson

**ANS: d          Pg: 419**
**LO: 9          Factual**

36.     According to Masters and Johnson, the four phases of the sexual response cycle are
a.      excitement, arousal, orgasm, relaxation.
b.      excitement, plateau, orgasm, resolution.
c.      arousal, plateau, orgasm, refractory period.
d.      vasocongestion, plateau, orgasm, refractory period.

**ANS: b**              **Pgs: 420-421**
**LO: 9**               **Factual**

37.     _____ is the direct physiological cause of erection.
a.      Orgasm
b.      Refraction
c.      Ejaculation
d.      Vasocongestion

**ANS: d**              **Pg: 420**
**LO: 9**               **Factual**

38.     Vasocongestion (engorgement of blood vessels) begins during the_____ phase of the
        sexual response cycle.
a.      plateau
b.      orgasm
c.      resolution
d.      excitement

**ANS: d**              **Pg: 420**
**LO: 9**               **Factual**

*39.    Vasocongestion causes
a.      penile erection in males.
b.      clitoral swelling in females.
c.      orgasm .
d.      both penile erection in males and clitoral swelling in females.

**ANS: d**              **Pg: 420**
**LO: 9**               **Factual**

40.     During which stage of the sexual response cycle does the level of arousal escalate most
        rapidly?
a.      plateau
b.      orgasm
c.      resolution
d.      excitement

**ANS: d**              **Pg: 420**
**LO: 9**               **Factual**

41.	Which of the following phases of the sexual response cycle occurs immediately before the first orgasm?
a.	plateau
b.	refractory
c.	resolution
d.	excitement

**ANS: a**	**Pgs: 420-421**
**LO: 9**	**Factual**

42.	The refractory period is a
a.	post-orgasmic period when females are relatively unresponsive to sexual stimulation.
b.	post-orgasmic period when males are relatively unresponsive to sexual stimulation.
c.	pre-orgasmic period when males are relatively unresponsive to sexual stimulation.
d.	prepubescent period when males and females are relatively unresponsive to sexual stimulation.

**ANS: b**	**Pg: 421**
**LO: 9**	**Factual**

43.	The refractory period occurs during which phase of the sexual response cycle?
a.	plateau
b.	orgasm
c.	resolution
d.	excitement

**ANS: c**	**Pg: 421**
**LO: 9**	**Factual**

*44.	Around _____ % of women always or usually reach orgasm in their primary sexual relationships.
a.	25
b.	50
c.	65
d.	85

**ANS: c**	**Pg: 421**
**LO: 10**	**Factual**

*45.	When females masturbate then can reach orgasm in about _____ minutes.
a.	4
b.	14
c.	24
d.	Very seldom can females masturbate to orgasm.

**ANS: a**	**Pg: 421**
**LO: 10**	**Conceptual**

46.     A body area that is sexually sensitive or responsive is called
a.      a sensate focus.
b.      a refractory area.
c.      an autoerotic zone.
d.      an erogenous zone.

**ANS: d**              **Pg: 422**
**LO: 11**              **Factual**

*47.    The most common sexual fantasy
a.      involves having sex with a person other than the partner.
b.      involves dominance and submission.
c.      involves multiple partners.
d.      is different for males and females.

**ANS: a**              **Pg: 422**
**LO: 11**              **Factual**

48.     Which of the following statements regarding kissing and touching is accurate?
a.      Men often overestimate the importance of kissing and touching.
b.      Men often underestimate the importance of kissing and touching.
c.      Partners rarely have differing expectations about kissing and touching.
d.      For most couples, kissing and touching are not integral elements of sexual stimulation.

**ANS: b**              **Pg: 422**
**LO: 11**              **Conceptual**

49.     Which of the following terms does **not** belong with the others?
a.      cunnilingus
b.      masturbation
c.      autoeroticism
d.      self-stimulation

**ANS: a**              **Pg: 423**
**LO: 12**              **Conceptual**

50.     Which of the following statements regarding self-stimulation is **not** accurate?
a.      It is common in our society.
b.      Most people masturbate with no ill effects.
c.      It is less common among those with less education.
d.      Masturbation in marriage is typically associated with low marital satisfaction.

**ANS: d**              **Pg: 423**
**LO: 12**              **Conceptual**

51.    Research shows that self-stimulation
a.    tends to disappear after marriage.
b.    is common among married adults.
c.    is an indication of problems in a marriage.
d.    is often a focus of communication among married couples.

**ANS: b**          **Pg: 423**
**LO: 12**          **Factual**

52.    Oral stimulation of the female genitals is called
a.    coitus.
b.    fellatio.
c.    cunnilingus.
d.    autoeroticism.

**ANS: c**          **Pg: 423**
**LO: 13**          **Factual**

53.    Oral stimulation of the male genitals is called
a.    coitus.
b.    fellatio.
c.    cunnilingus.
d.    autoeroticism.

**ANS: b**          **Pg: 423**
**LO: 13**          **Factual**

54.    Which of the following statements regarding oral sex is **not** accurate?
a.    Oral sex plays a central role in homosexual relationships.
b.    It is possible to contract AIDS through mouth-genital stimulation.
c.    Oral sex is a major source of orgasms for many heterosexual couples.
d.    Oral sex is more common in older than younger teens.

**ANS: d**          **Pg: 423**
**LO: 13**          **Conceptual**

55.    Insertion of the penis into a partner's rectum is called
a.    coitus.
b.    fellatio.
c.    sensate focus.
d.    anal intercourse.

**ANS: d**          **Pg: 424**
**LO: 13**          **Factual**

*56.    Sodomy is the legal term for
a.      oral sex.
b.      anal sex.
c.      cunnilingus.
d.      oral and anal sex.

**ANS: b**          **Pg: 424**
**LO: 13**          **Factual**

57.     Which of the following sexual behaviors is least prevalent among gay men?
a.      fellatio
b.      oral sex
c.      anal intercourse
d.      mutual masturbation

**ANS: c**          **Pg: 424**
**LO: 14**          **Factual**

58.     Which of the following is the most common position for vaginal intercourse?
a.      rear-entry
b.      man-above
c.      side-by-side
d.      woman-above

**ANS: b**          **Pg: 424**
**LO: 14**          **Factual**

59.     Which of the following is the most common sexual activity among gay men?
a.      fellatio
b.      tribadism
c.      anal intercourse
d.      mutual masturbation

**ANS: a**          **Pg: 424**
**LO: 14**          **Factual**

60.     Which of the following is the most common sexual activity among lesbians?
a.      tribadism
b.      cunnilingus
c.      mutual masturbation
d.      use of an artificial penis

**ANS: b**          **Pg: 424**
**LO: 14**          **Factual**

61. According to your textbook, the changes in sexual attitudes and behavior that have occurred in the United States in the past 30 years are best characterized as
a. minimal.
b. mythical.
c. evolutionary.
d. revolutionary.

**ANS: c**      **Pg: 424**
**LO: 15**      **Conceptual**

*62. The teenage pregnancy rate in the U.S. is
a. one of the lowest in the world.
b. one of the highest in the world.
c. about average.
d. none of these.

**ANS: b**      **Pg: 424**
**LO: 15**      **Factual**

*63. About what percentage of Americans have had sex by age 22?
a. 25
b. 50
c. 75
d. 90

**ANS: c**      **Pg: 425**
**LO: 16**      **Factual**

*64. Who is less approving of sexual activity in women?
a. females
b. males
c. males and females
d. only older females and younger males

**ANS: c**      **Pg: 426**
**LO: 16**      **Conceptual**

*65. Sexual intimacy is a _____ predictor of relationship stability?
a. positive
b. negative
c. positive only in religious couple
d. negative only in religious couples

**ANS: a**      **Pg: 426**
**LO: 17**      **Factual**

66.     There appears to be a _____ relationship between sexual satisfaction and marital satisfaction.
a.      nonsignificant
b.      weak, negative
c.      strong, positive
d.      strong, negative

ANS: c          Pg: 426
LO: 17          Conceptual

67.     Which of the following is **not** a change in sexual response associated with aging?
a.      Orgasms tend to diminish in intensity.
b.      Females' vaginal lubrication decreases.
c.      Males' refractory periods become shorter.
d.      Arousal builds more slowly in both genders.

ANS: c          Pg: 427
LO: 17          Conceptual

*68.    Couples over 75 report having sex approximately
a.      once per week.
b.      once per month.
c.      once every 2-3 months.
d.      very, very rarely.

ANS: b          Pg: 427
LO: 18          Conceptual

*69.    Who is most likely to find casual sex acceptable?
a.      males
b.      gay males
c.      lesbians
d.      both gay males and lesbians

ANS: b          Pg: 427
LO: 18          Conceptual

70.     Which of the following groups is likely to have the most permissive attitudes about sexual activity outside of a committed relationship?
a.      lesbian couples
b.      married couples
c.      gay male couples
d.      heterosexual engaged couples

ANS: c          Pg: 427
LO: 18          Factual

386

71.    Data from several recent surveys on sex indicate that about _____ percent of American husbands have engaged in extramarital sexual activity at least once.
a.    10
b.    25
c.    50
d.    75

**ANS: b**          **Pg: 428**
**LO: 19**          **Factual**

*72.    Data from several recent surveys on sex indicate that about _____ percent of American wives have engaged in extramarital sexual activity at least once.
a.    10
b.    25
c.    50
d.    75

**ANS: a**          **Pg: 428**
**LO: 19**          **Factual**

73.    Experts speculate that approximately _____ percent of all divorces are caused by infidelity.
a.    20
b.    40
c.    60
d.    80

**ANS: a**          **Pg: 429**
**LO: 19**          **Factual**

74.    Which of the following is **not** one of the steps that intimate couples must negotiate through in order to use contraception effectively?
a.    define themselves as sexually active
b.    agree on the religious implications of contraception
c.    have accurate knowledge of fertility and conception
d.    have access to their chosen method of contraception

**ANS: b**          **Pg: 429**
**LO: 20**          **Conceptual**

75. Which of the following is a common explanation for the fact that many sexually active teenagers do not use contraception or use it only on occasion?
a. Ready access to contraceptive devices is often a problem for adolescents.
b. They can rationalize their sexual behavior by telling themselves that "we got carried away."
c. They harbor the illusion that pregnancy or sexually transmitted diseases "could never happen to me."
d. All of these are common explanations.

**ANS: d**           **Pg: 429**
**LO: 20**           **Conceptual**

*76. Which birth control method shows the least discrepancy between actual and ideal failure rates?
a. condoms
b. rhythm
c. IUDs
d. oral contraceptives

**ANS: c**           **Pg: 430**
**LO: 20**           **Conceptual**

77. Which of the following are the two most widely used birth control methods in the Western world?
a. IUDs and condoms
b. rhythm and condoms
c. condoms and oral contraceptives
d. diaphragms and oral contraceptives

**ANS: c**           **Pg: 430**
**LO: 20**           **Factual**

78. Oral contraception refers to
a. taking pills that inhibit ovulation in women.
b. engaging in oral sex rather than intercourse.
c. talking about sex with a member of the clergy.
d. attending sex education classes at which contraception is discussed.

**ANS: a**           **Pg: 431**
**LO: 20**           **Conceptual**

79. Which of the following contraceptive methods is likely to yield the greatest degree of sexual spontaneity?
a. rhythm
b. condoms
c. oral contraceptives
d. diaphragms with spermicidal cream

**ANS: c**           **Pg: 431**
**LO: 20**           **Conceptual**

80. Which of the following statements regarding the relationship between oral contraceptives and cancer is accurate?
a. There is a slight risk for ovarian cancer in women over the age of 35.
b. Using oral contraceptives does not appear to increase a woman's risk for cancer.
c. The risk of uterine cancer is increased with the use of low-dosage oral contraceptives.
d. When taken in high doses, oral contraceptives have been found to increase the risk of breast cancer.

**ANS: b**        **Pg: 431**
**LO: 20**      **Factual**

81. Which of the following statements about condoms is accurate?
a. Polyurethane condoms are impervious to oil-based creams and lotions.
b. If used correctly, the condom is highly effective in preventing pregnancy.
c. Condoms made of animal membranes don't protect against sexually transmitted diseases.
d. All of these statements are accurate.

**ANS: d**        **Pg: 431**
**LO: 20**      **Factual**

82. There are about _____ different sexually transmitted diseases.
a. 5
b. 20
c. 50
d. 90

**ANS: b**        **Pg: 431**
**LO: 21**      **Factual**

83. Which of the following statements regarding sexually transmitted diseases is **not** accurate?
a. Even monogamous partners can develop some STDs.
b. People can be carriers of STDs without being aware of it.
c. Engaging in anal, as opposed to vaginal, intercourse will reduce the risk of AIDS.
d. The risk of contracting an STD is directly related to the number of sexual partners you have.

**ANS: c**        **Pg: 432**
**LO: 21**      **Conceptual**

84. Which of the following is a good suggestion for engaging in safer sex?
a. Avoid engaging in anal intercourse.
b. Don't have sex with someone who has had lots of previous partners.
c. Wash your genitals with soap and water before and after sexual contact.
d. All of these statements are good suggestions.

**ANS: d**        **Pg: 432**
**LO: 22**      **Conceptual**

85. Which of the following is **not** suggested as a way of enhancing sexual relationships?
a. Communicate about sex.
b. Enjoy your sexual fantasies.
c. Review your sexual values system.
d. Set clear goals for each encounter.

ANS: d          Pg: 434
LO: 23          Conceptual

86. Which of the following statements about sex is **not** true?
a. Fantasizing during a sexual encounter is normal in both men and women.
b. Few couples have disagreements about basic issues such as how often to have intercourse.
c. Despite the interest in sex today, many people are ignorant about basic sexual functioning.
d. Many sexual problems stem from a negative sexual values system that associates sex with immorality.

ANS: b          Pg: 435
LO: 23          Conceptual

87. It is probably most accurate to conclude that sexual problems belong to the
a. male.
b. female.
c. couple.
d. individual's culture.

ANS: c          Pg: 436
LO: 24          Factual

88. The technically correct term for male impotence is
a. erectile difficulties.
b. retarded ejaculation.
c. orgasmic difficulties.
d. premature ejaculation.

ANS: a          Pgs: 436-437
LO: 24          Factual

89. A man who has never had an erection sufficient for coitus is said to have
a. orgasmic difficulties.
b. retarded ejaculation.
c. lifelong erectile difficulties.
d. primary erectile difficulties.

ANS: c          Pg: 437
LO: 24          Factual

90.    A man who has experienced coitus in the past but is currently having problems achieving erection is said to have
a.    acquired erectile difficulties.
b.    retarded ejaculation.
c.    primary erectile difficulties.
d.    secondary erectile difficulties.

ANS: a            Pg: 437
LO: 24            Factual

91.    Which of the following has been found to contribute to erectile dysfunction?
a.    organic factors
b.    common diseases such as diabetes
c.    medications used to treat physical illnesses
d.    all of these

ANS: d            Pg: 437
LO: 24            Factual

92.    The most common psychological cause of erectile difficulties is
a.    a depressed mood.
b.    too much stress at work.
c.    an argument with one's partner.
d.    anxiety about sexual performance.

ANS: d            Pg: 437
LO: 25            Factual

93.    _____ occurs when sexual relations are impaired because a man consistently reaches orgasm too quickly.
a.    Impotence
b.    Sensate focus
c.    Erectile dysfunction
d.    Premature ejaculation

ANS: d            Pg: 437
LO: 24            Factual

94.    Which of the following is generally **not** considered a possible cause of premature ejaculation?
a.    anger at one's partner
b.    drinking too much alcohol
c.    low threshold to stimulation
d.    not exerting enough effort to prolong intercourse

ANS: b            Pg: 437
LO: 25            Conceptual

95. Women who formerly experienced orgasms but are currently unable to do so are said to have
a.    situational orgasmic difficulties.
b.    hypoactive sexual desire.
c.    primary orgasmic difficulties.
d.    generalized secondary orgasmic difficulties.

**ANS: a**          **Pg: 437**
**LO: 24**          **Factual**

*96. _____ is the lack of interest in sexual activity.
a.    Generalized lifelong orgasmic difficulties
b.    Hypoactive sexual desire
c.    Primary orgasmic difficulties
d.    Generalized secondary orgasmic difficulties

**ANS: b**          **Pg: 437**
**LO: 24**          **Factual**

97. Which of the following is the most likely cause of orgasmic difficulties in women?
a.    anger toward one's partner
b.    relationship difficulties
c.    anxiety about sexual performance
d.    overemphasis on sexual fantasies

**ANS: b**          **Pg: 438**
**LO: 25**          **Conceptual**

98. Which of the following is least likely to be a cause of orgasmic difficulties in women?
a.    fear of pregnancy
b.    negative attitudes about sex
c.    anxiety about sexual performance
d.    lack of authentic affection for the partner

**ANS: c**          **Pg: 437**
**LO: 25**          **Conceptual**

99. To overcome psychologically-based erectile difficulties, the key is to
a.    increase sexual motivation.
b.    decrease sexual motivation.
c.    increase performance anxiety.
d.    decrease performance anxiety.

**ANS: d**          **Pg: 438**
**LO: 25**          **Conceptual**

100. Often, the key to conquering orgasmic difficulties in women is
a.     a restructuring of values.
b.     increasing the tempo of intercourse.
c.     emphasizing the importance of having an orgasm during intercourse.
d.     all of these.

**ANS: a**          **Pg: 439**
**LO: 25**          **Conceptual**


## MULTIPLE CHOICE QUESTIONS FROM STUDY GUIDE

1. Research on sexual behavior is
a.     difficult to do because it is hard to get a representative sample of subjects.
b.     easy to do because people are always willing to talk about their sex lives.
c.     well advanced because it is one of the oldest areas of research in psychology.
d.     in its infancy because the variables are difficult to define.

**ANS: a**          **Pg: 407**
**LO: 1**           **Factual**

2. During prenatal development the sex hormones that are active are
a.     androgens (in males only).
b.     estrogens (in females only).
c.     both androgens and estrogens, in varying amounts.
d.     neither androgens nor estrogens, since they appear at puberty.

**ANS: c**          **Pgs: 408-409**
**LO: 2**           **Conceptual**

3. During prenatal development, the differentiation of the genitals depends primarily on the
       level of _____ produced.
a.     androgens
b.     estrogens
c.     testosterone
d.     neurotransmitters

**ANS: c**          **Pgs: 408-409**
**LO: 2**           **Factual**

4. One of the ramifications of "rational outness" for homosexuals is that they are likely to
a.     keep their sexual orientation a well-guarded secret.
b.     disclose their sexual orientation only to close friends and siblings.
c.     engage in sexual relations with those who are unaware of their sexual orientation.
d.     publicly reveal the sexual orientation of their homosexual friends.

**ANS: b**          **Pg: 416**
**LO: 6**           **Factual**

5. Homosexuality was initially classified as a psychological disorder by the mental health community. The pioneering research of Evelyn Hooker and others demonstrated that this view was
a. a myth.
b. fairly accurate.
c. accurate only for gay men.
d. accurate only for older homosexuals.

**ANS: a**      **Pg: 417**
**LO: 6**      **Factual**

6. Negotiating the terms of a sexual relationship
a. may not be explicit, but it's there.
b. occurs if there are problems and a counselor is consulted.
c. diminishes the intimacy of a sexual relationship and reduces spontaneity.
d. should be completed before entering a marriage to avoid problems later.

**ANS: a**      **Pg: 418**
**LO: 8**      **Conceptual**

7. Greater sexual satisfaction and satisfaction in the relationship come if
a. only nonverbal cue are used during sex.
b. there is open communication about sex.
c. both partners refrain from expressing themselves during sex.
d. both partners control their desires so as not to make the other uncomfortable.

**ANS: b**      **Pg: 419**
**LO: 8**      **Factual**

8. When a female experiences vaginal lubrication and swelling of the clitoris and vaginal lips, she
a. should consult a physician for treatment ovulation.
b. is likely to be pregnant.
c. is showing external evidence of.
d. is experiencing vasocongestion.

**ANS: d**      **Pg: 420**
**LO: 9**      **Factual**

9. The refractory period occurs
a. among males after an orgasm.
b. when a person has strong feelings of guilt and anxiety about sex.
c. when a person is subjected to unwanted and unwelcome sex.
d. between the first signs of puberty and actual fertility.

**ANS: a**      **Pg: 421**
**LO: 9**      **Factual**

10. Most two-person sexual activities begin with
a. oral sex.
b. kissing.
c. self-stimulation.
d. fondling the genitals.

**ANS: b**          **Pg: 422**
**LO: 11**          **Factual**

11. "Coitus" is the technically correct term for
a. oral sex.
b. self-stimulation.
c. anal intercourse.
d. vaginal intercourse.

**ANS: d**          **Pg: 424**
**LO: 13**          **Factual**

12. The incidence of infidelity in committed relationships is
a. virtually identical for both genders.
b. somewhat greater for males than females.
c. somewhat greater for females than males.
d. unknown because of the difficulty of collecting such data.

**ANS: b**          **Pg: 428**
**LO: 19**          **Factual**

13. Which of the following is <u>not</u> considered a hormone-based contraceptive?
a. condom
b. the pill
c. vaginal ring
d. transdermal patch

**ANS: a**          **Pgs: 429-431**
**LO: 20**          **Factual**

14. Which of the following statements regarding sexually transmitted diseases (STDs) is accurate?
a. People can be carriers of an STD without being aware of it.
b. The more sexual partners you have, the higher the risk of exposure.
c. People who know they have an STD often continue to be sexually active.
d. All of these statements are accurate.

**ANS: d**          **Pg: 432**
**LO: 21**          **Factual**

15. People use sensate focus when they
a. want to avoid pregnancy.
b. are treating sexual dysfunctions.
c. want to prolong the pleasure of sex beyond the orgasm.
d. are not in a situation where sex is appropriate; it is a form of self-stimulation.

**ANS: b**          **Pg: 439**
**LO: 25**        **Factual**

## MULTIPLE CHOICE QUESTIONS ON WEB SITE

1. _____ is comprised of the personal qualities, self-perceptions, attitudes, values, and preferences that guide an individual's sexual behavior.
a. Eroticism
b. Body image
c. Sexual identity
d. Sexual orientation

**ANS: c**          **Pg: 408**
**LO: 1**         **Factual**

2. _____ are the principal class of female sex hormones; _____ are the principal class of male sex hormones.
a. Estrogens; androgens
b. Androgens; estrogens
c. Pheromones; androgens
d. Androgens; pheromones

**ANS: a**          **Pg: 408**
**LO: 2**         **Factual**

3. Adolescents attain reproductive capability as hormonal changes lead to the full development of the
a. gonads.
b. primary sex characteristics.
c. secondary sex characteristics.
d. pubescent sex characteristics.

**ANS: b**          **Pg: 409**
**LO: 2**         **Factual**

4.      Open communication between parents and their children about sexual topics correlates
        with
a.      lower rates of teen pregnancy.
b.      lower rates of STDs among teenagers.
c.      less sexual activity in adolescence.
d.      more promiscuity among high school students.

**ANS: c**          **Pg: 410**
**LO: 3**           **Factual**

5.      Research findings indicate that exposure to erotic materials
a.      encourages pro-rape attitudes in both men and women.
b.      elevates permissive attitudes about sexual behavior.
c.      increases the likelihood that a male viewer will commit a sex crime.
d.      may lead to the development of conservative attitudes about sexual behavior.

**ANS: b**          **Pg: 411**
**LO: 3**           **Conceptual**

6.      Which of the following groups is most likely to emphasize "sex for fun" in casual
        relationships and reserve "sex with love" for committed relationships?
a.      men
b.      women
c.      lesbians
d.      bisexuals

**ANS: a**          **Pg: 411**
**LO: 4**           **Conceptual**

7.      _____ is the researcher who designed a seven-point scale to characterize sexual
        orientation.
a.      Alfred Kinsey
b.      Albert Bandura
c.      William Masters
d.      Virginia Johnson

**ANS: a**          **Pg: 413**
**LO: 5**           **Factual**

8.      Jay is clearly uncomfortable whenever he is introduced to a gay man. He frequently
        makes disparaging remarks about homosexuals and states that he would "punch out" any
        man who came on to him. Jay shows signs of
a.      bisexuality.
b.      homophobia.
c.      heterophobia.
d.      sensate focus.

**ANS: b**          **Pg: 415**
**LO: 5**           **Conceptual**

9.          _____ conducted groundbreaking research on the physiology    of the human sexual response.
a.     Alfred Kinsey
b.     Albert Bandura
c.     Carl Jung and Sigmund Freud
d.     William Masters and Virginia Johnson

**ANS: d**          **Pg: 419**
**LO: 9**          **Factual**

10.     A body area that is sexually sensitive or responsive is called
a.     a sensate focus.
b.     a refractory area.
c.     an autoerotic zone.
d.     an erogenous zone.

**ANS: d**          **Pg: 422**
**LO: 11**          **Factual**

*11.     The most common sexual fantasy
a.     involves having sex with a person other than the partner.
b.     involves dominance and submission.
c.     involves multiple partners.
d.     is different for males and females.

**ANS: a**          **Pg: 422**
**LO: 11**          **Factual**

12.     Which of the following groups is likely to have the most permissive attitudes about sexual activity outside of a committed relationship?
a.     lesbian couples
b.     married couples
c.     gay male couples
d.     heterosexual engaged couples

**ANS: c**          **Pg: 427**
**LO: 18**          **Factual**

13.     Which of the following are the two most widely used birth control methods in the Western world?
a.     IUDs and condoms
b.     rhythm and condoms
c.     condoms and oral contraceptives
d.     diaphragms and oral contraceptives

**ANS: c**          **Pg: 430**
**LO: 20**          **Factual**

14. Which of the following is a good suggestion for engaging in safer sex?
a. Avoid engaging in anal intercourse.
b. Don't have sex with someone who has had lots of previous partners.
c. Wash your genitals with soap and water before and after sexual contact.
d. All of these statements are good suggestions.

**ANS: d**        **Pg: 432**
**LO: 22**       **Conceptual**

15. To overcome psychologically based erectile difficulties, the key is to
a. increase sexual motivation.
b. decrease sexual motivation.
c. increase performance anxiety.
d. decrease performance anxiety.

**ANS: d**        **Pg: 438**
**LO: 25**       **Conceptual**

## TRUE/FALSE QUESTIONS

1. Sex education by parents has been shown to lead to more sexual activity in teenagers.

**ANS: false**       **Pg: 410**
**LO: 3**          **Conceptual**

2. Peers tend to be a source of highly misleading information about sex.

**ANS: true**       **Pg: 410**
**LO: 3**          **Factual**

3. Most schools' sex education programs could be termed comprehensive.

**ANS: false**       **Pg: 410**
**LO: 3**          **Factual**

4. The most common sex education programs could be termed "abstinence plus."

**ANS: true**       **Pg: 410**
**LO: 3**          **Factual**

5. It is a myth that aggression is linked to sexuality more commonly in males than females.

**ANS: false**       **Pg: 411**
**LO: 4**          **Factual**

6. Females' sexuality is more easily shaped by culture than males'.

**ANS: true**       **Pg: 411**
**LO: 4**          **Factual**

7.    Homosexual parents are slightly more likely to have homosexual children.

ANS:   false          Pg: 414
LO:    5              Factual

8.    Lesbians are more likely to have shown masculine behavior in childhood than homosexual males.

ANS:   false          Pg: 414
LO:    5              Conceptual

9.    The order of the phases theorized by Masters and Johnson are: excitement, plateau, orgasm, resolution.

ANS:   true           Pg: 420
LO:    9              Factual

10.   HIV cannot be transmitted through oral sex.

ANS:   false          Pg: 423
LO:    15             Factual

11.   Actual and ideal failure rates are nearly the same for most forms of contraception.

ANS:   false          Pg: 430
LO:    20             Factual

12.   Oral contraception shows an actual failure rate almost equal to their ideal failure rate.

ANS:   false          Pg: 430
LO:    20             Factual


## SHORT-ANSWER ESSAY QUESTIONS

1.    Explain how parents' behaviors can convey to their children that sex is "dirty."

**Pg: 409**

2.    Briefly describe the role of sex education classes in shaping the sexual behavior of adolescents.

**Pg: 410**

3.    Contrast the typical sexual socialization received by females and males in American culture.

**Pgs: 411-413**

4.    Briefly discuss the notion that heterosexuality and homosexuality are end points on a continuum.

**Pg: 413**

5.    List and briefly describe several explanations for the origins of homosexuality. For which of these explanations is the research support the most compelling?

**Pg: 414**

6.    Briefly describe the role of vasocongestion in the sexual response cycle.

**Pg: 420**

7.    List and briefly describe the kinds of sexual activities that homosexuals prefer in the absence of coitus.

**Pg: 424**

8.    List several characteristics of teenagers who engage in premarital sex and discuss the factors that promote use of contraception among sexually active teenagers.

**Pgs: 426, 429**

9.    Briefly describe the correlation between sexual activity and duration of relationship in dating couples.

**Pg: 426**

10.   Briefly describe the effectiveness, benefits, costs, and risks associated with oral contraceptives and condoms.

**Pgs: 430-431**

*11.  Discuss the four stages of the human sexual response cycle.

**Pg: 420-421**

*12.  Compare and contrast male and female sexual problems.

**Pgs: 436-439**

*13.  Discuss treatments for two sexual dysfunctions.

**Pgs: 436-439**

*14.  Why is it important to have multiple options for contraception? Give examples.

**Pgs: 429-431**

# Chapter 14
# PSYCHOLOGY AND PHYSICAL HEALTH

## LEARNING OBJECTIVES

1. Describe the Type A personality and evidence regarding its most toxic element.
2. Discuss possible explanations for the link between hostility and heart disease.
3. Summarize evidence relating emotional reactions and depression to heart disease.
4. Summarize evidence linking stress and personality to cancer.
5. Summarize evidence linking stress to a variety of diseases and immune functioning.
6. Discuss the strength of the relationship between stress and illness.
7. Give some reasons why people develop health-impairing habits.
8. Discuss the health effects of smoking and the dynamics of giving up smoking.
9. Summarize data on patterns of alcohol use and the short-term risks of drinking.
10. Summarize the major long-term health risks and social costs of drinking.
11. Discuss the health risks and determinants of obesity.
12. Outline the key elements in effective weight loss efforts.
13. Provide examples of links between nutrition and health and discuss the basis for poor nutrition.
14. List three general goals intended to foster sound nutrition.
15. Summarize evidence on the benefits and risks of exercise.
16. List five guidelines for embarking on an effective exercise program.
17. Describe AIDS and summarize evidence on the transmission of the HIV virus.
18. Identify some common misconceptions about AIDS and discuss the prevention of AIDS.
19. Summarize evidence on patterns of treatment-seeking behavior.
20. Explain the appeal of the "sick role."
21. Discuss the factors that tend to undermine doctor-patient communication and how to improve it.
22. Discuss the prevalence of nonadherence to medical advice and its causes.
23. Explain the concepts of drug tolerance, physical and psychological dependence, and overdose.
24. Summarize the main effects and risks of narcotics.
25. Summarize the main effects and risks of sedatives.
26. Summarize the main effects and risks of stimulant drugs.
27. Summarize the main effects and risks of hallucinogens.
28. Summarize the main effects and risks of marijuana and ecstasy (MDMA).

# MULTIPLE CHOICE QUESTIONS

1.    Before the 20th century, the principal threats to health in our society were
a.    farm accidents.
b.    heart diseases.
c.    contagious diseases.
d.    various forms of cancer.

**ANS: c**          **Pg: 443**
**LO: 1**           **Factual**

2.    Which of the following factors has been instrumental in the decline of contagious diseases in our society?
a.    improvements in nutrition
b.    improvements in public hygiene and sanitation
c.    evolutionary changes in human immune resistance
d.    all of these

**ANS: d**          **Pg: 443**
**LO: 1**           **Factual**

3.    The greatest threat to health in our society today is posed by
a.    homicide.
b.    chronic diseases.
c.    contagious diseases.
d.    environmental toxins.

**ANS: b**          **Pg: 443**
**LO: 1**           **Factual**

4.    Which of the following is **not** considered a chronic disease?
a.    cancer
b.    stroke
c.    influenza
d.    heart disease

**ANS: c**          **Pg: 443**
**LO: 1**           **Factual**

5.    Which of the following is known to be the principal cause of coronary heart disease?
a.    diabetes
b.    atherosclerosis
c.    Alzheimer's disease
d.    post-traumatic stress disorder

**ANS: b**          **Pg: 445**
**LO: 1**           **Factual**

*6.         _____ psychology is the area concerned with how psychosocial factors relate to the promotion and maintenance of health.
a.    Health
b.    Clinical
c.    Community
d.    Psychosociology

**ANS: a              Pg: 444**
**LO: 1                Factual**

7.         _____ is the gradual narrowing of the coronary arteries.
a.    Cancer
b.    Influenza
c.    Atherosclerosis
d.    Acquired immune deficiency syndrome

**ANS: c              Pg: 445**
**LO: 1                Factual**

*8.        The name of the condition when the heart is temporarily deprived of adequate blood flow is
a.    atherosclerosis.
b.    coronary heart disease.
c.    myocardial ischemia.
d.    myocardial infarction.

**ANS: c              Pg: 445**
**LO: 1                Factual**

*9.        A heart attack is called
a.    atherosclerosis.
b.    coronary heart disease.
c.    a myocardial ischemia.
d.    a myocardial infarction.

**ANS: d              Pg: 445**
**LO: 1                Factual**

*10.      Angina is
a.    a psychosomatic condition.
b.    chest pain.
c.    a mild heart attack.
d.    a heart attack.

**ANS: b              Pg: 445**
**LO: 1                Factual**

11. The Type A behavior pattern is most closely linked to which of the following physical ailments?
a. cancer
b. asthma
c. Alzheimer's disease
d. coronary heart disease

ANS: d    Pg: 446
LO: 1     Conceptual

*12. Hank continually loses his temper when waiting in lines. He has very little patients for other people and is driven to be highly successful. Hank's personality is called
a. Type A
b. Type AeH
c. hostile subtype
d. domineering subtype

ANS: a    Pg: 446
LO: 1     Applied

13. Which of the following characteristics is most closely associated with the Type A personality?
a. hostile
b. patient
c. permissive
d. cooperative

ANS: a    Pg: 446
LO: 1     Conceptual

14. Which of the following characteristics is most closely associated with the Type B personality?
a. impatient
b. easy-going
c. competitive
d. time-conscious

ANS: b    Pg: 446
LO: 1     Conceptual

15. Which of the following characteristics is least closely associated with the Type B personality?
a. patient
b. easy-going
c. competitive
d. relatively relaxed

ANS: c    Pg: 446
LO: 1     Conceptual

*16.    Which component of Type A behavior seems to be most responsible for the increased rate of heart attacks?
a.    hostility
b.    highly driven work goals
c.    competitiveness
d.    impatience

**ANS: a          Pg: 446**
**LO: 2           Conceptual**

17.    Which of the following statements regarding Type A individuals is **not** accurate?
a.    They probably create additional stress for themselves.
b.    They are likely to get more exercise than Type B individuals.
c.    Type A personalities tend to have less social support than others.
d.    They appear to exhibit greater physiological reactivity than Type B individuals.

**ANS: b          Pg: 448**
**LO: 2           Conceptual**

*18.    Bobby has had overwhelming feelings of sadness and despair for the last six months. A psychologist would likely categorize her as having
a.    Type A personality.
b.    dysthymic personality.
c.    persistent sadness disorder.
d.    depression.

**ANS: d          Pg: 449**
**LO: 3           Applied**

19.    _____ refers to malignant cell growth, which may occur in many organ systems in the body.
a.    Cancer
b.    Atherosclerosis
c.    Myocardial ischemia
d.    Coronary heart disease

**ANS: a          Pg: 450**
**LO: 4           Factual**

20.    The evidence linking psychological factors to the onset of cancer is
a.    strong.
b.    moderate.
c.    relatively weak.
d.    non-existent; little research has been done.

**ANS: c          Pg: 450**
**LO: 4           Factual**

*21. The immune response is
a. a series of steps taken by Type A personalities.
b. the body's defensive reaction to invasion.
c. one of the isolation effects of depression.
d. none of th.

**ANS: b**      **Pg: 450**
**LO: 5**      **Factual**

22. Which of the following has been found to impair immune functioning in animals?
a. shock
b. restraint
c. crowding
d. all of these

**ANS: d**      **Pg: 451**
**LO: 5**      **Factual**

23. Studies of the immune system in humans have found that stress
a. has very little effect on immune activity.
b. can lead to the destruction of lymphocytes.
c. is related to increased levels of immune activity.
d. is related to decreased levels of immune activity.

**ANS: d**      **Pg: 451**
**LO: 5**      **Factual**

24. Researchers have found a correlation between reduced immune activity and scores on
a. Weschler Intelligence Scale.
b. Somatic Rating Scale.
c. several occupational interest inventories.
d. the Social Readjustment Rating Scale.

**ANS: d**      **Pg: 451**
**LO: 5**      **Factual**

25. Researchers have found evidence of reduced immune activity among which of the following groups?
a. people recently traumatized by a hurricane
b. men who were recently divorced or separated
c. people who scored relatively high on a stress scale measuring daily hassles
d. all of these

**ANS: d**      **Pg: 451**
**LO: 5**      **Factual**

26. Virtually all of the research on stress and physical health in humans is
a. anecdotal.
b. correlational.
c. experimental.
d. observational.

**ANS: b**        **Pg: 451**
**LO: 6**        **Factual**

*27. The strength of the relationship between stress and health is
a. very weak.
b. weak.
c. moderate.
d. strong.

**ANS: c**        **Pg: 452**
**LO: 6**        **Factual**

*28. Dr. VanGundy is researching the relationship between stress and subsequent health in normal individuals. He is likely to find a correlation around
a. .10.
b. .25.
c. .40.
d. .60.

**ANS: b**        **Pg: 452**
**LO: 6**        **Applied**

29. The most likely explanation for people's tendency to act in self-destructive ways is that
a. people have an innate desire for sensation seeking.
b. most people tend to believe that bad things happen to bad people.
c. many health-impairing habits involve activities that are quite pleasant at the time.
d. people engage in health-impairing behavior "on the spur of the moment," without giving much thought to the consequences.

**ANS: c**        **Pg: 452**
**LO: 7**        **Conceptual**

30. People have a tendency to _____ the risk of their own health-impairing habits, and _____ the risks associated with others' self-destructive behaviors.
a. overestimate; underestimate
b. underestimate; overestimate
c. accurately view; overestimate
d. underestimate; accurately view

**ANS: d**        **Pg: 453**
**LO: 7**        **Conceptual**

*31. In the U.S., about _____ % of females and _____ % of males smoke.
a. 21; 26
b. 26; 21
c. 26; 26
d. 21; 21

**ANS: a**          **Pg: 454**
**LO: 8**           **Factual**

*32. In the U.S., college students smoke _____ compared to the general population.
a. more for males; less for female
b. less for males; more for females
c. less for males and females
d.. more for males and females

**ANS: d**          **Pg: 454**
**LO: 8**           **Conceptual**

33. Research shows that smoking increases the likelihood of developing
a. cancer.
b. heart disease.
c. arteriosclerosis.
d. all of these.

**ANS: d**          **Pg: 454**
**LO: 8**           **Factual**

34. Which of the following has been shown to increase the risk of such diseases as lung cancer, arteriosclerosis, and emphysema?
a. obesity
b. smoking
c. poor nutrition
d. lack of exercise

**ANS: b**          **Pg: 454**
**LO: 8**           **Factual**

35. Health risks after quitting smoking decline until they reach a normal level after about
a. 1 year.
b. 5 years.
c. 10 years.
d. 15 years.

**ANS: d**          **Pg: 454**
**LO: 8**           **Factual**

36.  Research shows that long-term success rates for efforts to quit smoking are about _____ percent.
a.  10
b.  25
c.  50
d.  80

**ANS: b**          **Pg: 455**
**LO: 8**           **Factual**

37.  On college campuses, alcohol appears to contribute to about _____ percent of student rapes.
a.  20
b.  50
c.  75
d.  90

**ANS: d**          **Pg: 458**
**LO: 9**           **Factual**

38.  In our society, alcohol is associated with which of the following crimes?
a.  murder
b.  child abuse
c.  spouse abuse
d.  all of these

**ANS: d**          **Pg: 459**
**LO: 9**           **Factual**

39.  Which of the following is considered one of the common warning signs of alcoholism?
a.  serving alcoholic drinks to close relatives
b.  drinking to relieve uncomfortable feelings
c.  having several drinks at a social gathering
d.  having dreams in which alcohol is consumed

**ANS: b**          **Pg: 459**
**LO: 10**          **Conceptual**

40.  Excessive drinking is correlated with which of the following?
a.  heart disease
b.  stomach cancer
c.  cirrhosis of the liver
d.  all of these

**ANS: d**          **Pg: 459**
**LO: 10**          **Factual**

41. Typically, people are considered obese if their weight exceeds their ideal body weight by _____ percent.
a. 20
b. 40
c. 60
d. 80

**ANS: a**      **Pg: 459**
**LO: 11**      **Factual**

42. Researchers have found that in terms of their weight, adult adoptees tend to resemble their_____ more than their _____.
a. adoptive parents; biological parents
b. biological parents; adoptive parents
c. adoptive siblings; biological siblings
d. biological siblings; adoptive siblings

**ANS: b**      **Pg: 460**
**LO: 11**      **Factual**

43. In order to lose one pound, you need to burn up _____ more calories than you consume.
a. 500
b. 1000
c. 3500
d. 5000

**ANS: c**      **Pg: 462**
**LO: 12**      **Factual**

44. Harry wants to lose 50 pounds. He should
a. sharply increase his exercise.
b. sharply reduce his food intake.
c. decrease his food intake and increase his exercise, both in moderate ways.
d. sharply increase his exercise while simultaneously reducing his food intake dramatically.

**ANS: c**      **Pg: 462**
**LO: 12**      **Factual**

45. Ahmed maintains a diet high in serum cholesterol, eating an abundance of eggs, cheese, butter, and shellfish. Ahmed may well be increasing his risk of
a. arthritis.
b. emphysema.
c. heart disease.
d. all of these.

**ANS: c**      **Pg: 462**
**LO: 13**      **Applied**

46.     High caffeine consumption is likely to elevate one's risk for
a.      depression.
b.      hypertension.
c.      prostate cancer.
d.      all of these.

**ANS: b**          **Pg: 463**
**LO: 13**          **Factual**

47.     High intake of Vitamin _____ may reduce one's risk for coronary disease.
a.      A
b.      B
c.      D
d.      E

**ANS: d**          **Pg: 463**
**LO: 13**          **Factual**

48.     Which of the following nutritional habits can increase susceptibility to a variety of diseases and health problems?
a.      obesity
b.      high fat diets
c.      low fiber diets
d.      all of these

**ANS: d**          **Pg: 462**
**LO: 13**          **Factual**

49.     Nutritional deficiencies among Americans are most likely a result of
a.      low income.
b.      lack of knowledge about nutrition.
c.      inability to find appropriate foods.
d.      emphasis in the media on "convenience" foods.

**ANS: b**          **Pg: 463**
**LO: 13**          **Conceptual**

50.     Which of the following is **not** considered a nutrient essential for physical well-being?
a.      fats
b.      starchoglycens
c.      proteins
d.      carbohydrates

**ANS: b**          **Pg: 464**
**LO: 13**          **Factual**

51. Which of the following groups of nutrients supplies the body with energy?
a. vitamins, minerals, fiber
b. proteins, fats, carbohydrates
c. cholesterol, vitamins, glucose
d. polyunsaturated, fiber, amino acids

ANS b        **Pg: 464**
LO: 13        **Factual**

52. The main function of vitamins and minerals is to
a. strengthen the immune system.
b. provide energy sources for the body.
c. help release energy from other foods.
d. provide roughage to facilitate digestion.

ANS: c        **Pg: 464**
LO: 13        **Factual**

53. _____ provide(s) roughage that facilitates digestion.
a. Fiber
b. Protein
c. Vitamins
d. Minerals

ANS: a        **Pg: 464**
LO: 13        **Factual**

54. It's a good idea to increase consumption of complex carbohydrates, natural sugars, and ample fiber. You can do this by eating more food from which of the following groups?
a. breads and cereals
b. fish, chicken, turkey
c. milk and milk products
d. fruits, vegetables, whole grains

ANS: d        **Pg: 464**
LO: 14        **Factual**

55. Recent studies suggest that physical fitness is associated with a decreased risk for which of the following?
a. colon cancer in men
b. breast cancer in women
c. reproductive cancer in women
d. all of these

ANS: d        **Pg: 466**
LO: 15        **Factual**

56.     Vigorous exercise is most likely to temporarily increase cardiac risk among people who
a.      don't eat red meat.
b.      are over the age of 40.
c.      don't exercise regularly.
d.      consume a large amount of natural sugars.

**ANS: c**          **Pg: 466**
**LO: 15**          **Factual**

57.     Eric's objection to exercise is that the dangers of muscular and skeletal injuries, not to
        mention heart attacks, far outweigh the benefits. Given the research, which of the
        following would be an appropriate response?
a.      He's right. All he really needs to do is monitor his diet.
b.      He's right. All he really needs to do is eliminate his health-impairing habits.
c.      He's wrong. The hazards he mentions have not been supported by research.
d.      He's wrong. The dangers can be minimized by carefully planning an exercise program.

**ANS: d**          **Pg: 466**
**LO: 15**          **Conceptual**

58.     An exercise activity that you find enjoyable
a.      is likely to increase the physical benefits of exercise.
b.      makes it easier to follow through and exercise regularly.
c.      tends to detract from the psychological benefits of exercise.
d.      reduces the likelihood that you'll get caught in the "competition trap".

**ANS: b**          **Pg: 466**
**LO: 16**          **Conceptual**

59.     Which of the following is **not** good advice for devising an exercise program?
a.      Increase your participation gradually.
b.      Exercise regularly without overdoing it.
c.      Look for an activity that you will find enjoyable.
d.      You should try to "exercise through" any minor injuries.

**ANS: d**          **Pg: 466**
**LO: 16**          **Conceptual**

60.     _____ is a disorder in which the immune system is gradually weakened and eventually
        disabled by the human immunodeficiency virus.
a.      HIV
b.      Hemophilia
c.      Myocardial ischemia
d.      Acquired immune deficiency syndrome

**ANS: d**          **Pg: 467**
**LO: 17**          **Factual**

61. AIDS is the final stage of the HIV infection process, which typically manifests itself about _____ years after the original infection.
a.   1
b.   5
c.   8
d.   15

**ANS: c**          **Pg: 467**
**LO: 17**          **Factual**

62. Treatment with which of the following has recently been found to hold promise for substantially longer survival for AIDS victims?
a.   Prozac
b.   exhibitory retrovirus therapy
c.   intease inhibitors
d.   highly active antiretroviral therapy

**ANS: d**          **Pg: 468**
**LO: 17**          **Factual**

*63. Where is HIV infection increasing the fastest?
a.   among U.S. heroin users
b.   among European homosexuals
c.   among South American prostitutes
d.   among African heterosexuals

**ANS: d**          **Pg: 468**
**LO: 17**          **Conceptual**

*64. U.S heterosexuals are generally _____ from HIV _____.
a.   safe; because it is generally confined to homosexuals and drug users
b.   unsafe; because HIV infection rates are relatively equal among most groups
c.   safe; if you share information about former lovers with your partner
d.   unsafe; because partners tend to not fullydisclose past sexual history

**ANS: d**          **Pg: 468**
**LO: 18**          **Conceptual**

65. Worldwide, which of the following is the most common mode of transmission of the HIV virus?
a.   sharing food
b.   heterosexual relations
c.   sexual contact among homosexual men
d.   the sharing of needles by intravenous drug users

**ANS: b**          **Pg: 468**
**LO: 18**          **Factual**

66.    Which of the following statements about AIDS is accurate?
a.     Having AIDS and being infected with HIV are basically the same thing.
b.     People who donate blood on a regular basis are in danger of contracting AIDS.
c.     AIDS can be readily transmitted through casual contact with infected individuals.
d.     HIV carriers often remain healthy and symptom-free for many years after they are
       infected.

**ANS: d**          **Pg: 468**
**LO: 18**          **Conceptual**

67.    Which of the following is good advice for minimizing the risk of developing AIDS?
a.     You should have sexual contact with fewer partners.
b.     Intravenous drug users should use sterilized needles for drug injection.
c.     You should curtail sexual behaviors that increase the probability of mixing semen and
       blood.
d.     All of these statements constitute good advice.

**ANS: d**          **Pg: 468**
**LO: 18**          **Conceptual**

68.    People who are eager to seek medical care are most likely to be which of the following?
a.     psychotic
b.     extraverted
c.     playing the sick role
d.     high in sensation seeking

**ANS: c**          **Pg: 470**
**LO: 19**          **Conceptual**

69.    For which of the following reasons is someone most likely to play the sick role?
a.     to escape the demands of others
b.     to deflect attention from themselves
c.     to establish the basis for a malpractice lawsuit
d.     to continue to receive medical insurance payments

**ANS: a**          **Pg: 470**
**LO: 20**          **Conceptual**

70.    Which of the following is least likely to be a consequence of playing the "sick role"?
a.     decreased demands from others
b.     delayed professional care
c.     increased concern from others
d.     increased affection from others

**ANS: b**          **Pg: 470**
**LO: 20**          **Conceptual**

71.    Which of the following is **not** considered a common barrier to effective provider-patient communication?
a.    Many providers use too much medical jargon.
b.    Medical visits are usually very brief, allowing little time for discussion.
c.    Some patients are evasive about their real concerns because they fear a serious diagnosis.
d.    Some providers are reluctant to challenge their patients' subjective interpretation of their own symptoms.

**ANS: d**          **Pgs: 470-471**
**LO: 21**          **Conceptual**

72.    People are most likely to follow the instructions they receive from health care professionals when
a.    the instructions are punctuated with impressive medical jargon.
b.    they like, respect, and understand the health care professional.
c.    they don't fully understand the instructions, but feel the need to do something.
d.    all of these.

**ANS: b**          **Pg: 471**
**LO: 22**          **Conceptual**

73.    Which of the following factors is likely to be the most important in increasing patients' adherence to medical advice?
a.    more detailed instructions from the practitioner
b.    a larger number of practitioners from which to choose
c.    the dissemination of literature about common medical problems
d.    the communication process between the practitioner and the patient

**ANS: d**          **Pg: 472**
**LO: 22**          **Conceptual**

74.    Tolerance involves
a.    physical dependence on a drug.
b.    psychological dependence on a drug.
c.    gradual increase in responsiveness to a drug with continued use.
d.    progressive decrease in responsiveness to a drug with continued use.

**ANS: d**          **Pg: 473**
**LO: 23**          **Factual**

75.    When a person must continue to take a drug in order to avoid withdrawal illness the person has developed
a.    abuse.
b.    tolerance.
c.    physical dependence.
d.    psychological dependence.

**ANS: c**          **Pg: 473**
**LO: 23**          **Factual**

76. When a person must continue to take a drug in order to satisfy an intense emotional and mental craving the person has developed
a.  abuse.
b.  tolerance.
c.  physical dependence.
d.  psychological dependence.

**ANS: d**          **Pg: 473**
**LO: 23**          **Factual**

77. Physical distress caused by the termination of drug use is called
a.  extinction.
b.  tolerance.
c.  withdrawal illness.
d.  reverse tolerance.

**ANS: c**          **Pg: 473**
**LO: 23**          **Factual**

*78. Abstinence syndrome is a synonym for
a.  abuse.
b.  withdrawal illness.
c.  physical dependence.
d.  psychological dependence.

**ANS: b**          **Pg: 473**
**LO: 23**          **Factual**

*79. Because he quit an addictive drug Michael is experiencing vomiting, diarrhea, chills, and tremors. Michael is probably withdrawing from
a.  barbiturates.
b.  stimulants.
c.  marijuana.
d.  LSD.

**ANS: b**          **Pg: 473**
**LO: 23**          **Applied**

*80. Because she quit an addictive drug Michelle is experiencing fatigue, apathy, and irritability. Michelle is probably withdrawing from
a.  barbiturates.
b.  stimulants.
c.  marijuana.
d.  LSD.

**ANS: a**          **Pg: 473**
**LO: 23**          **Applied**

81.     Drugs from which of the following groups carry the greatest risk of overdose?
a.      narcotics
b.      cannabis
c.      stimulants
d.      hallucinogens

**ANS: a          Pg: 474**
**LO: 24          Factual**

82.     Narcotics are
a.      drugs derived from opium that are capable of relieving pain.
b.      drugs that tend to increase activity in the central nervous system.
c.      drugs that are notable for distorting sensory and perceptual experience.
d.      sleep-inducing drugs that decrease activity in the peripheral nervous system.

**ANS: a          Pg: 474**
**LO: 24          Factual**

*83.    One of heroin's main effects is that it creates _____ in the user.
a.      a sense of invulnerability
b.      revelatory hallucinations
c.      unbounded energy
d.      euphoria

**ANS: d          Pg: 474**
**LO: 24          Conceptual**

84.     Which of the following drugs is **not** considered a narcotic?
a.      heroin
b.      cocaine
c.      codeine
d.      morphine

**ANS: b          Pg: 474**
**LO: 24          Factual**

85.     The most significant narcotics problem in modern Western society is the use of
a.      heroin.
b.      cocaine.
c.      codeine.
d.      morphine.

**ANS: a          Pg: 474**
**LO: 24          Factual**

86. Which of the following risks is **not** typically associated with narcotics use?
a. overdose
b. flashbacks
c. infectious diseases
d. physical dependence

ANS: b      Pg: 474
LO: 24      Conceptual

87. Drugs that induce sleep and decrease central nervous system activation are usually classified as
a. sedatives.
b. stimulants.
c. hallucinogens.
d. amphetamines.

ANS: a      Pg: 475
LO: 25      Factual

88. The use of sedatives may result in personal injury because they
a. trigger hallucinations such as flying.
b. produce a strong physical dependence.
c. cause motor coordination to deteriorate.
d. suppress pain warnings of physical harm.

ANS: c      Pg: 475
LO: 25      Conceptual

89. Which of the following groups of drugs tends to increase central nervous system activation and behavioral activity?
a. narcotics
b. sedatives
c. stimulants
d. barbiturates

ANS: c      Pg: 475
LO: 26      Factual

90. Which of the following drugs is considered a stimulant?
a. heroin
b. cocaine
c. morphine
d. marijuana

ANS: b      Pg: 475
LO: 26      Factual

91.     Which of the following is a risk associated with the use of stimulants?
a.      drug-induced psychosis
b.      deterioration of physical health
c.      strong psychological dependence
d.      all of these

**ANS: d**          **Pgs: 475-476**
**LO: 26**          **Factual**

92.     Use of which of the following groups of drugs is most likely to result in distortions in sensory and perceptual experience?
a.      sedatives
b.      stimulants
c.      hallucinogens
d.      all of these

**ANS: c**          **Pg: 476**
**LO: 27**          **Factual**

93.     Which of the following drugs is **not** considered a hallucinogen?
a.      LSD
b.      hashish
c.      psilocybin
d.      mescaline

**ANS: b**          **Pg: 476**
**LO: 27**          **Factual**

94.     A spontaneous, vivid recurrence of a previous drug-induced experience is called a(n)
a.      overdose.
b.      flashback.
c.      hallucination.
d.      psychotic episode.

**ANS: b**          **Pg: 476**
**LO: 27**          **Factual**

95.     Which of the following is least likely to be a risk associated with the use of hallucinogens?
a.      flashbacks
b.      death from overdose
c.      acute panic during a "bad trip"
d.      precipitation of psychological disorders

**ANS: b**          **Pg: 476**
**LO: 27**          **Conceptual**

96.     Marijuana, hashish, and THC are all derived from
a.      opium.
b.      cannabis.
c.      the peyote cactus.
d.      Central American mushrooms.

**ANS: b**              **Pg: 476**
**LO: 28**              **Factual**

97.     Which of the following is **not** a cannabis derivative?
a.      THC
b.      MDMA
c.      hashish
d.      marijuana

**ANS: b**              **Pg: 476**
**LO: 28**              **Factual**

98.     Which of the following is a risk associated with the use of cannabis?
a.      overdose
b.      chromosome damage
c.      physical dependence
d.      psychological dependence

**ANS: d**              **Pg: 476**
**LO: 28**              **Factual**

99.     The best known "designer drug" is
a.      LSD.
b.      THC.
c.      MDMA.
d.      heroin.

**ANS: c**              **Pg: 477**
**LO: 28**              **Factual**

100.    MDMA ("ecstasy") is most closely related to which of the following groups of drugs?
a.      narcotics
b.      cannabis
c.      stimulants
d.      hallucinogens

**ANS: d**              **Pg: 477**
**LO: 28**              **Factual**

# MULTIPLE CHOICE QUESTIONS FROM STUDY GUIDE

1. Recent studies suggest that _____ may be more important for coronary risk than other elements of the Type A personality.
a. ambition
b. anger and hostility
c. strong competitive orientation
d. impatience and time urgency

ANS: b          Pg: 446
LO: 1           Factual

2. Research consistently indicates that the strength of the relationship between stress and health is
a. weak.
b. modest.
c. strong.
d. negligible.

ANS: b          Pg: 448
LO: 5           Factual

3. People behave in self-destructive ways because
a. many health-impairing habits creep up on people slowly.
b. many health-impairing habits are quite pleasant at the time people engage in them.
c. the risks associated with health-impairing habits are in the distant future.
d. All of these are reasons that people behave in self-destructive ways.

ANS: d          Pg: 452
LO: 7           Factual

4. The percentage of people who smoke has _____ since the mid-1960s.
a. remained stable
b. declined noticeably
c. increased slightly
d. increased dramatically

ANS: b          Pg: 454
LO: 8           Factual

5. About _____ of the adult population in the United States drink alcohol.
a. 10%
b. half
c. two-thirds
d. 90%

ANS: b          Pg: 457
LO: 9           Factual

6.   That there may be a genetic vulnerability to obesity is supported by the finding that
a.   some people burn off calories faster than others.
b.   people who lose weight tend to gain back the weight they lost.
c.   adoptees resemble their biological parents more than their adoptive parents.
d.   obese people have more fat cells than other people.

**ANS: c**          **Pg: 460**
**LO: 11**          **Factual**

7.   The only way to lose weight effectively is to
a.   change the ratio of energy intake to energy output.
b.   stick to a reputable diet until the desired weight is reached.
c.   stop eating foods with cholesterol.
d.   engage in a vigorous exercise program.

**ANS: a**          **Pg: 462**
**LO: 12**          **Factual**

8.   A good exercise program should
a.   impose a little suffering –no pain, no gain!
b.   include daily workouts involving vigorous exercise.
c.   include some competitive activity for added motivation.
d.   be a physical activity that you find enjoyable.

**ANS: d**          **Pgs: 466-467**
**LO: 16**          **Factual**

9.   Which of the following statements regarding the treatment of AIDS with antiretroviral drugs is most accurate?
a.   Virtually all patients have responded favorably to the new drugs.
b.   The long-term efficacy of the drugs is yet to be determined.
c.   It is easy for patients to maintain the drug administration regimen.
d.   Antiretroviral drugs have transformed AIDS from a fatal disease to a manageable one.

**ANS: b**          **Pg: 468**
**LO: 17**          **Factual**

10.  The HIV virus can be transmitted
a.   through the exchange of bodily fluids, especially semen and blood.
b.   by the sharing of needles by intravenous drug users.
c.   through unprotected sexual contact with affected individuals.
d.   through all of the these means.

**ANS: d**          **Pg: 468**
**LO: 17**          **Factual**

11. One factor that is positively related to adherence to medical advice is the patient's
a. personality.
b. family income.
c. social support.
d. medical history.

**ANS: c**      **Pg: 471**
**LO: 22**      **Factual**

12. Noncompliance with instructions received from physicians
a. accounts for the vast majority of serious illnesses in our society.
b. may be due to the patients' failure to understand the instructions.
c. is generally caused by lack of confidence in the medical delivery system.
d. is not a major factor in the medical care system.

**ANS: b**      **Pg: 471**
**LO: 22**      **Factual**

13. When people need to consume larger and larger doses of a drug to obtain the desired effect, they have developed _____ on/for the drug.
a. physical dependence
b. tolerance
c. psychological dependence
d. all of these

**ANS: b**      **Pg: 473**
**LO: 23**      **Factual**

14. Technically, cocaine is considered a
a. narcotic.
b. sedative.
c. stimulant.
d. hallucinogen.

**ANS: c**      **Pg: 475**
**LO: 26**      **Factual**

15. Which of the following statements about hallucinogenic drugs is not accurate?
a. Psychological dependence is a common problem.
b. They have no potential for physical dependence.
c. They temporarily impair intellectual functioning.
d. Repetitious, frightening flashbacks can be troublesome.

**ANS: a**      **Pg: 476**
**LO: 27**      **Factual**

**MULTIPLE CHOICE QUESTIONS ON WEB SITE**

1.    Which of the following factors has been instrumental in the decline of contagious diseases in our society?
a.    improvements in nutrition
b.    improvements in public hygiene and sanitation
c.    evolutionary changes in human immune resistance
d.    all of these

**ANS: d**          **Pg: 443**
**LO: 1**            **Factual**


2.    The greatest threat to health in our society today is posed by
a.    homicide.
b.    chronic diseases.
c.    contagious diseases.
d.    environmental toxins.

**ANS: b**          **Pg: 443**
**LO: 1**            **Factual**


3.    Researchers have found evidence of reduced immune activity among which of the following groups?
a.    people recently traumatized by a hurricane
b.    men who were recently divorced or separated
c.    people who scored relatively high on a stress scale measuring daily hassles
d.    all of these

**ANS: d**          **Pg: 451**
**LO: 5**            **Factual**


4.    Virtually all of the research on stress and physical health in humans is
a.    anecdotal.
b.    correlational.
c.    experimental.
d.    observational.

**ANS: b**          **Pg: 452**
**LO: 6**            **Factual**


5.    Which of the following has been shown to increase the risk of such diseases as lung cancer, arteriosclerosis, and emphysema?
a.    obesity
b.    smoking
c.    poor nutrition
d.    lack of exercise

**ANS: b**          **Pg: 454**
**LO: 8**            **Factual**

6. Health risks after quitting smoking decline until they reach a normal level after about
a. 1 year.
b. 5 years.
c. 10 years.
d. 15 years.

**ANS: d**          **Pg: 454**
**LO: 8**           **Factual**

7. Typically, people are considered obese if their weight exceeds their ideal body weight by
_____ percent
a. 20
b. 40
c. 60
d. 80

**ANS: a**          **Pg: 459**
**LO: 11**          **Factual**

8. The main function of vitamins and minerals is to
a. strengthen the immune system.
b. provide energy sources for the body.
c. help release energy from other foods.
d. provide roughage to facilitate digestion.

**ANS: c**          **Pg: 464**
**LO: 13**          **Factual**

9. Which of the following is **not** good advice for devising an exercise program?
a. Increase your participation gradually.
b. Exercise regularly without overdoing it.
c. Look for an activity that you will find enjoyable.
d. You should try to "exercise through" any minor injuries.

**ANS: d**          **Pg: 466**
**LO: 16**          **Conceptual**

10. Which of the following statements about AIDS is accurate?
a. Having AIDS and being infected with HIV are basically the same thing.
b. People who donate blood on a regular basis are in danger of contracting AIDS.
c. AIDS can be readily transmitted through casual contact with infected individuals.
d. HIV carriers often remain healthy and symptom-free for many years after they are
infected.

**ANS: d**          **Pg: 468**
**LO: 18**          **Conceptual**

11. Which of the following is **not** considered a common barrier to effective provider-patient communication?
a. Many providers use too much medical jargon.
b. Medical visits are usually very brief, allowing little time for discussion.
c. Some patients are evasive about their real concerns because they fear a serious diagnosis.
d. Some providers are reluctant to challenge their patients' subjective interpretation of their own symptoms.

**ANS: d**      **Pgs: 470-471**
**LO: 21**      **Conceptual**

12. Tolerance involves
a. physical dependence on a drug.
b. psychological dependence on a drug
c. gradual increase in responsiveness to a drug with continued use.
d. progressive decrease in responsiveness to a drug with continued use.

**ANS: d**      **Pg: 473**
**LO: 23**      **Factual**

*13. Because he quit an addictive drug Michael is experiencing vomiting, diarrhea, chills, and tremors. Michael is probably withdrawing from
a. barbiturates.
b. stimulants.
c. marijuana.
d. LSD.

**ANS: b**      **Pg: 473**
**LO: 23**      **Applied**

14. The most significant narcotics problem in modern Western society is the use of
a. heroin.
b. cocaine.
c. codeine.
d. morphine.

**ANS: a**      **Pg: 474**
**LO: 24**      **Factual**

15. Use of which of the following groups of drugs is most likely to result in distortions in sensory and perceptual experience?
a. sedatives
b. stimulants
c. hallucinogens
d. all of these

**ANS: c**      **Pg: 476**
**LO: 27**      **Factual**

## TRUE/FALSE QUESTIONS

1. Atherosclerosis is sometimes called a heart attack.

**ANS: False**     **Pg: 445**
**LO: 1**       **Factual**

2. Inflammation has been recently implicated in coronary heart disease.

**ANS: True**     **Pg: 445**
**LO: 1**      **Factual**

3. Type B personalities tend to be patient and easy going.

**ANS: True**     **Pg: 446**
**LO: 1**      **Factual**

4. Depression is associated with heart disease.

**ANS: True**     **Pg: 449**
**LO: 3**      **Factual**

5. Research has shown a very strong relationship between stress and health.

**ANS: False**     **Pg: 451**
**LO: 6**      **Factual**

6. In the U.S., female college students smoke less than the general population but male college students smoke more.

**ANS: False**     **Pg: 454**
**LO: 7**      **Factual**

7. On average, smoking decreases life expectancy by a little over 20 years.

**ANS: False**     **Pg: 454**
**LO: 8**      **Factual**

8. It is nearly impossible to transmits HIV through casual sexual contact.

**ANS: False**     **Pg: 468**
**LO: 17**     **Factual**

9. In heterosexual relations, the transmission rate of HIV is about eight times higher in male-to-female than female-to-male.

**ANS: True**     **Pg: 468**
**LO: 17**     **Factual**

10. Abstinence syndrome occurs after a person withdraws from a psychologically dependent drug.

ANS: False     Pg: 473
LO:   23       Factual

## SHORT-ANSWER ESSAY QUESTIONS

1. Compare and contrast the Type A and Type B personalities and discuss the health risks that are associated with Type A behavior.

**Pg: 446**

2. Briefly discuss several reasons why people who smoke are reluctant to give it up.

**Pgs: 455-456**

3. Identify and briefly describe some of the chief warning signs associated with problem drinking.

**Pgs: 458-459**

4. Briefly explain the set point theory of obesity.

**Pg: 461**

5. Briefly discuss the notion of dietary restraint as a contribution to obesity.

**Pg: 461**

6. Briefly explain why it's a good idea to consume a balanced variety of foods.

**Pg: 464**

7. Briefly explain why it is that physical exercise can both improve cardiovascular health and cause a heart attack.

**Pgs: 465-66**

8. Explain why heterosexuals are at risk for HIV infection.

**Pg: 468**

9. Discuss the problems that arise in clear doctor-patient communication and ways to ensure better patient assertiveness and treatment compliance.

**Pg: 471**

10. Briefly describe several controversial aspects of marijuana use.

**Pgs: 476-477**

# Chapter 15
# PSYCHOLOGICAL DISORDERS

## LEARNING OBJECTIVES

1. Describe and evaluate the medical model of abnormal behavior.
2. Explain the most commonly used criteria of abnormality.
3. Discuss the history of the DSM system and describe the five axes of DSM-IV.
4. Summarize data on the prevalence of various psychological disorders.
5. List and describe four types of anxiety disorders.
6. Discuss the contribution of biological factors and conditioning to the etiology of anxiety disorders.
7. Discuss the contribution of cognitive factors and stress to the etiology of anxiety disorders.
8. Describe three types of somatoform disorders.
9. Summarize what is known about the causes of somatoform disorders.
10. Describe three types of dissociative disorders.
11. Summarize what is known about the causes of dissociative disorders.
12. Describe the two major mood disorders and discuss their prevalence.
13. Explain how genetic and neurochemical factors may be related to the development of mood disorders.
14. Explain how cognitive processes may contribute to mood disorders.
15. Explain how interpersonal behavior and stress may contribute to mood disorders.
16. Describe the prevalence and general symptoms of schizophrenia.
17. Describe four schizophrenic subtypes.
18. Distinguish between positive and negative symptoms in schizophrenia.
19. Identify factors related to the prognosis for schizophrenic patients.
20. Summarize how genetic vulnerability and neurochemical factors may contribute to the etiology of schizophrenia.
21. Discuss the evidence relating schizophrenia to structural abnormalities in the brain and neurodevelopmental insults to the brain.
22. Summarize how expressed emotion and stress may contribute to schizophrenia.
23. Explain the reasoning underlying the insanity defense, and how often it is used.
24. Explain the legal grounds for involuntary commitment.
25. Describe the symptoms and medical complications of anorexia nervosa and bulimia nervosa.
26. Discuss the history, prevalence, and gender distribution of eating disorders.
27. Explain how genetic factors, personality, and culture may contribute to eating disorders.
28. Explain how family dynamics and disturbed thinking may contribute to eating disorders.

## MULTIPLE CHOICE QUESTIONS

1.      According to the medical model it is useful to think of abnormal behavior as
a.      a disease.
c.      treatable only by physicians.
b.      resulting from deficiencies in brain chemicals.
d.      all of these.

**ANS: a**          **Pg: 482**
**LO: 1**           **Factual**

*2.     The _____ model proposes it is useful to think of abnormal behavior as a
        disease.
a.      physiological
b.      medical
c.      psychosocial
d.      bio-neurological

**ANS: b**          **Pg: 482**
**LO: 1**           **Factual**

*3.     Which of these models of abnormal behavior became the dominate way of thinking
        during the 19$^{th}$ and 20$^{th}$ century?
a.      physiological
b.      bio-neurological
c.      psychosocial
d.      medical

**ANS: d**          **Pg: 482**
**LO: 1**           **Factual**

*4.     A particularly  vocal critic of the medical model cited in the textbook is
a.      Thomas Szasz.
b.      Sigmund Freud.
c.      Eugen Bleuler.
d.      John Simon.

**ANS: a**          **Pg: 482**
**LO: 1**           **Factual**

*5.     Part of _____ is distinguishing one illness from another.
a.      diagnosis
b.      etiology
c.      prognosis
d.      none of these

**ANS: a**          **Pg: 483**
**LO: 1**           **Factual**

*6. . _____ is a forecast about the probable course of an illness.
a. Diagnosis
b. Etiology
c. Prognosis
d. None of these

**ANS: c** **Pg: 483**
**LO: 1** **Factual**

*7. Susan, a person suffering from mood swings, goes to see a psychologist. The psychologist tells Susan his first step will be to diagnosis her disorder; after that, he will provide her with a prognosis. Most likely this psychologist subscribes to the _____ model of abnormal behavior.
a. physiological
b. medical
c. psychosocial
d. bio-neurological

**ANS: b** **Pg: 483**
**LO: 1** **Factual**

*8. _____ is the apparent causation and developmental history of an illness.
a. Diagnosis
b. Etiology
c. Prognosis
d. None of these

**ANS: b** **Pg: 483**
**LO: 1** **Factual**

9. A prognosis
a. is a plan for treating an illness.
b. involves distinguishing one illness from another.
c. is a forecast about the probable course of an illness.
d. refers to the apparent causation and developmental history of an illness.

**ANS: c** **Pg: 483**
**LO: 1** **Factual**

*10. Dr. Richards explained to his client that obsessive-compulsive disorder appears to be heavily influenced by biological causes. Dr. Richards is explaining the _____ of obsessive-compulsive disorder.
a. diagnosis
b. etiology
c. prognosis
d. none of these

**ANS: b** **Pg: 483**
**LO: 1** **Factual**

11.      _____ is a psychological disorder in which a man achieves sexual arousal by dressing in women's clothing.
a.      Bisexuality
b.      Transvestic fetishism
c.      Homosexuality
d.      Bulimia nervosa

**ANS: b          Pg: 483**
**LO: 2            Factual**

12.      Transvestic fetishism is considered to be a psychological disorder primarily because it
a.      is maladaptive.
b.      is socially deviant.
c.      is a medical problem.
d.      causes great personal distress.

**ANS: b          Pg: 483**
**LO: 2            Conceptual**

13.      Michael gambles nearly every day, completely neglecting his family and his job.  His behavior best satisfies which of the following criteria of abnormality?
a.      deviance
b.      personal distress
c.      physical discomfort
d.      maladaptive behavior

**ANS: d          Pg: 483**
**LO: 2            Conceptual**

14.      The judgment of the normality of an individual's behavior can be based on whether
a.      he or she experiences personal distress.
b.      the behavior deviates from accepted social norms.
c.      his or her everyday adaptive functioning is impaired.
d.      any of these.

**ANS: d          Pg: 483**
**LO: 2            Conceptual**

*15.      Which of these is NOT a criteria for abnormal behavior?
a.      deviance
b.      maladaptive behavior
c.      personal distress
d.      bizarre behavior

**ANS: d          Pg: 483**
**LO: 2            Conceptual**

16. Although Cari always feels high levels of dread, worry, and anxiety, she still manages to meet her daily responsibilities. Which of the following conclusions regarding Cari's behavior is appropriate?
a. It should not be considered abnormal, because her adaptive functioning is not impaired.
b. It should not be considered abnormal, because everyone experiences worry and anxiety on occasion.
c. It can be considered abnormal, because she obviously feels great personal distress.
d. It can be considered abnormal, because the behavior meets the three criteria of the medical model.

ANS: c        Pg: 483
LO: 2        Conceptual

*17. Kenny believes that his dog often tells him important messages from God about how to prepare his food. The dog's orders are not a problem for Kenny to carry out and Kenny does not seem to mind the extra trouble. Under which criteria could Kenny's behaviors be considered a disorder?
a. deviance
b. maladaptive behavior
c. personal distress
d. bizarre behavior

ANS: a        Pg: 483
LO: 2        Conceptual

*18. Which of these statements is true?
a. It is usually not easy to divide people into distinct normal vs. abnormal groups.
b. People with psychological disorders usually behave in bizarre ways.
c. An abnormal behavior in one culture is always an abnormal behavior in other cultures.
d. The criteria for normal and abnormal behavior is value-free.

ANS: a        Pgs: 483-484
LO: 2        Conceptual

19. Which of the following statements regarding the definition of abnormal behavior is **not** accurate?
a. Everyone acts in deviant ways once in a while.
b. It is often difficult to draw a line that clearly separates normality from abnormality.
c. People are judged to have psychological disorders only when their behavior becomes extremely deviant, maladaptive, or distressing.
d. For the most part, people with psychological disorders behave in bizarre ways that are very different from the behavior of normal people.

ANS: d        Pgs: 483-484
LO: 2        Conceptual

20. In what year was the first version of the Diagnostic and Statistical Manual of Mental Disorders published?
a. 1879
b. 1932
c. 1952
d. 1974

**ANS: c**       **Pg: 485**
**LO: 3**       **Factual**

21. The DSM classification system is said to be "multiaxial." This means that the system
a. permits multiple diagnoses of a single individual.
b. allows many different potential methods of diagnosing people.
c. asks for judgments about individuals on a number of distinct dimensions.
d. recognizes that people can be considered both normal and abnormal at the same time.

**ANS: c**       **Pg: 485**
**LO: 3**       **Conceptual**

*22. The American Psychiatric Association publishers a book with a classification scheme of mental disorder called
a. Mental and Behavioral Disorders Checklist.
b. Minnosota Multiphasic Personality Inventory.
c. Diagnostic and Statistical Manual of Mental Disorders.
d. Personality and Abnormal Behavior Manual.

**ANS: c**       **Pg: 485**
**LO: 3**       **Factual**

*23. The DSM-IV uses _____ axes in its classification scheme.
a. three
b. four
c. five
d. six

**ANS: c**       **Pg: 485**
**LO: 3**       **Factual**

*24. In the DSM-IV axes _____ and _____ are used to diagnose disorders.
a. I; II
b. II; III
c. IV; VI
d. I; V

**ANS: a**       **Pg: 485**
**LO: 3**       **Conceptual**

25. The current classification system for psychological disorders (DSM-IV)
a. avoids giving people potentially stigmatizing diagnostic labels.
b. contains fewer disorders than previous systems, making it easier to use.
c. recognizes the importance of information other than a traditional diagnostic label.
d. provides specific criteria that allow therapists to classify individuals simply as normal or abnormal.

**ANS: c**      **Pg: 485**
**LO: 3**      **Factual**

26. According to the DSM-IV, mood disorders would be classified on the axis that includes
a. clinical syndromes.
b. personality disorders.
c. general medical conditions.
d. psychosocial and environmental problems.

**ANS: a**      **Pg: 486**
**LO: 3**      **Factual**

27. Epidemiology is the study of
a. treatments for psychological disorders.
b. how cultural values affect judgments of abnormality.
c. epidemics involving specific mental or physical disorders.
d. the distribution of mental or physical disorders in a population.

**ANS: d**      **Pg: 485**
**LO: 4**      **Factual**

28. Estimates of lifetime prevalence suggest that psychological disorders are
a. very rare.
b. more common than most people realize.
c. particularly common in non-Western cultures.
d. more common in higher socioeconomic classes.

**ANS: b**      **Pg: 486**
**LO: 4**      **Conceptual**

*29. Recent studies have found psychological disorders in roughly _____ % of the population.
a. 5 to 15
b. 15 to 25
c. 25 to 35
d. 35 to 45

**ANS: d**      **Pg: 485**
**LO: 4**      **Conceptual**

*30. The class of disorders marked by feelings of excessive apprehension and anxiety is
a. anxiety disorders.
b. somatoform disorders.
c. affective disorders.
d. phobic disorders.

**ANS: a**     **Pg: 487**
**LO: 5**      **Conceptual**

31. Which of the following categories of psychological disorders includes phobic and obsessive-compulsive disorders?
a. mood disorders
b. anxiety disorders
c. dissociative disorders
d. somatoform disorders

**ANS: b**     **Pg: 487**
**LO: 5**      **Factual**

32. Which of the following is an anxiety disorder marked by a chronic, high level of anxiety that is not tied to any specific threat?
a. panic disorder
b. phobic disorder
c. generalized anxiety disorder
d. obsessive-compulsive disorder

**ANS: c**     **Pg: 487**
**LO: 5**      **Factual**

33. Lila seems to "like to worry." She will usually find a reason to worry about something – her schoolwork, her boss, her parents, and whether the bus will come on time. Lila may be suffering from
a. panic.
b. phobic.
c. generalized anxiety.
d. obsessive-compulsive.

**ANS: c**     **Pgs: 487-488**
**LO: 5**      **Applied**

*34. The anxiety disorder brought on by specific stimuli is
a. obsessive-compulsive disorder.
b. generalized anxiety disorder.
c. phobic disorder.
d. stress disorder.

**ANS: c**     **Pg: 488**
**LO: 5**      **Factual**

35. Jerry is terrified of snakes, even though he lives in midtown Manhattan and only sees snakes at pet shops and zoos. He is probably suffering from
a. panic disorder.
b. phobic disorder.
c. generalized anxiety disorder.
d. obsessive-compulsive disorder.

ANS: b          Pg: 488
LO: 5           Factual

36. The main difference between a phobic disorder and a generalized anxiety disorder is that
a. the phobic disorder is more severe and more difficult to treat.
b. anxiety has a specific focus in a phobic disorder, but is "free-floating" in a generalized anxiety disorder.
c. generalized anxiety disorders depend on past conditioning, whereas phobic disorders tend to be genetic.
d. the generalized anxiety disorder occurs primarily in men and the phobic disorder occurs primarily in women.

ANS: b          Pgs: 487-488
LO: 5           Conceptual

*37. Vinnie often takes several minutes to leave his house. Every morning he finds he cannot quit worrying if he locked the door until he checks the lock 7 times, each time taking exactly seven steps from his car to the front door. Vinnie probably has
a. phobic disorder.
b. generalized anxiety disorder.
c. stress disorder.
d. obsessive-compulsive disorder.

ANS: d          Pg: 489
LO: 5           Applied

*38. Jenny can't quit wondering if she unplugged her iron this morning. Jenny is experiencing
a. a compulsion.
b. panic ideation.
c. an obsession.
d. a delusion.

ANS: c          Pg: 489
LO: 5           Applied

*39.    Every time Betty washes her hands she rubs them together 17 times, rinses for 32
        seconds, and dries with 3.5 paper towels. Betty's behaviors are
a.      compulsions.
b.      delusions.
c.      obsessions.
d.      delusions.

**ANS: a**          **Pg: 489**
**LO: 5**           **Applied**

40.     Compulsion is to "action" as obsession is to
a.      fear.
b.      thought.
c.      emotion.
d.      behavior.

**ANS: b**          **Pg: 489**
**LO: 5**           **Conceptual**

41.     An unwanted thought that repeatedly intrudes upon an individual's consciousness is
        called a(n)
a.      delusion.
b.      obsession.
c.      compulsion.
d.      hallucination.

**ANS: b**          **Pg: 489**
**LO: 5**           **Factual**

42.     The famous industrialist Howard Hughes devised extraordinary rituals to minimize the
        possibility of being contaminated by germs. For example, he would sometimes spend
        hours methodically cleaning a telephone. Hughes's behavior exemplifies which of the
        following disorders?
a.      agoraphobia
b.      panic disorder
c.      generalized anxiety disorder
d.      obsessive-compulsive disorder

**ANS: d**          **Pg: 489**
**LO: 5**           **Conceptual**

43.     A person who checks his alarm clock 20 times before going to sleep is being
a.      phobic.
b.      amnesic.
c.      obsessive.
d.      compulsive.

**ANS: d**          **Pg: 489**
**LO: 5**           **Conceptual**

44. Tanya thinks constantly about dirt and germs. She washes her hands hundreds of times a day. Tanya is most likely suffering from which of the following disorders?
a. phobic disorder
b. hypochondriasis
c. somatization disorder
d. obsessive-compulsive disorder

**ANS: d**          **Pg: 489**
**LO: 5**          **Conceptual**

45. Research suggests that _____ temperament in infants is a risk factor for the development of anxiety disorders later in life.
a. a difficult
b. an inhibited
c. a sensitive
d. a slow-to-warm-up

**ANS: b**          **Pg: 490**
**LO: 6**          **Factual**

*46. The genetic predisposition to anxiety disorders can be characterized as
a. weak to moderate.
b. moderate to strong.
c. strong to very strong.
d. non-existent.

**ANS: a**          **Pg: 490**
**LO: 6**          **Conceptual**

47. _____ are chemicals that carry signals from one neuron to another.
a. Neurochemicals
b. Poly-transmitters
c. Neurotransmitters
d. Psychoactive drugs

**ANS: c**          **Pg: 490**
**LO: 6**          **Factual**

48. Recent research has related disturbances in the neurotransmitter _____ to anxiety disorders.
a. GABA
b. serotonin
c. epinephrine
d. dopamine

**ANS: a**          **Pg: 490**
**LO: 6**          **Factual**

49.     Phobic responses tend to be acquired through _____ and maintained through _____.
a.      classical conditioning; operant conditioning
b.      operant conditioning; classical conditioning
c.      classical conditioning; observational learning
d.      operant conditioning; observational learning

**ANS: a            Pg: 490**
**LO: 6              Factual**

50.     People are more likely to develop phobic responses to snakes and spiders than to hot irons or electrical outlets. This finding is most consistent with which of the following concepts?
a.      neuroticism
b.      preparedness
c.      classical conditioning
d.      observational learning

**ANS: b            Pg: 491**
**LO: 6              Conceptual**

*51.    Preparedness is the idea that people are biologically prepared by their _____ to acquire some fears of specific objects much more easily than fear of other objects.
a.      evolutionary history
b.      learning history
c.      ego comparison history
d.      experience

**ANS: a            Pg: 491**
**LO: 6              Factual**

*52.    The fear of snakes and spiders is very common in people. Seligman (1971) would probably explain this with the idea of
a.      experience.
b.      learning history.
c.      ego comparison history.
d.      preparedness.

**ANS: d            Pg: 491**
**LO: 6              Conceptual**

53.     According to cognitive theorists, some people are prone to suffer from problems with anxiety because they tend to
a.      focus excessive attention on perceived threats.
b.      misinterpret harmless situations as threatening.
c.      selectively recall information that seems threatening.
d.      all of these.

**ANS: d            Pg: 491**
**LO: 7              Factual**

54. Which of the following statements best reflects the relationship between stress and anxiety disorders?
a. High stress may help precipitate the onset of anxiety disorders.
b. People with anxiety disorders tend to be unaffected by stress.
c. The relationship between stress and anxiety disorders is largely a myth.
d. Stress appears to exert its influence on the severity, rather than the onset, of anxiety disorders.

**ANS: a**          **Pg: 491**
**LO: 7**           **Conceptual**

55. Which of the following groups of disorders includes hypochondriasis and conversion disorders?
a  schizophrenia
b  mood disorders
c  dissociative disorders
d. somatoform disorders

**ANS: d**          **Pg: 492**
**LO: 8**           **Factual**

56. Someone whose behavior is dominated by excessive worry about developing physical illnesses and an excessive preoccupation with health concerns probably has
a. paranoia.
b. hypochondriasis.
c. a substance abuse disorder.
d. an obsessive-compulsive disorder.

**ANS: b**          **Pg: 493**
**LO: 8**           **Factual**

57. Which of the following personality types is most closely associated with the tendency to develop somatoform disorders?
a. avoidant
b. histrionic
c. dependent
d. narcissistic

**ANS: b**          **Pg: 493**
**LO: 9**           **Factual**

58. Which of the following reinforcements is most likely to play a role in the development and maintenance of somatoform disorders?
a. praise
b. attention
c. monetary rewards
d. promotions at work

**ANS: b**          **Pg: 493**
**LO: 9**           **Conceptual**

59. People who lose contact with portions of their consciousness or memory, and experience disruptions in their sense of identity, would most likely be considered as having which of the following types of disorders?
a. schizophrenia
b. anxiety disorders
c. dissociative disorders
d. somatoform disorders

ANS: c      Pg: 494
LO: 10      Factual

*60. Disorders in which people lose contact with their sense of identity are
a. dissociative disorders.
b. schizophrenic disorders.
c. mood disorders.
d. precipitating disorders.

ANS: a      Pg: 494
LO: 10      Factual

61. Which of the following groups of disorders includes psychogenic amnesia and multiple personality disorder?
a. paranoid disorders
b. dissociative disorders
c. somatoform disorders
d. schizophrenic disorders

ANS: b      Pg: 494
LO: 10      Factual

62. Kim is a successful lawyer who suddenly forgot who she is and most of the important details of her life after she survived a terrible car accident that killed three of her colleagues. Kim may be suffering from
a. bipolar disorder.
b. conversion disorder.
c. dissociative amnesia.
d. multiple-personality disorder.

ANS: c      Pg: 494
LO: 10      Factual

63. Which of the following is considered a dissociative disorder?
a. schizophrenia
b. bipolar disorder
c. phobic disorder
d. multiple-personality disorder

AN: d      Pg: 494
LO: 10      Factual

64.  Which of the following disorders features the coexistence in one person of two or more largely complete, and usually very different, identities or personalities?
a.  schizophrenia
b.  bipolar disorder
c.  dissociative fugue
d.  multiple-personality disorder

**ANS: d**          **Pg: 494**
**LO: 10**          **Factual**

65.  Some clinicians maintain that most cases of multiple-personality disorder are rooted in
a.  early reinforcement for avoiding reality.
b.  a genetic predisposition for engaging in fantasy.
c.  a deficiency in certain neurotransmitters in the brain.
d.  severe emotional trauma that occurred during childhood.

**ANS: d**          **Pg: 496**
**LO: 11**          **Factual**

*66.  The two basic types of mood disorders are
a.  major and minor.
b.  somatoform and cognitive.
c.  unipolar and bipolar.
d.  disruptive and non-disruptive.

**ANS: c**          **Pg: 497**
**LO: 12**          **Factual**

*67.  Ernest is deeply sad. He does not eat much, doesn't seem to want to take care of himself, and believes his life's work is useless. You think this is strange because several weeks ago Ernest was very excited about his life. He talked and talked about his new book and even seemed to stay up an entire week writing. Ernest probably has
a.  major depression.
b.  schizophrenia.
c.  obsessive-compulsive disorder.
d.  bipolar disorder.

**ANS: d**          **Pgs: 498-499**
**LO: 12**          **Factual**

68.  Which of the following is considered a mood disorder?
a.  schizophrenia
b.  phobic disorder
c.  bipolar disorder
d.  all of these

**ANS: c**          **Pg: 498**
**LO: 12**          **Factual**

69.     People with unipolar disorders experience _____; people with bipolar disorders experience _____.
a.      alternating periods of depression and mania; mania only
b.      depression only; alternating periods of depression and mania
c.      mania only; alternating periods of depression and mania
d.      alternating periods of depression and mania; depression and mania simultaneously

**ANS: b**          **Pg: 497**
**LO: 12**          **Factual**

70.     In _____ disorders, people show persistent feelings of sadness and despair and a loss of interest in previous sources of pleasure.
a.      manic
b.      phobic
c.      depressive
d.      conversion

**ANS: c**          **Pg: 497**
**LO: 12**          **Factual**

71.     Which of the following statements regarding the prevalence of depressive disorders is **not** accurate?
a.      Evidence suggests that the prevalence of depression is increasing.
b.      The prevalence of depression is about twice as high in men as it is in women.
c.      Evidence indicates that the lifetime prevalence of depression may be as high as 16%.
d.      People born since World War II appear to have an elevated risk for depression.

**ANS: b**          **Pg: 498**
**LO: 12**          **Conceptual**

72.     Which of the following statements regarding the prevalence of bipolar disorders is accurate?
a.      Bipolar disorders are seen more frequently in women than in men.
b.      Bipolar disorders are much more common than unipolar depression.
c.      Research indicates that bipolar disorders affect about 20% of the population.
d.      The peak of vulnerability for bipolar disorders is between the ages of 20 and 29.

**ANS: d**          **Pg: 499**
**LO: 12**          **Factual**

73.     Research suggests that heredity can create
a.      a predisposition to mood disorders.
b.      the hormonal imbalance associated with depression.
c.      a genetic "map" that determines the onset of mood disorders.
d.      a cognitive mindset that fosters the development of bipolar disorder.

**ANS: a**          **Pg: 499**
**LO: 13**          **Conceptual**

74. Which of the following statements regarding neurochemical factors in the development of mood disorders is accurate?
a. Correlations have been found between mood disorders and levels of several neurotransmitters in the brain.
b. Most of the drugs that are effective in the treatment of mood disorders are known to affect the availability of specific neurotransmitters.
c. Alterations in neurotransmitter activity probably depend on our reactions to environmental events.
d. All of these statements are accurate.

**ANS: d**      **Pg: 500**
**LO: 13**      **Factual**

75. Depressed people who _____ tend to remain depressed longer than those who don't.
a. try to distract themselves
b. engage in passive attribution
c. ruminate about their depression
d. discuss their depression with family members

**ANS: c**      **Pg: 500**
**LO: 14**      **Factual**

76. The evidence available today suggests that there is _____ between stress and the onset of mood disorders.
a. no relationship
b. a moderately strong link
c. a curvilinear relationship
d. a weak negative correlation

**ANS: b**      **Pg: 502**
**LO: 15**      **Conceptual**

77. Which of the following groups of psychological disorders is characterized by irrational thinking, poor reality contact, disturbed emotion, and hallucinations?
a. mood disorders
b. anxiety disorders
c. somatoform disorders
d. schizophrenic disorders

**ANS: d**      **Pgs: 502-503**
**LO: 16**      **Factual**

78.     Richard is a clerk who works at a music store. He believes that the CIA is regularly
        breaking into his apartment to plant listening devices into his telephone, stereo, and PC.
        Richard is exhibiting
a.      delusions.
b.      repression.
c.      hallucinations.
d.      displacement.

**ANS: a**              **Pg: 503**
**LO: 16**              **Factual**

79.     Sarah hears voices that tell her to shoot Dr. Laura. She is experiencing
a.      delusions.
b.      compulsions.
c.      a phobic reaction.
d.      hallucinations.

**ANS: d**              **Pg: 503**
**LO: 16**              **Factual**

80.     Delusions of grandeur and persecution are features that characterize the _____ subtype
        of schizophrenia.
a.      catatonic
b.      paranoid
c.      disorganized
d.      undifferentiated

**ANS: b**              **Pg: 503**
**LO: 17**              **Factual**

81.     Raymond tends to remain completely motionless for long periods of time, during which
        he seems oblivious to his environment. Raymond would most likely be diagnosed as
        having which of the following subtypes of schizophrenia?
a.      paranoid
b.      catatonic
c.      disorganized
d.      undifferentiated

**ANS: b**              **Pg: 503**
**LO: 17**              **Conceptual**

82.     _____ schizophrenia is characterized by a severe deterioration of adaptive
        behavior.
a.      Paranoid
b.      Catatonic
c.      Disorganized
d.      Undifferentiated

**ANS: c**              **Pg: 504**
**LO: 17**              **Factual**

83.    Marta sits alone all day, babbling incoherently and giggling to herself. Marta would most likely be diagnosed as having which of the following subtypes of schizophrenia?
a.    paranoid
b.    catatonic
c.    disorganized
d.    undifferentiated

ANS: c            Pg: 504
LO: 17            Conceptual

84.    Hallucinations and delusions are classified as _____ of schizophrenia
a.    negative symptoms
b.    positive symptoms
c.    temporary symptoms
d.    dangerous symptoms

ANS: b            Pg: 504
LO: 18            Factual

85.    Schizophrenic disorders usually emerge
a.    during early childhood.
b.    by the age of 12.
c.    during adolescence or early adulthood.
d.    between the ages of 30 and 45.

ANS: c            Pg: 504
LO: 19            Factual

*86.    About _____ percent of people with schizophrenia enjoy a full recovery.
a.    5-15
b.    15-20
c.    20-25
d.    more than 25

ANS: b            Pg: 505
LO: 19            Factual

87.    Which of the following statements regarding the etiology of schizophrenia is supported by research?
a.    Concordance rates for schizophrenia are virtually 100% for identical twins.
b.    Some people inherit a genetically transmitted vulnerability to schizophrenia.
c.    Schizophrenia has been linked to a recessive gene that must be contributed by both parents.
d.    If two schizophrenic parents have a child, it is a 90% certainty that the child will develop schizophrenia.

ANS: b            Pg: 505
LO: 20            Factual

88.     Which of the following has been identified as a major factor in the etiology of
        schizophrenia?
a.      genetic vulnerability
b.      observational learning
c.      exposure to high-anxious peers at an early age
d.      an extensive number of avoidance-avoidance conflicts

ANS: a                  Pg: 505
LO: 20                  Factual

89.     Recent findings indicate that the _____ larger in schizophrenic patients than in normal
        control subjects.
a.      thalamus is
b.      ventricles are
c.      adrenal gland is
d.      frontal lobes are

ANS: b                  Pg: 506
LO: 21                  Factual

90.     The prognosis is poorer for schizophrenics who return to families characterized by
        _____ expressed emotion.
a.      no
b.      low
c.      high
d.      erratic

ANS: c                  Pg: 508
LO: 22                  Factual

91.     Insanity is a
a.      legal term.
b.      medical diagnosis.
c.      DSM-IV classification.
d.      myth.

ANS: a                  Pg: 508
LO: 23                  Conceptual

92.     The principle that insanity exists when mental illness causes a person to be unable to
        distinguish right from wrong is called
a.      the insanity principle.
b.      the schizophrenia policy.
c.      the M'Naughten rule.
d.      the myth of mental illness.

ANS: c                  Pg: 508
LO: 23                  Conceptual

93.	It is most accurate to say that the use of the insanity defense
a.	is an easy way for criminals to avoid punishment.
b.	is a strategy that is abused and over-used by criminal defendants.
c.	is increasing in most state legal systems.
d.	is rarely used by defendants, and is very rarely successful.

ANS: d		Pg: 508
LO: 23		Conceptual

94.	In order for a person to be involuntarily committed to psychiatric treatment, it must be possible to demonstrate that the person
a.	is socially deviant.
b.	has a diagnosable disorder.
c.	is a danger to themselves, to others, or severely disoriented.
d.	would truly benefit from hospitalization and psychoactive medication.

ANS: c		Pg: 509
LO: 24		Conceptual

95.	_____ involves intense fear of gaining weight, disturbed body image, refusal to maintain normal weight, and dangerous measures to lose weight.
a.	Amenorrhea
b.	Osteoporosis
c.	Bulimia nervosa
d.	Anorexia nervosa

ANS: d		Pg: 510
LO: 25		Factual

96.	Anorexia nervosa can eventually lead to which of the following medical problems?
a.	a loss of bone density
c.	gastrointestinal problems
b.	a loss of menstrual cycles in women
d.	all of these

ANS: d		Pg: 510
LO: 25		Factual

97.	_____ involves habitually engaging in out-of-control overeating followed by unhealthy compensatory efforts, such as self-induced vomiting and excessive exercise.
a.	Amenorrhea
b.	Osteoporosis
c.	Bulimia nervosa
d.	Anorexia nervosa

ANS: c		Pg: 510
LO: 25		Factual

98.    Eating disordered behaviors
a.    have always existed but are now more common in affluent Western societies.
b.    began to appear in America in the 1980's.
c.    are now disappearing due to increased awareness and prevention strategies.
d.    are easily treated with cognitive-behavioral therapy.

ANS: a                Pg: 510
LO: 26                Conceptual

99.    As a result of cultural values in Western society, the vast majority of young women
a.    are generally satisfied with their weight.
b.    believe that extreme thinness is unattractive.
c.    exhibit symptoms of anorexia nervosa or bulimia nervosa.
d.    are dissatisfied with their weight and feel that they need to diet.

ANS: d                Pg: 511
LO: 27                Conceptual

100.   A young woman who says to herself, "I must be thin to be accepted," is demonstrating
       which of the following factors in the etiology of eating disorders?
a.    cultural
b.    cognitive
c.    biological
d.    evolutionary

ANS: b                Pg: 513
LO: 28                Conceptual


**MULTIPLE CHOICE QUESTIONS FROM STUDY GUIDE**

1.    Thomas Szasz has criticized the medical model because he believes that abnormal
      behavior
a.    involves deviation from social norms rather than an illness.
b.    does not really exist since it is the society that is abnormal.
c.    has a psychological rather than a physical cause.
d.    has a physical cause and is therefore a physical illness.

ANS: a                Pg: 482
LO: 1                 Factual

2.    When David Rosenhan studied accuracy of diagnosis, he found that
a.    even mental health professionals had difficulty distinguishing normality from
      abnormality.
b.    mental health professionals were able consistently to distinguish normal from abnormal.
c.    any normal person could recognize abnormal behavior.
d.    abnormality can be easily diagnosed by consulting the DSM.

ANS: a                Pg: 484
LO: 1                 Factual

3.     The current version of the DSM was introduced in
a.     1952.
b.     1974.
c.     1994.
d.     1998.

**ANS: c**          **Pg: 485**
**LO: 3**           **Factual**

4.     The current DSM uses a system of classification that asks for judgements about
       individuals on five separate dimensions.  This approach is termed a _____ system.
a.     multiaxial
b.     dimensional
c.     statistical
d.     multi-tasking

**ANS: a**          **Pg: 485**
**LO: 3**           **Factual**

5.     The study of the distribution of mental or physical disorders in a population is called
a.     etiology
b.     epidemiology
c.     psychopathology
d.     biopsychology

**ANS: b**          **Pg: 485**
**LO: 4**           **Factual**

6.     Obsessions are
a.     thoughts that repeatedly intrude into consciousness.
b.     actions that one feels forced to carry out.
c.     both thoughts and actions that cause subjective distress.
d.     stereotyped rituals that temporarily relieve anxiety.

**ANS: a**          **Pg: 489**
**LO: 5**           **Factual**

7.     The typical age of onset for obsessive-compulsive disorder is
a.     early childhood.
b.     early adolescence.
c.     early adulthood.
d.     middle adulthood.

**ANS: c**          **Pg: 490**
**LO: 5**           **Factual**

8.      Physical ailments that have no organic basis but are due to psychological factors are
        called _____ disorders.
a.      anxiety
b.      somatoform
c.      dissociative
d.      schizophrenic

ANS: b                  Pg: 491
LO: 8                   Factual

9.      A person suffering from a loss of hearing with no organic basis probably has which of the
        following disorders?
a.      hypochondriasis
b.      conversion disorder
c.      somatization disorder
d.      obsessive-compulsive disorder

ANS: b                  Pg: 492
LO: 8                   Factual

10.     According to your textbook, Abraham Lincoln, Ernest Hemingway, and Kurt Cobain all
        suffered from
a.      schizophrenia.
b.      severe mood disorders.
c.      obsessive-compulsive disorder.
d.      dissociative identity disorder.

ANS: b                  Pg: 496
LO: 12                  Factual

11.     Bipolar mood disorders were formerly known as
a.      schizophrenia.
b.      depressive disorders.
c.      manic-depressive disorders.
d.      multiple-personality disorders.

ANS: c                  Pg: 498
LO: 12                  Factual

12.     The idea that learned helplessness may contribute to depressive disorders is most
        consistent with which of the following theoretical approaches?
a.      cognitive
b.      interpersonal
c.      neurochemical
d.      evolutionary

ANS: a                  Pg: 500
LO: 14                  Conceptual

13. A person whose behavior is marked by striking motor disturbances, ranging from muscular rigidity to random motor activity is most likely suffering from the _____ type of schizophrenia.
a. paranoid
b. catatonic
c. disorganized
d. undifferentiated

**ANS: b**         **Pg: 503**
**LO: 16**         **Factual**

14. Schizophrenic disorders usually emerge during
a. early childhood.
b. adolescence or early adulthood.
c. a midlife crisis.
d. late adulthood.

**ANS: b**         **Pg: 504**
**LO: 16**         **Factual**

15. Which of the following statement concerning bulimia nervosa is not accurate?
a. Bulimia nervosa shares many features with anorexia nervosa.
b. Anorexia nervosa is more prevalent in Western societies than is bulimia nervosa.
c. People with bulimia are more prone to cooperate with treatment than are anorexics.
d. People suffering from bulimia nervosa typically maintain a reasonably normal body weight.

**ANS: b**         **Pg: 511**
**LO: 25**         **Factual**

1.      The process of distinguishing one illness from another is called
a.      etiology.
b.      diagnosis.
c.      prognosis.
d.      somatization.

ANS: b              Pg: 483
LO: 1               Factual


2.      _____ refers to the apparent cause(s) and developmental course of an illness.
a.      Etiology
b.      Diagnosis
c.      Prognosis
d.      Concordance

ANS: a              Pg: 483
LO: 1               Factual


3.      Which of the following is **not** one of the main criteria of abnormal behavior?
a.      deviance
b.      personal distress
c.      maladaptive behavior
d.      psychological affiance

ANS: d              Pg: 483
LO: 2               Conceptual


4.      The Diagnostic and Statistical Manual of Mental Disorders is published by the
a.      American Psychiatric Association.
b.      American Psychological Society.
c.      American Psychological Association.
d.      American Psychoanalytic Association.

ANS: a              Pg: 485
LO: 3               Factual


*5.     In the DSM-IV axes _____ and _____ are used to diagnosis disorders.
a.      I; II
b.      II; III
c.      IV; VI
d.      I; V

ANS: a              Pg: 485
LO: 3               Conceptual

6. The current DSM system includes which of the following as a specific type of psychological disorder?
a. extreme sadness or anxiety
b. difficulty controlling one's gambling
c. distress that results from attempting to quit smoking
d. all of these

**ANS: d**      **Pg: 486**
**LO: 3**      **Factual**

*7. The class of disorders marked by feelings of excessive apprehension and anxiety is
a. anxiety disorders.
b. somatoform disorders.
c. affective disorders.
d. phobic disorders.

**ANS: a**      **Pg: 487**
**LO: 5**      **Conceptual**

8. Compulsion is to "action" as obsession is to
a. fear.
b. thought.
c. emotion.
d. behavior.

**ANS: b**      **Pg: 489**
**LO: 5**      **Conceptual**

9. An unwanted thought that repeatedly intrudes upon an individual's consciousness is called a(n)
a. delusion.
b. obsession.
c. compulsion.
d. hallucination.

**ANS: b**      **Pg: 489**
**LO: 5**      **Factual**

10. The famous industrialist Howard Hughes devised extraordinary rituals to minimize the possibility of being contaminated by germs. For example, he would sometimes spend hours methodically cleaning a telephone. Hughes's behavior exemplifies which of the following disorders?
a. agoraphobia
b. panic disorder
c. generalized anxiety disorder
d. obsessive-compulsive disorder

**ANS: d**      **Pg: 489**
**LO: 5**      **Conceptual**

*11.    The fear of snakes and spiders is very common in people. Seligman (1971) would probably explain this with the idea of
a.    experience.
b.    learning history.
c.    ego comparison history.
d.    preparedness.

ANS: d            Pg: 491
LO: 6            Conceptual

12.    Psychosomatic diseases involve
a.    the deliberate faking of physical illness.
b.    a pseudo-illness caused by psychological factors.
c.    genuine physical ailments caused in part by psychological factors.
d.    a tendency to misinterpret minor body changes as indicative of serious illness.

ANS: c            Pg: 491
LO: 8            Factual

13.    People who lose contact with portions of their consciousness or memory, and experience disruptions in their sense of identity, would most likely be considered as having which of the following types of disorders?
a.    schizophrenia
b.    anxiety disorders
c.    dissociative disorders
d.    somatoform disorders

ANS: c            Pg: 494
LO: 10            Factual

14.    People with unipolar disorders experience _____; people with bipolar disorders experience _____.
a.    alternating periods of depression and mania; mania only
b.    depression only; alternating periods of depression and mania
c.    mania only; alternating periods of depression and mania
d.    alternating periods of depression and mania; depression and mania simultaneously

ANS: b            Pg: 497
LO: 12            Factual

15.    Sarah hears voices that tell her to shoot Dr. Laura. She is experiencing
a.    delusions.
b.    compulsions.
c.    a phobic reaction.
d.    hallucinations.

ANS: d            Pg: 503
LO: 16            Factual

**TRUE/FALSE QUESTIONS**

1.  Sigmund Freud was highly critical of the medical model of psychological disorders.

    **ANS: false**      **Pg: 482**
    **LO:   1**         **Conceptual**

2.  One criticism of the medical model is that it converts moral and social questions into medical ones.

    **ANS: true**       **Pg: 482**
    **LO:   1**         **Factual**

3.  Deviance by itself is no longer accepted as criteria for clinical diagnosis of a psychological disorder.

    **ANS: false**      **Pgs: 483-484**
    **LO:   2**         **Factual**

4.  Etiology is the cause of a disorder.

    **ANS: true**       **Pg: 483**
    **LO:   1**         **Factual**

5.  Prognosis is the likely course and outcome of a disorder.

    **ANS: true**       **Pg: 483**
    **LO:   1**         **Factual**

6.  Diagnosis is the likely course and outcome of a disorder.

    **ANS: false**      **Pg: 483**
    **LO:   1**         **Factual**

7.  Phobic disorder involves a generalized dread or anxiety.

    **ANS: false**      **Pg: 488**
    **LO:   5**         **Factual**

8.  Obsessions are reoccurring, uncontrollable, intruding behaviors.

    **ANS: false**      **Pg: 489**
    **LO:   5**         **Factual**

9.  Multiple personality disorder is classified separately from schizophrenia.

    **ANS: true**       **Pg: 494**
    **LO:   10**        **Conceptual**

10. The prognosis for schizophrenia is better when the person had a sudden (rather than gradual) onset of the symptoms.

ANS: **true**      **Pg: 504**
LO:  **19**       **Factual**


## SHORT-ANSWER ESSAY QUESTIONS

1.      Explain the medical model of mental illness.  What are its strengths? Its weaknesses?

**Pg: 482**

*2.      Discuss the criteria for abnormal behavior.  Cite some examples of behaviors that some people would consider "abnormal" yet would seem perfectly normal to other people.
**Pg: 483**

3.      Discuss the continuum concept as it applies to the distinction between normal and abnormal behavior.

**Pg: 483**

*4.      List the different types of anxiety disorders.  Compare and contrast the differences between them.

**Pgs: 487-491**

5.      Briefly explain how classical conditioning and operant conditioning may play a role in
the      development of anxiety responses.

**Pgs: 490-491**

6.      Briefly describe the notion of preparedness as it applies to the development of phobic disorders.

**Pg: 491**

7.      Distinguish between psychosomatic diseases and somatoform disorders.

**Pgs: 491-493**

146.     Discuss the controversy concerning the true prevalence of multiple personality disorder.

**Pgs: 494-496**

8.      Compare and contrast depressive disorders and bipolar disorders in terms of their symptoms and prevalence.

**Pgs: 497-499**

9.      Briefly describe the theorized role of attribution in the development of depression.

**Pgs: 497-498**

*10. What are the different types of schizophrenia?  Contrast the positive and the negative symptoms of each.

**Pgs: 502-504**

11. List and briefly describe several factors that are related to the likelihood of recovery from schizophrenic disorders.

**Pgs: 504-505**

12. Briefly describe the main similarities and differences between anorexia nervosa and bulimia nervosa.

**Pgs: 510-511**

*13. Discuss the biological etiology of the major classes of mental disorders.

**Pgs: 490-507**

# Chapter 16
# PSYCHOTHERAPY

## LEARNING OBJECTIVES

1. Identify the three major categories of therapy.
2. Discuss why people do or do not seek psychotherapy.
3. Describe the various types of mental health professionals involved in the provision of therapy.
4. Explain the logic of psychoanalysis and describe the techniques used to probe the unconscious.
5. Discuss interpretation, resistance, and transference in psychoanalysis.
6. Explain the logic of client-centered therapy.
7. Describe therapeutic climate and process in client-centered therapy.
8. Discuss the logic, goals, and techniques of cognitive therapy.
9. Describe how group therapy is generally conducted.
10. Identify some advantages of group therapy.
11. Summarize evidence on the efficacy of insight therapies.
12. Summarize both sides of the recovered memories controversy.
13. Summarize the general approach and principles of behavior therapies.
14. Describe the three steps in systematic desensitization and the logic underlying the treatment.
15. Describe the use of aversion therapy and social skills training.
16. Summarize evidence on the efficacy of behavior therapies.
17. Describe the principal drug therapies used in the treatment of psychological disorders and summarize evidence on the efficacy.
18. Discuss some of the problems associated with drug therapies and their overall value.
19. Describe ECT and discuss its efficacy and risks.
20. Discuss how managed care has affected the provision of therapy.
21. Discuss the merits of blending approaches to therapy.
22. Explain why therapy is underutilized by ethnic minorities.
23. Discuss when and where to seek psychotherapy.
24. Discuss the potential importance of a therapist's gender and professional background.
25. Summarize the evidence whether therapists' theoretical approach influences their effectiveness.
26. Discuss what one should expect out of therapy.

# MULTIPLE CHOICE QUESTIONS

1. Which of the following is **not** among the major approaches to therapy discussed in your textbook?
a. insight therapies
b. behavior therapies
c. biomedical therapies
d. transpersonal therapies

ANS: d          Pg: 518
LO: 1          Conceptual

2. The main goal of behavior therapy is to
a. alter the client's brain chemistry by prescribing specific drugs.
b. change the client's thought patterns so that negative emotions can be controlled.
c. alter the frequency of problem behaviors using conditioning techniques.
d. identify the early childhood unconscious conflicts that are the source of the client's symptoms.

ANS: c          Pg: 518
LO: 1          Factual

3. The prescription of drugs in the treatment of psychological disorders is a feature of
a. insight therapy.
b. behavior therapy.
c. biomedical therapy.
d. transpersonal therapy.

ANS: c          Pg: 518
LO: 1          Conceptual

*4. Andre has recently been prescribed Xanax for a psychological disorder. His provider must believe in
a. insight therapy.
b. behavior therapy.
c. biomedical therapy.
d. transpersonal therapy.

ANS: c          Pg: 518
LO: 1          Applied

5. Traditionally, biomedical therapies are usually provided by
a. counselors.
b. psychiatrists.
c. psychologists.
d. social workers.

ANS: b          Pg: 518
LO: 1          Factual

6. The two most common problems among those who seek psychotherapy are
a. loneliness and phobias.
b. excessive anxiety and depression.
c. low self-esteem and irrational thinking.
d. marital conflict and a sense of loneliness.

ANS: b          Pgs: 518-519
LO: 2          Factual

7. Which of the following statements regarding treatment for psychological problems is most accurate?
a. Men are more likely than women to receive therapy.
b. Many people who need therapy don't receive it.
c. Only people who have an identifiable psychological disorder are eligible for therapy.
d. People with less education are more likely to enter therapy than those with more education.

ANS: b          Pg: 519
LO: 2          Conceptual

8. Which of the following statements reflects the theoretical difference between a clinical psychologist and a counseling psychologist?
a. A clinical psychologist can prescribe drugs, but a counseling psychologist can't.
b. A clinical psychologist has a doctorate, whereas a counseling psychologist has a master's degree.
c. Clinical psychologists are trained to provide insight therapy whereas counseling psychologists are trained to provide behavior therapy.
d. A clinical psychologist specializes in the treatment of psychological disorders, whereas a counseling psychologist specializes in the treatment of everyday adjustment problems.

ANS: d          Pg: 520
LO: 3          Conceptual

9. In their provision of therapy, psychiatrists tend to emphasize _____ treatments.
a. group
b. behavioral
c. biomedical
d. humanistic

ANS: c          Pg: 521
LO: 3          Factual

10.	Today, psychoanalysis is most likely to be practiced by which of the following types of mental health professionals?
a.	psychiatrists
b.	social workers
c.	clinical psychologists
d.	counseling psychologists

**ANS: a**	**Pg: 521**
**LO: 3**	**Factual**

*11.	Ms. Harding has a master's degree and usually treats people with minor depression and communication problems.  Ms. Harding probably is a
a.	counselor.
b.	clinical psychologist.
c.	social worker.
d.	psychiatrist.

**ANS: a**	**Pgs: 521-522**
**LO: 3**	**Conceptual**

*12.	Dr. Benoitte has an MD and usually treats people with bipolar disorder and schizophrenia.  Dr. Benoitte probably is a
a.	counselor.
b.	clinical psychologist.
c.	social worker.
d.	psychiatrist.

**ANS: d**	**Pg: 521**
**LO: 3**	**Conceptual**

*13.	Dr. Jones has a Ph.D and usually treats people with depression and phobic disorders.  Dr. Benoitte probably is a
a.	counselor.
b.	clinical psychologist.
c.	social worker.
d.	psychiatrist.

**ANS: b**	**Pgs: 520-521**
**LO: 3**	**Conceptual**

14.	Which of the following statements about the role of counselors in providing therapy is **not** accurate?
a.	Counselors typically have a master's degree.
b.	Counselors tend to emphasize the biomedical approach to treatment.
c.	Counselors often specialize in particular types of problems, such as marital conflict.
d.	Counselors are usually found working in schools, colleges, and human service agencies.

**ANS: b**	**Pgs: 521-522**
**LO: 3**	**Conceptual**

15. Which of the following individuals is credited with developing psychoanalysis?
a. Carl Jung
b. Alfred Adler
c. Sigmund Freud
d. Richard Lazarus

**ANS: c**      **Pg: 522**
**LO: 4**      **Factual**

*16. Psychoanalysis is a therapy that emphasizes
a. self-fulfillment.
b. behavioral intervention.
c. self-concept congruency.
d. unconscious conflict.

**ANS: d**      **Pg: 522**
**LO: 4**      **Factual**

17. Which of the following concepts is least closely associated with psychoanalytic treatment?
a. transference
b. free association
c. negative thinking
d. unconscious conflict

**ANS: c**      **Pgs: 522-525**
**LO: 4**      **Conceptual**

18. Freud believed that neuroses were caused by
a. negative thinking.
b. classically conditioned fear responses.
c. unresolved conflicts in the unconscious.
d. incongruence between a person's self-concept and reality.

**ANS: c**      **Pg: 522**
**LO: 4**      **Factual**

19. Which of the following terms refers to a psychoanalytic technique involving spontaneous expression of thoughts with as little censorship as possible?
a. resistance
b. transference
c. interpretation
d. free association

**ANS: d**      **Pg: 522**
**LO: 4**      **Factual**

20.   In psychoanalysis, free association is used to
a.    overcome resistance.
b.    explore the unconscious.
c.    modify maladaptive habits.
d.    clarify clients' feelings about their self-concept.

**ANS: b**          **Pg: 522**
**LO: 4**           **Factual**

21.   According to Freud, which of the following was/were the "royal road to the unconscious"?
a.    the id
b.    dreams
c.    free association
d.    defense mechanisms

**ANS: b**          **Pg: 523**
**LO: 4**           **Conceptual**

*22.   _____ is spontaneously expressing thoughts and feelings exactly as they occur.
a.    Relaxation analysis
b.    Dream analysis
c.    Free association
d.    Connection mechanisms

**ANS: c**          **Pg: 522**
**LO: 4**           **Conceptual**

23.   According to the system of psychoanalysis, _____ involves the therapist's attempts to explain the inner significance of the client's thoughts, feelings, memories, and behaviors.
a.    resistance
b.    transference
c.    interpretation
d.    free association

**ANS: c**          **Pg: 523**
**LO: 5**           **Factual**

*24.   _____ are unconscious defense maneuvers intended to hinder the progress of therapy.
a.    Resistance
b.    Transference
c.    Interpretation linkage
d.    Free association linkage

**ANS: a**          **Pg: 524**
**LO: 5**           **Factual**

*25.   Meagan has been receiving psychotherapy. Lately she has been showing up late and has become hostile to such an extent that it is interfering with her therapy. She is likely showing
a.   resistance.
b.   transference.
c.   interpretation.
d.   free association.

**ANS: a**          **Pg: 524**
**LO: 5**           **Applied**

26.    If a client in psychoanalysis attempts to lead the therapist away from sensitive issues, the client is displaying
a.   resistance.
b.   transference.
c.   over-interpretation.
d.   free association linkage.

**ANS: a**          **Pg: 524**
**LO: 5**           **Factual**

27.    In _____, clients relate to their therapist in ways that mimic key relationships in their lives.
a.   congruence
b.   transference
c.   interpretation
d.   free association

**ANS: b**          **Pg: 524**
**LO: 5**           **Factual**

*28.   Paul's father was always very competitive with Paul. Lately, in therapy, Paul have been trying to prove that he makes more money and is smarter than the therapist. Paul is showing
a.   resistance.
b.   transference.
c.   over-interpretation.
d.   free association linkage.

**ANS: b**          **Pg: 524**
**LO: 5**           **Applied**

29. When a client starts behaving as though the psychoanalyst were a parent or a lover, it is likely that _____ is taking place.
a. resistance
b. transference
c. interpretation
d. free association

**ANS: b**　　　　**Pg: 524**
**LO: 5**　　　　**Conceptual**

30. Because Suzanne has always felt an unconscious rivalry with her mother, she is hostile to her therapist who is just a little younger than her mother and a female. Suzanne's behavior is most likely a form of
a. resistance.
b. transference.
c. free association.
d. misinterpretation.

**ANS: b**　　　　**Pg: 524**
**LO: 5**　　　　**Conceptual**

*31. Psychoanalysis, Freudian style, usually takes
a. less than 6 months.
b. 6 months to 1 year.
c. 1 to 3 years.
d. 3 to 5 years.

**ANS: d**　　　　**Pg: 524**
**LO: 5**　　　　**Factual**

32. The "descendants" of Freud's classical version of psychoanalysis are collectively known as _____ approaches to therapy.
a. cognitive
b. behavioral
c. client-centered
d. psychodynamic

**ANS: d**　　　　**Pg: 524**
**LO: 5**　　　　**Factual**

33. Client-centered therapy was developed by
a. Carl Jung.
b. Aaron Beck.
c. Carl Rogers.
d. Sigmund Freud.

**ANS: c**　　　　**Pg: 524**
**LO: 6**　　　　**Factual**

34.     According to the client-centered approach to therapy, personal distress and neurotic anxieties are usually caused by
a.      conflicts centering on sex.
b.      conflicts centering on psychosocial issues.
c.      incongruence between self-concept and reality.
d.      maladaptive habits that have been previously reinforced.

ANS: c          Pg: 524
LO: 6           Factual

35.     Client-centered therapy is based on the assumption that incongruence between the client's self-concept and reality is caused by the client's
a.      lack of ego strength.
b.      dependence on others for approval.
c.      inability to overcome conditioned habits.
d.      tendency to engage in negative thinking.

ANS: b          Pg: 524
LO: 6           Conceptual

36.     Which of the following is **not** one of the conditions Rogers felt was necessary for a positive therapeutic climate?
a.      empathy
b.      genuineness
c.      conditional free association
d.      unconditional positive regard

ANS: c          Pg: 525
LO: 7           Conceptual

37.     In client-centered therapy, the therapist must demonstrate a complete, nonjudgmental acceptance of the client as a person.  This approach is most consistent with which of the following conditions of therapy?
a.      empathy
b.      genuineness
c.      conditional free association
d.      unconditional positive regard

ANS: d          Pg: 525
LO: 7           Conceptual

38.     According to Carl Rogers, which of the following is the major force promoting healthy change in therapy?
a.      a supportive emotional climate
b.      the extinction of negative self-talk
c.      conditional positive regard for the client
d.      the transference of the client's negative feelings to the therapist

ANS: a          Pgs: 525-526
LO: 7           Conceptual

39.     According to Carl Rogers, the therapist's key task in helping clients sort out their feelings
        is
a.      clarification.
b.      dream analysis.
c.      directing free association.
d.      providing conditional positive regard.

**ANS: a**              **Pgs: 525-526**
**LO: 7**               **Factual**

*40.    Lenny's therapy is progressing very quickly. Lenny's likes to go in and openly explore
        his problems rapidly, and his therapist seems open to that. He also feels very supported
        during the therapy. Lenny is probably in _____ therapy.
a.      psychodynamic
b.      client-center
c.      cognitive
d.      behavior

**ANS: b**              **Pgs: 525-526**
**LO: 7**               **Factual**

41.     Which of the following individuals is most closely associated with the cognitive approach
        to therapy?
a.      Carl Jung
b.      Albert Ellis
c.      Carl Rogers
d.      Sigmund Freud

**ANS: b**              **Pg: 526**
**LO: 8**               **Factual**

*42.    Albert Ellis is most closely associated with _____ therapy.
a.      psychodynamic
b.      client-centered
c.      rational-emotive
d.      cognitive depression treatments

**ANS: c**              **Pg: 526**
**LO: 8**               **Factual**

*43.    Aaron Beck is most closely associated with _____ therapy.
a.      psychodynamic
b.      client-centered
c.      rational-emotive
d.      cognitive depression treatments

**ANS: d**              **Pg: 526**
**LO: 8**               **Factual**

44. Cognitive approaches to therapy tend to focus on
a. increasing one's self-awareness and self-acceptance.
b. uncovering unconscious conflicts that may be causing anxiety.
c. reliving childhood trauma as a way to alleviate long-term anxiety.
d. recognizing and changing negative thoughts and maladaptive beliefs.

ANS: d          Pg: 526
LO: 8           Factual

45. According to Beck, which kind of thought process tends to produce depression?
a. focusing selectively on positive experiences
b. making unduly pessimistic projections about the future
c. blaming setbacks on circumstantial factors without considering personal inadequacies
d. all of the above

ANS: d          Pg: 526
LO: 8           Factual

46. The main goal of cognitive therapy is to
a. change the way clients think.
b. uncover unconscious conflicts.
c. provide a supportive environment.
d. foster self-acceptance and personal growth.

ANS: a          Pgs: 526-527
LO: 8           Factual

47. A therapist openly challenges a client's statement that she is a failure as a woman because her boyfriend left her, insisting that she justify it with evidence. This is characteristic of
a. behavior therapy.
b. cognitive therapy.
c. client-centered therapy.
d. psychodynamic therapy.

ANS: b          Pgs: 526-527
LO: 8           Conceptual

48. Cognitive therapy is most often paired with which of the following approaches to therapy?
a. medical
b. behavior
c. client-centered
d. psychodynamic

ANS: b          Pg: 527
LO: 8           Conceptual

49.    In group therapy, the participants' most important role is to
a.    set goals for the group.
b.    provide acceptance and emotional support for each other.
c.    gently reprimand group members who don't make progress.
d.    use free association to explore each other's unconscious conflicts.

**ANS: b**          **Pg: 527**
**LO: 9**           **Factual**

50.    Which of the following statements about group therapy is **not** accurate?
a.    Each participant helps select other members of the group.
b.    A therapy group typically consists of five to ten participants.
c.    The participants essentially function as therapists for one another.
d.    The therapist may share his or her own personal feelings with the group.

**ANS: a**          **Pg: 527**
**LO: 9**           **Conceptual**

51.    Which of the following is generally **not** considered an advantage of group therapy?
a.    Clients come to realize that their unhappiness is not necessarily unique.
b.    Group therapy is less expense for clients.
c.    All types of problems are well suited to it.
d.    Clients can practice their social skills in a safe environment.

**ANS: c**          **Pg: 528**
**LO: 10**          **Conceptual**

52.    Which of the following statements best reflects the current view of psychologists on the issue of recovered memories?
a.    Most psychologists accept recovered memories at face value.
b.    Psychologists tend to be sharply divided on the issue of repressed memories.
c.    Most psychologists blame psychiatrists for "creating" the controversy in the first place.
d.    There is very little controversy on the subject.

**ANS: b**          **Pgs: 529-530**
**LO: 12**          **Conceptual**

53.    Which of the following is a reasonable conclusion regarding the repressed memories controversy?
a.    Therapists can unknowingly create false memories in their patients.
b.    It seems likely that some cases of recovered memories are authentic.
c.    A significant portion of recovered memories of abuse are the product of suggestion.
d.    All of the above can reasonably be concluded.

**ANS: d**          **Pg: 532**
**LO: 12**          **Conceptual**

54.   Behavior therapy emerged from research fostered by which of the following individuals?
a.   B. F. Skinner
b.   Hans Eysenck
c.   Joseph Wolpe
d.   all of the above

**ANS: d**          **Pg: 532**
**LO: 13**          **Factual**

55.   Behavior therapy involves using the principles of _____ to change problem behavior.
a.   operant conditioning
b.   classical conditioning
c.   observational learning
d.   all of the above

**ANS: d**          **Pgs: 532-533**
**LO: 13**          **Factual**

*56.   Which of these is NOT an assumption of behavior therapies?
a.   Pathological behavior is learned.
b.   Pathological behavior can be unlearned.
c.   Parents often do not provide enough teaching of proper behaviors.
d.   All of the above are assumptions.

**ANS: c**          **Pgs: 532-533**
**LO: 13**          **Factual**

57.   Systematic desensitization was devised by
a.   Albert Ellis.
b.   Carl Rogers.
c.   Joseph Wolpe.
d.   Sigmund Freud.

**ANS: c**          **Pg: 533**
**LO: 14**          **Factual**

58.   _____ is a behavior therapy used to reduce clients' anxiety responses through counter-conditioning.
a.   Free association
b.   Self-modification
c.   Aversion therapy
d.   Systematic desensitization

**ANS: d**          **Pg: 533**
**LO: 14**          **Factual**

59.    Establishing an anxiety hierarchy is a critical element in
a.    free association.
b.    aversion therapy.
c.    systematic desensitization.
d.    all of the above.

**ANS: c**          **Pg: 533**
**LO: 14**          **Factual**

60.    The first step in the process of systematic desensitization is to
a.    train the client in muscle relaxation.
b.    help the client build an anxiety hierarchy.
c.    have the client work though the hierarchy and try to remain relaxed.
d.    expose the client to mild anxiety-arousing stimuli.

**ANS: b**          **Pg: 533**
**LO: 14**          **Factual**

*61.    The second step in the process of systematic desensitization is to
a.    train the client in muscle relaxation.
b.    help the client build an anxiety hierarchy.
c.    have the client works though the hierarchy and try to remain relaxed.
d.    expose the client to mild anxiety-arousing stimuli.

**ANS: a**          **Pg: 533**
**LO: 14**          **Factual**

*62.    The third step in the process of systematic desensitization is to
a.    train the client in muscle relaxation.
b.    help the client build an anxiety hierarchy.
c.    have the client works though the hierarchy and try to remain relaxed.
d.    expose the client to mild anxiety-arousing stimuli.

**ANS: c**          **Pg: 533**
**LO: 14**          **Factual**

63.    Evidence on systematic desensitization generally indicates that it is an effective
       procedure for eliminating
a.    negative self-talk.
b.    specific anxieties.
c.    generalized anxiety.
d.    drug and alcohol problems.

**ANS: b**          **Pg: 533**
**LO: 14**          **Factual**

64. _____ is a behavior therapy in which a noxious stimulus is paired with a stimulus that elicits an undesirable response.
a.   Free association
b.   Self-modification
c.   Aversion therapy
d.   Systematic desensitization

**ANS: c**          **Pg: 534**
**LO: 15**          **Factual**

65. Aversion therapy is most closely associated with which of the following processes?
a.   self-actualization
b.   operant conditioning
c.   classical conditioning
d.   observational learning

**ANS: c**          **Pg: 534**
**LO: 15**          **Conceptual**

66. Which of the following has been treated successfully with aversion therapy?
a.   schizophrenia
b.   alcohol dependence
c.   multiple-personality disorder
d.   obsessive-compulsive disorder

**ANS: b**          **Pgs: 534-535**
**LO: 15**          **Factual**

67. _____ is a behavior therapy, designed to improve interpersonal behaviors, that emphasizes shaping, modeling, and behavioral rehearsal.
a.   Aversion therapy
b.   Self-actualization
c.   Social skills training
d.   Systematic desensitization

**ANS: c**          **Pgs: 535-536**
**LO: 15**          **Factual**

68. Which of the following techniques is least likely to be used in social skills training?
a.   shaping
b.   modeling
c.   counterconditioning
d.   behavioral rehearsal

**ANS: c**          **Pg: 536**
**LO: 15**          **Conceptual**

69. Kerri's therapist has her practice her listening skills in structured, role-playing exercises. Later she is asked to practice these skills with family members, friends, and co-workers. Kerri is likely in a treatment program based on which of the following techniques?
a. self-modification
b. aversion therapy
c. social skills training
d. systematic desensitization

ANS: c          Pg: 536
LO: 15          Conceptual

70. Which of the following statements regarding the evaluation of behavior therapies is accurate?
a. Behavior therapists historically have placed little emphasis on measuring therapeutic outcomes.
b. Behavior therapies are well suited for the treatment of virtually any psychological problem.
c. There is favorable evidence on the efficacy of most of the widely used behavioral interventions.
d. Behavior therapists generally have a difficult time measuring progress, due to the nature of their therapeutic goals.

ANS: c          Pg: 536
LO: 16          Conceptual

71. Behavior therapies are least likely to be effective in the treatment of which of the following?
a. phobias
b. drug-related problems
c. vague feelings of discontent
d. obsessive-compulsive disorder

ANS: c          Pg: 536
LO: 16          Conceptual

72. Biomedical therapies involve
a. complex verbal interactions between therapist and client.
b. active confrontation of clients' inappropriate thought patterns.
c. attempts to manipulate behavior using reward and punishment.
d. physiological interventions intended to reduce symptoms.

ANS: d          Pg: 536
LO: 17          Factual

73.		_____ is the treatment of mental disorders with medication.
a.	Insight therapy
b.	Behavior therapy
c.	Psychopharmacotherapy
d.	Electroconvulsive shock therapy

**ANS: c		Pg: 536**
**LO: 17		Factual**

74.	Which of the following is **not** considered a type of therapeutic drug?
a.	antianxiety
b.	antineurotic
c.	antipsychotic
d.	antidepressant

**ANS: b		Pgs: 537-538**
**LO: 17		Factual**

75.		_____ drugs are used to relieve tension, apprehension, and nervousness.
a.	Antianxiety
b.	Antineurotic
c.	Antipsychotic
d.	Antidepressant

**ANS: a		Pg: 537**
**LO: 17		Factual**

76.	Valium, Xanax, and other tranquilizers are most likely to be used to treat which of the following disorders?
a.	depression
b.	schizophrenia
c.	anxiety disorders
d.	multiple-personality disorder

**ANS: c		Pg: 537**
**LO: 17		Factual**

77.	Which of the following is a common side effect of antianxiety drugs?
a.	nausea
b.	depression
c.	drowsiness
d.	all of the above

**ANS: d		Pg: 537**
**LO: 17		Factual**

78. Antipsychotic drugs
a. tend to produce an immediate, but short-lasting, effect.
b. are effective for only a small minority of psychotic patients.
c. are often prescribed even for individuals who have no psychotic disorder.
d. gradually reduce psychotic symptoms such as hallucinations and delusions.

**ANS: d**      **Pg: 537**
**LO: 17**      **Factual**

79. Studies suggest that about _____ percent of psychotic patients respond favorably to antipsychotic medication.
a. 10-20
b. 30-40
c. 50-60
d. 70-90

**ANS: d**      **Pg: 537**
**LO: 17**      **Factual**

80. _____ is a neurological disorder marked by chronic tremors and involuntary spastic movements.
a. Diazepam
b. Haloperidol
c. Schizophrenia
d. Tardive dyskinesia

**ANS: d**      **Pg: 538**
**LO: 17**      **Factual**

81. Some experts have predicted that a new class of antipsychotic drugs, called _____, will almost completely replace conventional antipsychotic medications in the near future.
a. tricyclics
b. MAO inhibitors
c. lithium derivatives
d. atypical antipsychotics

**ANS: d**      **Pg: 538**
**LO: 17**      **Factual**

82. Which of the following drugs has been found to be beneficial in the treatment of depressed patients while creating the fewest side effects?
a. tricyclics
b. serotonin reuptake inhibitors
c. diazepam
d. MAO inhibitors

**ANS: b**      **Pg: 538**
**LO: 17**      **Factual**

83. Prozac, which is commonly used to treat depression, belongs to a class of antidepressants called
a. diazepam.
b. MAO inhibitors.
c. atypical antidepressants.
d. selective serotonin reuptake inhibitors.

ANS: d          Pg: 538
LO: 17          Factual

84. Lithium is most frequently used in the treatment of individuals with which of the following disorders?
a. schizophrenia
b. bipolar disorder
c. bulimia nervosa
d. multiple-personality disorder

ANS: b          Pg: 539
LO: 17          Factual

85. One of the disadvantages of the use of lithium to treat mood swings is that
a. it doesn't work for older patients.
b. it causes mania.
c. it can be toxic.
d. it is not as effective as anti-psychotics for this purpose.

ANS: c          Pg: 539
LO: 18          Factual

86. One of the problems with the use of drugs in the treatment of psychological disorders is that they
a. work only for mild disturbances.
b. often have undesirable side effects.
c. can't be used along with other therapies.
d. are questionable regarding effectiveness.

ANS: b          Pg: 539
LO: 18          Conceptual

87. Which of the following is **not** a common criticism of drug therapies?
a. Drug treatment is effective only for a small minority of patients.
b. Many drugs are over-prescribed and many patients are overmedicated.
c. Drugs temporarily relieve symptoms without addressing the underlying problem.
d. The side effects of the drugs can be worse than the illnesses the drugs are supposed to cure.

ANS: a          Pgs: 539-540
LO: 18          Conceptual

*88.    SSRIs seem to cause a small rise in suicide rates among
a.      younger females.
b.      all males.
c.      all males and females.
d.      younger males and females.

**ANS: d**          **Pg: 539**
**LO: 18**          **Factual**

89.     Which of the following statements regarding the use of electroconvulsive therapy (ECT)
        is accurate?
a.      ECT is a rare form of therapy.
b.      ECT is used primarily for the treatment of schizophrenia.
c.      ECT involves the use of electrical shock to produce a cortical seizure accompanied by
        convulsions.
d.      All of the above statements are accurate.

**ANS: c**          **Pg: 540**
**LO: 19**          **Factual**

90.     The therapeutic efficacy of electroconvulsive therapy
a.      is a matter of debate.
b.      far outweighs any risks.
c.      is clear for individuals with schizophrenia.
d.      is minimal; thus, its use has been virtually discontinued.

**ANS: a**          **Pg: 541**
**LO: 19**          **Factual**

91.     ECT is used primarily to treat which of the following psychological disorders?
a.      depression
b.      schizophrenia
c.      dissociative fugue
d.      generalized anxiety disorder

**ANS: a**          **Pgs: 540-541**
**LO: 19**          **Factual**

92.     Therapists have become more eclectic in their approach mainly because
a.      they like to specialize in all types of treatments.
b.      many therapeutic approaches simple don't work.
c.      patients often respond better to a combination of treatments than to one alone.
d.      it is easier to practice several treatment approaches than to be an expert in one approach.

**ANS: c**          **Pg: 542**
**LO: 21**          **Conceptual**

93.      _____ is a therapeutic approach that involves borrowing ideas, insights, and techniques from a variety of sources while tailoring the intervention strategy to the unique needs of the client.
a.      Interpretation
b.      Free association
c.      Eclecticism
d.      Theoretical integration

ANS: c          Pg: 542
LO: 21          Factual

94.      Which of the following statements regarding ethnic minority utilization of psychotherapy is accurate?
a.      Minority group members will use psychotherapy services if no other choices exist.
b.      Minority group members use psychotherapy services more frequently than majority group members.
c.      Female members of an ethnic minority will use psychotherapy services if encouraged by males in their ethnic group.
d.      A variety of barriers exist that most likely result in members of ethnic minority groups underutilizing psychotherapy services.

ANS: d          Pg: 543
LO: 22          Conceptual

95.      Effective communication in therapy can be difficult for members of ethnic minorities because
a.      members of ethnic minorities refuse to learn to speak English.
b.      hospitals and clinics often lack staff members who understand the culture of those being served.
c.      ethnic minority group members don't open up in therapy.
d.      ethnic minority group members are often living in the US illegally and cannot disclose much information to therapists.

ANS: b          Pg: 543
LO: 22          Conceptual

96.      You should probably think seriously about obtaining professional therapy if
a.      you have no one to lean on.
b.      you feel helpless and overwhelmed.
c.      your life is seriously disrupted by your problems.
d.      all of the above.

ANS: d          Pg: 545
LO: 23          Factual

97.     In looking for therapeutic services, it is important to keep in mind that
a.      most therapists are in private practice.
b.      community mental health centers are good sources of information.
c.      available therapeutic services tend to be consistent across communities.
d.      all of the above.

**ANS: b**          **Pg: 545**
**LO: 24**          **Conceptual**

98.     Which of the following statements regarding the role of a therapist's profession is
        accurate?
a.      Only a clinical psychologist can prescribe drugs for disorders that merit drug therapy.
b.      There is no reliable association between therapists' professional background and
        therapeutic efficacy.
c.      Psychologists are generally considered more effective therapists than either counselors or
        social workers.
d.      Health insurance policies that cover psychotherapy generally specify that treatment must
        be provided by a psychiatrist.

**ANS: b**          **Pg: 545**
**LO: 24**          **Conceptual**

99.     A therapist's gender is important only
a.      for male clients.
b.      for female clients.
c.      if the client thinks it is.
d.      when the client and the therapist are not the same gender.

**ANS: c**          **Pg: 546**
**LO: 24**          **Factual**

100.    Martin Seligman has suggested that panic disorders are most amenable to treatment with
a.      drug therapy.
b.      insight therapy.
c.      cognitive therapy.
d.      systematic desensitization.

**ANS: c**          **Pg: 547**
**LO: 25**          **Factual**

101.    Variations in the effectiveness of psychotherapy appear to depend on individual
        therapists' _____ rather than on their theoretical orientation.
a.      age
b.      gender
c.      personal skills
d.      years of education

**ANS: c**          **Pg: 547-548**
**LO: 25**          **Factual**

102. Which of the following would be considered the least important characteristic of a potential therapist?
a. self-confidence
b. a doctoral degree
c. empathy and understanding
d. personal warmth and sincere concern

**ANS: b**          **Pg: 548**
**LO: 25**          **Conceptual**

103. Which of the following statements regarding therapy is **not** accurate?
a. Therapy is hard work.
b. Therapy is usually a slow process.
c. It's the therapist's responsibility to change your behavior.
d. In therapy, you may have to face up to some painful truths about yourself.

**ANS: c**          **Pgs: 548-549**
**LO: 26**          **Conceptual**

104. The best thing to do if you feel that you are making no progress in therapy is to
a. quit before you waste anymore time or money.
b. discuss your feelings honestly with your therapist.
c. request medication to help your mental state improve more quickly.
d. join a therapy group as an additional treatment to speed your progress.

**ANS: b**          **Pg: 548**
**LO: 26**          **Conceptual**


## MULTIPLE CHOICE QUESTIONS FROM STUDY GUIDE

1. The goal of insight therapies is to
a. change the patient's undesirable behaviors.
b. intervene in a person's biological functioning.
c. try to understand the nature of the client's difficulties.
d. All of the above are goals of insight therapy.

**ANS: c**          **Pg: 518**
**LO: 1**          **Factual**

2. The main reason why people who need therapy don't get it is that
a. it is simply too expensive.
b. there aren't enough qualified therapists available.
c. those who need help don't know where to find it.
d. many people equate being in therapy with personal weakness.

**ANS: d**          **Pg: 519**
**LO: 2**          **Factual**

3.     Freud believed that neurotic problems were caused by
a.     unconscious conflicts left over from childhood.
b.     recurring self-defeating behaviors.
c.     conscious conflicts with significant others.
d.     learned behaviors that become established early in life.

**ANS: a        Pg: 522**
**LO: 4          Factual**

4.     For Sigmund Freud, the most direct means of access to patients' innermost conflicts,
       wishes, and impulses was through
a.     resistance.
b.     transference.
c.     word association.
d.     dream interpretation.

**ANS: d        Pg: 523**
**LO: 5          Factual**

5.     Carl Rogers maintained that most personal distress is due to
a.     the lack of cooperation between the client and therapist.
b.     the inability of the client to follow the directions of the therapist.
c.     inadequate feedback about oneself from others.
d.     incongruence between a person's self-concept and reality.

**ANS: d        Pg: 524**
**LO: 6          Factual**

6.     In client-centered therapy, the relationship between the client and therapist is
a.     one of equals working together on the problem.
b.     much like that of a horse (client) and rider (therapist).
c.     the therapist directing the process through free association.
d.     one where neither plays an active role, allowing the process to unfold naturally.

**ANS: a        Pg: 525**
**LO: 7          Factual**

7.     The goal of cognitive therapy is to
a.     identify unconscious needs and desires through free association.
b.     recognize and change negative thoughts and maladaptive beliefs.
c.     help clients think about how therapy might help them.
d.     help clients learn how to be of help to others in need of therapy.

**ANS: b        Pg: 526**
**LO: 8          Factual**

8. A strength of group therapy is that it
a. has a better chance of succeeding than any other form.
b. places participants in challenging social situations while still in the therapy group.
c. stretches the therapy period over a longer time so that the client can make steady progress.
d. provides the participants an opportunity to try out new social behaviors in a safe environment.

**ANS: d**          **Pgs: 527-528**
**LO: 10**          **Factual**

9. The subject of the recovered memories controversy involves the recovery of repressed memories
a. from the collective unconscious.
b. of sexual abuse and other childhood trauma.
c. that appear to the patient in his or her dreams.
d. of viewing one's parents engaged in sexual intercourse.

**ANS: b**          **Pgs: 529-530**
**LO: 12**          **Factual**

10. Behavior therapies are based on the assumption that
a. behavior is a product of learning.
b. unconscious desires lead to most psychological problems.
c. negative self-talk is the root of most behavioral problems.
d. insights about one's behavior are necessary for constructive change.

**ANS: a**          **Pgs: 532-533**
**LO: 13**          **Factual**

11. When comparing behavior therapy with insight therapy, researchers conclude that the differences are
a. small, but favor behavioral approaches.
b. small, but favor the insight approaches.
c. large, favoring the behavioral approaches.
d. large, favoring the insight approaches.

**ANS: a**          **Pg: 536**
**LO: 16**          **Factual**

12. Antipsychotic drugs are a problem because
a. they work in fewer than half of the patients.
b. patients frequently suffer overdoses.
c. they work quickly but don't last very long.
d. they have many unpleasant side effects.

**ANS: d**          **Pgs: 537-538**
**LO: 18**          **Factual**

13. Critics maintain that the negative effects of psychiatric drugs are not fully appreciated because
a. medical researchers don't have access to representative samples.
b. most drugs are not around long enough to determine their long-term impact.
c. the pharmaceutical industry has undue influence over the research on drug testing.
d. drug testing on humans is illegal in the United States.

**ANS: c**      **Pg: 539**
**LO: 18**      **Factual**

14. Electroconvulsive therapy is considered a type of _____ therapy.
a. insight
b. cognitive
c. behavioral
d. biomedical

**ANS: d**      **Pg: 540**
**LO: 19**      **Factual**

15. In recent surveys of psychologists' theoretical orientations, the greatest proportion of respondents describe themselves as _____ in approach.
a. eclectic
b. cognitive
c. behavioral
d. client-centered

**ANS: a**      **Pg: 542**
**LO: 21**      **Factual**

## MULTIPLE CHOICE QUESTIONS ON WEB SITE

1. The prescription of drugs in the treatment of psychological disorders is a feature of
a. insight therapy.
b. behavior therapy.
c. biomedical therapy.
d. transpersonal therapy.

**ANS: c**      **Pg: 518**
**LO: 1**      **Conceptual**

2. Which of the following statements about the role of counselors in providing therapy is **not** accurate?
a. Counselors typically have a master's degree.
b. Counselors tend to emphasize the biomedical approach to treatment.
c. Counselors often specialize in particular types of problems, such as marital conflict.
d. Counselors are usually found working in schools, colleges, and human service agencies.

**ANS: b**      **Pg: 521**
**LO: 3**      **Conceptual**

3.  Freud believed that neuroses were caused by
a.  negative thinking.
b.  classically conditioned fear responses.
c.  unresolved conflicts in the unconscious.
d.  incongruence between a person's self-concept and reality.

**ANS: c**        **Pg: 522**
**LO: 4**         **Factual**

4.  According to the system of psychoanalysis, _____ involves the therapist's attempts to explain the inner significance of the client's thoughts, feelings, memories, and behaviors.
a.  resistance
b.  transference
c.  interpretation
d.  free association

**ANS: c**        **Pg: 523**
**LO: 5**         **Factual**

5.  If a client in psychoanalysis attempts to lead the therapist away from sensitive issues, the client is displaying
a.  resistance.
b.  transference.
c.  interpretation.
d.  free association.

**ANS: a**        **Pg: 524**
**LO: 5**         **Factual**

6.  Client-centered therapy was developed by
a.  Carl Jung.
b.  Aaron Beck.
c.  Carl Rogers.
d.  Sigmund Freud.

**ANS: c**        **Pg: 524**
**LO: 6**         **Factual**

7.  Which of the following individuals is most closely associated with the cognitive approach to therapy?
a.  Carl Jung
b.  Albert Ellis
c.  Carl Rogers
d.  Sigmund Freud

**ANS: b**        **Pg: 526**
**LO: 8**         **Factual**

8.      According to Beck, which kind of thought process tends to produce depression?
a.      focusing selectively on positive experiences
b.      making unduly pessimistic projections about the future
c.      blaming setbacks on circumstantial factors without considering personal inadequacies
d.      all of the above

**ANS: d**          **Pg: 526**
**LO: 8**           **Factual**

9.      Which of the following statements about group therapy is **not** accurate?
a.      Each participant helps select other members of the group.
b.      A therapy group typically consists of five to ten participants.
c.      The participants essentially function as therapists for one another.
d.      The therapist may share his or her own personal feelings with the group.

**ANS: a**          **Pg: 527**
**LO: 9**           **Conceptual**

10.     Behavior therapy involves using the principles of _____ to change problem behavior.
a.      operant conditioning
b.      classical conditioning
c.      observational learning
d.      all of the above

**ANS: d**          **Pg: 532**
**LO: 13**          **Factual**

11.     The third step in the process of systematic desensitization is to
a.      train the client in muscle relaxation.
b.      help the client build an anxiety hierarchy.
c.      have the client work though the hierarchy and try to remain relaxed.
d.      expose the client to mild anxiety-arousing stimuli.

**ANS: c**          **Pg: 533**
**LO: 14**          **Factual**

12.     _____ is a behavior therapy, designed to improve interpersonal behaviors, that
        emphasizes shaping, modeling, and behavioral rehearsal.
a.      Aversion therapy
b.      Self-actualization
c.      Social skills training
d.      Systematic desensitization

**ANS: c**          **Pgs: 535-536**
**LO: 15**          **Factual**

13.     Behavior therapies are least likely to be effective in the treatment of which of the following?
a.      phobias
b.      drug-related problems
c.      vague feelings of discontent
d.      obsessive-compulsive disorder

**ANS: c**          **Pgs: 536**
**LO: 16**          **Conceptual**

14.     Antipsychotic drugs
a.      tend to produce an immediate, but short-lasting, effect.
b.      are effective for only a small minority of psychotic patients.
c.      are often prescribed even for individuals who have no psychotic disorder.
d.      gradually reduce psychotic symptoms such as hallucinations and delusions.

**ANS: d**          **Pgs: 537**
**LO: 17**          **Factual**

15.     Which of the following statements regarding therapy is **not** accurate?
a.      Therapy is hard work.
b.      Therapy is usually a slow process.
c.      It's the therapist's responsibility to change your behavior.
d.      In therapy, you may have to face up to some painful truths about yourself.

**ANS: c**          **Pgs: 548-549**
**LO: 26**          **Conceptual**


**TRUE/FALSE QUESTIONS**

1.      Sigmund Freud focused on a client's unconscious motivations and needs.

**ANS:    true**          **Pg: 522**
**LO:      4**              **Factual**

2.      Classical psychoanalysis is commonly practiced today.

**ANS:    false**          **Pg: 524**
**LO:      5**              **Factual**

3.      Client-centered therapy emphasizes an emotionally supportive climate.

**ANS:    true**          **Pg: 524**
**LO:      6**              **Factual**

4.      Unconditional positive regard was one of Ellis' keys to therapy.

**ANS:    false**          **Pg: 526**
**LO:      7**              **Factual**

5.      The allegiance effect occurs when clients adapt their therapist's attitudes.

**ANS:   false          Pg: 528**
**LO:    11             Factual**

6.      Memory researchers tend to believe that "recovered" memories are usually implanted by therapists.

**ANS:   true           Pgs: 530-531**
**LO:    12             Factual**

7.      Behavior therapies assume parental conflict is the cause of most disorders.

**ANS:   false          Pg: 532**
**LO:    13             Conceptual**

8.      Aversion therapy is the most controversial behavior therapy.

**ANS:   true           Pg: 534**
**LO:    15             Factual**

9.      Antineurotics are a relatively new class drugs available for psychological treatment.

**ANS:   false          Pgs: 537-538**
**LO:    17             Factual**

10.     Prozac is an SSRI which is prescribed for depression.

**ANS:   true           Pg: 538**
**LO:    17             Factual**


## SHORT-ANSWER ESSAY QUESTIONS

1.      Distinguish between the training of a psychiatrist and a psychologist.

**Pgs: 520-521**

2.      Explain the significance of dream interpretation, resistance, and transference in the psychoanalytic approach to therapy.

**Pgs: 523-524**

3.      Identify and briefly describe the three conditions necessary for a supportive therapeutic climate in client-centered therapy.

**Pg: 525**

4.    Briefly describe several "errors" in thinking that have been identified by Aaron Beck and that are often seen in depression-prone individuals.

**Pg: 526**

5.    Compare and contrast the roles of the participants and the therapist in group therapy.

**Pg: 527**

6.    Identify and briefly describe the two basic assumptions of the behavioral approach to therapy.

**Pgs: 532-533**

7.    Briefly explain the role of the anxiety hierarchy and the concept of counterconditioning in systematic desensitization.

**Pg: 533**

8.    Briefly describe the benefits and drawbacks associated with drug therapies.

**Pgs: 539-540**

9.    Briefly describe the benefits and drawbacks associated with the use of electroconvulsive therapy.

**Pg: 541**

10.   Briefly discuss the relative importance of a therapist's personal skills and professional training as they apply to the effectiveness of therapy.

**Pgs: 547-548**